Morris Jacob Raphall

Post-Biblical history of the Jews from the close of the Old Testament

ISBN/EAN: 9783337131548

Printed in Europe, USA, Canada, Australia, Japan

Cover: Foto ©Lupo / pixelio.de

More available books at **www.hansebooks.com**

POST-BIBLICAL
HISTORY OF THE JEWS;

FROM THE

CLOSE OF THE OLD TESTAMENT, ABOUT THE YEAR 420 B. C. E.
TILL THE DESTRUCTION OF THE SECOND TEMPLE,
IN THE YEAR 70 C. E.

BY

MORRIS J. RAPHALL, M.A. Ph.Dr.

RABBI-PREACHER AT THE SYNAGOGUE, GREENE ST., NEW YORK.

IN TWO VOLUMES.—VOL. I.

NEW YORK:
D. APPLETON & CO., 443 & 445 BROADWAY.
1866.

CONTENTS.

INTRODUCTION.. 11

BOOK I.
JUDEA UNDER THE PERSIANS AND GREEKS.

CHAPTER I.

Return of the Jews from the Babylonish captivity—Policy of Cyrus and of his successors—Ezra—Nehemiah—Condition of Judea—Alexander the Great—His visit to Jerusalem—Authority of Jewish historians vindicated—Alexander's conquest of Egypt—Babylon—His death. (From 536 to 324 B. C. E.)................... 21

CHAPTER II.

Wars between Alexander's generals—Perdiccas—Ptolemy—Antigonus—Siege and Storm of Jerusalem by Ptolemy—Jews carried to Egypt—Demetrius—Battle of Gaza—Mosollamus—Credibility of Greek historians in reference to Jewish affairs; Jerom of Cardia; Hecatæus—The Nabathæans—Seleucus Nicator—His success in Upper Asia—Era of the Seleucidæ: *Minyan Staroth*—Extinction of the family of Alexander the Great—Battle of Ipsos. (From 326 to 301 B. C. E.).. 59

CHAPTER III.

Partition of Alexander's empire—Judea assigned to Ptolemy—The Syro-Grecian Empire—Jews on the Euphrates—The Egypto-Grecian Empire—Jews of Alexandria—Of Jerusalem—Simon the Just—The Septuagint—Berosus—Manetho—Rivalry and wars of the Ptolemies and the Seleucidæ—The Parthian Empire—*Young Judea*—Antigonus of Socho—The Sadducees—Ptolemy IV. Philopator—Antiochus III.—Battle of Raphia—Philopator at Jerusalem—His attempt on the Temple—His Flight—Persecutes the Jews of Egypt—His death—Antiochus III. invades Cœle-Syria—Battle of Mount Panias—Judea incorporated with the Syro-Grecian Empire. (From 301 to 198 B. C. E.)... 106

CHAPTER IV.

Antiochus III.—War with Rome—Hannibal—Antiochus defeated—His death—Seleucus Philopator—Onias III., the high-priest—Heliodorus attempts to plunder the temple—His miscarriage—Antiochus IV. Epiphanes—His intervention in Judean affairs—Conservatives and Destructives—Jason buys the office of high-priest—Attempted fusion of Judaism and Heathenism—Judeo-Grecian literature—Menelaus—War between Antiochus and the Egyptians—Troubles in Judea—Antiochus plunders the temple—Popilius Lœnas—Massacre at Jerusalem—The Jewish religion proscribed—The Haphtora—First religious persecution—Insurrection—Matathias the Asmonean declares self-defence lawful on the Sabbath—Holland, the United States, and Judea—Judah the Maccabee—His victories—The Syrians expelled—Public worship restored in the temple of Jerusalem. (From 198 to 166 B. C. E.)........................ 188

BOOK II.
THE MACCABEES.

CHAPTER V.

Death of A. Epiphanes—Polybius, the historian—Antiochus V. Eupator—Death of P. Macron—Judah's campaigns—Truce, and renewed hostilities—First siege of Acra—Death of Eleazar the Maccabean—Siege of Jerusalem—Lysias and Philip—Peace—Judah appointed governor for the king—Death of Menelaus—Alcimus.—(From 165 to 161 B. C. E.).. 265

CHAPTER VI.

Demetrius I. King of Syria—His flight from Rome—Death of A. Eupator—Invasion of Judea—Massacre of Hassidim—José ben Joëzer—Nicanor—His blasphemy, defeat, and punishment—First treaty between Judea and Rome—Discontent of the Hassidim—Bacchides—Battle of Elcasa—Death and burial of Judah the Maccabee—His character—Gentile testimony to his military talents.—(162 to 161 B. C. E.).. 297

CHAPTER VII.

Jonathan succeeds his brother—Battle of Tekoah, and retreat across the Jordan—Alcimus—His death—Ariarethes VI.—Jonathan returns to Judea—State of parties—Bacchides invited by the apostates—Siege of Bethlagan—Syrians evacuate Judea—Internal peace and good government restored—Troubles in Syria—Conspiracy of the three kings—Balas claims the crown of Syria—Immunities granted to the Jews—Jonathan high-priest—Defeat and death of Demetrius I.—Reign of Alexander Balas—Onias builds a temple in Egypt—Samaritan temple and controversy. (From 161 to 149 B. C. E.).. 332

CHAPTER VIII.

Demetrius II. recovers the crown of Syria—Battle of Azotus; Waterloo—Death of A. Balas, and of Ptolemy VI. Philometor—Treaty between King Demetrius and Jonathan—Troubles in Antioch suppressed by the assistance of Jonathan—Perfidy of King Demetrius—His expulsion from Antioch—Tryphon—Antiochus VI.—His treaty with Jonathan—Civil war—Battle of Azor—Jonathan renews the alliance with Rome, and treats with Sparta—The pirates of Cilicia—Jonathan entrapped and murdered by Tryphon—Simon elected to succeed him—Death of Antiochus VI.—Sepulchre of the Maccabees at Modin—King Demetrius II. declares Judea independent. (From 148 to 143 B. C. E.)... 372

INTRODUCTION.

THERE is one people, the sole survivor of the really olden times when mankind was in its infancy—a people unmixed in lineage, unchanged in religious belief and observance, and whose history, down to the present day, inseparably connects itself with those primeval and most sacred records from which the civilized portion of mankind derives its faith, and on which it rests its hopes. This people—the Jews—has, beyond all others, exercised the most lasting influence on the human mind—an influence that has outlived the philosophy of Greece and the statesmanship of Rome, and to which every succeeding century, every advance in knowledge, every discovery in science, every amelioration in the social system, affords greater strength and a wider scope. And yet, while this is not only true, but generally admitted so to be,—while all that is highest, holiest, most venerated, and most admired among men attaches itself to this people, its history, and its influence,—what is, what has so long been, the condition of this people? Expatriated and dispersed, deprived of its political existence long before any of the states that at present constitute the civilized world had sprung into being, the Jewish people has, during many centuries, been "the jest of folly and the scorn of pride," the victim of ignorance, fanaticism, and calumny; and even yet, in most countries, is not permitted to enjoy that absolute and unmulcted freedom of conscience which is man's highest, dearest birthright.

Ever since men have begun to throw off the trammels of prejudice and the fetters of ignorance, the history, the character, and the condition of the Jews have, in every land, excited the attention of the reflecting part of the community. We may say in every land, for there is no land which does not, or did not at some former period, number Jews among its inhabitants. Wherever Civilization dispenses its blessings, the Jew is found its harbinger or its immediate follower. Wherever Commerce spreads its sails, the Jew is foremost in cementing that bond which unites the most distant nations. Wherever the dignity of human nature has been respected in him, wherever he has been treated as a man and a brother, he has proved that he likewise is made in the image of God—that his bosom, too, can harbour every virtue that dignifies mankind. And even where the iron hand of Bigotry has crushed him to the dust, or the soul-chilling venom of Contempt and the "oppression (that) maketh a wise man mad" had gnawed his mind and cowed his better part of man, even there he strove, and strove not in vain, to preserve those nobler feelings inseparable from the memory of his former greatness. Even there he remained very different from what his oppressors laboured to render him, and his detractors would fain make him appear. And though full justice is still but too frequently denied to him, the truth, that he has been more sinned against than sinning,—that his failings have been forced upon him, while his virtues are his own,—is gradually working its way in the conviction of every one who, with unprejudiced mind, reflects on the severe ordeal that, during eighteen centuries, the Jew has passed through, and on the unyielding constancy with which he has maintained his principles.

The Post-Biblical History of the Jews begins at the

close of the Old Testament, and continues till the present day. It embraces a period of 2200 years, and extends to every quarter of the globe; and during this long space of time, what a number of events does this history embody! Events interesting, exciting, pleasing, harrowing, but all of them important and highly instructive, unfold themselves to our view. We behold the highest motives, the noblest feelings, the sternest energies of human nature, called into activity—patriotism, love of country and of freedom, bravery the most exalted, and religious fervour the most pure, arming the few against the many, the weak against the strong, the freeman against the oppressor, and inspiring the firm resolve "to do or die." Nor is it active courage only we are called to admire; for we also behold how, during centuries, the inflexible determination to suffer wears out the ruthless power to inflict, and the firmness of principle overcomes the obstinacy of prejudice. We behold how, under disadvantages the most overwhelming, mind triumphs over matter, the lofty hope over the crushing reality.

And what men shall we become acquainted with! Not only Alexander and Cæsar, Cromwell and Napoleon, are introduced to us, but we are also taught to know and to respect those less meteoric, though equally gifted and far more beneficent heroes of mind, who, during the struggle of centuries, could keep alive the inward spirit which bade defiance to the pressure from without. Let it not be supposed that, because eighteen hundred years have elapsed since the body politic of the Jews was destroyed, therefore their history can offer no scenes grand, impressive, or interesting. If it be true that the noblest sight in nature is that of a good man struggling against adversity, what must it be to see an entire people martyrs to principle, who, during nearly two thousand years, bear up against all the ills that flesh is heir to; who, when a few brief sentences

Vol I. 2

might have placed them on a level with their oppressors,—when a few short words would have converted their ruthless persecutors into friends and protectors,—disdained to violate their own conscience, or to utter those few words, because they feared God more than man, and valued truth more than life!

The reader must not feel surprised that we speak in terms of commendation so warm of the history of a people that, till within the last few years, has seldom presumed to raise its voice, even in self-defence. But it must be borne in mind that, from Josephus, who wrote in the first century of the Christian era, to Jost, who within the last thirty years published his work in Germany, no Jew has written the history of his people in any other language than Hebrew. And as thus the Jewish historians were not accessible to the general reader, the writers best known on that subject were not Jews. They were mostly churchmen, who copied from each other. The monkish rancour and prejudice that guided the pen of the first libeller bequeathed a portion of its venom to every succeeding calumniator. The oldest of them wrote in the spirit of his times, and thought he performed a meritorious act. Were not the Jews the enemies of God? Was it not evident that the Jew had been condemned to endless suffering by the retributive justice of Providence, which had at one time deigned to work so many and great miracles in his behalf, but which now had cast him forth, to suffer whatever pains the rest of mankind chose to inflict upon him? Did he not stand an outcast in the midst of the nations, marked, like the first fratricide, by the wrath of the Omnipotent? When, therefore, men punished the Jew for his stubborn rejection of the *true* faith, what more did they do, than execute the decrees of the Deity? And what office more noble can man assume, than that of champion of the Lord! With what function more sacred can man be invested, than that of working the vengeance of the Lord on his enemies? What greater claim can man have on the divine bounty and grace, than by promoting the designs of the Deity? Accordingly, those very acts which are criminal when undertaken against other men, become meritorious when against the Jew. For the robber who despoiled, the slanderer who belied him, the perjured informer who denounced him to unmerited punishment, the ruffian who shed his heart's blood with savage exultation—what were they but the chosen ministers of divine vengeance against an accursed race? And, therefore, their deeds were heaven-directed, pious, and honourable.

Such were the doctrines which, during centuries, were preached from the pulpit and proclaimed in the market-place. Such were the insidious means by which the still small voice of conscience was stifled in the breasts of those who were able to feel, while the loud anathema of the dominant faith silenced the murmurs of reason in the minds of the few who dared to think. The influence of these doctrines is but too evident in all that has been written concerning the Jews previous to the works of the German Dohm, and the Frenchman Gregoire, in the last quarter of the eighteenth century. With the writings of these two just and wise men a better spirit began to prevail; but, though in our days we have seen an honest churchman (like Millman) attempting to approach the truth, how many a Chiarini and Eisenmenger work hard to pervert that truth, and prostitute talent and research in the service of bigotry and falsehood.

When all this is borne in mind, it will not appear strange if the history of his fathers, written by a Jew, may not be exactly in accordance with what the public has been accustomed to read, or if his estimate of men and motives may differ somewhat from Basnage or Voltaire; for, by a singular fatality, the character of the Jew has been assailed by the infidel not less than by the bigot. Between the two, the condition of the luckless Hebrew has been not unlike that of the lion in the fable. A man called the attention of the grim king of the forest to a picture representing a lion vanquished by a man: "We have no painters," was his significant reply. In like manner, whether a Gibbon, in his bitter hatred of revealed religion, distorts the truth of history, and indulges in malignant sneers at the Jew,—or a MacCaul, in his bigoted or interested zeal for conversion—a zeal assuredly not according to knowledge—falsifies the opinions of the Jew, and holds his teachers up to unmerited scorn,—the only reply the Jew could long give to the general reader was still, "We have no historians accessible to you." But that time is fast going by. In Germany and France, Jost, Gratz, and Salvador have in a masterly manner written on the history of their people.

And what they have done for Frenchmen and Germans, the writer of these pages, though by far their inferior in learning, talent, and industry, presumes to attempt for his fellow-citizens in the United States. For here, more than anywhere else, it is the duty of the Israelite to bring himself, his past fortunes, and his present condition, fairly before the world. Here, where he owns no superior but God and the law,—here, where, *de facto* as well as *de jure*, he enjoys perfect equality with his fellow-citizens, and takes that rank in society to which his talents and virtues entitle him,—here, where religious freedom, like civil liberty, is his birth-right,—here it behoves him to prove that he is not unworthy of the advantages he enjoys. Here it is his duty, as it is his privilege, to appeal not only from the bigotry of the past to the common sense of the present, but from the sordid selfishness of despots to the justice and generosity of freemen—to proclaim, and to prove it, that in every estimable quality of the heart and of the mind his fathers have at all times been, he himself is, the peer of the most highly-gifted races that inhabit our globe. Here he may give utterance to those truths, and relate those facts which, while they cover the fanatic with confusion, may call the blush of shame on the haughty brow of the oppressor, and wring the conscience of the few—if any such there be in this home of freedom, of justice, and of reason—who still, in their heart of hearts, cherish the dark notions of the dark ages.

But it is not only to the native, but to the adopted citizens of this our glorious country, that the Jewish historian must address himself. Thousands arrive here from the old countries, who, with their mothers' milk, have imbibed the old scorn of the Jew. They come here in search of liberty, ready and willing to exercise the rights of freemen, and to claim perfect equality for themselves and all that belong to them; but carrying into the ordinary relations of society and of active life that supercilious hauteur, or that narrow-minded prejudice, to which, in all matters appertaining to Jews, they have so long been accustomed. To them, the Jewish historian must speak freely. He must show how the long inheritance of hatred was first begotten by an unholy alliance of Tyranny with Superstition, whose first-born were Rapacity and Ignorance; how, during many ages, the fathers of these immigrants found some consolation under the heavy oppression they themselves suffered, in retaliating on the unfortunate Jew,— a consolation that might befit despot-ridden *subjects*, but is altogether unworthy of those who aspired to the highest of all human titles, that of freemen—and whose guiding axiom must be, "Do as ye would be done by."

We have now sufficiently explained our motives in undertaking the present publication. It is not our intention that it should be a learned work, or that the minds of the readers should be wearied by long dissertations on Talmudic lore, or by uncalled-for polemics on points at issue between church and synagogue. We write for the people; and, the better to reach them, we will endeavour to amuse as well as to instruct them. Interesting narrations, a popular style, and respect for the belief and feelings of our readers, is what such a publication requires; and in these essentials we trust we shall not be found wanting. But while thus, at the very outset, our history disclaims the title of "learned," it is determined at all times, and under all circumstances, to deserve and maintain the title of "veracious," and with fairness to distribute praise or blame wherever it may be due; for ours is a *history* of the Jews, not an *apology* for them. Rigid impartiality in opinions as well as in facts, is more than the author can undertake to promise; for he is not the abstraction of a Jew, but one living, acting, feeling warmly for them and with them: he is the son, the descendant of the men whose deeds and whose sufferings he is about to relate. The Past, with its manifold recollections; the Future, with its boundless anticipations, exercise their legitimate influence on his mind and on his feelings. But, though he cannot promise that perfect absence of all bias which in his position would be more or less than human, he can, and does pledge himself, in the words of immortal Shakspeare, that he will "nothing extenuate, nor set down aught in malice;" that he will advance nothing on doubtful authority, and that he will, in no instance, allow his feelings to distort facts, so that, though some of his readers may dissent from his views or inferences, none of them shall have cause to question his truthfulness, or to reject his statements.

We are great believers in the perfectibility of human nature, and therefore we highly prize the privilege of living at a time when progress of mind is the order of the day. But still higher do we appreciate the permission to co-operate, in some degree, and according to the slender measure of our ability, toward the general progress. Coming generations will, we know, witness its further development, and behold its highest triumphs; for where *we* only taste the first fruits, *they* will reap and enjoy the fulness of the harvest. But the seed of their harvest will have been sown by us, the men of the present times. We prepare for them a rich inheritance, and the greatness of future ages will date its rise from ours; for the errors which we root out will not mislead them; the prejudices which we overcome, will not narrow their minds. And among those errors and prejudices from which our efforts are to emancipate our descendants, those against which this "POST-BIBLICAL HISTORY OF THE JEWS" is directed, as they are among the oldest, are assuredly not the least pernicious. We therefore fully expect that good men of every creed and every lineage will bid us "God-speed;" that wise men will approve of our design; and that both will strengthen our hands in our honest endeavour to break down that icy barrier which Pride and Ignorance have raised, which Bigotry and Prejudice have so long upheld, between those who are children of one Father, creatures of one God.

M. J. R.

NEW YORK, *January* 25, 1854.

POST-BIBLICAL HISTORY

OF

THE JEWS.

CHAPTER I.

Return of the Jews from the Babylonish captivity—Policy of Cyrus and of his successors—Ezra—Nehemiah—Condition of Judea—Alexander the Great—His visit to Jerusalem—Authority of Jewish historians vindicated—Alexander's conquest of Egypt—Babylon—His death. (From 536 to 324, B. C. E.)

THE Biblical history of the Jews closes with the second administration of Nehemiah, whose high favour at the court of Persia had obtained the boon of being permitted to rebuild the walls of Jerusalem, one hundred and thirty-eight years after they had been destroyed by Nebuchadnezzar, King of Babylon. The tribes or nations adjoining Judea had long and successfully exerted their influence with the kings of Persia, to prevent the Jews from recovering that centralization and national consistency which must result from the possession of a large and fortified city. Accordingly, as often as the Jews attempted to rebuild the walls of Jerusalem, denunciations from their old hereditary foes, the Ammonites, Moabites, and Syrians, and especially from their latest but most rancorous enemies, the Samaritans, called forth an order from the king of Persia to suspend the work. It is true that a daughter of their race (Esther) had been raised to the throne of Persia; that her uncle

Mordecai, the Jew, became grand vizier at the court of Susa; and that, by the address and piety of the queen, the greatest danger to which the Jews had ever been exposed—the plot of Haman for their extermination—was happily averted. But, beyond this certainly most highly important instance of her patriotism and influence, there is no proof that, for a time at least, Queen Esther or Mordecai gave a different direction to the policy of the court of Persia; which consisted in gratifying the larger and more powerful of the subject tribes at the expense of the smaller and weaker ones; and which accordingly sacrificed the security of Jerusalem and its temple to the jealousy and resentment of their adversaries—"the men on this side the river," as the various tribes leagued against the Jews designated themselves.

The change in this policy on the part of King Artaxerxes may, however, as Hales justly remarks, be accounted for on sound political principles, and not merely from regard for the solicitations of his cup-bearer, Nehemiah. "Four years before, King Artaxerxes—who, after the reduction of the revolted Egyptians, had prosecuted the war against their auxiliaries, the Athenians—suffered a signal defeat of his forces by sea, and land from Cimon the Athenian general, which compelled the king to sue for peace, and to subscribe to the following humiliating terms:—1. That the Greek cities throughout Asia should be free and enjoy their own laws; 2. That no Persian governor should come within three days' journey of any part of the sea with an army; and, 3. That no Persian ships of war should sail between the northern extremity of Asia Minor and the boundary of Palestine," (according to Diodorus Siculus, lib. xii., whose authority, however, is in this instance controverted by modern criticism; and the fact that such a treaty was ever made is altogether denied by Dahlman, a German writer.) "Thus excluded from the whole line of sea-coast, and precluded from keeping garrisons in any of the maritime towns, it became not only a matter of prudence, but of necessity, to conciliate the Jews,—to attach them to the Persian interest, and detach them from the Grecians by further privileges,—that the Persians might have the benefit of a friendly fortified town, like Jerusalem, within three days' journey of the sea, and a most important pass to keep up the communication between Persia and Egypt; and to confirm this conjecture we may remark that, in all the ensuing Egyptian wars, the Jews remained faithful to the Persians, and even after the Macedonian invasion; and surely some such powerful motive must have been opposed, in the king's mind, to the jealousy and displeasure this measure must unavoidably excite in the neighbouring provinces hostile to the Jews, whose remonstrances had so much weight with him formerly. It was necessary, therefore, to intrust the important mission to an officer high in former trust and confidence, such as Nehemiah, whose services at court Artaxerxes reluctantly dispensed with, as appears from his appointing a set time for Nehemiah's return, and afterward, from his return again to Persia in the thirty-second year of his reign." (Howe's Critical Observations on Books, ii. 82.) This change in the policy of the Great King, as the monarchs of Persia were proudly styled, was a return to the sound and statesmanlike views which, in his dealings with the Jews, had acted on the mind of Cyrus, the founder of the Persian Empire.

The Persians were the victors and heirs of those Assyrian and Babylonian conquerors who had spread their sway over the greater part of Central and Western Asia—a sway which was still farther extended by Cyrus and his successors, until it reached from the Indus on the south to the Caspian Sea on the north, and from the Jaxartes on the east to the Mediterranean on the west. All the conquered nations inhabiting this vast extent of land, were idolaters. The Persians themselves, followers of Zoroaster, believed in two independent and rival principles,—the one, *Ormuzd*, of light and good; the other, *Ahriman*, of darkness and evil. Both principles were objects of adoration; but, while certain rites attested their dread of *Ahriman*, their worship was addressed to the Sun as the visible emblem of *Ormuzd*. They bowed to the everlasting fire that burnt on the altar of *Mithra*, the Sun, but admitted no idols or images into their temples; and to the animal-worship of the Egyptians they were so intolerant, that a later Persian king sacrificed the ox-god *Apis* to an ass. Among all the tribes and nations that obeyed his sceptre, Cyrus found but one people that, like himself, bowed not its neck before any image the workmanship of human hands; and that people was the Jews, who had been subdued and exiled from their own land by his conquered enemies, the Assyro-Babylonians.

That land, however, was of great importance, from its geographical position between the Euphrates and the Mediterranean, and as the only avenue to Egypt. The Assyro-Babylonians, in their day of power, had appreciated that importance, and had located, in the central regions of Palestine, colonists from Syria and the highlands of Asia, who subsequently were known by the name of Samaritans, or Cutheans. But in these colonists—attached to the Assyro-Babylonians, who had first planted them in the land, and idolaters like them—King Cyrus could have no confidence. As he was preparing for the invasion and conquest of Egypt, which his son and successor, Cambyses, subsequently undertook, Cyrus saw the importance of locating in Judea—his sole line of retreat in case of non-success in Egypt—a population that should have some feeling in common with him and his Persians. And it did not escape his penetrating mind that, if he restored their land—from which they had been expelled by idolaters—

to the Jews, they would prove the most faithful subjects he could place therein. Surrounded by idolatrous tribes, against the rancour of whom they were protected by his Persians—like themselves, non-idolaters,—necessity, as well as gratitude and fellow-feeling, would create and keep alive, in the mind of the Jews, an attachment to himself and his empire not easily to be shaken. He had, moreover, the merit in their eyes of having delivered them from captivity, and revenged their sufferings on their proud enslavers in Babylon. And when Cyrus was informed how— above a century before he was born—the prophet of the Lord had designated him by name as the future deliverer, whose triumph was to set free the captives of Zion and cause them to return to their own land,—when Cyrus thus beheld his name and connection with the Jews plainly announced in a prophecy, (Isaiah xliv. 28; xlv. 1-7,) the authenticity of which—whatever modern rationalism may do—he saw no reason to doubt, he at once prepared to obey the behest of a God whom he and his people did not serve; and he did this the more readily, as the promptings of his own interest and the dictates of the soundest policy so strongly and manifestly enforced obedience to that behest.

Cyrus issued a proclamation, in which, after setting forth that the Lord God of heaven, who had given him all the kingdoms of earth, had directed him to build for him a house at Jerusalem, he invites all Jews who might feel so inclined, to return to that city and to rebuild their temple, assuring them of his support and protection. It is a remarkable fact, and strong proof of the exact and literal manner in which this proclamation is preserved in Scripture, that the designation here officially given to the God of the Jews by Cyrus, and repeated by his successors in their decrees, "the God of heaven," is the self-same designation by which to this day—throughout China, Mongolia, Tartary, and in all countries of Central Asia which are not Mohammedan—the God of the Bible, of Jews and of Christians, is known. (Huc, Journey in Tartary, Thibet, &c., *passim*.) Some Jews availed themselves of the proclamation, but the bulk of the people remained located in the cities of Chaldea, on the rivers Tigris and Euphrates. The whole number of the first immigration did not quite reach fifty thousand persons, including men, women, children, freeborn and slaves. They were mostly poor, for all the horses and mules in their caravan numbered less than one thousand. Yet from this small and mean beginning there sprung a nation which, in a comparatively short period of time, filled the land with some millions of wealthy inhabitants.

The successors of Cyrus lost sight of his policy. Egypt conquered, Judea was no longer of the same importance to them. The kings of Persia gave ear to the hostile reports of the Samaritans and other enemies of the Jews, who were more wealthy and powerful, and, therefore, possessed greater influence at the court of Susa. The building of the city and temple was frequently interrupted, and the condition of the colony so precarious, as to hold out no encouragement for further immigration. At so remote a distance from the eye of the sovereign, the provincial governors were guilty of great extortions. Accordingly Nehemiah, on his arrival at Jerusalem, pathetically laments the condition of his people, who were in great distress because, though in their own land, they were servants to governors who had dominion over their persons and property, and whose exactions had burdened them with debts ruinous and continually increasing.

From this state of misery they were raised by Nehemiah. He had been commissioned to build walls and gates to the town, to erect a mansion for himself and future governors, and to rebuild the city. All this he accomplished with singular zeal, ability, and disinterestedness, during his administration of twelve years, to which his leave of absence from court extended. Threatened with hostilities by the adversaries of Judah, he piously encouraged the people to rely on the Lord, and "to fight for their brethren, their sons and their daughters, their wives and their homes," (Neh. iv. 8.) Dividing all the people into two bodies, he appointed one to labour and build, and the other to watch and fight. Even the builders "with one hand wrought in the work, and with the other held a weapon." Thus, by the most energetic and noble exertions, the whole wall, which had been distributed in lots among the priests and chiefs of the people, was, with all its gates and towers, finished in the short space of fifty-two days. And the great work which the Athenians, enriched by the spoils of the East, and inspirited by the eloquence and abilities of Themistocles, had a few years before undertaken, and which has so frequently called forth the praise and admiration of historians, (Thucydides, Diodorus, Plutarch, Gillies, Mitford, Grote, &c.,) was fully emulated by the poor Jews under Nehemiah, whom no one has ever thought it worth while to praise or admire.

Having raised the walls on the old foundations, Nehemiah found that, although within the enclosure "the city was large and great," yet "the people were few therein, and the houses not builded." He had begun his administration by relieving the poorer classes from the load of debts that had crushed them to the ground, and of which, by a successful appeal to the patriotism of the rich, he had obtained the remission; and to enable all classes to improve their circumstances, he declined to receive the usual dues of a governor; but, while he travelled with a great retinue, maintained a large number of servants, and kept open table at Jerusalem, the heavy charges were entirely borne from his own private fortune, (Neh. v. 18, *et pass.*) This disinterestedness, together with his piety, courage, and patriotism, had given him a strong hold on the affections of the people; so that when, in order to give inhabitants to the city, he caused the families to be registered, and required one in ten—to be chosen by lot—to come to reside in Jerusalem, the numbers obtained were increased by many volunteers, who came forward to please the governor, and were received with particular favour. Thus the city was filled with inhabitants, and its walls with defenders.

While Nehemiah was thus active in restoring the fallen city and providing for its security and defence, he was equally intent on giving stability to the principles by which the revived nationality of the Jews was to be guided. Some years before his appointment as governor, the king of Persia had commissioned Ezra, the priest and sopher, or scribe, to proceed to Jerusalem to regulate the worship and the sacrifices in "the house of the God of heaven." The governors beyond the Euphrates were commanded to supply him with whatever of silver, corn, wine, and oil (within a specified quantity) he might require, and salt in any quantity; and he himself, together with all the "priests, Levites, singers, gate-keepers, and temple servants," had been exempted from "tax, tribute, or toll," and thus put on an equality with the dominant nations, the Persians and the Medes. Lastly, this important commission authorized Ezra to appoint judges—he himself being their chief—and magistrates, who were to judge the people according to "the laws of his God," (Ezra vii. 12–27;) or, in other words, that the Jews were to be judged according to Jewish, and not according to Persian laws; a fact which goes far to dispose of the assertion of those skeptics who try to persuade us that the law of Moses was not known until its introduction by Ezra, though the Talmud itself admits (*tr.* Succah, p. 20, A.) that the law had fallen into oblivion, and that Ezra brought it into vogue again.

This pious man, who, before the arrival of Nehemiah, had laboured to improve the religious condition of the Jews chiefly by annulling matrimonial connections with heathens, —a measure harsh to the natural affections, but indispensably necessary to secure the people against a relapse into idolatry,—now exerted all his influence and authority to co-operate with the new governor in his zealous efforts to improve the social condition, and to consolidate the institutions of their people. There is no period in their post-biblical history so important, and at the same time so obscure, as that of the joint activity and administration of Ezra and Nehemiah, from whom several of the most important liturgical enactments still in force among the Jews bear date. Tradition—which, however, has been much contested, but which has the great preponderance of evidence in its favour—places in the days of Ezra the great constituent council known as "The men of the great assembly," of which hereafter we shall have occasion to speak more fully. One of Ezra's labours was the exchange of the old Hebrew character of writing for the more striking and shapely Assyrian or square character, which ever since has remained in use with the Jews; while the old character, retained by the Samaritans, has since been known by their name. The language, likewise, spoken by the Jews who returned from Babylon, was very different from that beautiful, concise, and energetic language that had been used by their fathers, in which the Lord had spoken, and which still survives in the imperishable records of the Bible. During the seventy years of their sojourn east of the Euphrates, daily intercourse with the inhabitants of the land had gradually estranged the Jews from their own noble language; and those who returned from Babylon had nearly all been born there, and imbibed the East-Aramæan, or Chaldee dialect, as a mother tongue. The Hebrew was well known to, and spoken by, educated persons; but Chaldee was used in all the ordinary intercourse of life, since that only was understood by all. This last-named language is indeed only a dialect of the Hebrew, which fact accounts for the ease with which the Jews adopted it during the captivity. It, however, assigned to words essentially the same such additional or new meanings, and such differing terminations and pronunciation, that the Hebrew could be but imperfectly intelligible to those who understood only the Chaldee. Accordingly, when on the first New-year's day after the building of the walls, Ezra stood forth to read the Law to the people, it was found desirable that the Levites should translate and expound to the multitude that which he read from the book in Hebrew; by which means the masses became more fully conscious of their religious obligations than they appear till then to have been.

Nehemiah, the expiration of whose leave of absence forced him to return to the court of Persia before his work was quite completed, caused the people to enter into a solemn league and covenant by which they pledged themselves—1. To walk in God's law as given to Moses; 2. Not to intermarry with the (heathen) people of the land; 3. To observe the Sabbath and holy days, and not to buy or to sell goods thereon; 4. To keep the sabbatical or seventh year, and to remit all debts therein; 5. Each man to contribute one-third of a shekel yearly to the support of the temple; 6. And to render first-fruits and tithes, as required by the law of God. But after his departure, his regulations, and even the solemn covenant, were gradually infringed upon and violated; so that, after an absence of some time, (according to Zunz, eight years after his return,) Nehemiah solicited and obtained from the king of Persia a reappointment to that office of governor which he had filled with so much zeal and success for the general good. This, his second administration, forms the last fact recorded in Scripture; for Malachi, the last of the prophets, and whom tradition asserts to have been no other than Ezra, is held by general opinion, supported by every probability of internal evidence, to have prophesied during this latter administration of Nehemiah. He continued in office till the third year of Darius Nothus, whom he designates as Darius the Persian, (420 B. C. E.,) when, having completed the restoration and settlement of the Jews in their own land, he left them in that condition in which, for a length of time afterward, they remained.

After the departure of Nehemiah, the land of Judea was annexed to the satrapy or province of Cœle-Syria, and no more governors were sent to Jerusalem from the court of Persia. For, as the kings of Persia wished to conciliate their Jewish subjects, and had granted them the privilege of living and of being judged by their own law, of which the Persians were ignorant, the right of self-government followed as a necessary consequence. And as the Persians were averse to popular or municipal administrations, the high-priest of Jerusalem, as first in rank among his own people, and recognised as such by the king and government at Susa, naturally became the chief magistrate and representative of the Jews. The temporal power, wealth, and dignity thereby attached to the high-priesthood, rendered it an object of competition to ambitious men, who, regardless of the holy character of the office, but too frequently resorted to violence and bribery—the fatal effects of which, on the morals of the people and on the welfare of the country, in process of time brought the Jews and their religion to the verge of destruction, as will hereafter be more fully related.

The history of the period under our immediate notice—from Nehemiah until Alexander of Macedon—is obscure, and the facts are few. It seems that, while the vast and unwieldy empire of Persia was suffering those intestine commotions which were the certain symptoms of its approaching dissolution; while Egyptians, Phœnicians, Cyprians, and other tributaries of Persia frequently broke out into ill-suppressed rebellion, in which they were supported by the Greeks,—who on more than one occasion insulted the power, defeated the arms, and devastated the dominions of the "Great King,"—the Jews, self-governed and subject to a moderate tribute, were the only people in Western Asia that remained steadfast in their loyalty and attachment to the kings of Persia. And though, in the reign of Darius Ochus, the provincial Jews seem to have been mixed up with the Sidonians and other Phœnician rebels whom that monarch defeated, and thus incurred his disfavour, yet the city of Jerusalem, which was not implicated, throve and prospered. The increase in wealth and population, throughout the whole of Judea, was great and rapid; and when the last Darius ascended the throne, his native Persians were not more faithful to his dynasty than the Jews. The frequent march of vast Persian armies through Judea, occasioned by the repeated, and often for a time successful, efforts of the Egyptians to recover their independence, must have been very grievous and burdensome to that country; and the stern manner in which military satraps exercised their authority, at times rendered the yoke of Persia most galling to the Jews. Nevertheless, and upon the whole, we cannot have a stronger proof of the quiet and prosperous condition of Judea, than that the only fact recorded is of a murder committed by a high-priest in the temple, and on the person of his own brother; and for which a fine was imposed in the shape of a tax on the sacrificial lambs, so heavy that, according to the estimate of Jahn, it must have produced a quarter of a million of dollars, but which was remitted by Ochus.

With this single exception, neither the traditions of the Jews nor the historians of the Gentiles know of any thing of consequence to relate of Judea, from the departure of Nehemiah till the invasion of Asia by Alexander the Great. This scarcity of events—forming so complete a contrast with every other period in the history of the Jews—has induced Rabbins to assume that there were but four kings of Persia, (those mentioned in Scripture,) whose sway over Judea lasted no longer than fifty-two years, at the end of which the Persian Empire was conquered by Alexander. Whereas, from the history of the Greeks, we know that from Cyrus, the first, to Darius Codomanus, the last of the kings of Persia, ten monarchs reigned over that empire—exclusive of the usurper Smerdis and the ill-fated Xerxes II., and his murderer Sogdianus—during a period of two hundred and ninety-two years. This has introduced a difference of two hundred and forty years between Jewish and general chronology—which some bigots have imputed to a design on the part of the Rabbins to abridge the period known as "the seventy weeks of Daniel:" a charge of which we, who are better acquainted with the character of the Rabbins, unhesitatingly acquit them. The discrepancy arises simply from the fact that, in their chronology, these Rabbins would admit of no other items than those furnished by Scripture.

But while the annals of the Jews during this period are thus "short and simple," those of the two empires which succeeded each other in the supremacy over Judea— the Persian and the Grecian—were all the more agitated. In the latter we behold the unceasing jealousies of Athens and Sparta, and the short-lived power of Thebes, preparing the way for the gradual but uninterrupted progress of Philip of Macedon, whose victory at Chæronea, while it forever destroyed the liberties of those turbulent communities, united under one leader the whole power of Greece, which thenceforth, menacing and ready for action, loudly proclaimed the approaching conquest of the East.

In Persia, Ochus, after having re-established his dominion over all the provinces which had newly or in former times revolted, considered his task as king of Persia completed; and, while he himself indulged in luxurious repose, abandoned the reins of government to his favourite Bagoas, an Egyptian eunuch, who, during the rebellion of his countrymen, had rendered important services to the king. But Bagoas was too much of an Egyptian ever to forgive the insults which Ochus had heaped on the religion of his country. Not content with having dismantled the towns, and plundered the temples of their treasures and public records, the king of Persia caused the great object of Egyptian adoration, the ox-god *Apis*, to be sacrificed to an *ass*—a severe practical satire upon the animal-worship of Egypt, and not less significant as an act of revenge upon the Egyptians for their having nicknamed himself *The Ass*, on account of his apparent sluggishness and inactivity.

This act of Ochus was an offence which Bagoas could neither forget nor forgive. He poisoned the king, and destroyed all his sons except the youngest. This horrid deed was followed by his sending back to Egypt such of the plundered archives as he could collect. Arses, the son of Ochus, whom the eunuch had spared, he placed upon the throne, with the intention of reigning in his name. But, discovering that the young king contemplated punishing the murderer of his father and brothers, Bagoas anticipated his intention, and in the third year of his reign destroyed him and all the remaining members of his family. Bagoas next tendered the blood-stained sceptre to Codomanus, a descendant of the royal family, who, after a life of poverty and vicissitudes,[1] had been appointed governor

---

[1] His grandfather was the brother of Darius II. Nothus; and his father was the only one of the family who escaped the massacre with

of Armenia, and who now, on his accession to the throne, assumed the name of Darius. (355 B. C. E.) The eunuch soon repented of his choice, and plotted the death of this king also; but Darius, having discovered his design, returned to his own lips the poisoned chalice he had prepared for the king.

Few kings of Persia ever enjoyed greater advantages at their accession than Darius. He had no competitors or opponents; his treasures, increased under Ochus by the plunder of many lands, seemed exhaustless; his dominion appeared well established all over the nations which abode from the Indus to the Isles of Greece, and from the cataracts of the Nile to the Caucasian mountains: and with all this, the personal bravery of Darius and his acknowledged merits made him universally respected and admired throughout his empire. But, bright as his star appeared, another had risen, before which his own grew pale and became extinct. Though he had assumed the appellation of *Darius*, he could not recall the principles or manners which distinguished his countrymen during the reign of the first monarch of that name. In the space of about two hundred and thirty years the Persians had been continually degenerating from the virtues which characterize a poor and warlike nation, without acquiring any of those arts and improvements which usually attend peace and opulence. · Their empire, as extended by Darius Hystaspes, still embraced the most valuable portion of Asia and

---

which Ochus opened his reign. He afterwards married, and had a son, who was this Codomanus. The young man lived in obscurity during most of the reign of Ochus, supporting himself as an *astanda*, or courier, by carrying the royal despatches. He at last had an opportunity of distinguishing his valour by slaying a Cardusian champion, who, like another Goliah, defied the whole Persian army. For this gallant exploit he was rewarded by Ochus with the important government of Armenia. (Diodorus, lib. xvii.)

Africa. The revenue paid in money was still estimated, as during the reign of that monarch, at fourteen thousand five hundred and sixty talents. Immense treasures had been accumulated in Damascus, Arbela, Susa, Persepolis, Ecbatana, and other great cities of the empire. The revenue paid in kind cannot be appreciated; but such was the extraordinary opulence of this great monarchy, that the conquests of Alexander are supposed to have given him an income of three hundred millions of dollars—a sum which will admit of every allowance for exaggeration, and still appear sufficiently great.

Although the extravagance and vices of Susa, Babylon, and other imperial cities corresponded to the extent and wealth of the monarchy, yet the Persians were prepared for destruction rather by their ignorance of the arts of peace and war, than by their effeminacy and luxury. The provinces, moreover, had ceased to maintain any regular communication with the capital or with each other. The standing military force proved insufficient to keep in awe the distant satraps or viceroys. The ties of a common religion and language, or the sense of a public interest, had never united into one system this discordant mass of nations, which was ready to crumble to pieces at the touch of an invader. When to these unfavourable circumstances we join the reflection that, under the younger Cyrus, twelve thousand Greeks had baffled the arms, and almost divided the empire, of Persia, our admiration of Alexander's magnanimity in undertaking his Eastern expedition will diminish, unless we are at the same time apprized that Darius, a brave and generous prince, beloved by his Persian subjects, was assisted by the valour of fifty thousand Greek mercenaries. (Gillies, iv. 255.)

His rival, Alexander of Macedon, holds so prominent a place in the history of the world, that it is needless for us to speak at length of his character and actions. Nor would it be necessary for us to say more of him or of his brief connection with Judea, than that, at the head of a small but veteran army, he conquered and overthrew the Persian Empire; and that, having established his own domination over Central and Western Asia, and part of India, he died, after a reign of twelve years, and left the Eastern world a prey to the reckless ambition of the chiefs who commanded his armies. This is all that it would be necessary for us to say of Alexander the Great, were it not that his intercourse with the Jews, short-lived as it was, and often disputed as it has been, showed us with what high-principled constancy, and respect for the sacred obligation of an oath, the Jews maintained their loyalty and attachment to the falling standard of Persia.

In the spring of the year 334 B. C. E., Alexander, at the head of an army of 30,000 foot and 5000 horse, entered Asia, the Persians having neglected to oppose his landing. Five days later their armies, numbering 100,000 foot and 20,000 horse, encountered him on the river Granicus, and were defeated. The year after, Darius in person took the field at the head of an army variously estimated at from four to six hundred thousand men. But, though the numbers engaged in this second battle were larger, the result was the same. The superior military skill of Alexander had enabled him, at Issus, to choose such a battle-ground, that the immense numbers of Darius became worse than useless to that unfortunate monarch. He lost the battle; and the thousands of his troops who had not been able to take part in the fight now incumbered the retreat; so that, in their eagerness of flight, more were crushed to death than had fallen by the swords of the Greeks. - Darius himself escaped with great difficulty; his camp, his mother, his wife, and his sons fell into the hands of the victor, who treated them with great kindness. The treasures of the Persians, their wives and children, who accompanied their husbands and fathers to the field, but had been left behind at Damascus, also came into the power of the conqueror, who took possession of that city immediately after the battle.

Darius fled to the interior of his empire, and, after a vain attempt at negotiation, began to raise another army. Alexander was in no hurry to follow him. Prudent as well as valiant, he determined to leave no enemies behind him. His original plan had been to reduce all the maritime provinces of the Persian Empire before he marched on Susa; and the great victory he had gained did not tempt him to alter his intention. In the spring of 332 B. C. E., he marched into Phœnicia, all the states of which tendered their submission, except Tyre. That great mart of the ancient world was the first city that offered serious resistance to his arms. He was compelled to besiege it in form, and the capture of that seaport town forms one of his most splendid operations, that to this day calls forth the admiration of military historians. Tyre, after the destruction of the ancient city by Nebuchadnezzar, had been rebuilt upon an island about four hundred fathoms from the shore. Its walls were high and strong, and additional defences had been erected. The city possessed a plentiful store of provisions, and fresh supplies could be brought by sea without any difficulty. The citizens of Tyre—encouraged by ambassadors from Carthage, who promised speedy and effectual succour—felt invincible within their seagirt isle, that seemed to bid defiance to any attack by an enemy destitute of shipping. Alexander, after the battle of Granicus, had discharged and dismissed his fleet, which was too small to cope with that of the Persians—collected from Egypt and Phœnicia—and yet too large for his slender treasury to maintain. He declared that he would render himself master of the sea by conquering the land; that is, by getting the ports and harbours of the Persians into his possession.

The *prestige* of his present power and future success was at stake before Tyre, but the resources of his genius were equal to the emergency; and, after a siege of seven months, in which attack and defence were conducted with equal valour and skill, the proud and wealthy city was taken by storm. Many of the Tyrians fled to Carthage, but eight thousand fell by the sword; thirty thousand were sold into slavery, while two thousand of the principal citizens were crucified, and the city was plundered and laid in ashes—a terror-striking example of the conqueror's wrath to other cities that might contemplate resistance to his arms.

On his entrance into Syria, Alexander had summoned all the cities of that province to surrender, to pay to him the tribute they had hitherto paid to the king of Persia, and to supply his army with provisions. All obeyed. Samaria even went beyond the conqueror's desire: not only were provisions furnished and the tribute paid, but eight thousand Samaritan warriors swelled the ranks of Alexander's host. Not so Jerusalem. When Alexander's written order—issued from his camp before Tyre—reached Jaddua, the high-priest, he, as the chief magistrate of the Jews, replied that he and his people had sworn fealty to Darius, and that, so long as that monarch was alive, they could not violate their oath by yielding obedience and aid to his enemy.

The haughty conqueror felt offended. He vowed vengeance against the petty tribe that had dared to disobey his mandate. Tyre was soon subdued; and Jerusalem was next threatened by his arms. The long-continued tranquillity and prosperity of the Jews had excited the envy of the neighbouring tribes. The opulence of Jerusalem and its temple tempted their cupidity. When it became known that the victorious army of Alexander was marching against Jerusalem, numerous reinforcements of Samaritans and Syrians, Phœnicians and Chaldeans, hastened to join him. Jaddua, the high-priest, and the Jewish people, were in the utmost consternation and dismay. Public sacrifices were offered for the national welfare; public prayers arose to implore the protection of the Deity. A nocturnal vision revealed to Jaddua how to appease the incensed Macedonians. Accordingly, he caused the city to be ornamented with garlands and flowers, and the gates to be thrown open, while he himself, and the other priests, dressed in their sacred vestments, and the people clothed in robes of white, prepared to meet the dreaded conqueror. The solemn procession marched forth to Sapha, an eminence from whence the whole city and temple might be seen.

No sooner had Alexander beheld the high-priest in his hyacinthine robes embroidered with gold, wearing his mitre with the golden frontal, than he fell prostrate and adored the Holy Name which was there inscribed in golden characters. His attendants were astonished. The enemies of the Jews, who impatiently expected the signal of slaughter and pillage, were struck with amazement. At length Parmenio, one of Alexander's principal leaders, addressed him, and said: "How comes it that thou, before whom every one prostrates himself, shouldst kneel before the priest of the Jews?" Alexander replied, "I worship not this man, but his God." He further related how, previous to his entering on his expedition to Persia, he had, in a nocturnal vision at Dion in Macedonia, seen the Jewish high-priest, dressed as he was then before him; that the man who appeared to him in that vision had encouraged him, and promised him the conquest of all Asia; and he concluded by saying, "Now that I see him before me, my vision recurs to my mind; and, as I am thus convinced of the divine protection, I no longer doubt but I shall fully succeed in my undertakings." He entered Jerusalem as a friend, offered sacrifices, and granted the nation all those favours and immunities which they solicited from him. After a short sojourn, he departed to complete the final subjugation of the Persian monarchy, and thus to verify the prediction of the prophet, that the empire of Cyrus should be subverted by a Greek.

Such is the account of this singular transaction, handed down to us by two Jewish sources, perfectly independent of each other—Josephus and the Talmud; both of whom agree in the main features of the narration. On the other hand, its truth has been positively denied; and even the visit of Alexander to Jerusalem has been set down as Talmudic fable, and self-glorification on the part of the Jews and their historian, Josephus. On an impartial examination of the proofs adduced for and against the Jewish writers, we are of opinion that the weight of circumstantial evidence strongly preponderates in their favour, and we doubt not but our readers will join with us in that opinion.

The objections urged against the truth of this Jewish narration are chiefly: 1. The tinge of the marvellous which attaches to the whole affair. 2. Anachronisms, conflicting with the known history of Alexander. 3. The total silence of the Greek historians and biographers of Alexander, who nowhere speak of his visit to Jerusalem. Each of these objections we will examine separately; for, as Alexander's interview with Jaddua is the first event related on the authority of post-biblical Jewish historians, and as their truthfulness is so bitterly attacked that the whole of their narration on this occasion is rejected as fabulous and false, it behoves us to examine whether this sweeping condemnation can be sustained before the tribunal of dispassionate inquiry. And should it appear that, even as to this narration, their trustworthiness has far greater claims in its favour than the clamour that has been raised against them, we shall then, and on other occasions, avail ourselves of their evidence, as an authority entitled to respect; but which, if they had been convicted of falsehood in their very first narration, we should not again have presumed to adduce.

And first, with respect to the tinge of the marvellous that is interwoven with the affair. This objection is chiefly urged by those who also question the supernatural events recorded in the Bible itself. But these objectors forget that, if we reject from the history of Alexander every thing that appears marvellous, but which, nevertheless, is attested by writers generally considered as trustworthy, we shall have to retrench full one-half of the details that have reached us of his progress. We should also deprive ourselves of our knowledge of the skill with which, in order to facilitate his success, Alexander availed himself of the powerful influence that the marvellous exercises over the human mind. The love of the marvellous was not only the characteristic of his age, but has at all times characterized the Oriental nations. Alexander, undertaking the conquest of a great empire with but small material means, enlisted in his aid every moral auxiliary that he knew; and of these, the marvellous was one of the most potent. Alexander not only used it as an instrument to act on the minds of others, but we find that it also most powerfully reacted on his own mind. Even his philosophical historian, Arrian, is forced to acknowledge that "the many concurring instances of singular good fortune in the life of Alexander seemed to be produced by the immediate interposition of divine power, which, in effecting an important revolution in the Eastern world, rendered the operations of nature and the volitions of men subservient to the secret purposes of its providence." (Gillies's Hist. of Ancient Greece, iv. 272.)

Such is the admission of philosophical history, wrung from it by facts so strangely marvellous, that the High-Priest Jaddua's nocturnal vision appears quite simple at the side of them. The recital of some of those facts will fully bear out our assertion.

On his advance, after the battle on the river Granicus, Alexander in person led a division of his army along the sea-coast from Phasellis to Perga. "On this foaming shore the sea commonly beats against the rocks, and renders the passage impracticable, unless when the waves are repelled by a strong north wind. When Alexander began his march, the wind blew from the south. Yet he advanced fearless, confiding in his fortune. His troops cheerfully followed him, encouraged by many artful prodigies[2] which announced success to his undertaking. The event which next happened was well fitted to strengthen their credulity and confirm their implicit obedience. Before they had reached the main difficulties of the pass, the south wind gradually ceased, a brisk gale sprung up from the north, the sea retired, and their march thus became alike easy and expeditious." (Ibid.) To the lively Oriental imagination of Josephus, (Antiq. xi.) this exploit of Alexander's suggests a comparison with the passage of the Israelites through the Red Sea. The evidence of

---

* "While Alexander deliberated whether he should march forward to attack Darius, a measure which promised glory and plunder to his troops, or proceed along the sea-coast and reduce the maritime cities, which would prevent the enemy from profiting by his absence in Upper Asia to conquer Greece or Macedon with their fleet, a fountain near the city Xanthus, in Lycia, boiled up and threw out a copper-plate engraved with ancient characters, signifying that the time was come when the Persian Empire should be overthrown by the Greeks. Plutarch adds, 'Encouraged by this prodigy, he hastened to subdue the coast.' It would, perhaps, have been more worthy of a historian to say, 'Encouraged by this prodigy, the Greeks and Macedonians readily obeyed the commands of their prudent, not less than valiant, general.'" (Gillies, iv. 272.)

Arrian explains the marvellous in this occurrence; while we, at the present day, are inclined to look upon this opportune change of wind, though perfectly natural, as a signal interposition of Providence in favour of the man whose success had been predicted by Daniel.

As a converse to the above fact, let us take the following legend: The city of Gordium was famous in remote antiquity as the principal residence of the Phrygian kings, and the chief seat of their opulence and grandeur. "Alexander had not long arrived in that place, when a desire seized him of ascending to the ancient castle or palace of Gordius, and of beholding the famous knot on his chariot, which was believed to involve the fate of Asia. Gordius, as the story went, was a man of slender fortune among the ancient Phrygians, who had but a small piece of land and two yokes of oxen, one of which he employed in the plough, and one in the wagon. It happened to Gordius, while he was one day ploughing, that an eagle alighted on his yoke, and sat on it till evening. Alarmed by the prodigy, Gordius had recourse to the Telmessians, a people inhabiting the loftiest mountains in Pisidia, and celebrated over all the neighbouring countries for their skill in augury. At the first village of the Telmessians he met a virgin drawing water at a fountain, to whom having communicated his errand, she ordered him to ascend the hill and there sacrifice to Jupiter. Gordius entreated her to accompany him, that the sacrifice might be performed in due form. She obeyed. Gordius took her to wife. She bore him a son, Midas, who, when arrived at manhood, was distinguished by his beauty and valour. It should seem that the father of Midas had, in consequence of his marriage, settled among the Telmessians, with whose arts his son would naturally become acquainted. The Phrygians at that time were harassed by cruel seditions; they consulted an oracle, who told them that a chariot should soon bring them a king, who would appease their tumults. While the assembly still deliberated on the answer given them by the oracle, Midas arrived in his chariot, accompanied by his parents. The appearance of Midas justified the prediction, and announced him worthy of royalty. The Phrygians elected him king; their seditions ceased; and Midas, in gratitude to Jupiter, consecrated his father's chariot, and suspended it by a cord made of the inner rind of the cornel-tree, the knot of which was so nicely tied that no eye could perceive where it began or ended.

"Whether Alexander untied or cut the knot, is left uncertain by historians;³ but all agree that his followers retired with the complete conviction that he had fulfilled the oracle. A seasonable storm of thunder confirmed their credulity; and the belief that their master was destined to be lord of Asia, could not fail to facilitate that event." (Gillies, iv. 276.)

This legend is at once marvellous and silly. The asses' ears, for which in after life King Midas became so famous, cast their shadow over the whole tale. And yet it is unquestionably true, that in popular belief the empire of Asia was bound up in the knot that tied the old chariot suspended in the castle of Gordius; and the presence of mind with which Alexander got over the difficulty which this belief might have caused him, is still perpetuated in the universally proverbial expression of "cutting the Gordian knot."

After these marvels, it is hardly necessary to speak of the swallow that helped to discover a plot formed to assasinate Alexander, (Arrian, p. 25;) or of the prediction of

---

* Curtius (lib. iii. c. 1) says he cut it with his sword. Plutarch (vit. Alexand., p. 1236) says he untied it. Arrian (p. 81) gives both accounts; and the latter on the authority of Aristobulus, which is therefore the more probable.

Calanus, who, having directly, previous to his self-inflicted death, embraced all present, refused to take leave of Alexander, saying, "he should again see him in Babylon," (Ib. l. vii. c. 3,) the spot where Alexander shortly afterward expired; and many other similar incredible circumstances related by, and believed on the authority of those very historians, whose silence on the subject of Alexander's visit to Jerusalem is adduced as the strongest objection against the trustworthiness of the Jewish writers. But if with these *outré* narratives we compare the account of Alexander's interview with Jaddua, the high-priest, we shall find that, though tinged with the characteristic of the times—the marvellous—this account is, nevertheless, perfectly credible.

That Jaddua's mind should have been strongly agitated by the impending fate of his city, his people, and himself, is quite natural; that, as resistance was out of the question, his thoughts must have been altogether absorbed in devising the most effectual mode of appeasing the conqueror's wrath by some striking act of submission, is also quite natural. This being granted, is it so incredible that in the silence of his chamber, and while his body was at rest, his mind should continue active; that the subject of his waking thoughts should be seized upon and worked out by his imagination, until his mind's eye saw the city ornamented with garlands, the gates thrown open, and the long procession of inhabitants clothed in white passing through them, preceded by the priests in their vestments, and the whole headed by himself, arrayed in all the splendour of his high dignity? Is it unlikely that the strong impressions produced by this VISION should have remained stamped on his memory after he awoke, and that his judgment should have approved of that which his imagination had suggested?

We repeat, that in all this we see nothing incredible.

Even in our days, we all know or have heard of remarkable instances of dreams and of their influence; nor is the present theory on the subject so clear and certain that it affords any satisfactory explication of such marvels. We use the word VISION advisedly; because we believe that the thought which arose in Jaddua's mind during his repose, though perfectly natural, was nevertheless a signal interposition of Providence for the preservation of Jerusalem, its people, and temple.

With respect to the second marvel, the vision which Alexander had, or professed to have had, at Dion, we also see no insuperable difficulty. It is certain that the pupil of Aristotle, preparing for the conquest of Persia, and naturally of an inquiring turn of mind, would seek to acquire the fullest information respecting such portions, at least, of that empire as the success of his arms would first lay open to him. The geographical position of Judea, together with the anomalies of a great and strong city like Jerusalem, governed by a priest, and of a celebrated temple in which there was no image, would be sure to strike him; and the impression thus produced, joined to the constant preoccupation of his sleeping and waking thoughts—the conquest of Persia—may at night have placed before his mind's eye the high-priest, whose peculiar vestments had perhaps been described to him during the day.

Moreover, and to us it appears more probable, that consummate politician, Alexander, "who so often employed superstition as an instrument of policy," (Gillies, iv. 380,) may here have treated his troops and allies to a second edition of "cutting the Gordian knot." His first ebullition of anger evaporated, it could not fail to strike him, that the solemn submission of the high-priest of Jerusalem would much more advance his interests than the destruction of the city could do; inasmuch as the submission of the priest would prove that "the God of heaven," in whose temple he ministered, and for whose worship the kings of Persia had so respectfully provided, had now forsaken those kings, recognising Alexander as their successor; and that this recognition, confirmed by the seasonable recollection, on his part, of a nocturnal vision at Dion previous to his entering on his expedition, would be certain to act on the mind of Darius and his native Persians, whose predecessors in former ages had been so careful to avert "the wrath of the God of heaven against their kingdom." (Ezra vii. 23.)

Whichever of those two views of Alexander's vision be adopted, there is nothing absolutely incredible in either; and we thus find that the first objection, the tinge of the marvellous, is not of sufficient weight to destroy the evidence of the Jewish historians.

The second objection, anachronisms, will not be found more tenable. They are chiefly three: First, Parmenio could not have asked Alexander "Why he, before whom every one prostrated himself, should kneel to the priest?" as Alexander did not require prostration—the mark of respect exacted by the kings of Persia—till long after the period alluded to by Josephus. Next, that the conqueror cannot have been accompanied by Chaldeans. And, lastly, that the high-priest could not, with propriety, have addressed to Alexander any requests in favour of the Jews settled in Babylon and Media, before that prince had conquered those countries or even passed the Euphrates. (Moyle's Letters, ii. 415 *et seq.;* Examen Critique des Historiens d'Alexander, 65–69.)

These objections appear to us futile and unworthy of those who offer them. Though Alexander did not at that time exact prostration, that mark of respect was certainly offered to him by the Orientals, even by those of highest rank. (Arrian, lib. ii. p. 39.) Consequently, Parmenio's remark, as reported, was correct; though the homage on the part of "every one" was voluntary and in conformity with the ancient custom of the East. Chaldeans from Babylon were among the colonists settled in the land of Israel, and are, long before Alexander's time, enumerated among the tribes who assumed the designation of "The men on this side the river," (Ezra iv. 9–11,) and who subsequently were known by the general name of Samaritans. And, lastly, that the high-priest should consider Alexander as already in possession of countries which he had not yet even approached, was, under the circumstances, by no means improper or unlikely. The high-priest knew and believed the predictions of Daniel, which proclaimed Alexander to be the destined conqueror of the whole Persian Empire. These predictions he imparted to Alexander, who had always announced himself as the man of destiny. It was therefore perfectly in keeping with the character of both, and goes far to confirm the truth of the whole narrative, that the high-priest should have asked, and that Alexander should have granted, favours, not only to the extent of that monarch's actual power, but also to the much greater extent of his future possessions.

The last objection, the silence of the Greek writers, has by some, even of the modern Jewish historians, been held so weighty, that they allow it to prevail over the positive evidence of Josephus and the Talmud. We confess we cannot adopt their views. The silence of Greek writers, whenever any circumstance creditable to Jews is to be related, proves nothing except the malice and partiality that dictated the omission. If we were to allow the silence of Greek historians to afford proof positive of the nonoccurrence of any event, we should have to reject from the annals of history the wars of the Maccabees, for these, likewise, are nowhere mentioned by any Greek writer. In the instance of Alexander's intercourse with Jaddua, the

Jewish authorities are supported by circumstantial evidence too decisive to leave any room for doubt as to the favour with which Alexander treated the Jews, and the honours which, in return, they decreed to him. He granted them the privilege that during the sabbatical year, in which they did not cultivate the ground, they should be exempt from tribute. This exemption they actually enjoyed during the whole time they were subject to the Egypto-Grecian and Syro-Grecian kings; nor can any other origin be shown for this important privilege. Indeed, had it been granted by any other and less authority than that of Alexander himself, the successive and hostile possessors of Judea—but who all claimed to be the successors of Alexander—would not have continued to respect an immunity so greatly at variance with their own interest. In return for his kindness to them, the Jews decreed that every male child born to the *Cohanim* (or descendants of Aaron the priest) in the year of his visit to Jerusalem, should, in honour of him, be named Alexander. Thenceforth this name—a truly Greek one—is found in frequent use among the Jews, and continues so unto this day; nor can any other reason be assigned for its introduction.

These two facts, which have never been denied, confirm the friendship between Alexander and the Jews, as related by their historians; while the silence of the Greeks is easily accounted for by their inveterate hatred of the Jewish people, which, on more than one occasion, prompted them not only to suppress facts, but also to invent falsehoods, of which we shall furnish abundant proof as we go on.

Little as the question, whether Alexander visited Jerusalem or not may concern us of the present generation, we deemed it right to subject it to a searching investigation, because in that question the truthfulness of the much-abused Talmudic historians is involved; a truthfulness which, in this instance, we trust we have fully vindicated.

Josephus relates that the Samaritans, who had early submitted to Alexander, and sent him auxiliaries at the siege of Tyre, on seeing the favour with which the Jews were treated by him, came forward, as followers of the same law, to solicit the same privilege. For—as the Jewish historian with equal asperity and truth remarks—the Samaritans were always ready to profess themselves Jews when the descendants of Abraham were prosperous, and equally ready to disown and disavow the connection when the Jews were in distress or difficulty. They also advanced to meet Alexander in solemn procession; and, as they were graciously received, they also requested exemption from tribute on the sabbatical year, since they, as well as the Jews, then left their land uncultivated. But, on being pressed, they could not give a direct and satisfactory answer to the question, whether they were Jews? Alexander, therefore, told them he would take time to consider the matter, and let them know his decision when he returned from Egypt.

It was not his policy to encourage such applications; as others, under the same or other pretences, might make similar claims to exemption, to the great injury of the public revenue. When, in addition to this, we remember that Alexander's natural disposition was sufficiently prone to anger, of which he had shortly before given dreadful proofs in his treatment of Thebes and Tyre, we may be sure that nothing short of an overwhelming influence would have induced him not only to pardon the defiance the Jews had offered to him, but even, and to his own loss, to grant them privileges which he refused to their time-serving neighbours.

After the submission of Syria, Alexander departed for the conquest of Egypt, which—after the storming of Gaza, the only place that offered resistance to his arms, and where he himself was wounded—the mere terror of his name accomplished for him. But, though he had no occupation for his arms, his talents for civil administration were all the more actively and favourably exerted. Continually occupied with the thoughts not only of extending, but also of improving his conquests, his discerning eye soon perceived what all the boasted wisdom of Egypt had never been able to discover. The inspection of the Mediterranean coast, of the Red Sea, of the Lake Marœotis, and of the various branches of the Nile, suggested the idea of founding a city, the geographical advantages of which would enable it to become the great mart of the world,— and thus to take the place of Tyre, which city he had so recently destroyed.

Fired with this idea, he not only fixed the situation[4] and traced the plan of his intended capital, but decreed of what nations its citizens should consist. And here we have the remarkable fact, that while to the eight thousand Samaritans who had joined Alexander at the siege of Tyre, and had accompanied him to Egypt, he assigned lands in the Thebaid, (Upper Egypt,) he directed that, in the city he destined to bear his name, to become the capital of his empire, and his own residence, two colonies should be located with equal privileges,—the one of Mace-

---

[4] "Egypt was formed to reunite the commerce of Europe, Africa, and the Indies. It stood in need of a harbour, vast and easy of access. The mouths of the Nile afford neither of these advantages. The only proper situation was distant twelve leagues from the river, and in the heart of a desert. On this spot, which none but a great genius could have pitched on, Alexander built a city, which, being joined to the Nile by a navigable canal, became the capital of nations, the metropolis of commerce. The trading nations of earth still respect its ruins heaped up by barbarism, and which only require the operation of a beneficent hand to restore the boldest edifice the human mind ever dared to conceive." (Mem. du Baron de Tott, t. ii. p. 179.)

donians, the other of Jews.[5] This was the greatest proof he could possibly give of his appreciation of their high principle, and value as loyal citizens. "Such was the sagacity of his choice, that, within twenty years, Alexandria rose to distinguished eminence among the cities of Egypt and the East; and continued through all the subsequent ages of antiquity the principal bond of union, the seat of correspondence and commerce, among the civilized nations of the earth." (Gillies, iv. 306.)

As the converse of this remarkable instance of his genius and talents for business, history relates that, during his sojourn in Egypt, Alexander was seized with an inclination to visit the revered temple and oracle of Jupiter Ammon. Whether he was impelled by curiosity alone, or guided by his usual policy, historians do not decide. The latter was probably the case; for, among the African and Asiatic nations, the oracle of Ammon enjoyed an authority similar and equal to that which Delphi so long held in Greece; and, perhaps, the conquest of the East could not have been so easily accomplished by Alexander had he not previously obtained the sanction of that venerated shrine. After a long, toilsome, and dangerous march through the burning and sandy desert of Lybia, Alexander reached the *oasis*—a fruitful spot in the midst of that desert—on which the temple of Ammon was situated, consulted the oracle, and received a very favourable answer. Plutarch (vit. Alex., p. 680) relates that the priest or prophet meant to address Alexander by the affectionate title of *paidion*, child, son; but not being sufficiently acquainted with the Greek tongue, he said *pai dios*, son of Jupiter. On this wretched blunder were founded Alexander's pretensions to

---

[5] These privileges, which, in the confusion arising after the death of Alexander, seem to have been withheld, Ptolemy I. Soter subsequently renewed and confirmed to the Jews. (Joseph. Ant. lib. xli. cap. 1, et con. Apion, lib. i. cap. 22.)

divinity. Ammon was worshipped under the form of a ram; hence the ram's horns which appear on the head of Alexander in most figures of him, and which are perpetuated in the designation by which he is best known among the Orientals—*Dhulkarnain* "of the two horns."[6] We must leave it to our readers, either, with Plutarch, to attribute all this to motives of policy, or to adopt the narrative of Curtius, (lib. iv. cap. 7,) together with that impression of Alexander's understanding which the whole affair is calculated to convey to us of the present day.

During his stay in Egypt, some Samaritans, enraged, probably, that they had not at once obtained the same immunities as the Jews, set fire to the house of Andromachus, whom Alexander had appointed their governor, and who perished in the flames. The other Samaritans delivered up the offenders to Alexander, who, on his return to the *rendezvous* of his army at Tyre, again passed through Palestine, (331 B. C. E.) But so highly enraged was he, that, not satisfied with the punishment of the actual culprits, he removed the Samaritans from their city, and transferred thither a Macedonian colony. (Curtius, iv. 21.) The Samaritans thus expelled from Samaria, thenceforth made Shechem their metropolis, as that city was at the foot of Mount Gerizim, on which the Samaritan temple stood. Under these circumstances they would hardly dare to remind him of their previous claim respecting exemption from tribute on the sabbatical year, though he had promised he would consider it. Accordingly they never obtained that immunity, which is an additional proof that this privilege had been actually conferred on the Jews

---

* Abul-pharagius, however, (Compend. Dynast. p. 96,) explains this designation as indicating Alexander's sway in the East and the West, "quod assecutus est Orientem et Occidentem." Alexander is indeed the only European monarch who ever, in person, reigned in the great central regions of Asia.

by Alexander in person, and on the occasion of his first and only visit to Jerusalem.

The operations and victories of Alexander beyond the Euphrates are not so directly connected with the history of the Jews as to require that we should speak of them at any length. The battle of Arbella, fought on the 1st of October, 331 B. C. E., gave Alexander possession of the Persian throne. Darius, who, after the battle, fled into Media to raise new levies, was prevented from carrying out that design by the rapid pursuit of the Greeks, and was shortly afterward basely and treacherously murdered by his own attendants. This foul deed Alexander subsequently punished. Bessus, the principal culprit, previous to his execution, was treated with a barbarity better merited by his own crimes than in accordance with the character of Alexander.

It was not till after his return from his expedition to India (324 B. C. E.) that the great conqueror again came in contact with the Jewish people. After having extended his conquests to the Indies, the Danube, the burning sands of Lybia, and the bleak Scythian desert, Alexander fixed on Babylon as the seat of his empire, of which, locally, that city formed the centre, being at an intermediate and nearly equal distance from its four boundaries. That great, populous, and wealthy city, taken by storm, and in part destroyed by Cyrus, who plundered its treasuries and profaned its temples, had frequently revolted, and was therefore always viewed with suspicion and treated with severity by the kings of Persia. They even went so far as to destroy two ancient sources of Babylonian wealth, by obstructing the navigable courses of the rivers Euphrates and Tigris.[7]

---

[7] The kings of Persia treated the merchants of Babylon precisely in the manner that a merchant of London, in the reign of Charles II., pretended ludicrously to fear lest that great commercial city might be treated

All ancient historians (Herodotus, Strabo, Diodorus, Curtius, Pliny) agree in stating that, at the time of its great prosperity under Nebuchadnezzar, Babylon contained upwards of two millions of inhabitants, and that the walls formed a circuit of forty-eight, or, as the Midrash states, sixty miles. A great part of this vast space, probably one-half of it, was occupied by gardens, or rather parks, spacious reservoirs of water, temples and palaces of great extent, vast squares, and market-places. Two of these royal palaces occupied the space of two and a half square miles; the principal one stood on the western bank of the Euphrates, directly opposite the temple, sepulchre, and tower of Belus, a portion of which still stands erect amid the surrounding mounds that cover the vast plain, and affords us convincing proof of the solidity and vastness of these Babylonian structures. Indeed, so solid were they, that the utmost rage of the Persians failed to demolish them: a feat which the powerful hand of time has not, even yet, after the lapse of twenty-five centuries, fully accomplished.

In the days of Alexander, the city of Babylon, though shorn of its splendours and its most gorgeous edifices ruined, still contained a numerous and industrious population, and only needed the fostering hand of a friendly government to recover its ancient prosperity. This friendly hand Alexander prepared to extend to the fallen city. The temple of Belus, so stupendous in its remains,—that ancient tower, indestructible, though ruined,—attracted his attention. With that energy and decision which formed the leading traits in his character, he gave orders for the immediate restoration of the temple and tower. In order to hasten the work, his Asiatic soldiers were employed, in turn, to remove the rubbish; these workmen were nume-

---

by the king. On being told, "His majesty is very angry with the citizens of London," the merchant's reply was: "Indeed! then I fear he will take the river from us!"

rous, for an army of fifty thousand men was stationed at Babylon. To gratify the king's well-known desire, all worked zealously—all but the Jews. The prophets of the Lord had, in former days, predicted that the prosperity of Babylon should never be restored; that the temple of the idol Belus should never rise from its ruins; and nothing could induce the Jews to join in the work Alexander had so zealously at heart. With patience and resignation these sufferers for conscience' sake endured many stripes, and paid heavy fines. Their passive resistance at length overcame Alexander's fiery will; his commands were powerless before their steadfastness of principle, and, shortly before his death, he exempted them from any participation in the hateful labour, though with characteristic ardour he persevered in his design. But, in the midst of his power, and while preparing to subjugate the West, the angel of death smote him at Babylon in the thirty-third year of his age, (28th May, 324 B. C. E.) His influence on the Eastern world is best expressed by his philosophical historian, (Arrian, lib. vii. sub. fin.) who declares that Alexander was "sent into the world by the particular disposition of Providence; a man singular and matchless, whose enterprises, justifiable in him alone, could not have reasonably been undertaken by any other."

CHAPTER II.

Wars between Alexander's Generals—Perdiccas—Ptolemy—Antigonus—Siege and Storm of Jerusalem by Ptolemy—Jews carried to Egypt—Demetrius—Battle of Gaza—Mosollamus—Credibility of Greek historians in reference to Jewish affairs: Jerom of Cardia; Hecatæus—The Nabathæans—Seleucus Nicator—His success in Upper Asia—Era of the Seleucidæ: *Minyan Staroth*—Extinction of the family of Alexander the Great—Battle of Ipsos. (From 326 to 301, B. C. E.)

HISTORIANS differ as to the causes of Alexander's death. According to some, he had been poisoned by the emissaries of Antipater, one of his *lieutenants*, whom he had shortly before displaced from the government of Greece and Macedon. Others, and with more truth, consider debauchery, and the excessive use of wine, as the only poison that destroyed him. With him died the project of restoring the prosperity of Babylon and the temple of Belus, the present condition of which strikingly attests the truth of prophecy. He had permitted the passively-refractory Jews to return to their homes, where, as their historian relates, "they pulled down the temples and altars which had been erected by the colonists in their land, and paid a fine for some to the governors, and received a pardon for others." (Hecatæus in Joseph.: contra Apion, i. 22.)

Aristobulus, a contemporary biographer, relates (apud Arrian, cap. 26) that Alexander being asked, immediately before his dissolution, "to whom he bequeathed the empire?" replied "to the strongest, for my obsequies, I know, will be celebrated by strenuous funeral games among my generals." This report was greedily embraced by the Greeks, whom Homer (Iliad. lib. xvi. 850) had taught to believe that the soul, at taking its flight from the body, often clearly predicted the secrets of futurity, and all acknowledged the characteristic fitness of a reply which veiled Alexander's melancholy forbodings under his accustomed magnanimity.

Yet he had not been guilty of the omission to which able and busy men are peculiarly liable. Sleep and love, he used, according to Plutarch, to say, kept him in mind of his mortality; and, impressed with this reflection, he had made a full and clear testamentary disposition with regard to his whole dominions. (Diodorus. lib. xx. s. 81.) This important document he had deposited in the city of Rhodes, capital of the island of that name, the inhabitants of which Alexander regarded with much fond partiality, and with whom he entertained a cordial correspondence. But in the matter of his testament, these Rhodians did not justify his confidence and good opinion. Their descendants, with preposterous vanity, always boasted that Rhodes had once been in possession of a document so important to the world. (Ibid.) But the will itself, which many powerful persons had the strongest interest to cancel, never made its appearance. His succession was left, as a prize, to be contended for by the ambition of his lieutenants.

The struggle between them is the most memorable warfare ever waged in Asia in point of duration and obstinacy, and the only general conflict in that quarter of the globe during which the resources of wealth and numbers were steadily directed by scientific skill and disciplined valour. During the twenty-two years that this struggle continued, "Evils were multiplied in the earth," (1 Mac. i. 19;) and the Jews, from their intermediate situation, between the two powerful kingdoms, as they speedily became, of Syria, northward, and of Egypt, southward, were alternately harassed by both. According to the imagery of Josephus, (Antiq. xii. 3,) "they resembled a ship tossed by a hurricane, and buffeted on both sides by the waves, while they lay in the midst of contending seas."

It is not our intention to enter into the details of the wars that devastated the wide extent of Alexander's empire, or, indeed, to notice them, except inasmuch as they influenced the condition of the Jews, which they did to a very considerable degree. At a military council held directly after the death of Alexander, it had been decided that Aridœus, his illegitimate brother, but a man of no capacity, should be king, assuming the name of Philip; that a posthumous son of Alexander's, called Alexander Ægus, should share the sovereignty with him; and that Perdiccas, a prince of the Macedonian blood-royal, to whom the dying Alexander had handed his signet-ring, should be regent and guardian of the two kings, who both were incapable of reigning—the one being an imbecile, and the other an infant. After this settlement of the supreme power, the provinces of the empire were distributed as satrapies among the principal generals and ministers of Alexander. Syria and Palestine fell to the share of Laomedon. His most powerful neighbour was Ptolemy Soter in Egypt, of whose character and actions we shall presently have to speak more fully. Among the other great officers of Alexander's, the two most entitled to our notice are Antigonus, who, for a time, seemed in a fair way of re-establishing the unity of Alexander's Asiatic empire; and Seleucus, the youngest, and destined to become the most powerful of them all, but to whom, at the first distribution, no satrapy was assigned.

It was scarcely possible that the authority of two such kings, vested in a regent who had been lifted over the heads of his equals in rank and abilities, should hold in check the powerful and ambitious soldiers who had been appointed governors over provinces equal in extent and resources to independent monarchies. Within a year after Alexander's death, his veterans were opposed to each other in a furious battle fought near the plain of Troy, in which Craterus, the oldest and most respected of his lieutenants, was slain. The year following, a combination was formed against the regent Perdiccas, on account of the design which he betrayed of appropriating the crown of Macedonia. In order to discomfit this combination by vanquishing its most formidable chief, Perdiccas, who kept the two kings constantly with him, marched at the head of a large army through Syria into Egypt, to attack Ptolemy. This expedition miscarried, and terminated fatally for the regent. His own soldiers slew him and went over to Ptolemy, who determined to make the best use of the advantages which this great accession of force and the death of the regent Perdiccas placed in his hands. Accordingly he invaded and conquered Syria.

Ptolemy was a natural son of Philip, King of Macedon, and, as such, the brother of Alexander, but was contented to be thought the son of Lagos, and had been treated by Alexander with the more fraternal regard because he never boasted the name of brother. Present in Babylon at the time of Alexander's decease, Ptolemy, the son of Philip, highly honoured by Alexander, and singularly beloved by the troops, might, at the military council which disposed of the kingdom, have aspired, with no mean prospect of success, to fill the vacant throne. But the abilities which rendered this prudent and lettered prince most worthy of that high honour, also enabled him to calculate its uneasiness and danger. His sagacity was too discerning to allow him for a moment to provoke a comparison with his gifted brother; he wished rather to spread and confirm the opinion that the sceptre of that extraordinary favourite of the gods was too heavy for any one individual to wield.

His circumspection was rewarded with the secret object of his dearest wishes—the possession of the wealthy and secure kingdom of Egypt. (Pausanias, Attic. p. 3.) For, defended on three sides by deserts, marshes, and a great river, and the fourth side formed by a difficult seacoast, which might easily be protected by a watchful fleet, that country had been chosen by him as exactly adapted to carry out his plan of founding a separate monarchy; and in this he eventually succeeded, not, however, without acting his full share in that scene of bloodshed and oppression which desolated a great part of Asia. For, though popular, and seemingly humane, he concealed, under the mild semblance of indulgent affability, a mind of unrelenting severity, not to be deterred by any conscientious scruples in pursuing the views of his ambition. On his arrival in Egypt, he rid himself, by murder, of Cleomenes, whom Alexander had appointed to the financial administration of that country, and who, by his vices and the extortions he practised, was become exceedingly odious to the people, but who, nevertheless, was sufficiently capable of thwarting Ptolemy's projects of independence. (Ibid. cap. vi.) The treasury in Alexandria, which contained eight thousand talents, was seized by Ptolemy, who augmented his provincial troops, courted the affection of his subjects, and so firmly fortified himself by fleets, armies, and garrisons, that thenceforward his country alone remained exempt from the storms that shook the rest of Alexander's empire.

His first enterprise, beyond the limits of his own satrapy, had been the conquest of Cyrene, a wealthy and populous Greek city, and capital of the Greek colonies on the northeast coast of Africa. (Strabo, lib. xvii. p. 836.) This conquest, achieved through his general Ophellas, was, however, only the prelude of the great glory which Ptolemy gained in person, not only by his skilful defence of Egypt against Perdiccas, commanding the royal army of Alexander—till then unfoiled in any combat,—but also by the laudable sympathy which he evinced with the distresses of the invaders. Such of the bodies of their dead as could be recovered from the waters of the Nile—the scene of their discomfiture—he caused to be burnt, according to custom, with due lamentations; and their ashes were, in solemn pomp, restored to their friends. The captives who had fallen into Ptolemy's hands were treated like brethren. This show of humanity was soon to reap its reward. The Macedonians were struck with the contrast between him whom they had come to combat, and their own stern, unfeeling leader, the regent Perdiccas. A conspiracy against him was the consequence. The regent's tent was surprised in the night; and he who had for three years been a terror to his opponents in every part of the empire, fell, as we have already related, an easy victim to the hatred of his faithless followers. (Diodorus, lib. xviii. s. 35.)

Of this emergency Ptolemy availed himself with equal dexterity and boldness. Upon the day following his adversary's death, he came unguarded to the hostile camp, addressed the soldiers as countrymen and old companions in arms, and embraced affectionately their commanders as his dearest personal friends. His camels and wagons then made their appearance, loaded with all sorts of necessaries for men who, having undergone incredible hardships, were invited to a peaceful entertainment instead of being challenged to a fresh battle.

By this pleasing and unexpected transition they were filled with joy and gratitude. They could see no motive in Ptolemy but a concern for their happiness. None of the admired companions of Alexander, absent or present, could thenceforth bear a competition in their affections with the brave and generous satrap of Egypt. Through the acclamations of the admiring multitude he was encouraged to assume the envied title of regent and protector of the kings and of the empire. But he prudently declined an insecure and anxious office, which must have withdrawn him from the government of his flourishing province; recommending, however, to this high dignity a friend and benefactor, who, a few months before Perdiccas' hostile invasion, had marched to Egypt on a very different errand.

By the same military council—held immediately after the death of Alexander—which regulated the succession and fixed the regency, the funeral honours of the great deceased were intrusted to Aridæus, who is not to be confounded with his namesake, the king. This officer, high in credit with the Macedonians, employed nearly two years in preparations for this august solemnity. To convey the remains of Alexander from his palace in Babylon to the temple of Jupiter Ammon in the desert of Lybia, where he had expressed a desire to be interred, Aridæus provided a colossal chariot thirty-eight feet high, fourteen in breadth, and twenty-two in length, drawn on four wheels by sixty-four mules of conspicuous beauty. In the design and decorations of this gorgeous vehicle the rich magnificence of the East was united with the taste of Ionia and the skill of Athens. The golden canopy breathing precious perfumes, the golden throne supporting the arms of Alexander, and the burnished gold which composed its resplendent peristyle, formed but vulgar ornaments in a pageant variegated with Oriental gems, profusely studding even the collars of the mules. Painting and sculpture—arts highly indebted to the discerning munificence of Alexander—in representing with impressive energy the unrivalled series of his matchless victories, outshone the rubies of Asia. The perfection of the more useful arts, which he had so zealously encouraged, was displayed in the construction of the chariot itself, suspended on a flexible spring that humoured every inequality of surface, so as to retain the foliated diadem, crowning the canopy, in the same horizontal position. This mechanical achievement will be more readily admired than imitated—or, according to the opinion of the celebrated Count Caylus, even explained—by the skilful machinists of the present day.[8]

But whatever were the exact means by which the equilibrium was preserved, (and sixty-four mules were made to act in concert on so enormous a weight,) it is certain that this moving mausoleum was safely transported nine hundred miles, from Babylon to Memphis, in Egypt, and thence to Alexandria. (Pausanias, Attic. cap. 6, 7.)

In disregarding Alexander's command to bury him in the temple of Ammon, all his lieutenants were unanimous; but this seeming disobedience was, in reality, more respectful than would have been the most implicit submission. Shortly after his demise, a prophecy was circulated and believed, that the country which received his remains should surpass all other kingdoms of the earth in splendour and prosperity. (Ælian, V. H. lib. xii. cap. 64.) Each provincial governor wished to become the depository of so valuable a treasure; while the regent Perdiccas, himself a native of Alexander's birthplace, Pella, and who aspired and hoped soon to reign in that capital, insisted with much vehemence that the bones of Alexander ought to repose near those of his fathers in Macedon. But Aridæus, who had been intrusted with a considerable body of troops to

---

[8] We would recommend this fact to the notice of our readers. Perhaps some skilful machinist may think it worth his while to refute the assertion of Count Caylus, and explain to us the principle on which this chariot and its spring were constructed. Such an explanation, especially if the implements and tools required were noticed, would greatly add to the knowledge possessed of the state of the mechanical arts in the age of Alexander.

escort the funeral convoy, persevered inflexibly in his duty, and was proceeding through Syria and Egypt on his way to the temple of Ammon, when he was met and treated with much respect by Ptolemy. This adroit politician succeeded in gaining the confidence of Aridæus, and acquired so great an influence over his mind, that, yielding to flattering entreaties that which he had alike refused to menaces and promises, he was prevailed upon to make Memphis his goal.

From Memphis the precious relics of Alexander were slowly conveyed to the new capital of Egypt, which bore his name. There, in a lofty temple dedicated to him, he was worshipped with such ceremonies and sacrifices as the superstition of the Greeks had appropriated to departed heroes in the cities which they had founded. (Diodor. lib. xx. s. 102.) The consecrated grove surrounding the temple was distinguished by the magnificence of its games and festivals. Allured by these favourite entertainments, by the commercial advantages of the city and country, and, above all, by the security enjoyed under Ptolemy's administration, multitudes of new inhabitants from all quarters resorted to Egypt. We shall presently have to relate the manner in which many thousands of Jews became located in that country. Alexandria became the seat of industry and wealth, of ingenuity and learning, in short, of every advantage that adorns and gives importance to an imperial metropolis; and Egypt eventually derived from the policy of the first Ptolemy, and the concurrence of Aridæus in his views, benefits so substantial, that they almost realized the prophecy—if so we may call it—connected with the mortal remains of Alexander.

To requite a favour, the value and importance of which Ptolemy's sagacity enabled him duly to appreciate, he recommended Aridæus, together with Python, an officer of high rank, who had been chief of the conspiracy against the regent Perdiccas, as joint protectors of the empire. The soldiers provisionally⁹ ratified their nomination; and the two persons thus exalted to the highest situations in the state and army, listened only to the suggestions of ambition, and accepted with eager delight the dangerous dignities conferred on them, but which they found it more easy to acquire than to maintain. Euridicé, the wife of King Aridæus, was a woman of a bold and active character, ambitious and eager for power. So long as Perdiccas held the regency, her mutinous spirit had been overawed. But, now that inferior men, and one of them her personal enemy,[10] exercised the pre-eminent function, she determined to vindicate the rights of her imbecile husband; and her intrigues proved so successful, that the joint protectors Aridæus and Python were compelled to abdicate the regency, and, wonderful to relate, the soldiers of Alexander were for a time commanded by a woman. This state of things continued until Antipater, the oldest and most powerful of Alexander's lieutenants, arrived at the royal camp; nor was it without danger or difficulty that this veteran commander could succeed in assuming that supreme authority to which his dignity, his years, his experience, and the choice of the armies entitled him. (Gillies, v. 408.)

While thus the royal army of Alexander and the govern-

---

* It was determined that Antipater should be first protector and regent, and that Aridæus and Python should be his coadjutors; but as he was absent, it was determined that they should exercise all the power and functions of the office while leading the army to Syria to meet him. (Arrian, p. 22.)

[10] Python, who, in the military council and debate concerning Alexander's succession, had warmly opposed Aridæus; and when that prince was declared king, had boldly expressed his indignation, "that in seeking an heir to the crown, the *family* of Alexander should have been preferred to his wishes." (Curtius, lib. x. cap. 7.) This insulting remark, which made no impression on the imbecile king, rankled deep in the mind of his wife, whose character in every respect was the reverse of his own.

ment of his vast empire passed from the hands of Euridicé to those of Antipater—from a woman to a man seventy-seven years of age,—their authority was found altogether unequal to the task of ruling their ambitious subordinates, or of restraining the powerful satraps whose fierce conflicts agitated the whole of Western and Central Asia. Amid the general confusion, Ptolemy, the most astute politician of his age, and the one whose prudent perseverance most carefully but undeviatingly advanced its purpose, prepared to extend his power, and with it his means of personal security and eventual independence. Though he had in the first instance confined his sober views to Egypt, favourable circumstances induced him to undertake the conquest of Cyrene. And after the death of the regent Perdiccas, Syria, in its extensive sense, comprehending Palestine and Phœnicia, as well as Syria proper, offered him a tempting prize.

Its near neighbourhood to Egypt, adjoining the only vulnerable boundary of that country, has at all times rendered the possession of Syria an object of extreme importance to the rulers of Egypt. The fertility, wealth, and populousness of Syria proper, as well as of Phœnicia and of Palestine, in those days—so strongly contrasting with the present desolate condition in which misgovernment so long has kept these countries—rendered them desirable acquisitions. But in addition to this, there were motives peculiar to the position of Ptolemy which rendered it highly necessary for him to make himself master of Syria. Phœnicia still abounded with mariners and well-constructed harbours; the mountains of Palestine were rich in useful metals, particularly in iron; and Syria proper, especially the lofty ridges of Libanus and Anti-Libanus, overhanging intricate vales and extensive plains, produced in great plenty the finest timber.

Ptolemy had early discerned the channels through which

wealth was destined to flow into his country, and had earnestly begun to prepare a great naval force. In the pursuit of this object, he could not fail to cast wishful eyes on the harbours of Phœnicia, and to covet with equal avidity the profusion of iron and timber in Palestine and Syria—articles peculiarly essential to his plan, but of which Egypt was altogether destitute. And, as if all this had been insufficient to tempt him, Laomedon, the governer of Syria, commanded forces so inconsiderable as to be utterly inadequate to the defence of the country. Accordingly, Ptolemy endeavoured without any struggle to gain him to his views; but Laomedon rejected rewards and promotions from a man whom he considered as merely his equal. He fought, was defeated, and made prisoner, but found means to escape. All Syria proper and Phœnicia at once submitted to the conqueror. (Diod. lib. xviii. s. 43.)

But, while the unwarlike tameness and easy conscience of their neighbours felt no hesitation in transferring their allegiance to a new master, the Jews, influenced by the oath recently tendered to Laomedon, manfully resisted the troops Ptolemy sent against them. This is the second time, in the course of our narration, that we have had occasion to relate how the Jews withstood the stronger or winning side, because they had sworn fealty to the weaker and losing party.

Their condition, at the time when Ptolemy undertook the conquest of their country, was far superior to what it had been for some centuries before, and, in many respects, to what at any subsequent period they have experienced. Self-governed, and paying but a moderate tribute to the Persians, the burthen of that tribute had been greatly lessened by the exemption Alexander granted them during the sabbatical year; while their self-esteem as a people, and their reverence for their religion and its principal minister, the high-priest, must have become greatly increased, not only by the respect and kindness with which the great conqueror treated that official, but also, and even in a higher degree, by the truth of prophecy and the predictions of Daniel, which, contrary to all human probability, were realized before their eyes.

Moreover, the policy of Alexander, systematically the reverse of that pursued by the Persian dynasty, tended to raise the importance and welfare of the tributary nations. Under his immediate predecessors, the kings of Persia, and under the Medes, who preceded the Persians, individuals of these nations, who themselves trembled at the frown of a master, governed despotically other nations whom they looked upon as their natural inferiors. In this manner the extended possessions of Asiatic monarchies formed a wide political circle, of which the dominant nation was the centre, and of which the parts nearest to this centre rose in respectability above the provinces more remote from it. (Herod. lib. i. cap. 183 and 192; Conf. Xenoph. Cyropæd. lib. vii. p. 193.) Natives of Persis, the Persia proper, thus governed the territories in its immediate neighbourhood, and natives of these territories were appointed satraps over countries more distant from the Persians, and on one side contiguous to themselves. Vested with this commission, they held both the sword and the purse, were accountable for their administration to satraps nearer Persia, while the nearest and last of these, always themselves Persians, were amenable to none but the great king and his ministers.

The same national pre-eminence had been claimed of old by the Assyro-Babylonians; and has been exercised with stern cruelty over Asia by all the conquering dynasties of Scythian or Saracen descent down to this day.[11] Nor

---

[11] So extensive in point both of time and place, are Asiatic maxims, that the Tartars, with their emperor at their head, still continue to act toward

were the Jews, down to the administration of Nehemiah, in anywise exempted from this subjection. And though subsequently their internal affairs were administered by their own high-priest, yet the satraps of Cœle-Syria, of whose government Judea formed a part, sometimes caused the Jews to feel the heavy hand of irresponsible power: as, for instance, when the governor Bagoses, to punish the crime of an individual, punished the whole people by imposing a tax on the lambs used in their public worship; which, unjust and burdensome as it was, remained in force till repealed by the king in person, as we have already related. (Vide p. 32.) Alexander, the only European conqueror who personally governed in Asia, determined to destroy this most invidious of tyrannies—the tyranny of nation over nation; and he persevered unmovably in his purpose, notwithstanding the perpetual and turbulent remonstrances of his Greeks and Macedonians. The proudest of his lieutenants were compelled to respect the customs and local institutions of the vanquished. Their ordinary affairs, whether civil or sacred, were left to the management of persons appointed from their own number, and, therefore, the best qualified to take charge of all matters of domestic concern.

To the Jews, the boon of self-government, which they had enjoyed under the Persians, and which was confirmed

---

the Chinese with the same systematic nationality. Two hundred years and a succession of several emperors have not made the sovereign a Chinese. The place of his nativity is looked upon as an accident of mere indifference. It is not locality, but nationality; not the place in which he drew breath, but the blood from which he sprung; not the people among whom he lives, but his own family and tribe. "The Tartar conqueror never loses sight, for a moment, of the superiority of his caste; his impartiality is a mere pretence; he conducts himself at bottom with a systematic nationality." (Barrow, China, p. 415.) Accordingly, the struggle at present going on in China is not simply an insurrection, but a conflict between two nationalities.

and augmented by Alexander, became a benefit higher in value than to any of their neighbours; because the Law of Moses, which at this period was carried out in its purity, had qualified them, beyond all other people of the East, to profit by the blessings of rational liberty and municipal self-government. It does indeed appear, from the few and meager notices to be gleaned from the record of the times, that the precepts of their law were observed by them with scrupulous conscientiousness. Cured of that hankering after idolatry which they had so often displayed in the earlier period of their nationality, freed of the pernicious influence which wicked kings and unprincipled courtiers had exerted over them during the sway of monarchy, not yet torn to pieces by sectarianism, nor corrupted by the impure lessons of Greek sophistry and the fallacious varnish of Greek manners, the Jew, toward the end of Alexander's reign, was a fair specimen of what the training and discipline of the Law of Moses could do.

Industrious and simple in his habits, the land he inhabited was cultivated with the utmost care and assiduity. Its natural productiveness, every advantage of soil and climate, was fully brought out, while the barren rocks were rendered fruitful by the well-regulated toil of the husbandman; and perhaps no agricultural country so limited in extent as Judea ever maintained so numerous a population in comfort and abundance. The situation of the country made it the main route of the traffic carried on between Tyre and the ports of the Red Sea, the staple marts for India and Arabia; while the overland commerce between Babylon and the Phœnician cities of the Mediterranean Sea, in part at least, passed through Judea. So that, in the larger cities, especially in Jerusalem, numerous merchants interchanged their commodities, and placed the elegancies as well as the necessaries of life within the reach of the people. But to the corruption of morals and manners, which but too frequently abound in the crowded resorts of traders from different countries, the Jews as yet remained strangers; for the severe restraints of their law, and their horror of idolatry, limited their intercourse with idolatrous strangers to that brief communion which the purposes of trade exacted and the dictates of hospitality did not permit absolutely to withhold, while it did not at all suffer the intimacy and interchange of ideas that alone could infect the Jew with the vices of the heathen. Accordingly, his physical as well as his moral condition contrasted favourably with all other Oriental nations.

His body was strong, inured to exertion, and very different from that of the effeminate Syrian. His mind was sound, and his morals were pure. The intercourse between the sexes was regulated, and the sanctity of domestic relations maintained, to a degree that called forth alike the envy and surprise of the lascivious Babylonian and the dissolute Greek.

But what raised the Jews highest above all other nations, was their faith in One Eternal, Immaterial, and Omnipotent God, and the delighted devotion with which they adhered to and carried out the precepts of the law of God. The rigid observance, not only of the Sabbath day, but of the sabbatical year, proved that they possessed sufficient self-command to sacrifice interest on the shrine of duty. The different tithes, first-fruits, and other offerings enjoined in the law, were cheerfully paid; and the descendants of Aaron, the *Cohen*, or priest, who alone ministered at the altar, and their attendants, the Levites, were not only numerous,[12] but respected and affluent. The

---

[12] According to Hecatæus (in Joseph. cont. Apion, i. 22) the number of *cohanim* (priests descended from Aaron) receiving tithes, about the time of Ptolemy's invasion of Judea, was 1500. He must, however, have meant those resident in Jerusalem only; and which, according to 1 Chron ix. 13,

numerous Jews who had remained in Mesopotamia and Babylon also contributed largely to the support of the public worship in the temple of Jerusalem; and as the kings of Persia, and after them Alexander, had allowed a considerable annual sum for the same purpose, the temple gradually accumulated treasures, which in process of time excited the cupidity of later kings of Syria.

The excellent Jaddua, the high-priest who had so nobly sustained the character of his sacred office in his intercourse with Alexander, had entered the last year of his life; but his successor, Onias, trained up in his principles, conducted the public affairs of his people in the same spirit. Accordingly, Ptolemy's summons to the Jews to transfer their allegiance to him met with a decided refusal, and Jerusalem was put in a posture of defence. The city at that time contained one hundred and twenty thousand inhabitants, and was strongly fortified. The large army with which Ptolemy entered Judea enabled him easily to subdue the subordinate towns; but his siege of Jerusalem for some time proved unsuccessful. It is related that, finding his numerous and well-directed attacks foiled by the strength of the place and the valour of its defenders, he, as a last resource, determined to profit by the rigid strictness with which the Jews adhered to the precepts of their religion; for, having observed that on the seventh day of the week, the Sabbath, no resistance was offered by the besieged to the approaches of the besiegers, and that the walls on that day were left without defenders, he made his preparations for a grand final assault on that day; and, as he expected, meeting with no

---

numbered 1760, while all the priests that returned with Zerubbabel, and took up their residence throughout Judea, numbered not less than 4289, as enumerated in Ezra ii. 36–39.

resistance, he thus easily gained possession of a wealthy, populous, and strongly fortified city.

It must, however, be observed, that this narration rests chiefly on the authority of Agatharchidas, a writer otherwise unknown, but quoted by Josephus. (Cont. Apion, i. 22.) This obscure Greek introduces this *on dit* in order to indulge in a laugh at the superstition of the Jews, who thus lost their city and freedom because they observed the "silly custom," as he calls it, of losing one day in seven in their temple in religious observances. Josephus, in quoting Agatharchidas, contents himself with offering some remarks in defence of the Sabbath, but does not otherwise impugn or contradict the circumstance related; which, however, some modern historians reject, not considering Agatharchidas as sufficient authority.

To us it seems that, however unworthy his motive, his statement may not be altogether destitute of truth; for at a much later period we find (as will hereafter be related) that it required a declaration on the authority of the universally venerated patriot-priest Mathatias, the Asmonean, to convince the people of the lawfulness of self-defence on the Sabbath day. (1 Macc. ii. 40, 41.) And even long after they had ceased to have any scruples about fighting defensively on the Sabbath, they still refused to desecrate the day by acting on the offensive, or disturbing any operations short of actual assault. It was by taking advantage of this (as the Talmud, tr. Erubin, fo. 45, declares) erroneous view of the duties of the Sabbath, that the Roman Pompey succeeded in his attack on Jerusalem. So that, however little weight may be due to the unsupported authority of Agatharchidas, subsequent and well-authenticated facts in Jewish history do not permit us to reject his statement in silent disdain, as Kitto and some others have done.

Some historians assume that Ptolemy obtained possession of Jerusalem by treaty, and that, in imitation of Alexander, he paid a friendly visit to the temple and offered sacrifice. (Kitto, Palestine, i. 665.) But this is contradicted by the best ancient authorities. Whether by means of the stratagem imputed to him by Agatharchidas or not, Ptolemy certainly took Jerusalem by storm, and on a Sabbath day; and, according to the horrid customs of warfare in all ages, including the present, the doomed city was handed over to an infuriate soldiery. The worst passions of human nature—rapine, lust, murder—had free scope; and the obstinate resistance of the Jews, while it exasperated the victors, added greatly to the sufferings of the vanquished.

But Ptolemy was determined to possess the city, not to destroy, or altogether to depopulate it. He therefore put a stop to the outrages committed by his soldiers, and extended pardon and protection to the surviving inhabitants. But, to secure to himself a lasting benefit from a momentary success, he adopted a measure frequently resorted to by Asiatic conquerors—that of transplanting the inhabitants, whose obstinate bravery and love of independence they had experienced, to countries where, dispersed among the victors, these newly-acquired subjects would have patiently to bear the yoke imposed upon them.

Such had been the policy of the Assyrians, and, after them, of the Babylonians. The Persians, in the consciousness of their strength, had left the subject-nations in possession of their lands; so had Alexander. But Ptolemy, who feared he might not be able to maintain his new conquest, and doubted whether he could wean the citizens of Jerusalem from their allegiance to the family of Alexander, determined to derive the greatest possible advantage from the temporary possession of their city and country. Accordingly, he carried away into Egypt upwards of one hundred thousand Jews. His choice chiefly fell on the young and warlike—on all, indeed, who might prove dangerous in Judea, but useful in Egypt, by their energy, their industry, or their talents. The old, the timid, the feeble, were left to cultivate their fields and their vineyards, and were protected in their useful labours without enduring any oppressive imposts.

The captives whom he carried away were likewise treated kindly by a prince who never acted from impulse, and with whom humanity or rigour were alike the results of system and calculation. He knew how faithfully the Jews had kept their oath to Darius; he had just experienced how bravely they had upheld their sworn allegiance to Laomedon and the house of Alexander. Fidelity was a rare quality in those times; and Ptolemy was too wise to neglect any opportunity of attaching such a people to himself.

His treatment of the Jews became celebrated for its clemency. A number of those he had carried away he located in Cyrene, that he might have some faithful subjects in that newly-acquired territory; others he employed to garrison his principal fortresses; and the greater number had their residence assigned to them in his new metropolis, Alexandria, in which city Ptolemy renewed to the Jews the privileges originally granted them by Alexander, which placed them on a level with the Macedonian inhabitants of that city. Under his rule "the Jewish nation flourished in domestic peace, and their expatriated countrymen, by their virtuous and manly behaviour, especially by their unwearied industry and inviolable fidelity, gained such credit with their new master, that he promoted them to civil offices of the highest trust, and committed to their defence the most important strongholds in his dominions." (Gillies's Hist. of Greece, v. 428.)

The fears of Ptolemy that he might not be able to maintain possession of Syria, were, in part at least, soon realized. Eumenes, acting for the regent Antipater and the royal house of Alexander, expelled the Egyptians from Phœnicia. He, in his turn, was dispossessed by Antigonus, who acted for himself and his own aggrandizement, but was prevented from seizing on Cœle-Syria and Palestine by the doubtful conflict he had to wage against Eumenes, and which, eight years after the death of Alexander, terminated in the ruin and murder of Eumenes and the triumph of Antigonus.

Within that period, King Aridæus and his energetic wife Euridicé had been murdered by Olympia, the mother of Alexander the Great, who, in her turn, was put to death by Cassander, a son of Antipater, the regent, who died of old age. The young king Alexander Ægus and his mother were kept in prison, and Polysperchon, one of Alexander's lieutenants, appointed regent by Antipater, was also stripped of power by Cassander, who claimed and assumed the government of Greece and Macedon in right of his wife Thessalonica, the youngest sister of Alexander. Thus Ptolemy in Egypt, Cassander in Macedon, and Antigonus in Asia, seemed about to become the principal inheritors of Alexander's empire. Lysimachus, who had obtained the government of Thrace, was kept so fully occupied by the warlike but unruly inhabitants of that country, that he could for a length of time take no share in the struggle for supremacy that was carried on by the other three. Seleucus—whom Antigonus had appointed satrap of Babylonia, where he rendered himself greatly beloved by the inhabitants—was dispossessed of that government by the same hand that had bestowed it; and was, moreover, forced to escape by night from the rapid pursuit of Antigonus.

That crafty and ambitious veteran did not at first endeavour to impede the flight of Seleucus, but deemed it a piece of good fortune to have so easily rid himself of an enemy whose just and mild government had gained the love of the Babylonians, and whose flight rendered Antigonus master of the rich provinces of Central Asia. From the Grecian sea to the Indus, his will was now to be the only law; and he fully determined to crush every obnoxious vassal, to break every unbending rival. These lofty thoughts were, however, checked by the Chaldean priests, who had predicted that not Antigonus, but Seleucus, should possess the empire of Asia. When Antigonus learned this prediction, though less enslaved by superstition than most of his contemporaries, he instantly sent a nimble detachment of cavalry in pursuit of the fugitives. But Seleucus and his attendants—they numbered but forty horsemen—carried on the wings of fear, escaped its grasp; and travelling by rapid journeys upward of nine hundred miles, they arrived safely in Egypt, where Seleucus was received with open arms by Ptolemy. (Appian. Syriac, cap. 35, and Diodorus, lib. xix. s. 55.)

Ptolemy's conduct may have been influenced by that compassion for Seleucus to which it is wholly ascribed by historians; but the character of Ptolemy, who never suffered his humanity to be at variance with his policy, will reveal to us a less generous but more vigorous motive. If Egypt was ever to become a great maritime power, the possession of Syria was indispensable; and this could only be maintained by the ruin of Antigonus, or at least by the lessening of his power, which recent success had rendered so formidable. For this purpose, Ptolemy was active in forming a combination against Antigonus, the last regent, similar to that which had been formed against Perdiccas, the first; and of such a combination, the valour, great fame, and military talents of Seleucus—even though a powerless fugitive—rendered him a most valuable auxiliary. Both Cassander and Lysimachus readily joined Ptolemy. Their safety and greatness, like his own, required that the overgrown power of Antigonus should be checked.

The four princes addressed ambassadors to Antigonus with four separate demands. Seleucus claimed the restitution of Babylonia; Ptolemy required that his right to Syria—part of which he had now possessed seven years—should be acknowledged; Lysimachus insisted on the annexation of Lesser Phrygia to Thrace, that he might command both sides of the Hellespont; Cassander, until recently in alliance with Antigonus, declared himself contented with his possessions in Greece and Macedon, but joined his new allies in urging one most important point—that the sums of money taken from the royal treasuries should be faithfully accounted for, and equitably divided.

To these multifarious demands, Antigonus—assuming the tone of regent and protector of the empire—gave one general and short reply: "He was actually marching against Ptolemy, and after he had settled his differences with that satrap, he would proceed in due time to deal with his perfidious and insolent confederates." As the ambassadors were departing from Antigonus, they were met by his son Demetrius, then in his nineteenth year, just returned from hunting. Slightly regarding the strangers, and without laying aside his javelins, Demetrius flew to embrace his father. "Tell this, also," said the old man, "at your return to your several masters, that they may know on what terms I live with my son,"—an observation expressive of the odious character of the times, when, among the Greeks, fathers feared to be embraced by their armed children, and when even the great Alexander was strongly suspected of not having been altogether a stranger to the untimely end of his own father, Philip. When, subsequently, Plutarch (in Demet.) admiringly looks upon these words of Antigonus as prophetic of the *wonderful* harmony that afterward prevailed in the family of that prince, "which reigned one hundred and twenty years in Macedon with *only* one example of parricide,"[13] the historian unconsciously chronicles the strongest proof and condemnation of the foul and horrid depravity that so long corrupted and destroyed all natural feeling among the Greeks.

After this haughty answer to the ambassadors, Antigonus hastened to Syria to make good his threats. The whole of that country lay at his mercy. Jerusalem, stripped of its defenders by Ptolemy himself, was incapable of resistance. Of the three fortified cities garrisoned by the Egyptians—Tyre, Joppa, and Gaza,—the two last, feebly defended, were taken by assault. Tyre alone, though it had been sacked only eighteen years before, had already recovered such a portion of its former opulence and commerce as enabled it to make the most of its insular position, and to offer a stout resistance. But after a siege and blockade of fourteen months, the surrender of Tyre made Antigonus master of all Syria.

Leaving his son Demetrius at the head of a considerable army, and assisted by the councils of confidential friends and able generals to govern his new conquests, Antigonus hastened to confront his other enemies, Cassander and Lysimachus, over both of whom he gained considerable advantages, but imprudently rejected the proposals for peace which the allies separately made to him. He purposed to reduce them all to unconditional submission, and might have succeeded in this design, had not events in Syria given a new turn to the war that threatened a total ruin to his affairs.

The Jews, during the seven years that Ptolemy held possession of their country, had gradually become reconciled to his sway. The respect he expressed for their peculiar

---

[13] The word parricide is used in its largest acceptation; for the last Philip of Macedon, to whom Plutarch alludes, killed his son. (Gillies, Greece, v. 518.)

usages, the security they enjoyed under his protection while the adjoining countries were suffering all the horrors of war, attached them to his person and government; and the short experience they had of the rule of Antigonus, and of his son Demetrius, made them but the more strongly regret the change. The consequence was, that thousands of Jews quitted their country and sought refuge with Ptolemy. Like their fathers in the wilderness, they again exclaimed, "Let us appoint a chief and return to Egypt," where already so many thousands of their brethren had found a safe and happy home.

The vast extent of this immigration afforded a strong proof to Ptolemy of the affection his former subjects entertained for him, and convinced him that any effort of his to recover Palestine would be seconded by the natives to the utmost of their ability. He had, till then, been occupied with appeasing the troubles that Antigonus had excited against him in Cyrene. His natural caution, moreover, made him slow to show himself in the foreground of the war; but, in proportion to his prudent delay, he appeared at length with higher dignity and more decisive effect. By means of his great superiority at sea, he completed the conquest of Cyprus, the harbours of which island were conveniently situate for invading Syria and Cilicia. In the former country he gained the seaport of Posideum; in the latter, he carried with much bravery the strong fortifications of Mallos.

Ptolemy determined to mark his indignation at the frivolity with which the Syrians—after having so long experienced the benefits of his own administration—had not only hailed the conquest of their country by Antigonus, but had, with great zeal, seconded his designs against Egypt. Accordingly, both the places Ptolemy had taken were plundered, the inhabitants made slaves, and the districts dependent on them desolated by fire and sword.

After this success in the north of Syria, Ptolemy prepared to invade the south of that region, Palestine and Phœnicia. At the head of a large army he marched from Pelusium, the frontier-key of Egypt, penetrated through the wilderness a distance of one hundred and twenty miles, and encamped near a place called Old Gaza, distant a few miles from the strongly-fortified city of that name, now garrisoned by the troops of Antigonus.

Young Demetrius, exasperated by the loss of Posideum and Mallos, collected all his forces and hastened to meet the invader. His father's friends, however, strongly dissuaded him from risking a battle against superior forces, commanded by such generals as Ptolemy and Seleucus. But Demetrius was not of a temper to listen to such prudent advice. He fought, was entirely defeated, and fled northward to Gaza; but was so closely pursued by the victors, that he could not with safety enter that place, and had to continue his flight until he was sheltered within the friendly walls of Azotus, thirty miles distant from the field of battle.

In this city Demetrius ascertained the full extent of his loss. Five thousand of his bravest soldiers had fallen; eight thousand were made prisoners. The whole of his camp-equipage and treasures fell into the hands of Ptolemy, at Gaza; and in addition to all these losses came the disgrace, that the bodies of the slain, and among them two of the companions of Alexander the Great, still lay unburied on the field of battle.

To remedy this last—and, according to the ideas of the times, worst—disaster, heralds were sent to Ptolemy to crave permission to inter the slain. Together with this permission, which it would have been impious to deny, the heralds brought back to Demetrius his camp-equipage and effects, and the sad remnant of his surviving friends, with a generous message from Ptolemy, "that he contended not at once for all things with the son of his ancient partner in arms and formerly faithful ally." Demetrius accepted his bounty, but implored the gods that they would relieve him from a gratitude burdensome because due to the enemy of his father. (Diod. lib. xix. s. 81.)

His prayer was granted: he was enabled in a short time to repay Ptolemy's favour. Yet the consequences of his defeat were irreparable, since it enabled Seleucus to regain possession of Babylonia, which ever after he maintained. And thus the battle of Gaza was the first step towards fulfilling the prediction of the Chaldeans, which promised the empire of Asia to Seleucus. It is probable that in this, as in most other instances of the kind, the prophecy worked out its own fulfilment, since it inspired Seleucus with the courage and perseverance inseparable from lofty hopes. While at the same time, acting on the mind of the Babylonians, it made them embrace his cause with a degree of ardour and fidelity unrivalled in history till the destruction of Moscow during the French campaign in 1812, and which we shall hereafter have occasion to relate. We notice the fact of the prediction, however, to point out to our readers the great extent to which the marvellous enters into the real history of those times,— a circumstance which it is well to bear in mind when facts are related which it may not always be easy to explain.

The battle of Gaza seemed to have finally decided the mastery of all Syria. From Azotus, Demetrius found it necessary speedily to retreat to Tripoli, thus at once abandoning two hundred miles of the *litorale* to Ptolemy, who now reaped the fruits of the impression which both his former kindness and his recent severity had raised in the minds of the Syrians. Ascalon, Joppa, Acca, Samaria, and Sidon opened their gates to the conquerors. Andronicus, a favourite of Demetrius, who, escaping from Gaza, had assumed the command at Tyre, was the only one who ventured resistance. He even presumed to answer Ptolemy's summons with insult. But a revolt of the citizens compelled him to surrender; and Ptolemy, who, though a brave and skilful general, attached greater importance to the duties of civil administration than to the personally heading of his armies, and who saw no enemy in the field that called for his presence, returned to Egypt, intrusting the command of his army to Killes, an officer in whom he placed great confidence.

Among the different nationalities in Syria, none had watched the progress of events with greater sympathy for Ptolemy than the Jews, not only because of that inexplicable but active predilection which, on so many occasions, had induced their fathers to direct their views to Egypt, but also, and even in a much higher degree, from their own experience of the contrast between the mild government of Ptolemy and the stern rule of Antigonus. Accordingly, when the fortune of arms appeared to have decided between the rival claimants at Gaza, the Jews were in ecstasies. They determined not to rest satisfied, like the other tribes of Syria, with passively passing from the sway of Antigonus to that of Ptolemy, but resolved to form a treaty with Ptolemy which should forever after bind them to his fortune.

For this purpose the priest Hezekiah was deputed to attend Ptolemy on his return to Egypt, to conclude with him a treaty of alliance of the closest kind. And in order to acquaint Ptolemy with the means which the Jews could place at his disposal, and with the rights which their law rendered it incumbent to maintain, Hezekiah carried with him the necessary documents, and was accompanied by confidential councillors.

Hecatæus, to a fragment of whom (in Joseph. con. Apion. i. 22) we are indebted for our knowledge of this embassy, thus describes Hezekiah: "The high-priest of the

Jews, a man sixty-six years of age, held in the highest esteem by his people, of mind superior, of eloquence powerful, of experience in affairs of state second to none." And in a second fragment, Hecatæus further remarks, "Hezekiah, the high-priest, who was greatly respected, and was held in friendship by us, summoned some of his companions, to whom he submitted all points of difference; for he carried with him, in writing, the territory and constitution (of the Jews.)"

The sharp eye of modern criticism (Frankel's Monatschrift, Nov. 1851, p. 48) here discovers a trace of the Synedrion, or council, co-ordinate with the high-priest in public affairs. In opposition to Archbishop Usher, who assumed that Hezekiah was only *segan* or deputy of the high-priest, Dr. Frankel is of opinion that Hezekiah himself held the office of high-priest, and that, as such, he in person went to negotiate and conclude the alliance with Ptolemy personally. The high-priest, however, was not an absolute and unlimited ruler, but only chief magistrate; consequently he could not, by his own authority, concede every demand that the powerful ruler of Egypt was likely to make; and therefore councillors, members of the Synedrion, were appointed to attend him, to whom he was required to submit the various points at issue as they arose. We shall hereafter have occasion to return to this subject.

The mission of Hezekiah proved premature, as, before any treaty could be concluded, the fortune of war had turned. Demetrius, with defeated troops but a mind undismayed, used every exertion to retrieve his father's affairs. It was his character to harden under the blows of fortune; dissolute and careless in prosperity, he became vigilant and enterprising in adversity. By one of those rapid marches in which he equalled Alexander himself, he crossed Mount Taurus, assembled the veteran garrisons of Asia Minor, and suddenly appeared in the heart of Syria. Killes, who commanded the Egyptians, committed the greatest of all military errors, that of despising the enemy. Marching to encounter Demetrius, he advanced rashly, and encamped carelessly near the obscure town of Myons. His vigilant adversary, duly apprized of his security and negligence, contrived, by well-conducted movements, to surprise Killes in his defenceless camp at midnight, gained a large booty, and made seven thousand prisoners. His success filled Demetrius with inexpressible joy, as the means of *disburdening* his gratitude to Ptolemy, whose confidential friend, Killes, was instantly released, and with some other officers of distinction sent back to Egypt loaded with presents. (Diodor. lib. xix. s. 93.)

The defeat of Killes proved fatal to the supremacy of Ptolemy in Syria. Antigonus, who had met with great success, both against Cassander and Lysimachus, no sooner heard of the disaster of Gaza, than, at the head of a large army, he hastened to the support of his son. On his arrival, however, he found that Demetrius had already, in a great measure, retrieved his affairs; and the junction of their two armies placed Antigonus at the head of forces against which Ptolemy not only found it impossible to maintain any part of Syria, but even became alarmed for the security of Egypt; for the great army of Antigonus had become hardened in many a victorious campaign, while their admired commander, in a life of continued warfare, had passed his seventieth year without once losing a battle.

With that prudence which entered so largely into his character, Ptolemy determined at once to give up what he had no prospect of successfully defending. His generals received orders to evacuate Syria, to avoid all encounters with the enemy, and to concentrate their forces for the defence of Egypt and the banks of the Nile.

The departure of their Egyptian friends caused the utmost consternation among the Jews. Their attachment to Ptolemy had been too openly pronounced, their measures in his behalf had been too active, to permit them to expect forbearance from the stern and implacable Antigonus. He had been cruel enough to cause one of his own ancient companions-in-arms, Antigenes, a favourite of Alexander the Great, to be nailed up in a coffer, in which he was burnt alive. (Diodor. lib. xix. s. 44.) And those Jews who had most prominently committed themselves by their partisanship for Ptolemy, felt that their only hope of safety lay in flight. But not only they: the experience of Antigonus's rule, contrasted with the friendship which Ptolemy evinced for their nation, induced many Jews of all classes to prefer a residence in the flourishing capital of Egypt, where the discernment of Ptolemy had endowed their brethren with many valuable immunities. The march of the retreating Egyptians thus became followed by Jewish families in vast numbers.

Hecatæus, to the fragment of whose history, quoted by Josephus, (cont. Apion, i. 22,) we have such frequent occasion to refer, relates an anecdote connected with this retreat, interesting from the striking contrast between the common sense of the Jews and the superstition of the Greeks, which it places before us; and which plainly shows us how the Law of Moses acted on the mind of the Jew, and how the follies of idolatry influenced the heathen. Among the Jews who attended his detachment of the retreating army, Hecatæus, who commanded, makes especial mention of Mosollamus, a warrior "of great valour and strength, and, according to general and unanimous acknowledgment, the most skilful archer among the Greeks or barbarians." On the march to the Red Sea, the soothsayer, consulting the flight of birds, suddenly commanded a halt. Mosollamus inquired the cause of this unseasonable stoppage; on which the soothsayer pointed out a bird to him, and said, "Should this messenger of the gods remain at rest, it is necessary for our welfare that we should likewise, for the present, repose. If he rises and flies onward in the line of our march, we may then proceed with confidence; but should our sure guide take a contrary direction, it becomes incumbent upon us to return to the place from whence we last came." The grave admonition was scarcely uttered, when an arrow from the unerring hand of Mosollamus brought down the poor bird fluttering in its blood.

The diviner and many among the Grecian detachment were aroused to indignation, and curses, loud and many, against the *infidel*, found ready utterance. Amid the blind rage of a capricious multitude, glory or disgraceful death depend on the decision of the moment. Mosollamus was saved by his intrepidity and presence of mind. "How unreasonable you are!" he exclaimed, holding up the bird in his hand: "you think that this bird was acquainted with the destiny that awaits us on our march, when, in fact, it was ignorant of its own fate. Had it been able to foreknow or to foretell the future, it would never have come to this fatal spot, or run the risk of being killed by Mosollamus the Jew." There was too much common sense in this argument to be controverted even by a soothsayer, with all his superstition to back him. And Mosollamus, who so often challenged the admiration of the Greeks by his skill as an archer, now, and with equal justice, challenged their admiration for the boldness with which he evinced his contempt of their puerile superstition.

History thus places before us three distinct immigrations of large numbers of Jews into Egypt within the short space of ten years. The first, and most numerous, was compulsory; the second and third were voluntary. These Jews never returned to their own land: they remained in

Egypt, chiefly in Alexandria, where they throve and prospered, so that their numbers soon exceeded a million. Gradually they assumed the language of the country, an idiom of the Greek, in consequence of which they became designated by the name of Hellenists; and thenceforth the Jewish people were divided into three great masses, each speaking its own idiom, with a literature of its own; and each exercising a considerable influence on the minds of the whole people, which, notwithstanding this division, remained united in its faith in one God, and its adherence to the Law of Moses. The three distinct bodies we speak of are the Babylonians, or Eastern Jews, in the cities on and between the rivers Tigris and Euphrates; the Palestine, or Western Jews, in Judea; and the Hellenists, chiefly in Egypt and Cyrenaica, though there is reason to assume that the Jews who gradually spread over Asia Minor were also known by that designation.

As we have so often had occasion to quote Hecatæus, some account of him, and of another contemporary historian, may not be altogether unacceptable; especially as it will show us the principle (or rather the want of principle) which governed the Greek writers of the age of Alexander, and will prove to us the little weight that ought to be attached to their silence on any subject that other writers, less biassed, speak of.

"From conversation with the Jews who accompanied the retreat of the Egyptian army, Hecatæus of Abdera, a Grecian colony on the coast of Thrace, was enabled to compose his elaborate and faithful history of a people whose transactions and institutions have been strangely disfigured by the vain prejudices of Greece, and more strangely overlooked and calumniated by the proud ignorance of Rome. Hecatæus of Abdera, as well as Jerom of Cardia, assiduously cultivated letters amid the cares and labours of warfare, like Ptolemy, Eumenes, Aristobulus, and other generals of an age equally pre-eminent in arts and arms. After the death of Alexander, Hecatæus attached himself solely to Ptolemy; while the compliant Jerom followed successively the fortunes of Eumenes, Antigonus, and Seleucus, the first of whom was destroyed by the second, as was the second by the third. Under the empire of Seleucus, Jerom, who lived to the age of a hundred and four years, was employed as governor of Syria, in which Palestine was included. Yet, in his history of Alexander's immediate successors, it was remarked that Jerom had passed over the wonderful peculiarities of the Hebrew race in total and incomprehensible silence—a silence, however, that may, in some measure, be accounted for, if we consider that the natives of Judea were either open enemies or reluctant subjects to the princes whom he tamely and anxiously served. Whereas Hecatæus— being the friend of Ptolemy, the beloved protector of the Jews—deduced the memorable series of their exploits and sufferings from the age of Abraham to his own times:[14] a work, the loss of which is the more unfortunate, because the religion and polity of Palestine must have been placed in a light equally striking and new by the candid impartiality of this curious and well-informed stranger." (Gillies's Greece, v. 544.)

After this exposition of the probable motive for Jerom's silence, any comment of ours on the *fidelity* of Grecian historians becomes unnecessary. But it fully defends our attaching greater faith to the *assertion* of certain facts by Jewish writers than to the *silence* of Greeks.

The retreat of Ptolemy's forces left Antigonus in undisputed possession of all Syria, which he retained until his death, at the battle of Ipsos, eleven years later. Judea,

---

[14] Joseph. Antiq. lib. i. cap. viii. Euseb. Prœpar. Evang. lib. ix.; and Orig. contra Cels. lib. i. p. 13.

almost depopulated by the frequent emigrations of its ablebodied inhabitants to Egypt, and Jerusalem, which had not yet recovered from the effects of its capture by Ptolemy, were alike unable and unwilling to offer resistance; nor does history record any great or public measure of severity by which Antigonus punished the Jews for their attachment to his rival, Ptolemy, whose satrapy of Egypt he intended to attack.

Preparatory to the invasion of that country, Antigonus determined to obtain the command of the deserts between Syria and Egypt, that had witnessed the long wanderings of the Israelites under the leadership of Moses. The Nabathæan Arabs, who inhabited, or rather roved about, these deserts, derived their name from Nabaioth, the eldest son of Ishmael. (Gen. xxv. 13.) Six centuries before the time of Alexander, their decaying institutions were restored to their primitive vigour, and thenceforward perpetuated with a tenacity that even yet is in no wise relaxed. With a submission to the stern laws of Jonadab, the son of Rechab, (Jer. xxxv. 6, 10; Conf. Diodor. lib. xix. s. 94,) powerfully enforced by their country and climate, the Nabathæans neither built houses, nor planted fruit-trees, nor drank wine, nor sowed corn. They lived wholly in tents; their food consisted of flesh and milk; their luxuries were pepper, and wild honey found on the leaves of trees; sheep, camels, and horses, the noblest and swiftest in the world, formed their principal wealth. Their first great passion was to live independent and fearless; their second, to inspire terror into all their neighbours. Genuine sons of the wilderness, "their hand was against every man, and every man's hand against them." Still they were no strangers to peaceful pursuits and the avocations of commerce.

From time immemorial the great nomadic nation of which they were a powerful branch—the Arabs—served as carriers in the inland trade between Egypt and Phœnicia on the one hand, and Ethiopia and Assyria on the other. The southern part of the Arabian peninsula—the pastoral kingdom of Yemen—abounded in precious aromatics. The myrrh and frankincense furnished by its happy shores were, at stated fairs, supplied by the southern tribes to the Nabathæans, who deposited their costly merchandise in hugh caverns, particularly those of the rock Petra, distant about one hundred miles from the Mediterranean, and half that distance from the Dead Sea, called by the Greeks the Lake Asphaltites. From these magazines they supplied, with spices and perfumes, the commerce of Phœnicia, the luxury of Egypt, the magnificence of Babylon, and the costly wants of all those countries whose inhabitants they alternately overreached in peace or plundered in war. (Diod. lib. xix. s. 94, and lib. ii. s. 48.)

Against these Nabathæans, Antigonus—although they had given him no particular provocation—despatched an expedition, often undertaken by the greatest conquerors both before and afterward, but in which it should seem that no laurels were destined ever to be won. Having selected four thousand foot and six hundred horse—the best adapted for that species of service,—he waited till the main body of the Nabathæans travelled southward to one of their great periodical fairs. Their wives and children, together with their most precious effects, were left at their stronghold, Petra, under a feeble guard, consisting chiefly of old men. Athenæus, who conducted the invading expedition, in a forced march of thirty-six hours, surprised Petra, put its obstinate defenders to the sword, and returned toward Gaza loaded with much valuable merchandise, besides five hundred talents of silver and a large number of young captives. The whole account in Diodorus (lib. xix. s. 95) reads precisely like the report of some modern French commander of a *razzia* against the Kabyles of Algeria. But the final success of the enterprise was equal to its justice. Before this military caravan had proceeded twenty miles on its route, the fatigue of a sandy road, and the almost vertical blaze of the sun, necessitated a hasty encampment, in the full confidence that little danger was to be apprehended from so distant an enemy.

But the Arabs had already taken the alarm. Their attention was attracted by the smoke of the camp-kitchen. Accustomed to clear skies and naked plains, their experienced eyes discerned from afar the faintest shadows of warriors to avoid or of travellers to plunder; and whether they wished to fight or fly, the extreme swiftness of their horses and camels was always ready to second their purpose. Hastening back to Petra, they learned from their fathers, yet weltering in their blood, the full extent of their disaster; and they flew with fury to avenge it. To the number of eight thousand, they assailed the unguarded tents of the invaders; and, of the whole expedition, only fifty horsemen, wounded and bleeding, escaped with difficulty.

Antigonus, who, as he boasted of himself, "knew better than any other man how to eke out the lion's with the fox's skin," (Arrian, 225,) sought to pacify the incensed Arabs with fair words; and in reply to their indignant remonstrance, he loudly condemned Athenæus, who, without any orders from himself, had undertaken a mad and wicked enterprise that had been justly punished. At the same time, he equipped a new expedition far more numerous, and amply provided with food not requiring preparation by fire, and intrusted the command to the zeal and boldness of his son Demetrius.

But the smooth professions of Antigonus had not for one moment deceived the Nabathæans, or lulled that suspicious caution which is the characteristic of professed robbers. Sentinels, supplied with torches, were posted on the rocks skirting the Nabathæan desert; and as soon as Demetrius came within their sight, a general blaze announced the approaching foe, and gave time to prepare for his reception. Demetrius's first assault met with so vigorous a resistance, that he found it necessary to retreat. Next day the attack was on the point of being repeated, when the loud and clear voice of an Arab chief was heard, strongly urging the folly of wasting human lives on the conquest of a territory so desolate and worthless. Demetrius listened to the reason, accepted a nominal submission, and instantly withdrew his army. (Diod. lib. xix. s. 97, 98.)

But Antigonus was not yet satisfied. A third expedition was fitted out under the command of our acquaintance, the anti-Judean historian, Jerom of Cardia. The purpose was not indeed to conquer the desert, but, by a more lucrative foray, to collect the asphaltus or bitumen on the Lake Asphaltites, the dreary shores of which had been taken possession of by Demetrius. The Arabs looked on quietly, and offered no interruption till a large quantity had been collected, and preparations were made for carrying it away. Then they came down with six thousand men, attacked and destroyed Jerom's boats, and killed the greater number of his men. Jerom himself escaped, and was artful enough to varnish his disgrace. But his representations prevailed with Antigonus to relinquish all prospects of revenue from the Lake Asphaltites, and all hopes of vengeance from a renewal of the war with the Nabathæans. And this the more readily, as the intelligence which reached Antigonus from other parts of his dominions called equally for his personal exertions and those of his son. In the west, both Cassander and Lysimachus were recovering their strength, while in the east Seleucus had reconquered his satrapy of Babylonia. So that while Antigonus was wasting time and means on impracticable and unprofitable attempts to conquer deserts, his richest provinces were irrecoverably wrested from him.

Seleucus had, at the battle of Gaza, afforded Ptolemy the assistance of his valour and great military skill to such a degree, that an important share of the glory of that brilliant victory was justly ascribed to him. And as his activity never slumbered, he availed himself of the good fortune and gratitude of Ptolemy, and, obtaining from him a small body of troops, determined to make an effort for the recovery of his satrapy of Babylonia, of which, three years before, Antigonus had deprived him. During the four years that Seleucus had held this government, his impartial justice and vigilance endeared him to the Asiatics. Imitating the liberal policy of Alexander, he paid little regard to national distinctions; the vanquished engaged his protection equally with his victors, and both were promoted in just proportion to their ability and zeal in the public service. At the same time, Seleucus paid every respect to the habits and feelings of his Asiatic subjects, though gradually and gently engrafting on the Oriental stock many simple but solid improvements, the utility of which daily experience clearly evinced. With energy and abilities equal to his ambition, Seleucus, of all Alexander's lieutenants, was the one who most nearly resembled his master; and in both of them the love of power was called "royalty of soul." His praises accordingly were sounded both by Greeks and Asiatics; and, as he was only twenty-eight years old at the death of Alexander—and consequently many years younger, not only than Antigonus, but also than Ptolemy,—the Chaldeans hailed *him* as the rising sun, and predicted his future greatness.

The prudence, or rather, perhaps, the selfishness of Ptolemy, while willing to reward the eminent services of his ally, did not permit his gratitude to interfere with his interests so as materially to weaken his own force. Eight hundred foot and three hundred horse was all the aid that Seleucus could obtain from him; and with such inconsiderable means, the utmost that he could be expected to perform was to annoy Antigonus for a time, and then be overwhelmed by the superior power arrayed against him. But fortune favours the brave. While Demetrius was yet stunned by his defeat, and before Antigonus, laboriously occupied in the west, could decide on the intelligence of passing events in the east, Seleucus, with his handful of men, crossed the desert and the Euphrates; and after a short halt in Mesopotamia, where he increased his army, he invaded Babylonia as seasonably as, during the ascending star of Antigonus, he had relinquished that valuable province. On their weary march, his troops had been refreshed and encouraged by the predictions of the Chaldeans, announcing their beloved leader as the destined lord of Asia, and the founder of a new and endless dynasty. (Diodor. lib. ii., et xix. passim.)

His entrance into Babylonia was like a triumphal procession; on the progress of his march he everywhere met with the welcome reception of an hereditary prince, who comes to rescue his birthright from a cruel usurpation. Not only the natives flocked to his standard in crowds, but many Macedonians and Greeks joined him, putting him in possession of the strongholds they garrisoned. The lieutenants of Antigonus, who commanded for him in Persia and Media, joined their forces, and marched against Seleucus with ten thousand foot and seven thousand horse. Seleucus, with all the accession of recruits and reinforcements that had joined him, could not muster half the number of men; but his consummate generalship compensated for the deficiency. He surprised the enemy's camp at night: numbers were slain; some few escaped, but most of the soldiers surrendered, and passed into his service. The camp, with all its treasures, was the reward of his followers; but the greatest treasure to Seleucus, the best fruit of his success, was the securing a considerable body of well-disciplined Macedonians, which enlarged his own power even in a greater degree than it diminished that of his enemies.

It is from this victory,[15] which secured to Seleucus the recovery of Babylonia, (October, 312 B. C. E.) twelve years after the death of Alexander, that chronologists date the celebrated "era of the Seleucidæ," at one time in general use throughout all Central and Western Asia, and still retained by the Christians of Syria under the name of the "era of Alexander." The Arabians, who called it the "era of the two-horned," (*Dhulkarnaim,*) meaning Alexander, did not relinquish it till long after the religion of Mohammed had arisen, and the era of the "Hegira" (the flight of Mohammed from Mecca to Medina) had been introduced. The Jews did not adopt this era till after they passed from under the dominion of the Egypto-Greeks to that of the Syro-Greeks, when they became obliged to employ it in their civil contracts, and therefore it was designated by them as the *Minyan Staroth,* "era of contracts." Thenceforth they retained its use upward of twelve centuries, and employed no other epoch till the final close of the schools on the Euphrates, (1040 C. E.;) since when, they date their era from the creation, though the *Minyan Staroth,* in the East, is not altogether dropped. This era it is which, in the Books of the Maccabees is designated as "the year of

---

[15] The Chaldeans, or priestly caste in Babylon, whose great privileges were peculiarly interested in the issue of the contest between Seleucus and Antigonus, did not begin their computation of this era till the spring of the next year, (311 B. C. E.) because, according to some authors, they did not consider their prediction fulfilled, or Seleucus's sovereignty secured, till after the repulse of Demetrius. It is, however, as Kitto justly remarks, more natural to resolve the difference into an adjustment of the era to the different times at which the year was commenced by different nations—some at the autumnal equinox, as the Jews; others at the vernal equinox, as the Babylonians.

the kingdom of the Greeks;" while the horn—that ancient and general emblem of power throughout the East—that had been adopted by Alexander himself, and is so conspicuous on his own coins, was also appropriated by his Babylonian successors, the Seleucidæ, as may still be seen on their coins, which, for beauty and perfection of finish, rival those of Alexander himself.

Seleucus, whose prodigious activity was second only to that of Alexander the Great, did not repose on his laurels. Not content with having secured Babylonia by his victory, he determined to invade and conquer Media. Accordingly, he pursued Nicanor, the satrap of that province, who had commanded against him at the last battle, reduced him to the necessity of fighting at great disadvantage, slew him with his own hand, and gained a complete victory, that procured for him the submission of all Upper Asia.

The arrival of these tidings of repeated loss in such rapid succession, compelled Antigonus to give up every idea of expeditions against the Nabathæans or against Egypt. He at once despatched his son Demetrius, at the head of twenty thousand veteran troops, to reconquer Babylon—a city long ago rendered defenceless by the jealousy of its Persian masters, and still altogether unprepared for resisting a vigorous assault. Patrocles—who, while Seleucus was absent on his distant expedition into Media, commanded for him in Babylon—was apprized of the enemy's advance, and without loss of time communicated the news to his master. But the rapidity of Demetrius would have anticipated a less distant foe. He had already passed the Euphrates, and was marching through Mesopotamia, when Patrocles proposed to the inhabitants of Babylon a very extraordinary measure, which was embraced with yet more extraordinary consent.

The measure proposed and adopted was nothing less than that the vast multitude of peaceful and industrious natives should abandon their city to an invader whom they had not arms to resist; and that they should patiently wait for a change of fortune, either through his own success against the enemy, or the return of Seleucus with his victorious army from the East. The whole body of the people—not excepting those privileged orders of men long proverbial for pomp and luxury—left their habitations and comforts, and fled in various directions with their families and treasures. Some took the road through the desert; others crossed the river Tigris, and sought a refuge in Susiana, or Persia Proper. Patrocles himself, with his Macedonians and such natives as had the courage to follow his standard, —after throwing garrisons into two strong palaces or castles,—lurked amid the canals and marshes of the Euphrates, watching for an opportunity of gaining some stolen advantages over an enemy he durst not openly encounter.

Demetrius, whose hurried advance had been impeded by no resistance, entered the city, but, to his great surprise, found it ransacked and deserted—a proof of affection on the part of the Babylonians for Seleucus that inspired the heir of Antigonus with the bitterest feeling of resentment against them. Of the two castles garrisoned by Patrocles, one was taken by assault; but the other resisted so obstinately and held out so long, that the patience and resources of Demetrius were alike exhausted. He had expected that the wealthy and populous city of Babylon would afford abundant supplies for his army, as the rapidity of his own advance had not permitted him to incumber himself with provisions or baggage. His disappointment and suffering were therefore commensurate with the greatness of his expectations. His expedition to Babylon finds a most striking parallel in the desertion of Moscow in the year 1812, when the great leader of the invaders, the emperor Napoleon, expected that the vast and opulent metropolis of Russia would supply the wants of his exhausted troops, and met with disappointment such as had awaited Demetrius in Babylon. Both invaders, after a brief occupation of either deserted city, were compelled to retreat; but here the parallel ceases—for, while the rigours of an unusually severe winter proved ruinous to the retreating French army, the retreat of Demetrius became ruinous, not to his troops, but to the wretched inhabitants of the countries on his line of march. Exasperated by his disappointment, and at the preference so strikingly given by the people to his father's foe, Demetrius indulged his soldiers in the utmost license of plunder. (Diodor. lib. xix. s. 100.) But the cruelty of his invasion, the disgrace of his discomfiture, and the vengeful desolation of his retreat, forever ruined the cause of Antigonus in Upper Asia, and so firmly riveted the Babylonians to Seleucus, that all subsequent efforts against him proved unavailing.

The countries through which the line of Demetrius's march carried him, both in his advance and on his retreat, were thickly inhabited by Jews. Indeed, the number of Jews located on and between the rivers Euphrates and Tigris was far greater than that of those dwelling either in Judea or in Egypt. History does not tell us of any distinguished part they took in this struggle. But, as we find that Seleucus, when firmly established in that power and supremacy for which he was indebted to the fidelity and love of all his subjects, extended his favour and confidence to the Jews in a higher degree than to most of the other nationalities under his sway, we may be sure that their claims on his gratitude must have been among the strongest; though, for the reason already stated, Greek historians have, as usual, kept silent with regard to the cause that induced Seleucus so greatly to distinguish and prefer the Jews.

The return of Demetrius from his fruitless and inglorious expedition, imposed on Antigonus himself the task of crushing the new rival who had so unexpectedly dispossessed him of Alexander's richest conquests. In order to do this effectually, he at length consented to listen to the pacific overtures which Cassander and Ptolemy had separately and repeatedly made to him. Victorious in three scenes of the war—in Syria, in Asia Minor, and in Greece,—the compactness of his dominions, as well as the superiority of his army, which, when commanded by himself had never suffered a defeat, threatened Egypt on one side and Macedon on the other. He seemed entitled, therefore, to dictate the terms of the peace which two of the confederates solicited, and to which Lysimachus gladly consented. In the treaty between them and him, each of the three confederates retained possession of the satrapies assigned to him, and the dominion of all Asia was conceded to Antigonus—an article by which the allies clearly abandoned Seleucus; while at the same time they tacitly renounced the demand for a fair division of the provinces or treasures which had given birth to the war. It was stipulated that the government of Macedon should be administered by Cassander, until Alexander Ægus, the posthumous son of Alexander the Great, then in his thirteenth year, should attain his majority. This condition was specified with the view that the heir of Alexander should establish his court in his ancient hereditary kingdom, from whence sovereign orders would be issued to the many dependent provinces; and that the empire, founded by the father, would still remain united under the supremacy of the son.

But whatever their professions of allegiance to the house of Alexander, the ambitious chieftains who signed this treaty were fully resolved to maintain their independence. Accordingly, the stipulations in his favour became fatal to the young son of Alexander. He, with his mother, Roxana, had, till then, been retained in strict confinement at the strong castle of Amphipolis, in Macedon. In consequence of the treaty, acknowledging his just title to the throne, the voice of the loyal Macedonians, who still, in every part of the empire, formed the sinews and pride of the various armies, became louder in his favour, and claimed not only his release from captivity, but demanded for him an establishment suitable to his high dignity. Provoked and alarmed by these clamours, Cassander, the scourge of the family of Alexander, at once secured the permanence of his own power, and gratified the views of his confederates, by procuring the death of the young prince and of his mother.

The circumstances of their murder were never clearly brought to light, as otherwise it would have been impossible to restrain the enraged multitude. (Diod. lib. xix. s. 105.) Hercules, the only surviving son of Alexander, was illegitimate, and deemed incapable of succeeding. Nevertheless, as he found adherents to enforce his pretensions, he was betrayed to Cassander, and put to death at his instigation. One surviving sister of the great Macedonian— Cleopatra, who, after the death of his sons, was solicited in marriage by Ptolemy with a view of uniting her claims to the succession with his own, fell a victim to the cruel ambition of Antigonus. And thus, within fifteen years from the death of Alexander, his own family, and that of his father Philip, had been foully doomed to death by men who professed to worship his memory, and who derived all their greatness from his favour. One sister of his only, Thessalonica, the wife of Cassander, still survived; and her end, sixteen years later, was violent, like that of her kindred, but far more tragical and heart-rending, since she was murdered by her own son.

Antigonus, who had only consented to a peace with Ptolemy that he might with the more certainty destroy Seleucus, lost no time in preparing an expedition into Upper Asia. It is on record that he fought a battle of doubtful issue; after which, Seleucus, by making his men sleep in their armour, surprised his adversary the next morning, and gained over him a decided advantage. (Gillies, vi. 6.) But neither the year in which this battle was fought, nor the place, nor its immediate consequences, are preserved in history. It is certain, however, that Antigonus's expedition proved fruitless. Strong in the love of his people, Seleucus offered a resistance that Antigonus was unable to overcome; and the latter was foiled and forced to retreat, as his son Demetrius had been before. During the next ten years, this turbulent old man and his son, who also could never be at rest, were engaged in incessant hostilities against Egypt or Macedon, while Seleucus was extending his dominions in the East.

After the extinction of the house of Alexander, the satraps who bore sway in his empire no longer deemed it necessary to cloak their ambition, or to disguise their independent sovereignties by a designation expressive of delegated power. Antigonus was the first among them to assume the title of king, and to bestow it on his son Demetrius; and he was speedily followed by Ptolemy. Subsequently both Seleucus and Lysimachus disdained to remain inferior in title to those whom they equalled in renown. Cassander alone, out of respect for the ashes of the Macedonian monarchs entombed in his province,—or rather, perhaps, dreading the prejudices of the Macedonian people, and their deeply-rooted attachment for the royalty of Alexander's house,—neither styled himself king nor employed the royal signet.

He, however, in imitation of his kingly compeers, indulged his vanity by building and bestowing his name on a city, where he took up his residence, and in which, according to the superstitious practice of the Greeks, his shade might receive heroic worship after his death. Cassandria and Lysimachia in Europe, Antigonia and Seleucia in Asia, were all built with the intention of perpetuating the names of their founders. Ptolemy was the only one of the kings who did not affect the honour of distinguishing a new capital by his name. He had a nobler pride in adorning Alexandria, the glorious monument of his great brother. But such is the vanity of human designs, that while Alexandria, though shorn of all its magnificence, still, after a lapse of twenty centuries, maintains a place among cities of note, and the name of Alexander himself is immortal, the other four capitals have disappeared, and their founders are rescued from oblivion chiefly by their connection with Alexander.

Antigonus had now passed his eightieth year, but his lust of power, and continual aggressions on his neighbours, had suffered no diminution. To curb, if not to crush him, a fresh confederacy was formed. Ptolemy, though he nominally joined the alliance, cautiously refrained from risking his army. Lysimachus, who, by the toil of twenty years, had consolidated his power over Thracia, was first in the field, and was reinforced by a considerable body of auxiliaries sent by Cassander. But it was Seleucus who brought the largest force to the battle at Ipsos, in Phrygia, which all determined should be decisive. (301 B. C. E.) Antigonus fought with his usual valour and conduct, but not with his usual success. Demetrius, victorious in the early part of the day, and carried away by his ardour in the pursuit of the fugitives that fled before him, was, by a skilful movement of Seleucus, prevented from properly supporting his father; and the final result was, that Antigonus was utterly defeated and slain, while Demetrius, with a small remnant of the army, escaped. He survived seventeen years, experienced many changes of fortune, and took an active share in the affairs of that time, but not so as again to bring him under our notice.

CHAPTER III.

Partition of Alexander's empire—Judea assigned to Ptolemy—The Syro-Grecian Empire—Jews on the Euphrates—The Egypto-Grecian Empire—Jews of Alexandria—Of Jerusalem—Simon the Just—The Septuagint—Berosus—Manetho—Rivalry and wars of the Ptolemies and the Seleucidæ—The Parthian Empire—*Young Judea*—Antigonus of Socho—The Sadducees—Ptolemy IV. Philopator—Antiochus III.—Battle of Raphia—Philopator at Jerusalem—His attempt on the Temple—His Flight—Persecutes the Jews of Egypt—His death—Antiochus III. invades Cœle-Syria—Battle of Mount Panias—Judea incorporated with the Syro-Grecian Empire. (From 301 to 198 B.C.E.)

THE defeat and death of Antigonus terminated, as far as the Jews were concerned, that period of violence and uncertainty which, since the death of Alexander, had afflicted Western and Central Asia, the regions in which they chiefly dwelt. The victory at Ipsos was followed by a treaty between the four chieftains who had weathered the storm, and who now divided between them the immense territories that constituted the empire of Alexander. The distribution was made on the principle that each of them was to retain what he already possessed, and take his due share of the monarchy that Antigonus had lost with his life; and, as the family of Alexander was quite extinct, each of the four was formally to assume the royal dignity. In accordance with this treaty, Cassander obtained Macedon and Greece, while Lysimachus had Thrace, Bithynia, and some of the adjacent provinces. Ptolemy had neither in person, nor by his troops, taken any part in the battle; still he was not excluded from the partition; but, in addition to Egypt, Cyrene, and Lybia, which he already held, he recovered Cœle-Syria and Palestine—appendages so essential to his kingdom; and he further acquired Arabia Petræa, or rather so much of that district as had submitted to Antigonus. All the rest of Alexander's conquests—Syria, part of Asia Minor, all the immense extent between the Euphrates and the Indus—remained in the possession of Seleucus, who thus obtained the lion's share, and became lord of Asia, as the Chaldees had predicted.

This division was not final. Cassander died within two years of the battle of Ipsos: his sons disputed the succession, and were finally expelled from Macedon by Demetrius, the son of Antigonus. He, in his turn, was dispossessed by Lysimachus, and died as the prisoner of Seleucus. But though these two sovereigns had united against Antigonus and his son, their enemies were no sooner fallen than they turned their arms against each other. The last battle between the lieutenants of Alexander was fought forty-three years after his death, at Corupedion, in Phrygia. Lysimachus was defeated and slain; and his army was so totally destroyed, that no request was made for leave to bury their dead. This victory made Seleucus master of three out of the four monarchies into which the empire of Alexander had been divided; and as Ptolemy, who was much his senior, had died the year before this last battle, Seleucus—the sole survivor of all the chiefs that had crossed the Hellespont in the train of Alexander—now, after an absence of fifty-four years spent in the East, prepared to return to Macedon to reign in the country where he had first drawn breath, and spent the innocent years of his humble youth.

This had been the object of his secret ambition ever since the first dawn of his greatness. The proud title of Nicator, (the victorious,) which he then assumed, had hitherto been fully justified by the event; and now he, the special favourite of the gods, was about to seat himself on Alexander's throne, the reward for all his toils and all his dangers. But how blind are the hopes of man! Seleucus was treacherously murdered by his guest, Ptolemy Keraunus, the banished son of the king of Egypt, under circumstances that afford us another proof of how much of the marvellous enters into the history of those times. As Seleucus—then in his seventy-seventh year—was proceeding to Lysimachia, the capital of his late rival, he was struck with the appearance of an altar of uncommon magnitude, erected at a place called Argos, because its principal feature, the altar, was said to have been erected by the Argonauts. While he curiously examined this remains of antiquity—and was the more inquisitive about its name and origin because it had been foretold, as a warning, that he was to avoid Argos as the place most fatal to him—Keraunus stepped behind his back and stabbed him to the heart.

The murderer fled to Lysimachia, where, announcing himself to the inhabitants and garrison as the avenger of their patron and founder of their city, Lysimachus, he was readily received. And so unsettled were all principles of right and wrong among the mercenaries who followed the Macedonian kings, that Keraunus could reconcile himself with the army of the murdered Seleucus by sharing with the soldiers the treasures of their late general. (Appian, Syriac, cap. 63.)

We have anticipated the course of events, in order at once to terminate our narration of Alexander's lieutenants and their dissensions, and now return to the point whence we started—the treaty of peace which followed the battle of Ipsos. The conditions of this treaty were highly satisfactory to the Jews. Those of Syria and Mesopotamia came under the sceptre of Seleucus, who had always shown himself friendly to the Asiatic nationalities; and those of Palestine were restored to the dominion of Ptolemy, with whose generally beneficent government and particular favour to themselves they had every reason to be satisfied. The prospects of durable peace, under the mild sway of two such great and friendly kings, must also have been contemplated with peculiar satisfaction by a people that had suffered so much of the horrors and penalties, without sharing in the contingent honours or advantages, of war.

Nor were they disappointed: both Ptolemy and Seleucus were actuated by the same policy: while they sought to *attach* to their rule all the different nations that had become subject to their sceptre, they placed especial confidence in those nationalities whose steadiness of principle and moral rectitude held out the greatest assurance of loyalty and fidelity to the person and dynasty of the ruler. In these respects the Jews ranked far above the rest of the Eastern nations. From this policy sprang the favours which both kings showered on the Jews, and the indulgence with which, notwithstanding its peculiarities, they always treated the Jewish nation.

Seleucus, in whose dominions many fine cities had been entirely destroyed, and others had greatly suffered by the ravages of war, now set about repairing these injuries, and for that purpose built thirty-five new cities; and, according to the vanity of the times, he sought to perpetuate the name of his father, Antiochus, by giving it to sixteen cities scattered over his vast dominions; to nine others he gave his own name; his mother Laodicea had her name illustrated by five cities; and the name of his two wives were honoured by three Apameas and one Stratonicca.[16]

---

[16] Some authors speak of thirty-nine cities of note built by Seleucus, and named after himself and his dearest relations; but this is a mistake. Appian (de Reb. Syr. cap. 57) enumerates them in the same order that we give them. His text has, however, given rise to the mistake. For he says, "Seleucus named four cities in honour of his wives: three Apameas

Of all these cities, the most important were Seleucia, on the Tigris, in Babylonia, and Antioch, on the Orontes, in Syria. The first-named city he intended as the capital of the eastern, and the second, of the western part of his empire. The building of Seleucia greatly contributed to the accomplishment of prophecy by the final ruin of Babylon. For the seat of the court, the consequent great traffic, and the important privileges which Seleucus granted to his new city, gradually induced the inhabitants of the old city (Babylon) to remove and swell the population of its young and flourishing rival. The precise period when Babylon became entirely deserted cannot now be ascertained. Seleucia flourished as the seat of Syrian, Parthian, and Persian kings, and contained a numerous Jewish population, on whom Seleucus bestowed privileges equal to those granted to his own countrymen, the Macedonians. The city was sacked by the followers of Mohammed in the year 637, A. C. E., and a century later, it was finally supplanted by the building of Bagdad, under the Caliph Almansor; and *now*, Babylon itself is not more desolate—is even less desolate—than the superseding city of Seleucia, so thoroughly and literally has the prophecy (Isa. xxxiv.) been fulfilled.

Antiochia, on the Orontes, in Syria, became the seat of all Seleucus' successors, especially after the revolt of the Parthians had severed so large a portion of Central Asia from the Syro-Greek empire. This city, which afterward became the seat of the Roman governors, still exists, and has retained some relative consequence by virtue of the corresponding decline of all population and prosperity in the country around it. In this city, likewise, Seleucus, by the great privileges and immunities he granted them,

---

and one Stratonicea." The latter half of the sentence is only explanatory of the first half; and the mistake has arisen from its being considered a distinct and independent sentence.

induced as many Jews as he possibly could to settle. And they were in consequence attracted in such numbers that, in the time of its greatest prosperity, Antioch contained a Jewish population nearly as large as that of Alexandria itself.

It is in this last-named city, however, that the Jews of this period most flourished and attained the greatest prosperity. During the twenty-two years that elapsed from the battle of Ipsos till his own death, (282 B. C. E.) Ptolemy devoted his talents and energies to promote the happiness of the nations whose ruler he was become. And though his kingdom of Egypt did not attain its meridian glory until the reign of his son, Ptolemy II. Philadelphus, there is abundant proof that the best foundations of public prosperity had been laid under the father. He it was who made Alexandria then what the United States are now—the asylum for all whom oppression, and the perturbed state of other countries, forced to seek a home far from their native land. To such fugitives Egypt offered a secure refuge; and those among them who were distinguished for learning and ability met with support and encouragement from a monarch who, highly educated and gifted himself, knew how to appreciate the talents of others. And thus, by the merit and discernment of its ruler, did Egypt, renowned as the mother of arts and sciences, receive back from foreign lands her full-grown and highly-improved children, whom the continued oppression of the Persian rule had not permitted her longer to bring up at home. It was by the fostering care of Ptolemy that the first museum and library were founded in Alexandria; and we shall presently relate how the establishing of this library, which under the last kings of his dynasty reached 700,000 volumes, deposited in two different temples, is said to have led to the translation from the Hebrew into the Greek language of a portion of the sacred Scriptures.

Ptolemy granted to all his subjects the most perfect religious equality; and while he clearly saw that it was his interest to harmonize the differences of religious practice and opinion which divided his Egyptian from his Greek subjects, he was wise enough to perceive that the superiority of the Jewish character resulted from institutions of higher authority and more deeply rooted. Accordingly, the chief synagogue of the Jews was as much respected as the temple of Jupiter and of Isis. The Talmud preserves a brief account of this synagogue, a masterpiece of Egypto-Grecian architecture, and of which eyewitnesses, who had seen Herod's temple in Jerusalem in its glory, declare that "He who has not seen the synagogue at Alexandria, has not yet seen that which is most beautiful." It is highly praised for its vast dimensions and splendour of decoration, was built like a basilica, and surrounded by colonnades. Seventy golden arm-chairs were appropriated to the seventy elders of Alexandria. Each trade, profession, and corporation occupied its own portion of the synagogue, so that every stranger could at once find and address himself to his fellowship. In the middle of the synagogue there was a balustrade on which the superintendent was placed; and so vast was the size of the synagogue, that, during service it was necessary to appoint a special officer, who, by the raising and waving of a banner, should, at the proper time, give a signal to the congregation to make the responses.

This remarkable synagogue was destroyed by the Roman, Martius Turbo, during the wars of the Jews against Trajan.[17] "Since then," remarks the Jewish

---

[17] The Babylonian Talmud (in loc. cit.) imputes the destruction to Alexander of Macedon. This is evidently an error of the transcriber. The Jerusalem Talmud (in loco) gives the destroyer's name correctly, Trajan, under whom M. Turbo served.

record, "the splendour of Israel is extinguished." (Talmud, tr. *Succah*, fo. 51, b. Jerus. ib.)

The arrangement here described, and according to which each trade or corporation occupied its peculiar place or division in the great synagogue at Alexandria, was the more necessary, both from the vast number of strangers who flocked to that city, and from the great variety of trades which were carried on by the citizens, the most praiseworthy characteristics belonging to whom were industry and ingenuity. Throughout the whole place none lived in idleness; and here many occupations were skilfully exercised, unknown or disregarded in most other Greek or Oriental cities. Many Alexandrians laboured in blowing glass; many others were employed in softening and smoothing the papyrus. Weaving linen and brewing beer were trades very extensively carried on. And these various occupations furnished employment not only to citizens and strangers, but even to persons whose corporal afflictions were in other cities considered as barring them out from useful work. The blind and the lame—even those lame in their hands—had tasks assigned to them not incompatible with their several infirmities. The rich were, in a different way, not less diligent: some superintending their large manufactories; others augmenting their fortunes by commercial enterprise, in both which sources of profit the Ptolemies were largely interested. (Gillies, vi. 341.) And though the picture here given us of the active and industrious life of Alexandria does not make especial mention of the Jews, yet we may rest fully assured that, as they largely shared in the general prosperity, their exertions must have been fully on a par with those of their fellow-citizens.

The Jews at Alexandria were so numerous, and formed so preponderating a portion of its inhabitants, that it is impossible to read a description of the industry of that city, without putting full one-half of what is related to their account. Out of the five districts, or quarters, into which the city was divided, two were occupied by Jews only, who also, and numerously, dwelt in the other quarters of the city; so that we are justified in assuming that nearly one-half of the entire population of the city consisted of Jews. These, by means of the immunities and privileges granted to them by Alexander, and confirmed by Ptolemy, were in every respect placed on an equality with the Macedonians and Greeks, the conquering nations. Indeed, it appears to have been the policy of the Ptolemies, when they so highly favoured the Jews, by their means, and by that of the many foreigners to whom these kings granted an asylum, to strengthen and reinforce their subjects of Greek origin, so that the whole body of settlers and their descendants might form a counterpoise to the native Egyptians, who were fickle, turbulent, and extremely hostile to foreigners. And in this respect the Ptolemies were not disappointed. The Jews of Egypt identified themselves with the best interests of the land in which they lived, and remained loyal and faithful to the Ptolemean dynasty, to whom, on many occasions, they rendered important services.

Their relation to Judea and Jerusalem is truly and beautifully described by Philo, (Advers. Flacc. § 7): "The Jews consider the city in which the temple of the Most High God is situated, as the metropolis (of their faith.) But the land in which their fathers and grandfathers dwelt, and in which they themselves have been born and bred, they call their fatherland."

It is not altogether uninteresting or uninstructive to compare this condition of the Jews some 2100 years ago, in a remote corner of Africa, with what it is at present in civilized Germany and Italy, not to speak of semi-barbarous Russia. Alexandria, with its two districts entirely occupied by Jews—and numbers of them residing in other parts of the city—will certainly appear more truly civilized than Rome with its Ghetto in the year 1854; while the Ptolemies, Soter and Philadelphus, will not only compare favourably with the Hapsburgs and Romanoffs of Austria and Russia, but will be found even more worthy of power than the House of Lords in Great Britain, who in this selfsame year still deprive the Jew of the most important privilege of citizenship, because he will not violate his conscience by prostituting the sanctity of an oath.

While the Jews of Alexandria were thus flourishing, those of Judea and Jerusalem were also, and greatly, benefited by the wise and liberal administration of the Ptolemies. The privilege of self-government conferred on Judea by the Persians, and not disturbed by Alexander, was fully confirmed by the Egyptian monarchs. The year after the battle of Ipsos witnessed the death of the aged high-priest, Onias I., who, from the storming of Jerusalem by Ptolemy, and during the alternate supremacy of that ruler and of Antigonus, had, upward of twenty non-prosperous years, conducted the internal administration with prudent firmness. His successor was the able, pious, and in every respect excellent high-priest Simon, whom the well-merited admiration of his people has dignified with the surname of "the Just"—a designation deserved or enjoyed but by very few among the rulers, spiritual and temporal, whose surnames are preserved in history.

In the traditions of the Jews, Simon is described as the last survivor of the "Great Assembly," that illustrious council which, since the days of Ezra and Nehemiah, had administered the ecclesiastical and civil polity of Judea, and with the full authority of which Simon entered on his important and sacred office. Thus, by a concurrence of fortunate circumstances, at the very time the great and wise king of Egypt was recognised as the lawful sovereign of Judea, and thus became able to carry out his good intentions toward that country, its internal affairs were placed in the hands of the pious and patriotic high-priest Simon, who was best qualified to give effect to those good intentions. Fully appreciating each other's merits, these two distinguished men united in their efforts to restore the prosperity of Judea, impoverished and almost depopulated as it was by long wars and extensive emigrations. The walls of Jerusalem, which had been breached by Ptolemy, and the repairs of which Antigonus had not permitted, first attracted the care of Simon. He felt that without security of person, of property, and of worship, no lasting prosperity could be expected; and that, surrounded by tribes hostile and jealous, Jerusalem, in order to thrive, must be protected. Accordingly, with the consent of Ptolemy, Simon repaired and fortified the city and temple of Jerusalem with strong and lofty walls; and, as in former sieges, the city had suffered much from the want of water —the aqueducts beyond the walls being at the mercy of besiegers—Simon remedied this defect by constructing a spacious cistern or reservoir of water, "in compass as a sea."[18]

His measures for reviving the prosperity of the people were attended with complete success. As the powerful protection of Ptolemy secured to them the blessings of peace, the Jews, by their industry and frugality, soon recovered from the losses they had sustained, while their population rapidly increased. At the same time the solemnity of their religious observances, and the purity of their doctrines, attracted the attention and commanded the respect of Gentiles in an age when learning, arts, and

---

[18] Ecclus. i. 1–3. The whole chapter, entitled "The praise of Simon, the son of Onias," is devoted to a splendid eulogium of his deeds and character.

sciences flourished in an uncommon degree. Simon is also supposed to have completed the canon of the Old Testament; though the lynx-eye of modern criticism, from internal evidence, deduces proof that many Psalms must have been composed upward of a century after the death of this great man. Many, however, are of opinion that the books of Haggai, Zechariah, Malachi, Ezra, Nehemiah, and Esther were by him placed among the records of Scripture; and some aver that the Books of Chronicles were also completed and so placed in their present state; while other biblical critics place the admission of the Chronicles and of Daniel into the Bible at a much later period.

Simon the Just held office about ten years; and as, at the time of his death, his son was too young to assume the functions of high-priest, his brother Eleazar succeeded to that high dignity, which he held fifteen years. During his administration, the first Ptolemy died, at the age of eighty-four, (283 B. C. E.,) having survived his brother Alexander, forty years.

The *Mesecheth Aboth*, "Ethics of the Fathers," a collection of maxims and apophthegms of "the Sages of Israel," begins with the sayings of the men of the Great Assembly, and of Simon the Just, who thus may be considered as the heads of the chain of tradition which, from them, is continued uninterruptedly till the compilation of the Mishna, (about 190 C. E.,) and (before them) derived the authority of its transmission from Moses. A modern writer (Frankel's Monatschrift, n. 6) justly remarks that, in order to eke out the scanty materials furnished by Jewish history during the long period between Nehemiah and the Maccabees, due attention should be paid to these "sayings of the sages," from which much useful information respecting the internal and external condition of the Jews is to be derived.

The maxims ascribed to the men of the Great Assembly are three: "Be deliberate in judgment; train up many disciples; and make a fence for the law;" in which three sayings the writer in question finds the emblem and indications of the objects at which the men of the Great Assembly chiefly aimed. In their first saying they place before us an indication of the position Judea then occupied with respect to her foreign policy, and the best means to preserve that position. The privilege of self-government, which the Persians and Macedonians had granted, rendered Judea—at home, at least—a species of republic governed by its own laws. But this great immunity could only be enjoyed so long as the foreign rulers were not appealed to, or called in to decide on matters of litigation between Jews; and such an appeal could only be prevented by an administration of justice so pure and equitable as to convince all litigants that their cases were sure to receive thorough and impartial investigation, and would be decided fairly and justly. Thus the saying, "Be deliberate in judgment," at once points out the best means for preserving self-government, and the necessity for appointing competent judges, who shall have acquired that acquaintance with the law, and that habit of thought, which alone can insure due deliberation. And it is a remarkable fact that the portion of the Mishna which treats of civil jurisprudence (a part of *Nezekin* "damages,") is the oldest in the whole compilation, and that the fundamental principles of this jurisprudence date from time immemorial.

But then the question would arise, Where are we to find these competent judges? And this question meets with its reply in the second saying, "Train up many disciples." If the last records of the Bible, relating to the early period of the second temple, be carefully examined, it will be found, in many respects, to resemble the early times after the conquest of the land by Joshua. At both periods the *Cohanim,* "priests," descendants of Aaron, were intrusted with the administration of the law. They had originally (Lev. x. 10, 11) been appointed its guardians and teachers; and similar functions were assigned to them in the second temple. (Ezek. xliv. 23, 24.) But in the early times of Israel's nationality they appeared less attentive to their duties as teachers and upholders of the law than to their own interests and revenues, as is sufficiently proved by the the severe rebuke "to fatten yourselves with the first of all offerings" addressed to them. (1 Sam. ii. 29.) Therefore Samuel, the man of God, arose, rescued the *Torah* from the malversation of its unfaithful custodians, and caused a knowledge of the law to become general among the people. He founded the schools of the prophets, and trained young men of piety and capacity, who became the teachers of the people and the faithful administrators of the law.

The same process of events we find repeated in the second temple. The priests, it appears, entertained friendly relations with the Samaritans, whose admission within the pale and privileges of the law the two inspired men, Ezra and Nehemiah, had rejected, in order not to open a door for the re-entry of paganism and its impure practices. The priests even went so far as to assign chambers within the temple to a leader of the Samaritans, (Neh. xiii. 4, *et seq.,*)—a measure, the aim of which was evidently to augment their own influence and revenues by increasing the number of visitors and donors to the temple and altar at Jerusalem. And the partiality with which these Cohanim abused their judicial functions, as well as the cupidity with which they degraded the sacred services, and thereby alienated the people from the temple and its worship, are plainly set forth in the bitter reproaches uttered by Malachi, the last of the prophets, in his second chapter.

To remedy this evil, the men of the Great Assembly—among the members of which tradition especially enumerates Haggai, Zechariah, Malachi, Ezra, and Nehemiah—had recourse to a measure similar to that which Samuel had adopted; they established a check to the corruption of the sacerdotal caste, which forever after set limits to its abuse of power. "Train up many disciples" was the motto of their practical measures for preserving the law in its purity. Once more the knowledge of the law is to become general; let the most highly gifted be properly instructed, and whosoever is the best qualified shall, in his turn, become a teacher and administrator of the *Torah*.

By this means the irresponsible supremacy of the hierarchy was forever broken. The priests were no longer the sole guardians of law and justice; but they themselves were under the guardianship of authorities learned in the law. The high-priest retained his dignity and just influence; the priests were not disturbed in their birthright and emoluments. But the possibility of hierarchal tyranny in Israel was forever prevented. And this boon all succeeding generations owe to the men of the Great Assembly. The crown of royalty was, and is still, the birthright of the house of David; the crown of the priesthood was, and is still, the birthright of the house of Aaron; but the crown of the law became, and is still, the birthright of every Israelite worthy of acquiring it by learning and piety. The disciples of the men of the Great Assembly formed a large and influential class called *Sopherim*, (scribes,) from which priests were not excluded. But, in order that no diversity of opinion among the administors might open the door to schism, they enforced their third saying, "Make a fence for the law"—protect the spirit of the law while you keep to the letter.

The good effects of this measure are attested by the recorded sayings of Simon the Just, himself at once the chief and ornament of the priesthood, and the representative of the Great Assembly: "The world (society at large) is upheld by three things: by the law, by the temple service, and by acts of philanthropy."

While one of the crowns, that of royalty, is in abeyance, he places the remaining two in that position which their relative importance and influence on the welfare of society entitle them respectively to hold, assigning the first rank to the law. But with that first crown he immediately and inseparably connects that of the priesthood—the temple service, with its offerings. And the spirit by which Simon the Just wished that service to be actuated, he indicates by the third requisite he mentions, "acts of philanthropy." The prophets, during the first temple, had but too often cause to rebuke the error of the people, who considered the performance of outward acts of devotion, such as offerings, first-fruits and the like, to be all that religion requires. Against this error, Simon directs his third saying; and that he perfectly entered into the spirit of his own apophthegms, is proved by an anecdote in which he is concerned, related in the Talmud, (Tr. *Nazir*, 4, b:)

"Simon, surnamed the Just, was wise as he was pious, zealous to maintain in its purity the worship of his God, and the precepts of his holy law, but equally zealous to promote the happiness of Israel by encouraging the people in the practice of virtue and obedience to the law, and by checking, as much as in his power laid, the tendency to hypersanctimoniousness which but too often engenders bigotry and superstition. Therefore, he always strove to prevent men from subjecting themselves to penances not commanded by the law, and to dissuade them from lightly taking upon themselves vows and burthens which the revealed will of God did not require. And, in order the more strongly to mark and express his disapprobation of such uncalled-for practices, he publicly declared that he had never partaken of the sin-offering which the law requires of the *Nazir*;[19] and that he deemed it his duty always to make use of every argument in his power, to induce the person intending to become a *Nazir* to forego his purpose.

"'There is only one instance,' he said, 'in which I departed from my usual practice, and not only approved of the *Nazir's* vow, but also partook of his sin-offering.' And he related: 'There once came a youth of transcendent beauty—whose noble and intellectual countenance seemed the index of a pure mind, and whose beauteous hair flowed in natural ringlets over his shoulders—and expressed his desire to pronounce his vows as a *Nazir*. . . I was astounded,' said Simon the Just, 'and I exclaimed, "What, young man! hast thou lost thy senses? What ails thee, that thou desirest to ruin thy health, and deprive thyself of thy natural and beautiful ornament, thy hair?" "I wish to be good," replied the youth; "my hair is an obstacle in the way of that wish, and therefore I am desirous to take the vows." My attention,' continued Simon, 'was excited, and I listened in silence while he continued: "From my earliest infancy I have tended the flocks of my father; I loved God, my parents, and my fellow-creatures, and was contented and happy in my mind. But one morning I led my flock to the brook; my eye enjoyed the beauties of nature, while the animals under my care refreshed themselves with the cooling beverage. But suddenly my eye, struck with ad-

---

[19] *Nazir*, "Abstinent," is the designation which sacred Scripture gives to him who voluntarily takes upon himself vows of abstinence, the precepts relating to which are enacted in Numbers, vi. 3–21. Throughout the duration of his vow, the Nazir was to abstain from wine and whatsoever grows on the vine; he was not permitted to approach a corpse or to cut his hair. But, at the expiration of his vow, his hair was cut off, and he had to bring a sin-offering. The Talmud (in loco) remarks, "The Nazir had to bring a sin-offering, because he had sinned, inasmuch as, through his abstinence, he had afflicted his body without lawful cause. For he who needlessly fasts even one day is called a sinner."

miration, rested on the liquid mirror. I beheld the image of myself. 'Silly boy, dost thou not know thyself?' was the insidious whisper of vanity. I stood gazing on myself, and sensations to which till then I had been a stranger arose within me. Lost in admiration of my own beauty, my enraptured eye was fixed on the watery surface, while I stood playing with the locks of my hair. Alternately I let them fall over my shoulders, or saw them floating on the air as the wind played around my temples. While my rapture was at the highest, a skipping lamb approached to drink. It sipped a little water; the calm surface of the brook became troubled, and my image vanished. With a dreadful imprecation, such as till then had never defiled my lips, I struck the poor lamb with my staff, and drove it away. Patiently it retired, and stood afar off, trembling, and in a posture which seemed to reproach me with my injustice and cruelty. This sight restored vigour to my better feelings, and my conscience, alarmed, addressed my beauteous figure, and said, 'Worthless wrapper, forget not thy origin or thy end. Know thy trifling beauty is transient and perishable, but the stigma of the deed thou now hast been guilty of is lasting, and such as thou will not soon blot out.' Contrition gnawed on my heart. I burst out into tears, and weeping, I vowed physically to humble that which had wellnigh destroyed me morally. I therefore wish to take upon myself the vows of a *Nazir*. The hair which excited my vanity shall fall under the scissors; and the roses of my cheeks shall become blanched through abstinence; for I wish to be not beautiful, but good."—With these words, the youth ended his narrative. But I embraced and blessed him, while I exclaimed: "Oh that many like thee in Israel might, with motives as pure and praiseworthy, take upon themselves the vow which I now shall be pleased and happy to hear thee pronounce.'" (Hebrew Review, vol. iii. 93.)

This pleasing anecdote proves not only the rational views and the purity of feeling entertained by Simon himself, but it also shows how high-souled a people the Jews of that period must have been.

There can be no doubt but that the transfer effected by the men of the Great Assembly, of the judicial functions from the sacerdotal caste to the general body of the people, greatly contributed to elevate the character and to purify the ideas and feelings of the masses, inasmuch as it much augmented the number of educated men among them. Accordingly, we have proof that not only the study of the law, but likewise of philosophy and science, was cultivated by the Jews, and this even prior to their acquaintance with the Greeks, which followed the invasion of Alexander. Josephus, (cont. Apion. i. 22,) on the authority of Clearchus, a well-known disciple of Aristotle, quotes that celebrated philosopher, who had been the tutor of Alexander, as speaking of a Jew, a native of Jerusalem, who came from the upper country to the sea-coast, where he became known to many distinguished persons, and who, by his language and mind, was a Grecian. "I happened," says Aristotle, "at that time to be in Asia; and as he arrived at the place where I was, he was introduced to me and to other scientific and learned men, with whose wisdom he wished to become acquainted. Thus he held confidential intercourse with many sages, to whom he imparted more than he received from them." This is no small praise, considering who is the speaker. And we may assume it as a fact not to be denied, that ever since the time the Great Assembly propounded the maxim, "Train up many disciples," education has been generally cultivated among the Jewish people.

The most important proof of the spread of education consequent on the labours of the Great Assembly, is afforded by the translation into the Greek of the sacred

JUDEA UNDER THE PERSIANS AND GREEKS. 125

Scriptures, which the vast Jewish population in Egypt and Cyrene soon rendered necessary. For these Jews had, even in a shorter period than their ancestors during Babylonish captivity, become estranged from their vernacular tongue, the Chaldee spoken in Judea. And as the masses knew not Hebrew, nor indeed any other language except that idiom of the Greek spoken in Egypt, a version of the law accessible to them became as indispensable as a Chaldee version had been to their fathers in the days of Ezra.

The *real* history of both translations is equally unknown; but, while the sober mind of the Judeans did not seek to eke out history by fable, the active imagination of the Hellenists could not rest till it had dressed up and adorned the *myth* of the great version, known as that of the Septuagint, with a halo of the wonderful, in which historical truth altogether disappears. There yet exists a letter purporting to have been written by Aristeas, an officer at the court of the second Ptolemy Philadelphus, and addressed to his brother Philocrates, in which a full and circumstantial history of this Greek translation is given.

It begins with stating that Demetrius Phalereus,[20] who had been placed at the head of the royal library and museum, first called the attention of the king, Philadelphus, to the importance of the Jewish writings, and to the

---

[20] This eminent scholar and statesman, the son of a slave, but the favourite disciple of Theophrastus, the successor of Aristotle, had been appointed governor of Athens by Cassander, King of Macedon, and held that office with high reputation, and with great advantage to the Athenians during ten years, when he was expelled by King Demetrius. He then sought refuge in Egypt, where the elder Ptolemy received him kindly, and placed him high in his councils. At his suggestion, the library and museum of Alexandria were established, and, though he held offices of greater power in the state, yet the title of librarian seems to have been considered the most honourable.

necessity of enriching the royal library, which is stated by Aristeas to have then consisted of 500,000 volumes,[21] with a translation of the Law of Moses; that, when the king had ascertained the difficulty of obtaining such a translation, he sent Aristeas, and another courtier, named Andreas, on a special mission to Eleazar, the high-priest, at Jerusalem, with an autograph letter from the king, to request that he should send to Alexandria six men out of each of the twelve tribes of Israel; and that these seventy-two men should be competent to undertake the faithful translation into Greek of the Jewish law. And, in order to render the high dignitary at Jerusalem more zealous to fulfil the king's desire, Philadelphus not only sent rich gifts to the temple, but caused all Jews that were slaves in Egypt to be manumitted, compensating the owners at a fixed rate per head out of the royal treasury. Aristeas, after a long description of the royal presents of which he was the carrier, and a short account of the city of Jerusalem, its temple and priesthood, goes on to relate how kindly he and his colleague were received by the Jews, and that his mission was completely successful. The high-priest, with the consent and assistance of the council, selected seventy-two elders, six of each tribe, who were not only expert in the Jewish Scripture but who were thoroughly conversant with the learning, language, and customs of the Greeks, and therefore every way qualified for the work of translation intrusted to them; that, moreover, they were men of profound thought, calm in argument, gentle in their manners, and upright in their conduct; that, when they arrived in Alexandria, they were honour-

---

[21] When here and on a former occasion, in speaking of the library at Alexandria, we used the word VOLUMES, we must guard our readers against being misled by the modern acceptation of this word; for, in writings of any extent, among the ancients, each book, and sometimes each chapter or section, was rolled into a separate volume. (Gillies's Greece, vi. 120.)

ably received by the king, who on seven successive days entertained them, ten each day, at banquets where their table was prepared in accordance with Jewish law. Each day the king put their wisdom to the test by submitting to them questions, which, together with their answers, are recorded by Aristeas. At the expiration of this week of feasting, the seventy-two elders were conducted to the Isle of Pharos, near Alexandria, where, having agreed on the rendering of each section, after a conference in which the separate translation made by each was diligently scrutinized and compared, the version unanimously adopted by them all was written down by Demetrius Phalereus himself, who was constantly with them, and to whom they dictated it; and thus, in the space of seventy-two days, the translation of the Pentateuch, or Five Books of Moses, was completed. Aristeas concludes with an account of the king's joy at the possession of this translation, and with a brief mention of the honours and rich gifts with which the translators were sent home.

Thus far the letter of Aristeas, which is very old, since it existed in the days of Josephus, who makes use of it in his Antiquities. The authenticity of Aristeas's letter, and the veracity of his narrative, were not questioned until one hundred or a hundred and fifty years ago. An eminent biblical critic, R'Azariah di Rossi, even translated Aristeas's letter into Hebrew (Meor. Aynayim, part ii.) at Ferara, in the year 1574. But, since then, doubts have been thrown on the authenticity of Aristeas's letter; and at present, after mature investigation, and by the almost unanimous decision of the learned, it is held to be a forgery, though a very old one. It is certain that, until Di Rossi's translation, the letter was not generally known to the rabbins.

Philo, the celebrated Jew of Alexandria, who wrote about two hundred and fifty years after the death of

Philadelphus, seems not to have been acquainted with most of the circumstances narrated by the *soi-disant* Aristeas; but he relates others which appear not less extraordinary. According to him, Philadelphus sent to Palestine for some learned Jews, the number of whom he does not specify; and these, going over to the Isle of Pharos, there executed so many distinct versions, all of which so exactly and uniformly agreed in sense, phrases, and words, as proved them to have been not common interpreters, but men prophetically inspired, who had every word throughout the entire translation dictated to them by the Spirit from on high. He adds that an annual festival was, until his time, celebrated by the Jews of Alexandria, in the Isle of Pharos, where the version was made, to preserve the memory of it, and to thank God for so great a benefit. (Vita Mosis, lib. ii.)

The most wonderful portions of each narrative are melted together into one by Justin Martyr, who flourished about one hundred years after Philo, and who adds *somewhat* to both. *His* seventy interpreters are shut up, each in his own separate cell, (which had been expressly erected for that purpose by order of Ptolemy Philadelphus;) and that here they composed so many distinct versions, word for word, in the very same expressions, to the great admiration of the king, who, not doubting that this version was divinely inspired, loaded the interpreters with honours, and dismissed them to their own country with magnificent presents. The good father adds that the ruins of these cells were still visible in his time. (Cohort, ad. Gentes.) But this narrative of Justin's is directly at variance with several circumstances recorded by Aristeas; such, for instance, as the previous conference or deliberation of the translators, and, above all, the very important point of the version being dictated to Demetrius Phalereus. Epiphanius, a writer of the fourth century, attempts to harmonize all these accounts by shutting up these translators, two and two, in thirty-six cells, where they might consider and deliberate, and by stationing a copyist in each cell, to whom the translators dictated their labours, the result of which was the production of thirty-six inspired versions agreeing most uniformly together. (Horne, Introduction, &c. ii. 173.)

That the Hellenists, who in process of time became very jealous of the Judeans, should have invented and encouraged a *myth* which declared the version of Scriptures read in their synagogues to be not only authentic as a translation, but divinely inspired, and, as such, of equal value with the Hebrew text itself, is not at all astonishing. That the early Christian fathers, both Greek and Latin, who uniformly quote this version, which was read in all the churches, should have adopted and embellished a *myth* which they found ready to their hand, is what might have been expected. But that the echo of this *myth* should have struck the ears of the rabbins, and worked its way into the Talmud, is indeed surprising.

In the Babylonian Talmud, (first chapter of the treatise *Megillah*,) we find the tale of seventy-two elders whom Ptolemy (Philadelphus) assembled and shut up in seventy-two cells, without letting them know his purpose in so doing; that, when all communication between them had ceased, he applied to each one of them, separately, for a translation of the Law of Moses; and that they were divinely inspired to render the law word for word alike; and, though they departed from the text in thirteen different passages, yet each of them, directed from on high, still rendered these texts in precisely the same words as his fellows. The Jerusalem Talmud (in loc. citat.) omits the introduction, and at once enters *in medias res* by the remark, "Thirteen texts were departed from in the version undertaken for King Ptolemy." And the same legend is also found in several other of the rabbinical writings, who speak of the Septuagint in terms of great respect.

In one place, however, (tr. *Sopherim*, ch. i.) the legend varies, and begins with the words, "Five elders translated the Law into Greek for King Ptolemy; but the day on which this was done was unpropitious to Israel, like the day on which the golden calf was made, because the rendering was not so perfect as it ought to have been." And it then goes on to relate in the words of the Babylon Talmud quoted above: "Seventy-two elders were assembled by King Ptolemy," and so forth. And at the end of the treatise *Taanith*, we find among the public fasts, the eighth day of *Tebeth*, (the 10th month,) "on which day the Law was translated into Greek, and darkness (affliction) prevailed in the world (Israel) during three days." Though no reason is assigned for this affliction, the very fact of the anniversary on which the translation was begun being classed among the *dies nefasti*, or calamitous epochs—and which must have been done shortly after the translation began to be generally promulgated—is a proof that the *Tanaim*, or elder rabbins, did not hold the Septuagint in equal veneration with their successors, the *Amoraim* of the Talmud.

As far as we of the present day are capable of forming any judgment on the merits of this version from that which now passes by the name of Septuagint, its claims to authority, or even to correctness, are very slender indeed. Of the thirteen texts noticed in the Talmud—in which the translation is said to have departed from the original—only four can be identified in the version now extant. But numberless other departures from the Hebrew original are to be found. Errors in numbers and names are countless. Indeed, so little correct is this wondrous version, that St. Jerome, one of the early fathers of the church, desirous of maintaining the high authority of a version continually quoted in the New Testament, has recourse to the hypothesis that the Egyptians purposely corrupted the Greek manuscripts, out of spite to the Jews.

It appears certain that the oldest or original portion of the Septuagint only comprised the *Torah*, or five books of the Law; and that the Prophets and Hagiographa were subsequently, and at different periods, rendered into Greek by translators of inferior ability. R'Azariah di Rossi is of opinion that the first translation of the Law into Greek was made, not from the original Hebrew, but from a Chaldee paraphrase, at that time popular in Judea.

This subject of the Septuagint and its authority has exposed the Jews to bitter reproaches on the part of some Christian churchmen of the last century, who tax the Jews with having corrupted or falsified the Hebrew text of the sacred Scriptures, in order to invalidate the authority of the Septuagint. It is, however, remarkable that St. Augustine, with greater liberality than has fallen to the lot of the philosophic divines of Germany, expressly acquits the Jews of this charge, which, indeed, is one of the most unfounded and unreasonable that could be brought against them. It appears (Gratz's History of the Jews, iv. 125) that both Jews and Christians used great freedom with the version of the Septuagint; altering, adding, or expunging as suited their purpose; so that, according to the admission of Origen, (Epistola ad Africanum, *and* Comment. in Mattheum,) as well as of St. Jerome, (Prologus Galeatus,) many texts quoted by early schoolmen are not to be found in the Hebrew original, nor yet in the oldest Greek version. And Eusebius (Hist. Eccles. v. 28) expressly mentions the school of a certain Artemion, who completely distorted the old Greek translation.

We shall have to return to this subject when we come to speak of Akylas and his Greek version. For the present, we need only add that whatever liberties were taken with the Greek translation, none were ever attempted with the Hebrew text. Some errors in transcript may have crept in, especially in the latest or Hagiographical books. But the labours of the *Massorites* have placed the genuine Hebrew text beyond the possibility of attaint, and preserved to Jew and to Gentile the inestimable and universal treasure of the word of God in its purity.

When we attempt to apply the test of critical investigation to the legends which—from the *soi-disant* Aristeas until the *Meor Aynayim* of Di Rossi—we find concerning this Greek translation, the truth appears to be, that the want of acquaintance with any other language than the Greek, rendered it necessary for the Hellenists that a translation or paraphrase of the sacred Scriptures, suitable to their wants, should be made public; and that, for this purpose, in the last years of Soter, and when his son Philadelphus was already associated with him in the government, some Jews of Alexandria undertook the translation. It is probable that they were assisted by some learned Jews from Palestine; it is possible that those magnificent patrons of literature, the Ptolemies, may have borne the whole, or contributed a part, of the expense of the undertaking. But it is certain that the only portion of Scripture then translated was the Law, or Five Books of Moses, which, indeed, until the persecution under Antiochus Epiphanes, formed the only portion of Holy Writ that was read in the synagogue, or used in public worship. Other parts of Scripture were translated by different hands, at different periods, and with ability greatly inferior to that evinced by the translators of the Law.

The importance of this Greek version, and its direct connection with and influence on the history of the Jews, as well as on the Christian church, will, we trust, exonerate us from the reproach of having devoted too much space to

JUDEA UNDER THE PERSIANS AND GREEKS. 133

myths and legends. No sooner did the Septuagint[22] begin to become popularly known to the Gentiles, than it produced consequences which the translators and their patrons probably never anticipated. The appearance of a work which reflected such unparalleled honour on a province so diminutive as Palestine, and on a people so little powerful as the Jews, seems to have piqued the national pride, and to have provoked the enmity of the Babylonians and Egyptians.

" These once illustrious cultivators of the arts and sciences found ready champions in the priests Berosus and Manetho, who, in the reign of the second Ptolemy, also translated into the Greek language the history and antiquities of their respective countries. Berosus, a priest of Belus at Babylon, dedicates his work, which, under the name of history, comprehends a strange admixture of mythology and astrology, to Antiochus Soter, the son and successor of Seleucus,[23] and the then master of Seleucia-Babylonia, and all the dependent provinces in Upper Asia; and he begins his history by tracing back the antiquity of Babylon to a period of four hundred and seventy-three thousand years before the Macedonian conquest. With regard to the flood, as well as the transactions of Noah, Nebuchadnezzar, and Cyrus, his narrative nearly coincided with the Hebrew annals. (Joseph. cont. Apion.

---

[22] Some critics are of opinion that the designation, *Septuaginta*, is an allusion, not to the number of the translators, but to that of the SEVENTY elders of Alexandria, under whose direction the translation may have been undertaken, and by whose authority it must have been introduced into the synagogue.

[23] The above is the opinion of Gillies, from whose history we quote. But other writers assume that the Antiochus in question was not *Soter*, but *Theos;* their authority for this is Tatian, who, in a fragment preserved by Eusebius, (Prœp. Evang. lib 10,) states that Berosus wrote his history in three books, and dedicated it to Antiochus, the third from Seleucus.

VOL. I. 12

lib. i. s. 19.) But, whenever forsaken by this aid, all was impenetrable obscurity or wild inconsistency. The dark chasm of fathomless ages was partly filled up by barren lists of fabulous kings, while the palpable defect of satisfactory information was excused by a fiction still more palpable—namely, that Nabonassar, who is said to have reigned in Babylon only 747 years B. C. E., desirous of passing with posterity as the founder of the Assyrian empire, had destroyed all the historical monuments of his numberless predecessors. Should this assertion be admitted, what are we to think of the records long anterior to Nabonassar, which Berosus, with strange impudence, professes to have carefully copied?" (Gillies, vi. 324.)

Well might the grave, judicious, and truth-loving Strabo (lib. 11) say of Babylonians, Syrians, Medes, "These nations have obtained no great credit in the world, by reason of the absurdity and fabulousness of their historians." Yet Berosus has, by some, been received and quoted as an ancient historian, whose authority might be adduced in opposition to Moses.

This Babylonish historian was not actuated by the desire to hold up the Jews to scorn and disgrace; nor, indeed, does he seem to have entertained any hostile feeling against them. But such was not the case with Manetho, high-priest of Heliopolis, in Egypt. The history of the Israelites, and of their sojourn in, and exode from, Egypt, as related in the Scriptures, was by no means flattering or soothing to the natives of that country, who, like every degenerate race, clung to the shadow of former greatness as a compensation for the want of present worth. The injustice, the cruelty, the treachery of Egypt's ancient kings, the degradation and want of power of Egypt's gods, were too fully and plainly set forth in the history of Moses; the people, because of whom the pride of Egypt had been so fearfully humbled, enjoyed too much of the respect and good-will of the actual dynasty, to permit Egyptian patriots or zealots to acquiesce in such a state of things.

Moreover, Berosus's history rendered it necessary to prove to King Philadelphus that the Egyptian nation was not less ancient or illustrious than the people governed by his rival in power and fame, Antiochus. To accomplish this two-fold object, Manetho Sebennyta wrote his Dynasties, which embrace a period of 53,535 years. And, while the history of Berosus—with the exception of some fragments preserved by Josephus, Tatian, and Eusebius—is lost, the "Dynasties" of Manetho are yet preserved.[24] A quaint writer of the early part of the last century (Stillingfleet, Orig. Sac. lib. i. cap. 2) remarks that "the Egyptians were a people so unreasonably given to fables, that the wisest action they ever did was to conceal their religion; and the best office their gods had, was to hold their fingers in their mouth to command silence to their worshippers." It had been well for their reputation, as a truth-loving people, if the priest Manetho had more strictly obeyed the injunction to keep silence thus tacitly conveyed by his speechless gods; since the fables and conceits he passes off as authentic history are to the full as absurd as those of Berosus, but infinitely more mischievous.

In order to secure belief for his statements, by ascribing them to an authority that is beyond doubt or reproach, Manetho tells us that he copied his history "from some pillars in the land of Seriad, on which, before the flood, certain records had been inscribed in the sacred dialect,

---

[24] These Dynasties are yet preserved, having been first epitomized by Julius Africanus, and from him transcribed into Eusebius's Chronicon. From Eusebius by Georgius Syncellus, out of whom they are produced by Joseph Scaliger, and may be seen both in his Eusebius and his Canones Isogogici. (Stillingfleet, *ubi supra*.) Josephus, (contra Apion.) who reviews Manetho's allegations, has also fragments of his work.

by the first Egyptian Hermes; and that, after the flood, the inscription was found, and translated out of the sacred dialect into the Greek tongue, in hieroglyphic characters, by Agathodæmon, the second Hermes, or Mercury, the father of Taut."

Now, though this statement may have been perfectly convincing to Manetho's countrymen, yet, to all others who are not so easy of faith, each assertion seems to carry an attestation of its falsehood on the face of it. Who was this first Hermes? Though he is also known by the names of Mercury and Thoyth, it is absolutely impossible to ascertain; indeed, the accounts respecting him are so hopelessly contradictory, that his existence has been altogether denied. Assuming that, according to the Egyptian account, he was a sacred scribe to Osiris, and the tutor of Isis, how can he have lived before the flood?

Then, again, the land of Seriad, where is it? Scaliger, that most indefatigable scholar, after a laborious research, declares he cannot find it; no such land is ever named by any writer of antiquity except Manetho, who thus improves on the Talmudic axiom, "That he who intends to tell an untruth should locate his particulars at a distance;" since his locality is so very distant that no one has ever been able to find it.

Then, again, the pillars! If, as is evidently intended, they are to command belief because they alone had outlasted the flood, the question arises, how could isolated pillars resist the pressure of waters so mighty that they overthrew structures the most solid, and destroyed cities the most extensive? Then, the sacred dialect, of which no mention was ever made by any other writer! This can have been no omission on the part of other historians, since they take care to tell us that the sacred writing or character of the Egyptians, was distinct and different from that commonly used; and it therefore appears certain that if a similar difference had existed in the dialect, some one writer (besides Manetho) would have mentioned it.

Then, as to the translation into the Greek tongue; why just into that, and into no other language? What was the motive of the preference? Was the Greek tongue known to the Egyptians *at all*, at the early period when this translation is assumed to have been made? We know that the Egyptians were extremely jealous of foreigners; that the Greeks, in particular, were not permitted to hold even commercial intercourse with Egypt, till under Psammetichus, of the 26th of Manetho's dynasties. What, then, could induce Hermes, whom no one knows, in the land of Seriad, which no one can find, to translate an inscription on pillars, which no one has ever seen, from a sacred dialect, of which no one has ever heard, into the Greek tongue, which no Egyptian then spoke? And, to crown the absurdity, Hermes, who lived before the flood, wrote the history of events that transpired in the days of Moses! Was this Hermes prescient, that he knew beforehand what would happen? Was he omniscient, that he could by anticipation write the continuous history of so many thousands of years as those recorded in the "Dynasties"? Verily, when Manetho claimed credence for his history, on authority such as that which he adduces, and we have dissected, he cannot have expected ever to have other readers than his own credulous and marvel-loving Greek and Egyptian contemporaries.

Our readers will probably owe us small thanks for having occupied their attention so long with an historian whom we ourselves declare unworthy of attention, and whom almost every writer of reputation, whether Jew or Christian, condemns as a slanderer. But, unfortunately, this Manetho the Egyptian was the first of a class of writers who, since then, have been but too numerous, and who delight in holding up the Jewish people to odium and contempt. In his own times, and during the reign of the Ptolemean dynasty, the mischief he did was but limited. But, after the lapse of a couple of centuries, the seed of rancour which his history had sown in the minds of Egyptians and of Greeks, produced, as its poisoned fruit, conflicts between Jews and Gentiles, that led to the slaughter of unoffending thousands. The work of Josephus against Apion, which we have so often quoted, was written at a time when the Jews throughout the Roman world were suffering every calamity, and in reply to a libel which, on the authority of Manetho, declares them to be the refuse of mankind, and undeserving of pity or mercy. Since then, every infidel that wishes to attack the authority of Scripture, lays great stress on Manetho. Those who strain at a gnat, and cannot believe Moses, swallow a camel, and take Manetho for their guide. Nay, more; in our own days we witness the attempt, in works that gravely claim to be history, to supersede, wholly or in part, the truth as it is in Scripture, for falsehood as it is in Manetho. And as it is but too probable that many of our readers may fall in with works of the kind to which we allude, it is but fair we should be permitted not only to enter our protest against the authority of the Egyptian slanderer, but also to state the reasons by which that protest is supported.

As, on the one hand, it was not practicable altogether to deny the fact that the Israelites in times of old had been sojourners in Egypt, had left that country, and taken possession of Palestine; and, as on the other hand, zeal for the gods of Egypt, so natural to the high-priest of Heliopolis, did not permit him to receive the scriptural account of the "judgments" inflicted on these gods as well as on their worshippers, Manetho deems it necessary to give, what he wishes us to receive, as Egyptian accounts of the sojourn of Israel in, and the exodus from, Egypt.

Such accounts he gives two; the one calculated to render the Jews hateful to the Egyptians, the second to render them at once odious and contemptible—both accounts being equally at variance with each other and with the truth of Scripture.

His first account is: "During the reign of our King Timaus, God, from some unknown cause, was wroth with us; and men of obscure origin, coming from the east, unexpectedly made a bold inroad into the land, which they conquered speedily and without combat. They subdued the chiefs, cruelly set fire to the cities, destroyed the temples, and treated the inhabitants with great ferocity; the men they slaughtered, the women and children they reduced to slavery. Then they elected a king from among themselves, whose name was Salatis. He took up his residence at Memphis, subjugated both the upper and lower country, and placed garrisons in such cities as he deemed proper. The eastern provinces he especially fortified; having in view the then greatly preponderating power of the Assyrians, who might feel inclined to invade the land. And, as in the district of Sais he found a city well adapted for his purpose, situated east of the river Bubasto, and in several old histories of the gods designated as *Avaris*, he rebuilt this city, fortified it with strong walls, and placed in it a garrison of 240,000 warriors. Thither he used to come every summer, partly to furnish the soldiers with corn and pay, and partly to train them to arms; and he disciplined them so carefully, that they became a terror to all foreigners. He died after a reign of nineteen years, and was succeeded by a king named Beon, who reigned forty-four years. After him Apachnas, thirty-six years and seven months; then Apophis, sixty-one years; next Janias, fifty years and one month; and lastly, Assis, forty-nine years and two months. These were their first six kings; they were continually engaged in war, and sought to destroy the root of Egypt. This people were all of them called 'Hyksos,' that is, 'King-shepherds'—for in the sacred language *Hyk*[25] denotes 'king,' and in the ordinary dialect, *sos* signifies 'shepherd;' thence the compound word 'Hyk-sos.' Some say they were Arabs. The above-named kings of the so-called shepherds and their successors reigned over Egypt five hundred and eleven years. After that the kings of Thebais and the rest of Egypt rose against the shepherds; a long and violent war broke out; until, finally, under King Alisphragmuthosis, the shepherds were vanquished, expelled from the rest of Egypt, and shut up in one place that had an extent of 10,000 acres. The name of this place is Avaris. This place they had fortified with strong and high walls, and there, as in a place of safety, they deposited their booty and all their property. Thumosis, the son of Alisphragmuthosis, endeavoured to conquer this city by siege, and surrounded the walls with an army of 480,000 men. But eventually he gave up the siege, and offered a treaty that they all should depart unmolested from Egypt, and go whithersoever they pleased. After due deliberation, they departed from Egypt for the wilderness of Syria, to the number of not less than two hundred and forty thousand men, with their families and possessions. And as they dreaded the power of Assyria, which at that time bore sway over Asia, they built, in the country now called Judea, a city sufficiently capacious for so many thousands—which city they called 'Jerusalem.'"

This is Manetho's first account; his second one is altogether different. He relates: "King Amenophis greatly

---

[25] Josephus (contra, Apion. i. 14,) remarks, "According to another Egyptian writer, the word *Hyk* does not signify 'kings,' but, on the contrary, 'captives.' For '*Hyk*,' aspirated, as the Egyptians do, and pronounced '*Hak*,' does signify 'captives,' 'prisoners.' This appears to me more correct, and in conformity with ancient history."

desired to see one of the gods, as his predecessor Orus had done. He communicated this desire to his namesake, Amenophis the son of Papis, a man who, from his wisdom and knowledge of the future, seemed to partake of the nature of the gods. This his namesake told him, he would become able to see the gods when he should have cleansed Egypt of lepers, and of all other impure and defiled persons. The king, greatly rejoiced, commanded that all persons deformed or mutilated throughout all Egypt should be collected together. The multitude of them numbered eighty thousand; and the king commanded they should be cast into the quarries east of the Nile, where, like other banished criminals, they were held to hard labour. Among them were likewise some learned priests afflicted with leprosy. This caused Amenophis, the sage and diviner, to fear that the treating of these priests with violence would draw down the wrath of the gods upon himself and upon the king. He further foresaw that the lepers would find confederates who would come to their assistance and hold dominion over Egypt during thirteen years. But as he was afraid to tell this to the king, he committed suicide, and left the entire prediction behind him in writing, which greatly alarmed the king. After the impure men had long toiled in the quarries, the king yielded to their entreaties, and granted them, as a residence and asylum, the city of Avaris, which had been quitted by the shepherds. This city, according to ancient mythology, belonged to Typhon. When the impure had taken possession of their new abode, the strength and situation of their city soon encouraged them to rebel. They elected one of the priests of Heliopolis, named Osarsiph, for their leader, and swore to obey him in all things. The first law he gave them was, not to adore the gods, nor to abstain from any of the animals worshipped as holy in Egypt, but to kill and eat all of them; and lastly, not to hold intercourse with any but their own confederates. After he had given these and other laws, most repugnant and opposed to the customs of Egypt, he commanded that the walls of the city should be carefully strengthened, and that diligent preparations should be made for war against King Amenophis. He then, taking counsel with the other priests and several of his impure confederates, dispatched messengers to the so-called city of Jerusalem, to the shepherds that had been expelled by Thetmosis, to communicate to them what he and his confederates had suffered, and to invite them to join him in a war against Egypt. He promised that, before all things, he would lead them to Avaris, their original native home; and that he would abundantly supply the warriors with whatever they stood in need of; that moreover, if necessary, he and his men would form their advanced guard, and easily subdue the land for them. The shepherds agreed to his proposals, and with an army of two hundred thousand men marched to Avaris, where they soon arrived. When King Amenophis heard of this mission, he became not a little alarmed, for he remembered the prediction of Amenophis the son of Papis. He began by causing the people of Egypt to assemble; and after having consulted with the chiefs of the army, he ordered that the animals deemed the most holy should be brought to him from the temples; and gave the priests a special charge carefully to conceal the images of the gods.

"He then consigned to the care of a friend, in a place of safety, his only son, then five years of age, whom he had named Rampses or Ramesses, after his own father; while he himself, at the head of three hundred thousand Egyptian warriors, advanced against the enemy, who marched forth to meet him. But the king declined the battle they offered, and the accepting of which he considered would have been fighting against the will of the gods. He therefore returned again to Memphis. There he took Apis and all the other sacred animals he had caused to be assembled. With these, and also with the entire army and the population of Egypt, he retreated to Ethiopia, the king of which country was connected with him in bonds of friendship and alliance. This king received him kindly; and during the thirteen years appointed by fate, provided for the wants of the Egyptians. In this interval, the Solymitan invaders, combined with the Egyptian lepers, treated the people very cruelly, and their victory appeared most detestable to those who witnessed the horrors they practised. They did not rest content with burning towns and villages, and with defiling the images of the gods, but they used these holy images for fuel, by which to roast the sacred animals. These had been slaughtered by their own priests, whom the enemy compelled to commit these murders, and then drove them away naked. The priest who gave them laws and a constitution, was, by his lineage, a Heliopolitan named Osarsiph, after the god Osiris, worshipped at Heliopolis; but, when he became the head of this people, he altered his name for that of Moses. After the end of the thirteen years, King Amenophis, with his son Rampses, returned, at the head of mighty armies, fought and conquered the allied shepherds and lepers, and pursued them to the boundaries of Syria."

We have now placed before our readers the two conflicting statements of Manetho, which subsequently were repeated and embellished by other Egyptian writers. One of them, Lysimachus, quoted by Josephus, (contra Apion. i. 26,) relates that "the city of the Jews was formerly called *Jerosyla*, from two Greek words signifying 'defiling of sanctuaries;' because of the many temples and holy objects which Moses and his people gloried in having defiled. Subsequently, however, they grew ashamed of this name, and so they turned it into Jerusalem." "This silly fellow, in his eagerness to slander, forgets that he is speaking of Jews, not of Greeks, and that, in the language of the former—the Hebrew—the word Jerosyla has no affinity whatever with defiling of sanctuaries." Such is the pertinent remark of Josephus (*in loco*) on this singular piece of archæology.

Manetho's purpose—dictated alike by zeal for the humiliation inflicted on his gods in the Scriptures, and by envy at the superior consideration and favour the Jews enjoyed with the Ptolemies—appears to have been twofold: first, to render the Jews hateful to the Egyptians, as descendants of those detested Hyksos, or shepherds, whose memory was still execrated in Egypt; and next, to render the Jews contemptible as well as odious by holding them up as the descendants of sacrilegious lepers. Josephus, urged on by the unfortunate circumstances in which his people were at that time placed, took the trouble to refute these fables of Manetho, absurd as they are. And to his defence (contra Apion.) we must refer our readers, while we content ourselves with two simple remarks: Had the Israelites invaded and subjugated Egypt, as the Hyksos did, sacred Scripture would no more have hesitated to state the fact than it hesitates to relate the invasion and subjugation of Canaan. Had the Israelites been expelled from Egypt by force of arms, as the Hyksos were, sacred Scripture would no more have hesitated to state the fact than it hesitates to relate how the ten tribes were expelled and carried away captive to Assyria by force of arms. There could be no possible cause for the Bible not noticing the identity of the Israelites with the Hyksos, except one; and that is, that these two nations were not identical.

Dr. Kitto (Hist. of Palestine, i. 83.) labours hard, and not without success, to prove that the Hyksos expelled from Egypt were the people known in the Bible by the name of the Philistines, who dwelt on the shores of the Mediterranean, and of whom it is stated that they came from Caphtor, which is now generally allowed to have been Lower Egypt. But, be the success of this hypothesis what it may, it appears certain the Hyksos were not Israelites. Then, again, as to the tale about the lepers: without stopping to dwell on the absurdities and incredible *myths* of Manetho, we would only remark that, had Moses himself, and the majority, or any considerable portion of his people, been afflicted with the foul and highly contagious disease of leprosy, it is not possible he could have laid down such stringent rules for the complete isolation of lepers, as we find in Leviticus, chapters xiii–xv. His legislation on this subject would not only have been utterly impracticable, but would have been directed against himself, and would have condemned him and a large portion—according to Manetho, the majority—of his people to a state of existence that may truly be designated a civil death.

We have already stated that Manetho and his absurdities have been again and again hashed up by enemies of the Jews and by enemies of the Bible. It is, indeed, difficult to attack the one without having a fling at the other; and therefore we see, in our days, pseudo-historians avail themselves of Manetho's tales, even though they quote not his authority. But the favourable notice his calumnies now obtain was in his own days denied to them. Though he dedicated his Dynasties to King Philadelphus, that monarch was too enlightened, too wise, too truly alive to his own interests, to allow his mind to be influenced against a people whom he always found loyal, industrious, and law-abiding. During his long reign he was frequently involved in war against his neighbour, Antiochus I. Soter, the son and successor of Seleucus, King of Syria; and after the death of that monarch—who fell in battle against the Gauls—with his son Antiochus II. Theos. No very decided advantages were gained by either monarch, though Antiochus lost much in another direction. For, draining his garrisons in the upper provinces that he might the more effectually carry on the war against the king of Egypt, Antiochus neglected to provide for the security of Parthia, Bactria, and other provinces beyond the Tigris; consequently these countries became exposed to the twofold evils of foreign invasion and domestic insurrection.

In Parthia the standard of revolt was raised by two brothers, Arsaces and Tiridates, in consequence of an abominable outrage committed on the person of the younger brother by Agathocles, the viceroy, who was slain by the brothers, (250 B. C. E.) And though the Parthians themselves computed their independence from the ensuing reign, it is from this period that we must date the beginning of the Parthian Empire, which was ultimately destined to set bounds to the Roman power, and to vanquish the vanquishers of the world. The immediate result of this rebellion was, that within a year after it broke out, Antiochus was compelled to make peace with Ptolemy, who, on his part, was also desirous of an accommodation, as he was grown old and could not command his armies in person. Yet he did not fail to take advantage of the necessity to which Antiochus was reduced of obtaining peace on any terms.

The king of Egypt compelled the king of Syria to repudiate his beloved wife, who was also his half sister, Laodicé, by whom he had two sons, and to marry Berenicé, a daughter of Philadelphus; and it was agreed that the first male issue of this marriage should succeed to the throne of Syria. As a dower to his daughter, Philadelphus gave Antiochus half the revenues of Palestine, Phœnicia, and Cœle-Syria. The Judeans thus became connected with the king of Syria, who may seem to have acquired some kind of dominion over them. But such was not in reality the case; for the internal administration was in the hands of the high-priest, who, also, and always, farmed the revenues of Judea; and the king of Egypt retained in his own hands not only one half of these revenues, but the sovereignty of the country; so that the condition of the Jews was in no wise affected by the transaction between the two kings, and which, moreover, was not destined to be of long duration.[20]

Philadelphus died after a glorious reign of thirty-eight years, during which his kingdom reached its greatest prosperity and power, while learning, science, and the arts of peace flourished in the highest degree. In his reign, the rising and powerful commonwealth of Rome first became connected with the successors of Alexander; for, when the Romans acquired the mastery of the southern coast of Italy, Philadelphus, with due attention to foreign affairs, sent an embassy of congratulation to Rome, and received from that republic an embassy in return. The transaction was, on both sides, conducted with much dignity; and though eventually, Egypt, like the greater part of the countries that formed the empire of Alexander, was devoured by Rome, yet the league of amity entered into by Philadelphus continued in force till the last of his successors, the worthless Cleopatra.

No sooner was Philadelphus dead, than his daughter Berenicé became the victim of the treaty of which she had been the bond. She had borne a son to Antiochus; but when the protection of her father ceased, the Syrian king dissolved a marriage that had been the work of interest or fear, and, recalling Laodicé to the throne, reinstated her children in their birthright. In committing this breach

---

[20] Biblical commentators are of opinion that this marriage of Berenicé, the daughter of Philadelphus, with Antiochus II. Theos, is the subject of a prediction in Daniel, (xi. 6,) by whom Egypt and Syria are respectively designated as the "South" and the "North."

of faith, Antiochus too rashly despised the youth and inexperience of the new king of Egypt, Ptolemy III., who prepared to take up arms and revenge the wrong done to his sister. But before he could put his forces in motion, Antiochus had already with his life expiated his perfidy. Laodicé, his queen, fearful of his fickleness, and of the probable influence which the approaching war with Egypt might exercise over his mind, determined to guard against the possibility of her own dignity and the prospects of her children ever again becoming the sport of his state policy. She therefore poisoned her husband; and she then engaged a Greek named Artemon, who strongly resembled him, to personate Antiochus in a pretended malady, and to name, at the seeming approach of death, her elder son Seleucus as successor to the kingdom.

Upon the first news of this transaction, of which Seleucus was supposed not to be ignorant, Berenicé fled in haste from Antioch to the neighbouring asylum of Daphné. In so sacred a retreat she hoped her infant son and her Egyptian attendants might remain for a short time in safety; but before she could be rescued by her brother, the king of Egypt, they, as well as her infant and herself, were seized and murdered by the emissaries of her triumphant rival. But the latter had no great cause to exult in her success. Ptolemy, exasperated by the sufferings and death of his sister and his nephew, at once took the field. The powerful army which he inherited would have insured success against an adversary better prepared than Seleucus. His parricidal usurpation had provoked and alienated the more liberal portion of the Syrians and all the Greeks. So long as the fate of Berenicé had been in suspense, the Greek cities of Asia Minor had not been sparing of menaces to insure her safety. When her cruel death became known, the Greeks invaded Syria from the north, while Ptolemy attacked the country from the south.

Seleucus, unable to resist, fled; but Ptolemy succeeded in capturing the more guilty Laodicé, whom he caused to be ignominiously executed.

He then continued his inroad, marching on from province to province, levying heavy contributions, until disturbances in Egypt compelled him to abandon his enterprise and return home. His plunder was estimated at 40,000 talents of silver, or nearly forty millions of dollars. But what appeared far more valuable to his Egyptian followers, was the recovery of their idols, detained disgracefully in the cities of Persia ever since Cambyses, the conqueror of Egypt, had torn them from their venerated shrines. These cumbrous images, to the number of 2500, Ptolemy caused to be carried back to Egypt, where their arrival caused an enthusiasm of joy, and obtained for the king the surname of *Euergetes*, "the Benefactor," with which the gratitude of the Egyptians saluted him. On his return to Egypt he passed through Jerusalem, where he offered many sacrifices, and made large presents to the temple. It is probable, as Kitto remarks, that the high-priest pointed out to him those predictions in Daniel that had been fulfilled in the late events and in his own achievements; and that this circumstance may have greatly influenced his generous bounties to the temple.

On his return to Egypt, Ptolemy projected an expedition to the south for the conquest of Ethiopia; and, in order to carry it on with undivided means, he granted Seleucus a truce for ten years. This last-named monarch had suffered severely for the crimes of his mother, in which he was suspected of having participated, at least as far as a guilty knowledge went. Not only had the king of Egypt plundered Seleucus's empire and shaken his throne—while the rebellion in Parthia spread and acquired a degree of stability which rendered its suppression hopeless—but the Greek cities in Asia Minor had declared their independence, and the several provinces of the Taurus mountain-chain transferred their allegiance from Seleucus to his younger brother Antiochus, surnamed *Hierax*, "the Hawk," from his extreme rapacity.

To re-establish his authority along the coast of Asia Minor, Seleucus, with great diligence and a vast expense of treasure, assembled a considerable fleet; but his armament was overtaken by a tempest, and great part of it shipwrecked. This disaster, however, which might have been expected to ruin him irretrievably, turned, on the contrary, to his advantage. The Greeks, considering the storm as a judgment inflicted by heaven, began to feel compassion for the grandson of Seleucus Nicator, the worthiest and most illustrious of all Alexander's successors. Their returning allegiance was doubtless hastened by the designs of Hierax, who, having entered into a close connection with the Gauls, prepared to extend his usurpations in Asia Minor by the mercenary aid of these odious barbarians.

These Gauls originated from those countries in Europe which form the present empire of France, from whence swarms of warlike youth emigrated to seek spoil and settlements in other countries. In Italy, in the north of which they made large conquests, they were long the terror of Rome, which city they even burnt, though they were finally subdued. Another horde of them penetrated through Illyria into Macedon, where they defeated and slew in battle Keraunus, the murderer of Seleucus Nicator. After plundering Macedon, they invaded Greece, where they committed great devastations, but were eventually compelled to retreat. In Thrace they took possession of a considerable tract of land, and established a kingdom, called by the Greeks *Thule*. But finding, after a time, that their limits were too narrow, they invaded Asia, where they seized, desolated, and then abandoned entire provinces, laid the richest territories under heavy contribution, and interfered with a high hand in the affairs of Syria. Their whole course was marked by rapacity, cruelty, and want of good faith. Merciless to their enemies, and treacherous to their allies, they often sold their troops to rival powers, easily quitted one service for another, and, in all this infamous traffic of blood, invariably preferred the highest bidder.

These ruthless and unprincipled freebooters, *Hierax*, not less rapacious and unprincipled than they, had taken into his pay. And as their exorbitant expectations could only be gratified by boundless plunder, all the adjacent cities and countries hastened to make their peace with Seleucus, in order that, uniting their forces with his, they might be able effectually to repel the fierce assailants by whom they were menaced. And there is little doubt but that the readiness with which Ptolemy consented to a truce of ten years, was, in a great measure, called forth by a desire to maintain a barrier against the possible inroads of the Gauls into the Egyptian possessions, the safety of which had already once been endangered by them in the reign of Philadelphus, who had taken a body of them in his pay, and against whom they rebelled with great loss and discomfiture to themselves.

The war between the two brothers, Seleucus and Antiochus, was carried on during three years with all the bitter rancour of fraternal discord, and attended by all the horrors that could be enacted by a fierce mercenary soldiery, whose leader's rapacity entitled him to the name of "Hawk." At first, fortune favoured him. Seleucus was defeated in a great battle at Ancyra. And as a report was circulated that he himself had been killed in the action, the Gauls began to deliberate on the advantage to be derived from destroying the victor Antiochus likewise, so that they might appropriate to themselves exclusively the fruits of the victory. Antiochus was compelled to ransom his life for a large sum, which he paid to his auxiliaries, whose mutinous conduct and treacherous designs prevented him from profiting by his victory.

Thenceforth the pride of the Gauls knew no bounds: they looked upon themselves as supreme disposers, not only of the great kingdom of Syria, but likewise of the smaller Grecian states in Western Asia. But as pride must have a fall, they were defeated in two successive campaigns by the Greek kings of Pergamus; and their second defeat was so decisive as to compel them to give up their predatory mode of life, and to resign that ambulatory dominion which they had held for the space of forty years in Asia Minor.

The most ferocious among them, however, to the number of upward of 100,000 warriors, still adhered to the standard of Antiochus Hierax, whom they followed to Seleucia-Babylonia, in hopes of plundering that wealthy capital. Their march led them through countries thickly inhabited by Jews, where the Gauls fully maintained their character of ruffianly devastators, until the peaceable, illused, and exasperated inhabitants took up arms against them. A body of eight thousand Babylonish Jews assembled and advanced to oppose the invaders. This body was powerfully reinforced by four thousand of their Macedonian fellow-citizens. King Seleucus hastened to join them with what few soldiers he could muster. And in the battle which ensued he gained a great and decisive victory, through the indomitable valour of the Jews, who fought for their wives and children, for home and freedom. (Justin. lib. xxvii. cap. 3; 2 Maccab. viii. 20.) The Gauls were routed, and so completely dispersed that Antiochus could not again rally them, but was obliged to seek refuge in Egypt, in which kingdom he was detained a prisoner thirteen years by Ptolemy Euergetes. At length he succeeded in escaping from his confinement; but in his attempt to return to Syria, he was attacked and slain by the Arabs of the desert.

This great battle, in which the Gauls were defeated, is the first instance on record, after the rebuilding of Jerusalem, of Jews taking the field as an army, and distinguishing themselves as warriors. For though we know that Jews served in the armies of Alexander, of the Ptolemies, and of Seleucus and his successors, yet we have no proof or account of their having formed distinct bodies of troops—much less of their having formed the whole or greater part of a victorious army—until we meet them encountering Hierax and his auxiliaries, whose overthrow on that occasion enabled Seleucus to exchange the surname *Pogon*, "Bushy Beard," by which, till then, he had been known, for the more high-sounding one of *Callinicus*, "illustrious victor," to which, however, subsequent events proved him but little entitled.

His truce with Egypt, and the defeat of his brother and of the Gauls, left him at liberty to direct the entire force of his great monarchy against the rebellious Parthians. During his wars against the Egyptians and Antiochus, the rebels, Parthians, and Bactrians had formed a close alliance. The former, after greatly strengthening the defences of their country, had taken possession of Hyrcania, and prepared to invade Media, the finest province of the Syrian monarchy. To resist them, Seleucus led forth a large army, which, during four years was strongly reinforced, and checked the progress of the Parthians. Eventually, however, Seleucus was defeated and made captive in a great battle, decisive of the future independence and dominion of Parthia. His life was spared, and he was even treated royally by the victor, Tiridates, who had assumed the name and place of his elder brother, Arsaces,[27] the first author and leader of the revolt; but the king of Syria never again recovered his liberty, and, after ten years' loose confinement, he was killed by a fall from his horse while hunting, the same year that his brother Antiochus the Hawk met with his death on his flight from Egypt. Death might appear beneficial to imprisoned kings; but even imprisonment was beneficial to Seleucus and Antiochus, so shamefully had their freedom been disgraced in acts of fraternal discord. (Gillies, vi. 468.)

Seleucus left two sons: the elder, his namesake, was surnamed *Keraunus*, "thunder," for some reason unknown, but most probably in derision of his stolidity and bodily impotency. During the ten years that King Seleucus lived as a prisoner in Parthia, the Syrian monarchy, out of loyalty to the house of Nicator, submitted to the vicarious rule of his imbecile son. But when Keraunus ascended the throne after his father's death, his unfitness for his exalted station became so evident, that his generals and courtiers removed him by poison. He was succeeded by his younger brother, Antiochus, who obtained the surname of "the Great," of which, at least in early life, he proved himself not altogether unworthy.

While discord and misfortune weighed thus heavily on the successors of Seleucus Nicator, their rival, the king of Egypt, was busy in expeditions to the south; so that as the commencement of his reign had been signalized by splendid but useless achievements in Asia, the latter part of it was occupied in vast but untenable and profitless conquests in Africa. These remote undertakings had prevented Ptolemy Euergetes from interfering in the affairs of Syria, while at the same time they explain the strange negligence with

---

[27] The kings of Parthia thenceforward assumed the name of Arsaces, which, like that of Cæsar by the emperors of Rome, became the designation of all of them; in addition to which they are distinguished by the names which each one bore before mounting the throne.

which he managed the affairs of the countries dependent on Egypt, and of which Judea offers a striking example.

After the death of Antiochus Theos, the division of the revenues of Judea between Egypt and Syria ceased, and the whole reverted to Euergetes. The high-priest Eleazar, who died 276 B. C. E., was succeeded, not by his own son Onias, but by Manasseh, the son of Jaddua. At his death, in 250 B. C. E., Onias became high-priest and farmer of the revenue of Judea; but as he succeeded to that high dignity at an advanced age, and was of a covetous disposition, which grew stronger as he grew older, he contrived to evade an anuual payment of twenty talents (about twenty thousand dollars) from year to year, during twenty-four years, and until the arrears had reached the heavy sum of four hundred and eighty talents, or nearly half a million of dollars. Careless as the Egyptian government had been during the long time the arrears were accumulating, it now, and all at once, became as urgent in enforcing liquidation. King Ptolemy despatched a confidential officer, Athenion, (whom Josephus styles ambassador,) as a special messenger to Jerusalem to demand the payment in full of what was already due, and to require greater punctuality in future; with the threat that, unless his demands were satisfied forthwith, he would confiscate all the lands in Judea, and send a colony of soldiers to occupy them. Old Onias, who during so many years had ruled supreme in Judea without any interference from the king of Egypt, could not bring himself to believe in the reality of the danger. His darling money-bags ranked higher with him than the possible result of the king's anger; he, consequently, was disposed to neglect the warning, and to brave the threat that filled the people with consternation.

Fortunately, the high-priest's nephew, Joseph, was a wiser man than his uncle; and finding that no remonstrance could induce the old man to part with his gold, young Joseph took upon himself the task of averting the royal anger. His pleasing manners, together with his liberality and public spirit, had gained for him the favour of Athenion, and he prevailed on this officer to return to Alexandria, and to pacify the king by the promise that Joseph would speedily appear at court and satisfy every demand. And shortly after Athenion's departure, Joseph followed him to Alexandria, according to his promise. In an audience he had of the king, Joseph apologized for the undutiful behaviour of his uncle, whose old age had reduced him to a state of second childhood. "But," continued he, "of me, who have not yet outlived my understanding, the king shall have no reason to complain." Ptolemy was pleased with his frankness, assigned him an apartment in his palace, and daily admitted him to his table. (Joseph. Antiq. lib. xii.)

On his way to Alexandria, Joseph had fallen in and become acquainted with several travellers from Cœle-Syria and Phœnicia, men of distinction in their respective cities, who were proceeding to the capital to take part in the auction for the provincial revenues, which annually were farmed out to the highest bidder. To inspire a higher opinion of their wealth, they travelled in splendid style, with numerous attendants; and were inclined to make merry at Joseph's mean appearance, whose whole equipage had been procured at no greater cost than two thousand drachmas, (about three hundred dollars.) He only laughed at their raillery, but was deeply attentive to their serious conversation; for as they did not apprehend a competitor in one apparently so little wealthy as Joseph, they freely discussed before him the results of their previous bargains in Alexandria; and thus Joseph, to his great surprise, ascertained that the amount for which the revenues had been farmed, and which they again were likely to bring, was considerably less than half of their real value.

When the day of the auction came—which was carried on in the presence of Ptolemy, and of Berenicé, his queen—the highest sum offered for the entire revenues of Cœlo-Syria, Phœnicia, and Palestine, was not more than eight thousand talents, (about eight millions of dollars.) Joseph, who was in attendance on the royal party, at once came forward and bid double that amount. Ptolemy was delighted to hear these provinces valued at double their former price, but asked, as usual on such occasions, what sureties Joseph could offer for the due fulfilment of his contract. The young Hebrew—who had discerned how much, in the king's deliberations, a jest was paramount to every serious reason—with much gravity declared that he would give sureties of unquestionable probity and unrivalled opulence. He then named Ptolemy himself, and Queen Berenicé, who, he said, would be mutually bound to each other for the exact performance of his engagements. The king smiled consent; and Joseph, upon the credit of court favour, easily procured five hundred talents at Alexandria to pay up the arrears due by his uncle, and to equip himself in a manner suitable to his new and important employment. He returned to Palestine, attended by a body of two thousand infantry. Excited by the collectors, whom Joseph had outbid, the cities of Ascalon and Scythopolis at first refused his demands; but the ringleaders at each place were punished, some with death, some with confiscation of their property. This exemplary severity prevented further resistance; and it may be assumed that Joseph performed his duty with justice to the king, and without unusual or great oppression to the provinces, since he held his office twenty-two years, during the reign of Euergetes and his successors.

This Joseph, with his polished address, his pliant adaptation to circumstances, his *facile* disposition, and boundless assurance, was the type and representative of a class already numerous, but which derived greater strength from his success. This class, in the parlance of the present day, would have to be designated as *Young Judea*, or the *party of progress*. The Jews, since the invasion of Alexander, and still more since the battle of Ipsos, had lived in close and amicable connection with the Greeks both of Egypt and Syria; and the influence which the latter exercised over the former gradually became considerable. Grecian arts, Grecian philosophy, and Grecian polish acted on the susceptible minds of the warm-hearted and imaginative Jews with an effect all the more powerful because it was friendly. The Greeks carefully abstained from coercing the Jews into any deviation from their own long-cherished customs. But the restraints of the Law of Moses were encountered by the pleasures and elegancies of Grecian life; and the authority of religion was opposed by that of philosophy.

The writer (in *Frankel's Monatschrift*, No. 6,) whose analysis of the apopthegms of the men of the Great Assembly, and of Simon the Just, we have already submitted to our readers, likewise calls our attention to the maxims of Antigonus of Socho, the disciple of Simon the Just, and his successor in the presidency of the synagogue. He used to say, "Be ye not like servants who wait on the master on condition of receiving a reward; but be ye like servants who wait on the master without the stipulation of any reward; and let the fear of heaven (God) be upon you." (Mes. Aboth. i. 3.) This maxim, of which the concluding portion appears loosely connected with the other parts, gives us an idea of the manner in which Grecian philosophy attacked Jewish habits of thought, by showing us how the Jewish teachers laboured to ward off these attacks.

Among the various systems of Grecian philosophy, the one that found most favour with the short-sighted was that of Epicurus. He taught that the greatest good was happiness, and that the chief ingredient of happiness, nay, the greatest good itself, was pleasure, and the enjoyment thereof. The component parts of the greatest good consequently consisted in various kinds of pleasure, which, however, were to be subjected to examination and comparison, as many a kind of pleasure might cause displeasure or pain. As the result of such comparison, Epicurus proclaimed Virtue to be the chiefest of all pleasures; but at the same time he declared that he could form no idea of "the good," if he subtract from it the pleasures which arise from taste or enjoyment, or those which are caused by hearing, or by the sight of the beautiful. In accordance with this view of the greatest good, is his doctrine concerning the gods. The highest beatitude is tranquillity, or the remaining undisturbed in a "most excellent condition;" and as the gods are in perfect beatitude, they can have nothing to do with the management of human affairs. Accordingly, they do not allow themselves to be disturbed by these, or to be in any way concerned with them.

Such a doctrine, which holds up pleasure and its enjoyments as the sole aim of all human exertions, and which meets and removes any scruples that might arise from thinking of the Deity, by the assertion that the beatitude of the gods themselves consisted in the enjoyment or pleasure of tranquillity, and that they did not concern themselves about human actions, be they good or bad, would be likely to find ready acceptance with many men of the world, especially among Orientals, who, from the influence of their climate, are of their own accord strongly addicted to sensual pleasures.[28] And co-operating with the agree-

---

[28] How completely the Syrian Greeks gave themselves up to the teachings of Epicurus, may be seen in the description of their manners and conduct in the Emperor Julian's Misopogon.

able and polished manners and elegant mode of life of the Greeks, this doctrine seduced many a child of Israel from his allegiance to the Law.

In opposition to these pernicious principles of Epicurus Antigonus propounded his maxims, which, as he was chief of the synagogue, may be considered as the orthodox doctrine and confession of faith of the conservative party that remained true to the Law. Epicurus had, to all appearance, yielded great homage to virtue, designating it as the chiefest pleasure; therefore, he says, virtue is to be cherished, not because of any extrinsic reward, but because virtue carries with her, intrinsically, her own highest recompense; and as this doctrine proclaimed the autonomy, supremacy, and independence of virtue, many a disciple might be caught, even from among those who cared but little for sensual enjoyments. But, as has already been stated, the sole object of Epicurus's theory was the gratification of man's desire for pleasure. Therefore the lowest of our propensities has the unquestionable right to insist on being gratified, as well as our purest joys. Consequently the Epicurean autonomy, or supreme independence of virtue, was a mere illusion and specious pretext.

In opposition to this mock supremacy, Antigonus establishes the real autonomy, the most purely supreme independence of religion: "Serve the master, (God,) not with a view to reward, but independent of any reward." Religion carries her own best reward intrinsically within herself. This reward, however, does not well forth from the impure fountain of pleasure, but has its high and holy source in the portion from the God on high that indwelleth man. And as the climax of the Epicurean creed was "that the gods do not take heed of the actions of men"—since their so doing would disturb the perfect tranquillity which constitutes their beatitude—Antigonus, in direct opposition to this doctrine of Epicurus, and as the concentrated result of his own teachings, adds the concluding portion of his maxim, "Let the fear of heaven (God) be upon you." God does take cognizance of human deeds, and punishes the guilty; consequently the doctrine of Epicurus of the divine indifference is false; and, as a further consequence, it is not true that earthly pleasure is the chiefest good; as that can only be found in the consciousness of eternal happiness, which springs from the divine favour.

In the apocryphal Talmudic treatise, (*Aboth* of R'Nathan, ch. 5,) the origin of the first schism[29] among the Jews is traced to the maxim of Antigonus, that we have quoted. The narrative, as there given, states—"Antigonus used to say, 'Be ye not like servants who wait on the master on condition of receiving a reward; but be ye like servants who wait on their master without the stipulation of any reward.' He had two disciples, named Zadock and Baithos. These heard the words of their master, but understood them not; therefore they said, 'Shall a labourer work all day, and not receive his wages in the evening? Surely if there were any reward or future state after death, or if the dead were ever to rise again, our teacher would not have directed us to expect no reward.' Accordingly, they collected disciples and founded the sect of the Sadducees or Baithosces, whose doctrine was that the soul perisheth with the body, and that there is no resurrection of the dead, nor angels, nor spirits."

The writer in the *Monatschrift*, whom we have already quoted, remarks that this account of the origin of the sect of Sadducees does not appear very satisfactory, inasmuch as the inference sought to be deduced from Antigonus's maxim does not necessarily result therefrom. At the same time, he thinks this account has an historical basis,

---

[29] The Samaritans or Cutheans were indeed the first schismatics, but they were not Jews, and were never recognised as such, either in lineage or faith.

inasmuch as the system of Epicurus was first opposed by Antigonus. For Epicurus denied the immortality of the soul, and taught that, "when death is, we are not; when we are, death is not,"—which is tantamount to the Sadducee doctrine, that the soul dies with the body. It was, consequently, not the maxim of Antigonus which gave rise to the doctrine of Epicurus; but, on the contrary, the prevalence of Epicurean doctrines called forth the maxims of Antigonus.

Now, though the views of this writer are doubtless correct, and the maxim of Antigonus was the effect, not the cause, of the circumstance that the belief in the immortality of the soul was denied by some Judeans, yet, as all Jewish authorities agree in tracing the origin of the sect of the Sadducees to the disciples and to the maxim of Antigonus of Socho, we think that the connection between the two and the sectarians is stronger than the writer in question seems disposed to admit. We deem it probable that Zadock and Baithos were originally disciples of Antigonus, but that they, in process of time, embraced the doctrines of Epicurus; that subsequently they sought, with perverse ingenuity, to strengthen their new creed by enlisting in its service the very maxims with which their old master had opposed it; and that they did this in the manner related in the *Aboth* of R'Nathan. Certain it is, that the doctrines of the Sadducees—whose influence as a powerful and long-dominant sect we shall have frequent occasion to mention—embodied as much of the views of Epicurus as could by any possibility be reconciled with the letter of the Law of Moses; and that they did not attempt to reconcile the two, until the desperate efforts of the "Go-a-head party" to get rid of the Law had irretrievably failed, as will hereafter be related.

One hundred years had now elapsed since the death of Alexander; and during eighty years of that time the

Jews had prospered and thriven in peace, not only in Judea and Egypt, under the beneficent rule of the three first Ptolemies, but also, where they were most numerous, throughout the extensive dominions of the Syro-Greeks. The Judeans, in particular, had greatly flourished. Self-governed, lightly taxed, and free from the terrors and disturbances of warfare, peace and plenty prevailed throughout their land, and their numbers and wealth had equally increased. But a great change for the worse was impending; and little as hitherto we have had to relate of their actions, we are now approaching a period when their sufferings, their fortitude, and their prowess will alike demand our attention.

The reign of the third Ptolemy, Euergetes, was suddenly and tragically brought to a close. He was assassinated by his own son, Ptolemy IV., who from this foul deed derived his satirical surname of *Philopator*—"the father-loving." With Euergetes the prosperity of the Egypto-Grecian monarchy perished. He is popularly and justly considered as the last good king of the Ptolemean dynasty; and if in many respects he was inferior to his great predecessors, Soter and Philadelphus, he was more than in the same degree superior to his successors. His assassin ascended the throne the year after Antiochus had become king of Syria—221 B. C. E. Each of the rival monarchs owed his crown to the assassination of his immediate predecessor. But Antiochus of Syria mounted the blood-stained throne of his murdered brother with clean hands; and though, from his youth and inexperience, he was obliged to submit to the guidance of ministers who abused his confidence, and committed great crimes under his authority, yet, as he grew older and became a man, he emancipated himself from the thraldom of his unworthy favourites. Subsequently, his actions, in restoring the power and prosperity of his kingdom, gained for him the surname of "the great," as we have already stated. Whereas Ptolemy, who had seized the crown with hands dyed in the heart's blood of his own father, proved himself, throughout the whole of his reign, not only capable of the most horrid crimes, but also abandoned to the most shameless vices. His first act on ascending the throne was the murder of his mother Berenicé, and his brother Magas; and having thus secured, as he fancied, his government at home, he despised the nonage of Antiochus, his natural rival, abroad; committed the carés of state to servants worthy of such a master; and claimed the perpetration of every enormity as the best of royal prerogatives. (Strabo, lib. xvii. p. 796.)

According to the incestuous custom and policy of his dynasty, he had espoused his own sister Arsinoe, a virtuous and high-spirited woman. Her, however, he soon neglected; and surrounding himself with harlots and buffoons, he spent his days and nights in the most profligate debaucheries; while his minister and favourite, Sosibius, was only intent on enriching himself and extending his own power.

Among the many grandees and officers high in trust with the late king, whom Philopator and his minister determined to destroy, was Theodotus, the governor of Cœle-Syria. He, however, obtained some notice of their purpose; and, thus reduced to the sad choice between destruction or treason, this brave but ill-rewarded officer anticipated the designs of a master whom he despised, and at once addressed himself to Antiochus, offering to put him in possession of the valuable Egyptian possessions in Cœle-Syria, Phœnicia, and Palestine. Antiochus readily closed with the offer; and Damascus, with great part of Cœle-Syria, Phœnicia, with the seaports of Tyre and Ptolemais, and forty sail of Egyptian ships of war, were the fruits of one short campaign; which, however, was terminated by a truce obtained through the mediation of the great trading communities of the Rhodians and Byzantines. They had long been connected with Egypt in bands of commerce and of amity, and now exerted themselves to negotiate a peace between the rival monarchies.

The conduct of the Egyptian ministers on this trying occasion proved that, however destitute they were of virtue, they were by no means deficient in the wiles and craft of diplomacy. The attack of Antiochus had taken them by surprise. They had never contemplated the possibility of Theodotus' treason, and were, therefore, altogether unprepared for war. Their first step, on hearing of the disasters in Cœle-Syria, had been to order the wells between Egypt and Syria to be destroyed, and to open the flood-gates of the Nile near Pelusium, that the inundation might stop the advance of an invading army. They next eagerly availed themselves of the mediation of the Rhodians, and at a congress held at Memphis they professed their willingness to accept peace on any terms.

But while every conference they held with the ambassadors of Antiochus confirmed the latter—who were treated with unbounded respect—in their opinion that the lazy, voluptuous Philopator would purchase peace by the meanest compliance, the time thus gained by Sosibius and his colleagues was employed with the utmost diligence. The as yet unbroken strength of Egypt was exerted to the utmost; numbers of Greek mercenaries, eager for profitable service, were enlisted; and gradually, during the four months the negotiations and truce continued, an army of seventy thousand foot, five thousand horse, and seventy-three elephants, with adequate magazines of arms and provision, were assembled near Alexandria, and ready to take the field.

As soon as their preparations were completed, the king of Egypt and his minister disdained all further temporizing. Cœle-Syria and its dependencies had, they averred, been assigned to Ptolemy Soter at the general peace that followed the battle of Ipsos. He and his descendants had been in possession nearly a century; and it was only through treason that these valuable appendages to the Egyptian monarchy had been severed from it. They consequently summoned Antiochus to surrender territories to which he had no right. Other conditions were dictated equally unpalatable to Antiochus, who at once rejected them. His army was scarcely less powerful than that of Philopator, as it numbered sixty-two thousand foot, six thousand horse, and upward of a hundred elephants. The king of Egypt roused all the energies he was capable of exerting, and, placing himself at the head of his army, advanced to Raphia, a place near Gaza, and not far from the borders of Judea. Antiochus pitched his camp at less than a mile from the Egyptians. Frequent skirmishes happened daily between parties sent out in search of provisions and water; and the ground between the hostile camps became the scene of fierce encounters, both of horse and foot.

But the exploit of Theodotus surpassed all others in boldness. To gratify his personal resentment, and to finish the war by an illustrious vengeance, he entered the Egyptian camp attended only by two daring companions; and favoured by darkness and disguise—the more easy to assume as the Egyptian troops were variously dressed and armed—he penetrated to the royal pavilion which Ptolemy used for giving audience, and in which he was in the habit of supping with his friends. But the king commonly slept in a more private tent; and as this circumstance was not known to Theodotus, he missed his purpose, and instead of killing Ptolemy he stabbed Andreas, the royal physician. After wounding two other courtiers, Theodotus gained the outer entrenchments, and finally escaped uninjured. (Polyb. lib. v. cap. 18.)

JUDEA UNDER THE PERSIANS AND GREEKS. 167

The danger to which he had been exposed, and which proved that, even in the midst of his camp, and surrounded by many thousands of brave and devoted warriors, his life was not safe, rendered Philopator impatient to terminate the war by a decisive battle; and Antiochus, whose supplies of provisions began to fail him, was equally eager for a decision. The battle which ensued is very graphically described by Polybius, (lib. v. cap. 84.) The troops in both armies were of the same description. Intermixed with Greeks and Macedonians, chosen men from the remotest dependencies of Syria and Egypt augmented the phalanx[30] of heavy infantry, which, in either line, amounted to nearly thirty thousand. On both sides there were Thessalian cavalry and Theban spearmen, crafty Cretans, fierce Thracians, and ferocious Gauls. The wealth of the two most powerful kingdoms of the East purchased martial auxiliaries wherever they could be obtained; and it is of interest and importance to the historian of the Jews, to become well acquainted with the composition of armies

---

[30] The Macedonian phalanx was a body of foot soldiers, carrying short swords fit either for cutting or thrusting, strong bucklers four feet in length, and two and a-half in breadth, and pikes eighteen feet long. Originally this heavy brigade, which formed the main battle, consisted of six thousand men drawn up sixteen deep; gradually these numbers were increased to sixteen thousand, and finally to thirty-two thousand men. By its depth, compactness, and the nature of its weapons, this heavy body of infantry long vanquished every enemy. But in the wars between the remote followers of Alexander and the Romans, the phalaux was proved to be, in itself, a very incomplete instrument of victory. It depended on the co-operation of light troops for removing obstacles, for covering its flanks, and for giving it a fair opportunity to exercise in front its matchless might. As its numbers were increased it became more unwieldy, and could only act on level ground. The defeats of the Macedonian phalanx by the Roman legion arose partly from the greater mobility of the latter, and partly from the Macedonian kings considering the phalanx complete and all-sufficient in itself. (Polybius, lib. xviii. caps. 12, 15.)

which presently he will find arrayed in all the terror of numbers, discipline, and warlike skill, against the few, unwarlike, barely half-accoutred, and altogether inexperienced champions of freedom in Judea.

Though the two armies were thus equal in point of arms and discipline, and nearly so in point of numbers, yet at the battle of Raphia the European auxiliaries of Ptolemy had one great advantage over those of his rival. They came more recently from their native lands, and carried with them that unbroken vigour and inborn bravery which always suffered decay through contact long continued with Egyptian and Asiatic softness.

Before the signal for action, the two kings, as if by mutual prearrangement, rode round their respective armies, and animated them to a battle which was to decide the pre-eminence between Syria and Egypt. In his progress along the line, Philopator was accompanied by his nobleminded wife, Arsinoe, eager to share the dangers of her unworthy husband, whose debased profligacy was utterly incompatible with every conjugal virtue. Having finished his review, Philopator took his post on the left; Antiochus placed himself on his right, directly opposite to the king of Egypt. Each of them, after the example introduced by Alexander the Great, was surrounded by troops of equestrian companions, though neither of the two rivals knew how to make that use of these select bands which invariably had made them the great instruments of Alexander's victories.

Ptolemy, as well as Antiochus, had placed a line of elephants in front of the cavalry. The battle began as these fierce and powerful animals advanced to the charge; a singular spectacle being exhibited by the spearmen fighting from towers on their backs; and one still more extraordinary, by the elephants themselves, who rushed against each other with the utmost fury, and strove with their implicated trunks to force the adversary from his ground; until the stronger having pushed aside the proboscis of the weaker, and forced him to turn his flank, then pierced him in many parts with his tusks, as a bull gores with his horns.* At length the Egyptian warriors were repelled by the superior size and strength and fury of their rivals from India;[31] and the confusion which their rout occasioned was followed by the defeat of Ptolemy's left wing, the king himself being obliged to retire for safety behind the phalanx of his heavy infantry. While Antiochus, hurried away by the ardour and inexperience of youth, was incautiously urging the pursuit, and eager to push to the utmost his partial advantage, Echecrates the Thessalean, a general of great skill and experience, and who commanded on Ptolemy's right, instructed by what had happened at the other extremity of the field, determined not to advance his elephants to an unequal combat. Instead, he ordered the Greek mercenaries to attack the same description of troops in Antiochus's line that were opposed to them; and by their furious onset he diverted the attention of the generals who commanded for Antiochus until he had caused his Thessalian and other cavalry to outflank the Syrian left wing, when the whole of this large body of horse poured, in one resistless attack on the flank and rear of the Syrians. This movement proved decisive, and Antiochus was defeated as completely on his left wing as he had proved victorious on his right.

---

[31] Seleucus Nicator, on the occasion of his treaty with Sandracottus, King of India, received from him, as a gift, five hundred elephants—a fact which explains the frequent appearance of that noble animal on the battle-fields of Syria and Palestine. Subsequent supplies were afterwards obtained from the same source, to keep up this favourite force in the armies of the Syrian kings. The ancient Egyptians do not appear to have known the elephant. We do not remember to have met with a single instance in which this animal is described as being figured on the old monuments of that country.

The phalanxes, thus stripped of both their wings, remained entire on the middle of the plain. Ptolemy Philopator, for the first and last time in his life, proved himself equal to the occasion, and with Arsinoe and his escort passed quickly from the rear to the front. Their sudden appearance infused ardour and courage into the Egyptian line, and dismayed the enemy. The battle on the side of the Syrians was sustained with vigour only by Theodotus, the personal enemy of Ptolemy, who commanded the select bands of Syria. But the heavier phalanx quickly yielded to the pressure of the Egyptians, and their flight compelled Theodotus to quit the field.

Antiochus, meanwhile, had been carried forward with juvenile ardour, as if the engagement had everywhere been successful, because his own wing was victorious. One of his more experienced attendants at length showed him clouds of dust flying in the direction of his camp. He hastened back from the pursuit toward the scene of action, but found the battle irretrievably lost, and retreated to Gaza. He had lost upward of ten thousand slain and four thousand prisoners; while the entire loss of Ptolemy did not exceed two thousand two hundred men. In acknowledgment of his defeat, Antiochus sent heralds from Gaza to Ptolemy to crave leave to bury his slain; and then, without attempting to defend any of his conquests, retired northward to his well-fortified capital on the banks of the Orontes, from whence a truce for a year, and afterward a lasting peace, was negotiated between himself and Ptolemy.

Such was the battle of Raphia—the first that for almost a century had been fought near Judea, and a prelude, as it were, to the many sanguinary conflicts that for nearly three centuries were to convert all Palestine into one vast battle-field. The countries the king of Egypt had lost by treason at once returned to their allegiance; and the Jews, who had remained steadfast in their adherence to Ptolemy, were in so far singled out as special objects of his regard, that he came to Jerusalem in person to offer sacrifices according to Jewish law, and presented gifts at the temple. Unhappily, the beauty of the building, and the peculiar order and solemnity of the worship, excited the curiosity of the king to see the interior; and when he was informed that no mortal except the high-priest, and *he* only once a year, (Lev. chap. xvi.,) entered the inmost sanctuary, the king's curiosity became ungovernable. Philopator's natural disposition was both haughty and tyrannous: his recent unexpected and signal victory had raised his arrogance to the highest extreme; so that when the high-priest, Simon II., who had but lately succeeded to that dignity, remonstrated, and the priests in solemn array and sacerdotal vestments entreated him to desist from a purpose not permissible even in the minister of the temple, he roughly answered, "that though *they* were deprived of that honourable privilege, it could not be withheld from *him*, as *his* authority was not to be controlled by *their* laws." He then pressed forward from the court of the Gentiles, to force his way into the inner sanctuary.

The whole city was in commotion; and while Simon prayed to the Lord to defend the chosen spot which, in the days of yore, he had dignified with a visible sign of his presence, and which still was consecrated to the most solemn rites of his worship, a promiscuous multitude of every age and of either sex filled the air with such loud and lamentable wailing, that it seemed as if not only human voices, but the walls and streets from their foundations, had deprecated the impious purpose of the king. That purpose appeared unalterable. But as he left the inner court, and was about to enter the building itself, he was "shaken like a reed by the wind, and fell speechless to the ground."

The writer who relates this circumstance, (3d book of Maccabees,) considers it as a supernatural dread and horror cast upon the king from above. It has, however, been wisely observed by one of the greatest judges of human nature, that "'Tis conscience that makes cowards of us all;" and what moment, what place more likely to act upon and to alarm the conscience of the parricide, than that sanctuary, untrodden by human foot, into which he was about to force his way, and where unbidden he intruded on the presence of that incomprehensible and awful Being, who dwelt invisible within that mysterious and time-honoured temple. Besides, by a combination, alas! but too frequent! the most beastly profligacy and the most heartless cruelty were in Philopator united with a great degree of superstition; and his own superstitious fears would suffice to prostrate him, body and mind.

Whichever of these reasons we adopt, it is certain that Philopator did not step over the threshold of the temple, which thus vindicated its awful and supreme sanctity. The king was raised from the ground by his body-guards, who carried him, half dead, out of the second court of the temple; and when he recovered he speedily left Jerusalem, full of displeasure against the Jewish people, and determined to let them feel the weight of his anger.

But if he was displeased with them, they were still more displeased with him. For upwards of eighty years no foreign master had issued his mandates in Jerusalem. The Egyptian supremacy under the three first Ptolemies had been so slightly perceptible in Judea, the Jewish people had been so little disturbed in their self-government, both political and religious, that they had gradually lost sight of the fact that they were a tributary people, dependent upon a foreign autocrat. Even the moderate taxation to which they were subjected, and which was farmed by the high-priest, was collected by Jewish tax-gatherers; so that their financial, as well as their judicial administration was apparently free from all foreign control; and as the Egyptians do not appear to have garrisoned Jerusalem, or any other city in Judea, while the authority of the high-priest and of the temple were alone in active operation, the people, or at least the generation then living, who had not on any occasion felt the weight of foreign domination, fancied themselves free.

From this dream of independence they were suddenly and most painfully aroused. The rude hand of a foreign master had pressed the yoke of slavery on the most sensitive spot in their national feeling. The veneration in which their religious system had always been held had now been violated by a proud heathen; the most holy temple had been insulted by an idolater; they had seen,. yet been unable to avert, the calamity. Grief and indignation struggled for mastery in the minds of the multitude: even those who, with the greatest ardour had embraced the lax principles of Epicurus, joined in the outcry raised against Philopator, because they felt and deeply resented the outrage committed on the national feeling of Israel by the Egyptian.

That day the bond of attachment that so long had united the Judeans to the Ptolemean dynasty was forcibly rent asunder. They began to contrast the insult to which their most pure and highly cherished feelings had wantonly been subjected by Philopator, with the high estimation in which the Jews were held in the neighbouring kingdom of Syria, where—especially since the important service they had rendered against the Gauls—the Jews stood foremost in the favour of the king and in the respect of the people. Thenceforth the determination gradually ripened in the minds of the Judeans, to transfer their allegiance from the house of Ptolemy to that of Seleucus Nicator—a de-

15*

termination which, on the first favourable occasion, they carried into effect.[32]

---

[32] Philopator's transactions at Jerusalem are related in Rufinus's Latin edition of Josephus, (contra Apion, lib. ii.,) and also in the 3d book of Maccabees, which latter further contains the only narrative extant of his persecution of the Jews in Egypt. There are in all five books of Maccabees, of which, however, only two possess that species of authority which is derived from their being received into the biblical Apocrypha. The first book of Maccabees is entitled to that full credence which is due to contemporary history confirmed by independent testimony, such as that of the Talmud. This first book of Maccabees is the only one of the Apocryphal writings known by that name that circulated among the people in Judea. It was originally composed in Chaldaic or Aramaic, which was the vernacular tongue of the Judeans, in which it bore the name of *Tsharbit Sar Bne El*, "The sceptre of the prince of the children of God," and is supposed to have been written toward the end of the reign of John Hyrcanus, and after the wars were concluded. From the Chaldaic it was translated into Greek, and subsequently into Latin. Into Hebrew it has been translated within the last few years by *Plessner*. This book is veracious history, narrated with great care and faithfulness; though some few errors in minor particulars, such as the writer could not well be acquainted with, (as, for instance, that Rome was governed by *one* consul annually chosen,) have been discovered by the lynx-eye of criticism. And it is the authority to which Josephus adheres in his history of that period. The second book of Maccabees is abridged from a larger work in five books, written in Greek by a Hellenist, Jason of Cyrene. It is less purely historical than the first, which it sometimes contradicts; the narrative is highly coloured, and embodies many legends and marvels. Still the book is entitled to respect, as it contains accounts of individual suffering and magnanimity confirmed by the *Medrashim* and others, which but for this second book of Maccabees would have been lost. The third book of Maccabees is in point of time the first, and relates the sufferings of the Jews under Philopator. It exists in Greek, and is found in some ancient manuscripts of the so-called Septuagint, particularly in the Alexandrian and Vatican manuscripts. There is also a Syriac version from the Greek, but it has never been inserted in the Vulgate, or in the English Bible, though English translations of it exist. It is apparently written by a Jew of Alexandria, abounds in marvels and absurdities, and is of itself but of little authority; still, in the outlines of the facts it relates, searching criticism has discovered sufficient internal evidence to receive them as substantially true.

Philopator returned to Alexandria, and as he was still under the influence of that terror which had driven him from Jerusalem, he forebore molesting the Judeans. But as he conceived that the Jews of Egypt were more completely in his power, he determined to wreak his vengeance on them. He began by causing a decree to be inscribed on brazen pillars at the palace-gate, that none should enter there who did not sacrifice to the gods he worshipped; which not only effectually excluded all Jews from access to his person, but, as the judges commonly sat in the palace, it also amounted to a sentence of outlawry against them. He next deprived the Jews of Alexandria of the high civil privileges they enjoyed, and which had been bestowed on them by Alexander the Great and by the first Ptolemy; and whereas till then they had ranked among the first or highest class of the inhabitants, Philopator degraded them into the third or lowest rank. Lastly, he ordered them to be formally enrolled, and that at the time of their enrolment the mark of an ivy-leaf (one of the insignia of *his* god Bacchus) should be impressed on them with a hot iron; if any refused this mark, they were to be made slaves; and whoever opposed the decree was to be put to death.

Having thus, as he imagined, disgusted them with the adherence to their ancient faith, he tempted them to apostasy by offering to restore to their former rank of first-class citizens such Jews as would worship his gods. But, notwithstanding these disgraceful and cruel penalties, scarcely three hundred, out of the many thousands of Jewish citizens in Alexandria, accepted his offer; and those who

---

The fourth book relates the history of the Asmoneans and of Herod; and though of doubtful authority, frequently serves to correct or complete the narrative of Josephus. Of the fifth book of Maccabees not much is known; it exists in Greek, in some few manuscripts of the Septuagint, and is a metaphysical treatise on reason, faith, and immortality.

were so mean as to embrace the *royal clemency* and barter their religion for worldly advantage, met with such ineffable disdain, and were so pointedly shunned and excluded from the society of their old associates, that the king, when acquainted with this contempt for his authority, was provoked almost to madness. He declared the conduct of the Jews to be rebellion and opposition to his royal dignity, and vowed he would extirpate the whole nation.

From all parts of Egypt, the Jews, as the worst of criminals, were dragged to Alexandria in chains. When they had been brought together to the number of many thousands, they were shut up in the Hippodrome, which was a very large enclosure outside of the city, built for the purpose of horse-racing and other public amusements. Here he intended to expose them as a spectacle to be destroyed by elephants. At the appointed time the people assembled in crowds. The writings of Manetho began to bear fruit. The Egyptians were delighted that the descendants of the cruel *Hyksos* should come to a cruel end; that the offsprings of the impious and impure lepers who had murdered, roasted, and actually made a meal of their divine animals, should at length meet with just retribution from the fury of animals inflamed with wine and frankincense. The elephants were on the spot, bellowing and roaring with rage; but the effects of a drunken bout the preceding night prevented the attendance of the king, and caused the postponement of the sports.

The next day a similar *disappointment* proceeded from the same *right royal* cause. The third day the king managed to be present, and the elephants were brought out. But though Philopator had contrived to overcome the effects of his repeated drunkenness, the nobler animals,— the elephants,—to whose nature intoxication was foreign, were affected by the stimulants that had been administered to them, in a manner the king had not foreseen. Instead of spending their fury on the unhappy Jews, the elephants first turned on their own keepers, whom they destroyed, and then attacked the Egyptian spectators, of whom they killed great numbers.

King Ptolemy, the parricide, was not less coward than ruffian, and his immediate attendants were like him. He and they, terrified by the unexpected catastrophe, fancied they saw angels descending of frightful form, goading on the elephants in their havoc among the spectators. The king, alarmed for his own safety, acknowledged the interposition of the divine power in behalf of the Jews, and hastened to set them at liberty: at the same time, rescinding all his odious decrees, he at once restored to them the rights of which he had so unjustly deprived them. In the true spirit of capricious despotism, Ptolemy sought to make atonement for his cruelty to the Jews, by the more cruel permission of retaliating it on their apostate brethren. And as the tardy reflection arose in his mind, that those who had so signally evinced their fidelity to their God, were not likely to prove unfaithful to their king, he tried to regain their good-will by many marks of his munificence and confidence. (3d Macc., iii. 4., 5.)

Such is the account of this persecution, as given in the 3d book of Maccabees. It is necessary to state that Josephus does not relate any portion of these transactions in Egypt; and his silence is a circumstance to which due weight should be given. But this objection has been met by the remark, that the history of this period (the reign of Philopator) is exceedingly brief in Josephus: while on the other hand it has been said, that though the third of Maccabees is so little authentic as to be excluded even from the Apocrypha, yet there is so much appearance of probability in the leading features, and so many small agreements with the accounts which history has preserved of the manners, and ideas, and circumstances of the times, as well as with the character of the king, as to outweigh the silence of Josephus.

Certain it is, that shortly after the catastrophe in the Hippodrome, as above related, a fierce rebellion against Philopator broke out among the Egyptians, which swelled into a civil war of some duration, not distinguished by any recorded exploits either of skill or valour, but abominably disgraced by the enormities perpetrated alike by the contending parties. Forty thousand of the Jewish inhabitants perished in this contest, which deluged Egypt with blood, and in which Ptolemy eventually prevailed through the relative superiority of his generals, and the real abilities of his unprincipled minister, Sosibius.

After a reign of seventeen years, Philopator died a victim to extreme debauchery at the early age of thirty-seven years. His son and successor, Ptolemy Epiphanes, was only five years old when he ascended the throne—the same year that Antiochus returned to Syria, after a sojourn of ten years in Upper Asia, where he had compelled Arsaces III. of Parthia, as well as Eutydemus, the third Greek king of Bactria, to sue for peace and to acknowledge the supremacy of the Seleucidæ. On the banks of the Indus he renewed the ancient alliance of his house with the kings of India, and returned to the West with a supply of one hundred and fifty elephants. Shortly afterward he rescued the commercial city of Gerra, on the Persian Gulf, from the grasp of Arab robbers; and, having re-established the independence and freedom of that city, he was, in return for these favours, rewarded by the Gerræans with a profusion of spices and perfumes, as well as with a large amount in gold and silver. With these vast treasures and mighty forces, Antiochus THE GREAT,—as he was now universally called—the fugitive of Raphia, returned to find his victorious rival dead, and the sceptre of Egypt in the feeble grasp of an infant. (204 B. C. E.)

During his absence in the far East, the Western world had been agitated by a fierce conflict between the two mighty commonwealths of Rome and Carthage. The second Punic war, which lasted seventeen years, and brought Rome to the very verge of ruin, showed the world how firmly based was the power, how inexhaustible the resources, of that all-conquering and rapacious republic. In vain Hannibal, the Carthaginian general, evinced military talents second only to those of Alexander the Great; in vain he defeated and destroyed the Roman armies again and again. After every defeat Rome rose with increased vigour, like a giant refreshed. At the battle of Cannæ, a Roman army of eighty thousand foot, with a proportionate number of horse, was so utterly and hopelessly routed that only seventy horsemen escaped with the consul Varro from the field. Battles less destructive had overturned many a powerful kingdom; but this fatal conflict shook not the stability of the Roman Commonwealth. When Hannibal marched suddenly to surprise Rome, he found three armies in order of battle prepared to receive him. Having encamped on the banks of the river Anio, scarcely four miles from the capitol of Rome, he learned that the ground occupied by his army had brought its full value at a public auction, and that a body of troops had left Rome through an opposite gate to reinforce the legions in Spain.

Such indomitable perseverance was certain of eventual success. And though Hannibal's admirable abilities gave the Romans no opportunities of combatting him with advantage, he could not wear out the spirit or exhaust the resources that enabled Rome to maintain armies in Spain, Sicily, Sardinia, and the country beyond the Adriatic Sea, in addition to the forces that defended the Italian peninsula. He maintained his ground in Italy fourteen years; but in the very year that Philopator died, and Antiochus returned from the East, a formidable Roman army, under Publius Scipio, who had just achieved the ruin of the Carthaginian power in Spain, landed on the north coast of Africa; and the rapid progress he made compelled the senate of Carthage to recall Hannibal from the scene of his triumphs in Italy, to the defence of his native city. His defeat at Zama laid Carthage prostrate at the feet of Rome; and the terms of peace granted by Scipio reduced Carthage to a state of dependence, that forever destroyed the possibility of her recovering her former weight in the balance of power, and left Rome supreme arbitress of the West, as far as at that time it was known.

Had the successors of Alexander the Great been gifted with common prudence, they must have foreseen that the insatiable lust for conquest, which had already extended the sway of Rome over so great a part of the West, would next turn itself to the East, especially as Philip, King of Macedon, the ally of Carthage, had already incurred the ill-will of Rome; and that the only means of safety against the encroachments of the all-subduing republic, was the intimate union of all the kings that had succeeded to portions of Alexander's empire. But these kings were incapable of appreciating the magnitude of the danger which threatened them. Ptolemy the Fifth of Egypt was an infant. Antiochus of Syria, intoxicated by the uninterrupted success that had gained for him the surname of " The Great," was burning with the desire, by some decisive advantage over Egypt, to blot out the disgrace of his defeat at Raphia, the only miscarriage in his splendid career. Philip of Macedon, who had, with credit to himself, resisted the Romans, and then withdrawn from his alliance with Carthage before the catastrophe of Zama, harboured projects of aggrandizement in the East. Both these kings were in the vigour of life; their natural ambition was heightened by prosperity. Antiochus was at the head of an army supposed the greatest in the world; and Philip possessed a most powerful fleet. It consisted of about two hundred sail, and contained vessels of such magnitude, that the trireme galleys, considered the most efficient in ancient naval battles, were scarcely thought worthy to fight in his line. With that frivolous vanity and unreasoning pride peculiar to Greeks, both kings despised the Romans as barbarians incapable of making head against Grecian skill, bravery, and discipline.[33]

Between monarchs thus prepared for action, and devoid of all scruples to restrain their rapacity, an alliance was formed for invading, by sea and land, the dominions of young Ptolemy, (203 B. C. E.,) and for guaranteeing to each other their respective conquests. (Polybius, lib. xv. cap. 20.) Accordingly, without the slightest pretence, and unsupported by any reason, Philip attacked and seized on the valuable possessions long held by the Ptolemies on the coasts of Thrace, Caria, and Asia Minor; while Antiochus entered, and made himself master of, Cœle-Syria and Palestine.

The insult which Philopator had offered to the feelings of the Judeans was now to be resented; the outrage he had committed against the sanctity of the temple was now to be expiated. Antiochus was everywhere throughout Judea received as a friend, and the wants of his army were abundantly supplied. He then marched to Asia Minor to restore the supremacy of his house over the

---

[33] At this time Philip had personally twice encountered the Romans in battle. On the first occasion, he attacked them between Corinth and Sicyon, defeated them, and drove them disgracefully to their ships. (Tit. Liv. lib. xxvii. cap. 31.) On the second occasion, he was surprised by them during his attack on Elis; but though he was outnumbered and obliged to retreat, no advantage of moment was gained over him, and he encamped only five miles from the former battle-field, without being disturbed by the Romans. Ibid.

Grecian cities, which had profited by the civil war between his father Callinicus and his uncle Hierax, to proclaim themselves independent.

But the regents who governed Egypt during the nonage of Ptolemy, prepared to take advantage of Antiochus's absence. They had beheld with regret the dismemberment of so important a portion of their master's dominions. Hopeless of recovering the lost provinces by cowardly Egyptians and degenerate Alexandrian Greeks, they had recourse to Scopas, formerly prætor or elective chief of the Etolians, who, restless and discontented at home, had come to Egypt in quest of riches and preferment. He was now despatched to Greece loaded with money, and with assurances of tempting pay to as many of his countrymen as he could engage to follow his standard. He succeeded in enlisting six thousand Etolians, the most warlike and ferocious of Greek mercenaries. At their head, and reinforced by numbers of other military adventurers, he returned to Egypt; and, without awaiting the usual season for taking the field, he immediately, and in the midst of winter, led his army into Cœle-Syria and Judea. The feeble garrisons left in those countries by Antiochus, were unable to resist the invaders. A great part of the coast, as well as the inland cities, submitted to Scopas, who did not fail to let the Jews feel that he was fully conscious of the leaning they had manifested toward the King of Syria. In those days of relentless cruelty and rapacity, the Etolians ranked high among the fiercest and most rapacious; the wealth of Judea, a country so long at peace, tempted their cupidity; and wherever they came, their devastations caused the Jews to experience all the severity with which war could be carried on.

Apprized of their proceedings, and alarmed by their unresisted progress, Antiochus hastened from Asia Minor into Palestine to encounter the Etolians, now reinforced by numerous bands of Egyptians. He attacked and defeated them at the foot of Mount Panias, and, after wresting from them most of their strongholds, he at length shut up Scopas, with ten thousand of his men, in Sidon. The defence of this city was obstinate, and Scopas did not surrender until compelled by famine. The Etolians and Egyptians only bargained for their lives, and were permitted to return, unarmed and half naked, to Egypt. (Polyb. lib. xv. cap. 39.)

The Judeans had been sufficiently averse to their connection with Egypt, ever since Philopator's attempt on the temple; the rapacity of Scopas and his Etolians, destroyed what little lingering hesitation might still have existed in the minds of the Jewish people and their chiefs. During the war they had greatly served the cause of Antiochus; and when the battle of Mount Panias had restored to him the mastery of Palestine, the Jews received him at Jerusalem with the most lively demonstrations of joy, (198 B. C. E.,) and expressed their desire of becoming united to the great mass of their people in Mesopotamia and Babylonia, who had so long been governed by the house of Seleucus Nicator. The king of Syria readily granted them important favours, that not only rewarded their services, but confirmed their attachment to his person and government. Aware that there were no points on which they were more anxious than in what concerned their city and temple, he declared his intention to restore the city to its ancient splendour and dignity, and thoroughly to repair the temple at his own cost. And to heighten the contrast between the persecuting Philopator and himself, Antiochus issued an edict guaranteeing the inviolability of the sacred place, by prohibiting all strangers from entering the temple at Jerusalem; at the same time, by liberal grants, he made ample provision for the due and orderly performance of the sacred services.

The effect of all these friendly measures, was to render the warm-hearted and single-minded Jews quite enthusiastic in their attachment to Antiochus, who, like a wise statesman, failed not to avail himself of their devotion to his government. Finding that Judea had a redundant and enterprising population, he induced the people, on very advantageous terms, to form colonies in such parts of his dominions as he considered of most doubtful allegiance—as Lydia, Phrygia, and other provinces—unsafe, because surrounded by the territories of his enemies. In all such places Antiochus relied on the firmness and fidelity of the Jews, and continually reinforced their colonies with new settlers, both from Judea and Mesopotamia; a circumstance that accounts for the great numbers of Jews that subsequently were found throughout Asia Minor. (Joseph. Antiq. lib. xii. cap. 3.)

Thenceforth the Judeans looked upon their political connection with Egypt as entirely dissolved; and such, in fact, proved to be the case. But at the very time that Antiochus professed to cherish them as the most firmly attached of his tributaries, he was negotiating with Egypt a treaty of peace, and also of marriage between his beautiful daughter Cleopatra and the young king of Egypt, Ptolemy V. Epiphanes, then in his eleventh year. The principal stipulation of this treaty was that, when Ptolemy should be of an age to consummate the nuptials, Cleopatra should bring him, for her dower, the restored allegiance of Cœle-Syria, Phœnicia, and Palestine.

It is probable that the Judeans, who so readily forwarded his plans of colonization, and quitted their country by thousands, were totally unacquainted with this double-dealing of Antiochus. And it appears equally probable, that as the motive which induced Antiochus to conciliate the Egyptians—whose power he had greatly underrated—was tardy alarm at the progress of Rome, so his secret purpose was to keep possession of his recent acqusitions, and to amuse the king of Egypt with promises and stipulations which he never intended to carry out. The princess Cleopatra was accordingly betrothed to Ptolemy; and six years after Antiochus had obtained possession of Jerusalem, when the young king had attained his eighteenth year, the marriage actually took place. (192 B. C. E.)

And here we meet with a singular discrepancy in history. Appian and Jerome say that Antiochus did surrender the three Syrian provinces, as stipulated; and Josephus seems to concur with them, intimating that the revenues were paid to the king of Egypt, (Antiq. lib. xii. cap. 4.) The Talmud has no account whatever of this transaction, which, perhaps, as we said before, never came to the knowledge of the Jews. But Polybius denies the surrender, (lib. xxviii. cap. 1 and 17;) and at a subsequent period Antiochus Epiphanes, the brother of Queen Cleopatra, altogether repudiated the existence of any treaty that restored to Egypt the three provinces conquered by his father; and these denials are confirmed by the fact, that these countries still remained in the possession of the sons and successors of Antiochus.

It is possible that, as on a former intermarriage between the houses of Ptolemy and Seleucus, the king of Egypt assigned half the revenues of these very provinces as a dower to his son-in-law, Antiochus Theos, while he himself retained the sovereignty, so in this second instance of intermarriage, the king of Syria retained the sovereignty, while he may have assigned the revenues as a dower to his son-in-law. This would explain Josephus's statement. But even this appears questionable, especially when we consider the extreme and desperate measures to which want of money reduced Antiochus the Great and his successors, and of which we shall presently have to speak.

Some weight has been attached to a circumstance related by Josephus, (Antiq. cap. 4,) that on the birth of a son and heir to Ptolemy and Cleopatra, (187 B. C. E.,) many principal men in Palestine and the neighbouring districts hastened to Alexandria with presents and congratulations. Among these visitants young Hyrcanus the Jew particularly distinguished himself, and gained as high favour with the then king and queen of Egypt, as his father Joseph had gained with Euergetes and Queen Berenicé thirty-four years before. But this circumstance is not by any means conclusive, as to any dominion exercised by the king of Egypt in the Syrian provinces; indeed, it does not even furnish presumptive evidence of such domination. It is natural that a dynasty which had so long and so mildly governed a country, as the Ptolemies had done in Palestine and the adjacent countries, should possess many friends and adherents, especially among families long and high in office in those countries; and that those friends and adherents—even after their country had passed under the sway of another dynasty—would be glad to avail themselves of the first opportunity that offered, when, without giving offence to the powers that be, they could present their tribute of respect and affection to the powers that had been. Such an event was the birth of a grandson to their present, of a son to their former, sovereign; and they profited by it, like well-bred and skilful courtiers.

Upon a full consideration of all these circumstances, we do not hesitate to declare, that with the battle of Mount Panias the political supremacy of the Egyptians in Judea terminated; and that after an uninterrupted connection of upwards of a century from the battle of Ipsos, the Judeans transferred their allegiance from the descendants of Ptolemy Soter to those of Seleucus Nicator. To this they were chiefly urged by the offence which Philopator attempted to commit against the temple. But for this,

Antiochus could never have gained the support of the Judeans, or retained possession of their land. But for this, the history of the Jews would have been quite different from what it is. The ungovernable curiosity and rudeness of Philopator thus produced consequences that in a great degree influenced the character, and, with it, the fortunes of the Jews; and, as such, the brief sojourn of the Egyptian parricide in Jerusalem is an event in the history of the Jews.

CHAPTER IV.

Antiochus III.—War with Rome—Hannibal—Antiochus defeated—His death—Seleucus Philopator—Onias III., the high-priest—Heliodorus attempts to plunder the temple—His miscarriage—Antiochus IV. Epiphanes—His intervention in Judean affairs—Conservatives and Destructives—Jason buys the office of high-priest—Attempted fusion of Judaism and Heathenism—Judeo-Grecian literature—Menelaus—War between Antiochus and the Egyptians—Troubles in Judea—Antiochus plunders the temple—Popilius Lœnas—Massacre at Jerusalem—The Jewish religion proscribed—The Haphtora—First religious persecution—Insurrection—Matathias the Asmonean declares self-defence lawful on the Sabbath—Holland, the United States, and Judea—Judah the Maccabee—His victories—The Syrians expelled—Public worship restored in the temple of Jerusalem. (From 198 to 166, B. C. E.)

THE resentment that caused the Judeans to withdraw their allegiance from the kings of Egypt, and to transfer it to the kings of Syria—however natural and just at the time it was most wantonly provoked—was one that should have died with its author, the tyrant and parricide, Philopator, especially as even he did not presume to repeat the outrage. To visit the misdeed of the father on the feeble head of his infant son, would be unjust in any case: in the instance of which we are speaking it was also unwise; and dearly had the Judeans to pay for having attached themselves to the falling fortunes of Antiochus the Great.

The partner in his unprincipled aggressions on the infant king of Egypt, Philip of Macedon, had not been as fortunate as Antiochus himself. The political foresight of Ptolemy II. Philadelphus, had early discerned and justly appreciated the rising power of Rome: he alone, of all the successors of Alexander, had entered into early relations of amity with that all-conquering republic; and now that their victory over the Carthaginians had made the Romans masters of the West, they were but too glad to avail themselves of any opportunity to interfere in the affairs of the East. They therefore affected to treat the infant king of Egypt with the regard due to a dear hereditary friend. In consideration of his youth, and of the merit of his great ancestor Philadelphus, they did not designate him merely by the cold name of ally, but extended to him the more affectionate and—as the senate declared—more honourable appellation of their pupil. (Justin. lib. xxx. cap. 3.) But notwithstanding this distinguished title, and the strong remonstrances of his tutors or protectors, Ptolemy V. Epiphanes had been stripped by Philip of Macedon of his possessions in Thrace and Caria; while Antiochus had dismembered Egypt of the valuable provinces of Cœle-Syria, Phœnicia, and Palestine.

The Romans had other causes of complaint against one, at least, of the two confederate kings. At the battle of Zama, four thousand of Philip's troops had been made prisoners fighting in the ranks of the defeated Carthaginians; although Philip, in his treaty of peace with the Romans three years before, had renounced his alliance with Carthage, and engaged to afford that commonwealth no aid or succour of any kind. He had also carried on hostilities against the Rhodians and the king of Pergamos, allies of Rome; and lastly, he had besieged and taken the thriving commercial city of Abydus—on the Asiatic shore of the narrow strait now called the Dardanelles—and had driven the inhabitants to destruction, notwithstanding the active intercession in their favour of a Roman ambassador. (Polyb. lib. xvi. cap. 32.) No sooner, therefore, had their victory at Zama enabled the Romans to conclude a treaty of peace with Carthage, on such terms as they themselves chose to dictate, than they prepared to turn their arms against Philip; and a few months after the ending of the war with Carthage, that against Macedon began, (200 B. C. E.) After the vicissitudes of three campaigns, which on the whole were rather in his favour than otherwise, Philip was finally defeated by the Romans in the fourth year of the war, at the decisive battle of Kynoscephaloe. And deeming it wisest and safest to submit while he had yet the means of resistance, Philip sued for, and obtained, peace on terms which reduced Macedon from a first to a second-rate power, and left the Romans supreme in Greece.

During this war, Philip had in vain solicited and expected assistance from his ally Antiochus; and every consideration of wise policy ought to have induced the king of Syria to strain every nerve in supporting an ally, like himself a Greek and successor of Alexander the Great, and who, moreover, was the best shield against the advancing sword of the Romans. But blinded by that grasping and narrow-minded selfishness which had induced him to court the alliance of Philip at the expense of Ptolemy, Antiochus now left Philip to his fate, fully determined to profit by that fate, whichever way it turned.

Should the Romans be unsuccessful, their allies of Rhodes and Pergamos would no longer have courage to oppose his usurpations in Asia Minor: should Philip's power, on the contrary, be greatly reduced by the war, the representative of Seleucus Nicator might revive, with good success, his claims on Macedon. And in order to be free of apprehension from Egypt while he pursued his designs in the West, King Antiochus made peace with Ptolemy, as we have already stated, giving his beautiful daughter Cleopatra as the bond of amity between them, and making fair promises of restitution, which probably he never meant to perform. But his selfish and treacherous policy met with the punishment it deserved; and when Philip had succumbed, Antiochus was compelled to confront the onward progress of Rome.

The great Hannibal, expelled from Carthage by the rancour of domestic enemies and the influence of Rome, had sought refuge with the king of Syria, who entertained him honourably; and as the war against Rome was become inevitable, this great warrior proposed a plan lofty and extensive like his own genius, and which, while it attacked or threatened the possessions of Rome in Spain, in Africa, in Illyria, and Sardinia, would also have struck at the root of her power by invading Italy with a small but chosen army, of which Hannibal offered to take the command.

But the mind of Antiochus was incapable of grasping or of carrying out designs so vast and daring. Prosperity, luxury, and the unrestrained indulgence of indolent and voluptuous habits, had destroyed the mental powers of Antiochus. The mistrust so natural to a despotic ruler, and which leads him to suspect his best and most faithful friends, had been skillfully aroused by Roman intrigues. Suborned calumniators, taking advantage of frequent interviews between Hannibal and Villius, one of the Roman ambassadors on a special mission at the court of Antiochus, and who is supposed to have solicited these conferences with the intent of their exciting the king's suspicion, accused the great Carthaginian of conspiring with Rome. It was long before the illustrious exile became acquainted with the cause that had estranged the king from him. But when, at length, he heard that he was accused of partiality to Rome, he at once and forever repelled the accusation by the following recital to Antiochus, equally simple and impressive:—

"My father Hamilcar, at his departure from Carthage to Spain, performed a sacrifice to Jupiter. I was present at the ceremony, though only a child, in my ninth year. Hamilcar asked me whether I would accompany him to the Spanish war. I assented with alacrity. He promised to take me, provided, on the present occasion, I showed my ready compliance with his will. Then, desiring all present to withdraw, he led me to the altar on which he had just sacrificed, and bidding me approach and touch it with my hand, commanded me to swear eternal enmity to the Romans. I swore the solemn oath, and my subsequent life for thirty-six years has been one unvaried act of performance. In the war with Rome, you may therefore safely trust Hannibal. But should you ever think of peace with that republic, it will be time to have recourse to other advisers." (Polyb. lib. iii. cap. 11, Cornelius Nepos, in Hannibal, and Tit. Liv. lxxv. cap. 19.)

But though Hannibal regained the king's confidence, his advice was not adopted; and Antiochus, defeated at Thermopylæ, was disgracefully driven out of Europe. On his return to Ephesus, Hannibal, the only one of his counsellors who had either sagacity to foresee coming events, or boldness to announce them, assured the trembling monarch that soon he would be called to fight the Romans *in* Asia and *for* Asia. The firm remonstrances of the Carthaginian at length roused the king to a full sense of his danger, and Antiochus prepared to defend himself by all the means yet at his command. But the *prestige* of his success and power was gone. His own daughter Cleopatra—now the wife of Ptolemy, King of Egypt, and entering fully into the views of her husband—joined in an embassy to Rome, in which the rulers of Egypt promised the most zealous co-operation, provided the Romans would carry their arms into Syria.

The ablest of the Roman generals, Scipio, surnamed *Africanus*, from his victory at Zama, accompanied his brother, the ostensible chief of the Roman army, and who, from his success against Antiochus, gained the surname of *Asiaticus*. Before their star, that of Hannibal again grew pale. Defeated by sea, Antiochus saw that he was no longer able to dispute the passage of the Romans into

Asia; and his fears almost deprived him of understanding. Every measure he took in his trepidation facilitated the advance of his irresistible enemies, and hastened the impending crisis. He had, in the early period of the war, captured the son of *Africanus*, who was still a prisoner, but treated by the king with every indulgence that could soothe his confinement. Of this circumstance Antiochus determined to avail himself, in order to obtain peace. He therefore sent ambassadors to the consul, offering not only to relinquish all that he yet possessed in Thrace and Lydia, but also to refund one-half of the expense which the Romans had incurred in prosecuting the war. He was answered, that the freedom of the Greek cities in Asia, which the Romans had proclaimed, required that he should relinquish all the territory he possessed north and west of Mount Taurus; and that, as the king's ambition only was to blame, not one-half, but the whole expense of the war, must be defrayed by him.

To obtain some abatement of these exorbitant demands, the king's ambassador had recourse privately to Africanus, endeavouring to tempt him with bribes, and giving him assurance of the speedy liberation of his son, a youth of great promise, but whose fame disappears between the splendour of his father, Africanus, and of his adopted son, Emilianus, the conqueror of Carthage. To the many promises and offers made to him by the king, the Roman father replied, "I am less surprised that you should not know the Romans, than that you should be ignorant of the condition of your own master. After relinquishing the defence of the Hellespont, and allowing the Romans to pass quietly into Asia, Antiochus may be compared to a horse that has not only admitted the rein, but has patiently received a rider. I shall accept my son at his hands as the highest personal favour, and shall be ready to repay him by every personal service in my power. But as to public affairs, I can do nothing for his interest, except by giving him this one advice: That he accept any terms of peace, however unreasonable they may appear to him." (Polyb. lib. xxi. cap. 11, 12.)

It was the singular fortune of Antiochus, that he had the advice of the two greatest men of his age—Hannibal and Scipio Africanus; the one counselled him how to make war, the other how to make peace. In each case their advice was the best that under the circumstances could be given. But the king could not and did not profit by either. The decisive battle of Magnesia, however,—in which he was routed with the loss of fifty thousand men, while the victors boasted a loss of less than four hundred—compelled him to beg, rather than to negotiate, a peace. The friendship of Africanus obtained for him terms which, with respect to territorial cessions, did not materially differ from those offered to him before the battle; but which, in every other respect, were so greatly aggravated by the senate, as to give the *coup de grace* to the independence of Syria as a first-rate power. Antiochus was compelled to pay fifteen thousand Eubœic talents[34] for the expenses of war; three thousand almost immediately, and the remainder in twelve equal annual payments, together with five hundred and forty thousand measures of wheat every year. He was required to surrender his elephants and all his ships of war, except ten only, which were not to sail beyond a certain limit. He was further to pay large sums to the king of Pergamos and to the Rhodians, the allies of Rome; and lastly, the Romans required that Hannibal the Carthaginian, and some other political refugees, should be surrendered to them.

---

[34] Ninety millions of dollars. In computing the tribute, the Eubœan talent was named as that of the greatest weight; but the senate further added, that the silver should be of the Attic standard, because this was the finest.

The whole of these conditions were accepted, and faithfully executed, in as far as they depended on the king of Syria; but the surrender of Hannibal was not in his power. Even before the final decision at Magnesia, the great Carthaginian foresaw the sad result; while his knowledge of the selfish character of Antiochus, placed it beyond a doubt that the king would not be restrained by any considerations of honour and magnanimity, from sacrificing his friend and guest as a scapegoat to his enemies. Hannibal therefore quitted the court of Antiochus, and successively sought refuge in Crete, in Armenia, and in Bithynia. Wherever he went, the relentless hatred of Rome pursued him; and finding that Prusias, King of Bithynia, was about to betray him to the Romans, and that any attempt at further escape was hopeless, Hannibal was driven to commit suicide by poison—a victim to the rancour, not unmixed with fear, of the mighty commonwealth which, in the midst of its triumphs, did not think itself safe while Hannibal lived.

Had the Romans been sincere in their professions of attachment to Ptolemy Epiphanes, they would have compelled Antiochus to restore to Egypt the three Syrian provinces of which, by force, and without a semblance of right, he had deprived that kingdom. But this it no longer suited the far-sighted policy of Rome to do. The power of Syria was broken; that of Egypt was, as yet, comparatively intact. Two out of the three provinces in question, Cœlo-Syria and Phœnicia, were especially valuable, from the naval supplies, the many harbours, and the experienced mariners with which they abounded. All these elements of a maritime force Rome preferred seeing in the possession of Syria,—bound by treaty not to fit out a larger fleet than ten ships—rather than to have them transferred to Egypt, which, by means of these very provinces, had raised itself to the rank of a first-rate naval power. The Senate, also, and most astutely, judged, that so long as Syria possessed these ancient appendages of the Egyptian monarchy, no cordial union of the two kingdoms, and consequently no serious attempt against Roman supremacy, was to be apprehended. The Romans, therefore, left Antiochus in undisturbed possession of all that he held east of Mount Taurus; and contented themselves with taking twelve hostages for the due observance of the treaty, among whom the king's younger son, Antiochus, was one.

Ruined, disgraced, stripped of every claim to his surname of "the Great," the King of Syria returned from his war against the Romans. Not only his fortunes, but his very character, were altered: in the beginning of life, active, temperate, and dignified; in his declining years, indolent, dissolute, and contemptible. Even at the height of his prosperity, he had not been able to obtain from the Parthians and Bactrians more than a nominal recognition of his supremacy. He had now lost all Asia Minor; and the western possessions of Seleucus Nicator had either been declared independent under the protection of Rome, or had been parcelled out among the inveterate enemies of the Syrian monarch, the Rhodians, and the king of Pergamos. But it was not only the present and immediate loss; there was, moreover, the heavy tribute, that for years to come would cripple the resources of the state. To provide for this last and pressing want, King Antiochus devised a scheme that cost him his life, and proved fatal to two of his successors: and this was to plunder the rich temples throughout his dominions.

These temples possessed not only vast treasures of their own, but were also places of deposit for money and merchandise belonging to private individuals, to whom the sacred character of these depositories afforded greater protection and assurance of safety, than their own dwellings or care.

The beginning was to be made with one of the richest—that at Elymais, at the meeting of the caravan roads connecting Media with Persia and Susianah, and which had been adorned by Alexander the Great. Antiochus made his assault in the night: the guards of the temple defended their treasures and idols, and were assisted by the hardy mountaineers, ever ready and armed, in their neighbourhood. A tumultuary combat ensued, in which Antiochus fell, fighting at once against the religion, the commerce, and the arts, of his country. (187 B. C. E.) On the news of his death, his elder son, Seleucus, immediately ascended the throne; and though he did not at once continue the plundering forays of his father, necessity and the comparatively defenceless condition of some of these temples, eventually tempted him to follow in his father's footsteps.

Assuming the surname of Philopator, Seleucus, during the first ten years of his reign, abstained from any attempts on temple property, while at the same time he continued punctual in discharging the annual contribution due to Rome; and he cautiously avoided giving any offence to that state, by confining his arms and exactions to his own side of Mount Taurus.

But intestine dissensions at Jerusalem, became the cause of directing the attention of Seleucus to the riches deposited in the temple of that city. Simon II., who was high-priest at the time Ptolemy IV. Philopator attempted to force his way into the temple, died 195 B. C. E., after an administration of twenty-two years. He was succeeded by his son, Onias III., a man of great piety, of a mild and amiable disposition, and well worthy of better times than those in which he lived, of a better end than it was his lot to experience.

During the first years of his administration, and when his excellent intentions received full effect from Antiochus, then newly master of Palestine, and after his death from his son and successor, "the holy city was inhabited in all peace, and the laws were kept very well." The Judeans were held in high estimation by the sovereigns of the neighbouring countries, who courted their friendship and made magnificent offerings to the temple. Seleucus Philopator was likewise favourably disposed toward the Jews; and notwithstanding his embarrassments, he had given orders that the public worship should be defrayed out of his own treasury. But toward the end of the tenth year of his reign, a violent quarrel broke out between Onias the high-priest and one Simon, who had been appointed governor of the temple at Jerusalem. The latter, in order to injure his antagonist, and to excite against him popular indignation, informed the king that the temple of which he was the governor was very rich—more than abundantly so, indeed, to bear the entire charge of the public worship, including all sacrifices and oblations.

This information reached the king at a time when he was greatly straitened for money to pay the tribute to the Romans; and, as if the surname of Philopator was doomed to come in hostile contact with the temple of Zion, the Syrian resolved to go a step farther than his Egyptian namesake had intended, and not only to penetrate into the temple, but also to plunder it of its great wealth. For this purpose he despatched his treasurer, Heliodorus, to Jerusalem, with orders to seize the reported treasure and to bring it to Antioch. Heliodorus concealed the object of his journey till he reached Jerusalem, when he communicated the king's orders to the high-priest Onias, and demanded the quiet surrender of the money, In reply, Onias informed him, that though there was a considerable treasure in the temple, it by no means reached the large amount reported; that great part of it consisted of holy gifts and offerings consecrated to God, the appropriation of which could not be disturbed without sacrilege;

the rest had been placed there, by way of security, for widows and orphans, who claimed it as their property—and that a considerable sum had been deposited there by Hyrcanus, (the son of that Joseph who obtained the farming of the revenues from Ptolemy Euergetes,) a man high in credit and favour with the king. He added, that being, by virtue of his office, the guardian of this wealth, he could not consent to its being taken from the right owners, and thereby disgrace his high office and profane that holy place, which was held in reverence by all the world.

Heliodorus, however, who was attended by a numerous armed escort, was not to be deterred from his purpose by any remonstrance of the high-priest. Indeed, the king's peremptory orders, and the pressing want of money which had extorted those orders, and with which no one could be better acquainted than the king's treasurer, left that officer no choice. Attended by his guards, Heliodorus marched to the temple; and, as the priests attempted to oppose his progress, he ordered the outer gates to be demolished. The whole city was in the utmost agonies of apprehension, and shrieks of woe were heard in all directions. But when the treasurer, at the head of his escort, was about to enter the hall of the temple, he was struck with a panic terror, and fell to the ground speechless, as Ptolemy Philopator had done; and, like him, had to be carried away insensible by his attendants. By the prayers of Onias, and the kind offices of the priests, he gradually recovered, and immediately quitted Jerusalem. The legend, preserved in the Second Book of Maccabees, (ch. iii.) relates that, as Heliodorus attempted to enter the temple, he was encountered by a warrior on horseback, accoutred in golden-armour, grand and terrible to behold. He rode against the audacious Syrian, and threw him down; when two youths, of superhuman beauty, magnificently arrayed, appeared and struck him with rods, so that he fainted;

that Heliodorus, lifeless, had to be carried away on a litter to his apartments; but that Onias, the high-priest, fearful that the king might suspect or accuse the Jews of having committed a criminal outrage on the person of his officer, offered an expiatory sacrifice, by which means, and by his prayers, he restored Heliodorus to life.

Certain it is, that the Syrian intruder left the temple and its treasures intact, and returned empty-handed to Antioch, where he assured the king that he would do well to send on that terrible errand any one who had offended him beyond the hope of pardon, and whom, therefore, he wished most signally to punish, as the chastisement inflicted rendered that employment only fit for the worst of villains. In the course of the same year, however, Heliodorus entitled himself to that infamous designation. It had, on the death of Antiochus the Great, been agreed between the Roman senate and Seleucus, that, after a certain time, he was to send his own son Demetrius as a hostage to Rome, in lieu of his brother Antiochus, who was then to return back to Syria. Shortly after the attempt on the temple, the time for this exchange arrived, and Demetrius left for Rome. Thus the two persons nearest in succession to the throne of Syria were both absent and out of the country. And of this interval between the departure of the king's son and the arrival of the king's brother, Heliodorus took advantage, and poisoned his unsuspecting master, in hopes of usurping the sovereignty. (175 B. C. E.)

Antiochus was visiting Athens on his way home when he heard of this. He immediately applied to the old enemy of his father, Eumenes, King of Pergamos—to whom the Romans had assigned the greater part of the territories in Asia Minor, which they had compelled Antiochus the Great to cede—who, with his brother Attalus, was easily persuaded to assist the legitimate prince against the usurper. Heliodorus, deserted by his adherents, was soon crushed; and Antiochus—who, to distinguish him from his vile competitor for the crown, had been surnamed Epiphanes "the illustrious"—ascended the throne of Syria, while his nephew Demetrius remained a hostage at Rome.

The Judeans had looked upon the sudden death of Seleucus and the destruction of Heliodorus as a judgment upon the two desecrators of the temple, and flattered themselves that thenceforth they would again be permitted to enjoy that undisturbed prosperity which so long had been their portion under the Ptolemies. But they were mistaken. Each year proved more strongly how pernicious the transfer of their allegiance was becoming, and how ill-advised they had been when they rejected the Egyptian king Log, because he had offended them, and preferred the Syrian king Stork, who not only offended, but eventually devoured them. The king and court of Syria were so much more needy than the Egyptians, the distance between Jerusalem and Antioch so much shorter, and the communication so much easier, and therefore so much more frequent than it had been with Alexandria, that the direct interposition of the Syrian monarch in the internal affairs of Judea, left the Jews but small scope for self-government. Add to this that the continuous intercourse with Antioch was at once the cause and effect of the prevalence of Grecian manners and innovation, which now reached their greatest extension, and caused intense hatred between two parties that struggled for mastery, and who, as far as regards Judaism and their religious tendencies, may justly be designated as the Conservatives and the Destructives.

The first intervention of the Syrian king in the internal affairs of Judea, was the immediate consequence of Heliodorus's foray on the temple. When Simon, the informer, saw his guilty plan frustrated, he had the audacity to charge the high-priest Onias himself with having, from motives of interest, invited this outrage on the temple. Some believed the calumny; and the consequence was, that parties were formed: the high-priest became an object of hatred to a portion of the people; and it was not long before hostile conflicts arose between the party of Onias and the faction of Simon, in which many lives were lost. At last Onias resolved to proceed himself to Antioch, and lay the whole matter before King Seleucus, than whom, in this dispute, no one could be better acquainted with the truth. It is an old axiom, that however much men may love the treason, they invariably hate the traitor. Onias was favourably received by the king; his complaints were heard, and Simon, whose treason had failed to enrich the king, was banished from his native country. Onias returned to Jerusalem and resumed his authority; but the confidence and affection of a great part of the people remained lost to him. The apopthegm of the sages of Israel "Calumny is the ruin of three—of him who utters, of him who listens, and of him who is its object"—was in this instance fully verified. Simon, the guilty calumniator, perished miserably in exile; Onias, the innocent victim, lost his office and his life; while the Judeans, who listened to the slander, saw their temple desecrated, their city in ruins, and their people slaughtered by idolaters.

Antiochus IV. Epiphanes had scarcely punished Heliodorus, and been firmly seated on the throne, when, from all parts of his empire, the leading men thronged to Antioch to assure the king of their allegiance. Among them came Joshua, better known by his Greek name Jason, a younger brother of Onias, the high-priest of Jerusalem. This young man was unprincipled, ambitious, and strongly imbued with the philosophy of Epicurus; at the same time, supple, insinuating in his manners, and highly polished in his address. He met with a friendly reception at court; and, availing himself of the penury of the royal treasury, drained as it was by the annual tribute to Rome, he tempted the new king by an offer of four hundred and forty talents of silver (about half a million of dollars) to depose the excellent Onias from the high-priesthood, and to appoint Jason to that most sacred and illustrious office.

Not content with thus making the highest dignity of the temple an object of traffic, and degrading the high-priest of the Lord into the nominee of an idolater, Jason, dreading the presence of his injured brother at Jerusalem, and the high estimation in which he still was held by the most estimable portion of the people, obtained an order that Onias should be summoned to Antioch, and commanded to dwell there.

Having thus secured, as he thought, the main object of his ambition—the high-priesthood—and removed from Jerusalem a man whose devotion to Judaism and great influence might stand in the way of his ulterior designs, Jason next took steps to secure the preponderance of his own opinions, which aimed at nothing less than a fusion of Judaism with Greek philosophy and civilization. Finding how acceptable money was to the king, Jason, at the price of one hundred and fifty talents, (about one hundred and fifty thousand dollars,) obtained,—first, license to erect at Jerusalem a gymnasium, or place for such public sports and exercises as were usual among the Greeks; next, the permission to establish an academy in which Jewish youth might be brought up after the manner of the Greeks; and lastly, the important privilege of making what Jews he pleased free of the city of Antioch. The obvious purpose of all this was as opposite as possible to that of the institutions of Moses; for while these sought to preserve the purity of morals and the orthodoxy of faith among the

Jews, by upholding strict nationality to the exclusion of every commixture with idolaters, the purpose of Jason was to facilitate that commixture, so as eventually to amalgamate Jew and Greek.

In this, however, he was guided by motives of policy and of self-interest, even more than by the spirit of innovation, of which he was so recklessly possessed. Admitted to the entertainments and social reunions at the court of Antioch, he had become familiar with the king and had read the secrets of the royal breast, which were no other than a restless and ever-burning desire to raise Syria from that state of prostration and tutelage to which it had been reduced by Rome. And as so large and important a portion of his possessions as the greater part of Asia Minor had been dismembered from his empire, nothing but the most intimate union of the various territories and nationalities which still obeyed the sceptre of the Seleucidæ, could render it possible that his uncontrollable longing for independence and power should ever be realized.

The Syro-Grecian monarchy was still sufficiently extensive, its population numerous, its resources vast enough, to rank as a first-rate power, provided the Oriental nations who formed the immense majority of its inhabitants could become, politically as well as socially and religiously, cemented into one nationality, animated by the same spirit and aspirations as himself. This, from the moment Antiochus ascended the throne, was the one all-absorbing object that filled his mind and engrossed his thoughts. Whoever could greatly assist him in the attaining of his important purpose, would have lasting claims on his gratitude and favour.

Among the various Oriental nations under his sway, none ranked higher, or offered greater obstacles to his plans, than the Jews. Numerous in Judea, still more so in Mesopotamia and Babylonia, wealthy, industrious, and generally respected, the gaining of their unqualified adhesion was an object of great importance; while from their ancient customs, and still more by their rigid morality and pure monotheism, they might be considered as the most stubborn opponents of the king's wish to supersede their nationality and to substitute his own. To employ force against them was what, at this early period of his reign, Antiochus had neither the intention nor the means of doing. To seduce them was a work of so much time and difficulty, as to appear almost hopeless, but for the aid which Jason was in a condition and willing to afford to his plans. Gradually but gently to turn the Jews into Greeks, was a service for which no reward could be too high; and this service the high-priest essayed to render.

The effects which resulted from the exertions of Jason, after he had established himself in the high-priesthood, were such as the king hailed with delight. The example of a person in his commanding position drew forth and gave full scope to the more lax dispositions which existed among the people, and especially among the younger class. They were at once enchanted with the ease and freedom of the Grecian mode of life, and weary of the restraints and limitations of their own. Accordingly, they abandoned themselves with all the frenzy of a new excitment, from which all restraint had been withdrawn, to the license which was offered to them. The exercises of the gymnasium seem to have taken hold of their minds with the force of a fascination. The priests neglected their service at the temple to be present at these spectacles. Some of these exercises were performed naked; and it is related that many of the Jewish competitors found means to obliterate the peculiar stamp of their nationality, in order that they might not be distinguished from Greeks and other champions in the sports of the gymnasium. The year after his promotion, Jason sent some young men on whom he had conferred the citizenship of Antioch, to assist at the games which were celebrated at Tyre, in honour of Hercules, and at which King Antiochus himself was present. To prove to the king how zealously the high-priest of Jerusalem laboured in promoting the religious amalgamation of the various nationalities in the Syro-Greek empire, Jason had intrusted his emissaries with a large sum of money to be expended in sacrifices to Hercules. But even the least scrupulous of the high-priest's followers were not prepared to go to this extent with him; and, instead of obeying his instructions, they presented the money to the Tyrians, as a contribution toward repairing their fleet.

The ferment of innovation in the minds of the Judeans at that time, was not unlike that which, some two thousand years later, agitated the continent of Europe after the spread of the French Revolution and its doctrines. A new and foreign standard of perfection was set up: whatever was Greek, was elegant, and beautiful, and desirable; whatever was not Greek, or opposed to its predominance, was superannuated, bigoted, contemptible. Even minds sincerely attached to Jewish faith and Jewish nationality did not altogether escape the contagion. And it is during this period that we must place the production of works which adhere to the Law and doctrines of Moses, but seek to adorn and popularize them by the help of Grecian muses and philosophy. Indeed, the desire to approximate externally as much as possible to the usages of the Greek world, without renouncing, internally, the essentials of Judaism, produced a Judeo-Grecian literature, which, in point of time, extended over nearly three centuries, and continued till the destruction of Jerusalem, (70 c. e.,) after which every trace of it disappeared from among the Jews; so that, at present, this literature is only known to us from fragments that have been preserved by Gentile writers.

Dr. Philipson, the learned and enterprising Rabbi of Magdeburg, in Germany, has lately collected and published these Greek fragments.[35] Among them we find tragedies on biblical subjects, by a writer named Ezekiel; an epic poem by the elder Philo, the subject of which is Jerusalem and the fortunes of its people; the history of the patriarch Jacob, versified by Theodotus. The writings of Aristobulus, of the sacerdotal family of Aaron, who is said to have lived at the court of the first Ptolemy, (325–284 B. C. E.,) and fragments of which are preserved by Eusebius, (Præp. Evang. vii.,) are by Philipson considered as of doubtful authenticity. But the letter of Aristeas— of which we spoke in our account of the Septuagint—is, by the acute critic of Magdeburg, declared to belong to the period of the Maccabean wars, and, most probably, to be the work of an Alexandrian Jew. The two first books of Maccabees, preserved in the Apocrypha of the Bible, are among the more important productions of this Judeo-Grecian literature, the last and greatest of which are formed by the writings of Philo and Josephus.

Dr. Philipson dwells at some length on the error of assuming that the Septuagint, the writings of Philo the Younger, and of Josephus, were isolated efforts which had neither predecessors, connecting links, nor successors. It is true that, except to a few ripe scholars, these works were all that was known of the writings of Hellenists; but the fragments preserved fully prove that there was a continuous series of works written in Greek by Jews, at the head of which stands the Septuagint, and the last of which is the history of Josephus. And it is a remarkable circum-

---

[35] "Ezekiel and Philo," Berlin, 1830. "Judeo-Grecian Literature," a sketch: Magdeburg, 1854.

stance, that the whole of this literature, tragic, epic, historical, or philosophical, treats of biblical and Jewish subjects only. It may, therefore, be considered as a concession made to the innovating spirit of the times, which required that even Judaism itself should, to some extent, assume a foreign garb, and deck itself out with foreign graces.

Jason only enjoyed his ill-gotten dignity for three years. The means he had used to supplant his worthier predecessors were, with similar effect, employed against himself. Having sent his younger brother Onias, who assumed the Greek name Menelaus,[36] to Antioch with tribute, this ambitious profligate took advantage of the opportunity to ingratiate himself with the king; and, by offering to pay annually three hundred talents (about $300,000) more than Jason did, he succeeded in removing Jason from the high-priesthood, and getting himself appointed in his stead. But in his attempt to assume that high office he was repulsed and compelled to return to Antioch. There he professed for himself and his associates an entire conformity to the religion of the Greeks, and by that means succeeded in persuading Antiochus to establish him by force. He returned to Jerusalem at the head of a detachment of the Syrian army, then marching against Egypt. Jason, disgracefully expelled, was forced to seek refuge in the land of the Ammonites. And Menelaus, who was not only less scrupulous even than Jason, but who, moreover, proved himself capable of the most atrocious crimes, triumphantly assumed the honours and powers of high-priest. Thus there were at one and the same time what had never been before, three high-priests,

---

[36] It became the fashion among persons of consequence, to adopt, in their intercourse with the Greeks, a Grecian name, in sound or meaning as like as possible to the Hebrew one by which they were known among the Jews.

of whom, however, only one, Onias, then living at Antioch, was legitimate; the other two were usurpers.

The Syrian monarchy had at length acquitted itself of the heavy annual tribute it had to pay to Rome, and to raise which every means of extortion, and even of plunder, had been adopted. But King Antiochus had become accustomed to these nefarious means of raising money; and as one of the instruments by which he hoped to restore the power of his empire consisted in a large army of mercenaries, the maintaining of which was very costly, the king continued to grind down his subjects by excessive taxation, and exacted from the farmers of the royal revenues—the high-priest of Jerusalem being one of the number—the most punctual payment of the largest possible amount that could be wrung from the people.

This king, Antiochus IV. Epiphanes, "the illustrious," but who subsequently gained for himself the surname of Epimanes, "the mad," was one of those wayward, fickle, but still obstinate and ruthless characters, that but too often are found among the inheritors and holders of irresponsible despotic power. Possessed of considerable abilities, and destitute neither of courage nor of conduct—according to the testimony of his contemporary, Polybius the historian, who by no means flatters him—the king of Syria on several occasions acted in a manner corresponding to the "illustrious" surname which he bore. (Polyb. lib. xxvi. frag. 8; lib. xxix. frag. 9.) But, to counterbalance his talents, he was immoderately fond of wine, and when under its influence, he became a madman. In his temper and disposition he combined the quick, versatile, and capricious character of the Greek, with the splendid voluptuousness and fierce despotism of the Oriental. His residence of twelve years at Rome had also produced a considerable impression on his mind. He brought home with him that ruthlessness of purpose, and that indifference to human suffering, for which the Romans were distinguished; and his natural stubbornness and haughty temper were carried to excess in the vain attempt to emulate Roman firmness.

Dishonest in his purposes, and utterly unscrupulous, like his father, in the means of accomplishing them, not the least among the many discrepancies of this worthless character was a degree of bigotry and consequent religious intolerance, all the more detestable because it was the offspring, not merely of feeling or conviction, but chiefly of policy and calculation. We have already spoken of his great design to effect the social, political, and religious amalgamation of all the different nationalities in his empire. As a principal means, he revived the splendour of public worship, especially of those gods who were considered as the most nationally Grecian. Among these he singled out the Olympian Jupiter as the object of his own special adoration, with such zeal and generosity, that his gifts to the temple of that god at Athens, his profuse liberality to the temple at Delos, and his general largess to the various temples, began to produce the effect at which he aimed; at least in Greece, whence the armies of his mercenaries were chiefly recruited. In the public assemblies of the Greek cities, the magnanimity and generous patriotism of Antiochus toward Greece were loudly proclaimed, and met with ready recognition, even by the political adversaries of the king of Syria.

The large sums of money which Antiochus extorted from his subjects, enabled him to avail himself of the popularity his zeal for religion had gained him in Greece, to enlist in his service numbers of military adventurers; and though he did not attempt to increase his fleet beyond the number of ships to which the treaty with Rome restricted him, his land forces daily became more formidable, both from numbers and military prowess. And he soon found the oppor-

JUDEA UNDER THE PERSIANS AND GREEKS. 211

tunity of employing them. It will be remembered that the king of Egypt, Ptolemy V. Epiphanes, who was stripped of his Syrian possessions by Antiochus the Great, had subsequently married Cleopatra, the daughter of that monarch, under a promise that the three provinces of Palestine, Phœnicia, and Cœle-Syria, which had been wrested from him, should be restored to him; a promise that never was fulfilled. After a profligate and troubled reign of twenty-four years, this Ptolemy V. was taken off by poison, (181 B. C. E.,) and left three children, Ptolemy Philometor, Ptolemy Physcon, and Cleopatra, who was successively married to her two brothers.

The eldest of them, Ptolemy VI., surnamed Philometor, "mother-loving," was but a child at the death of his father, and the government was conducted by his mother, Cleopatra, during eight years, with great ability. But when she died (173 B. C. E.,) the regency devolved on the tutors of the young king, who at once advanced a claim on his behalf to the possession of the three provinces, on the twofold ground that they had been secured to Ptolemy I. Soter by the partition treaty of the battle of Ipsos, (301 B. C. E.;) and that they had again been given by Antiochus III. the Great, in dowry with his daughter Cleopatra, on her becoming queen of Egypt. Antiochus IV. Epiphanes refused to listen to these demands, and both parties sent deputies to Rome to argue their respective claims before the senate.

When Philometor completed his fourteenth year, he was solemnly invested with the sovereignty, on which occasion embassies of congratulation were sent from all the neighbouring governments. Apollonius, the ambassador of Antiochus, was instructed to sound the dispositions of Ptolemy's court; and when he informed Antiochus that he was viewed as an enemy by the Egyptians, the king of Syria immediately proceeded to Joppa to survey his frontiers toward Egypt, and to put them in a state of defence. On this occasion he paid a visit to Jerusalem. The king was received by Jason, who was still high-priest, with every demonstration of respect; and the city was illuminated in honour of his presence. He afterward returned through Phœnicia to Antioch, where he began actively to prepare for the invasion of Egypt.

The time was well chosen. Rome had just begun war with the last king of Macedon; and with its usual diplomatic skill and duplicity, the senate had evaded pronouncing sentence on the conflicting claims of Syria and Egypt, lest, by deciding in favour of the one, it might drive the other to take part with Macedon. And as thus the possession by Antiochus of the three provinces in dispute, had at least the tacit sanction of Rome, he determined to avail himself of his military superiority, in order to compel the king of Egypt forever to relinquish claims on which Rome had declined to decide. It was while busy with these preparations, that Menelaus arrived at Antioch as the emissary of his brother Jason, whom, by the bribe of a larger tribute, he supplanted in the high-priesthood. And when, as we have already related, Menelaus had to be established in that office by force of arms, it was a detachment of the king's forces marching against Egypt, that installed the new dignitary in Jerusalem.

Menelaus soon found that he had overtaxed his resources in the sum he had engaged to pay for his promotion; and in consequence of the non-payment, he was summoned to Antioch by the king, who exacted strict punctuality from his debtors. On arriving at the capital, Menelaus found that Antiochus was absent, preparing for the campaign against Egypt; and that he himself could not hope to retain the king's favour, unless the promised payment was completed. Having exhausted his own coffers as well as credit, he privately sent directions to his youngest brother,

Lysimachus, whom he had left as his representative at Jerusalem, to withdraw some of the consecrated vessels of gold from the temple, to sell them at Tyre, or in some other city, and to send the money to him at Antioch.

This disgraceful affair could not be managed with so much secrecy as to remain altogether concealed; and eventually it came to the knowledge of the eldest of the brothers, Onias III., the legitimate high-priest, who had been supplanted by Jason, and who, compelled to reside at Antioch, was highly respected by the numerous Jews inhabiting that city. Indignant at the sacrilegious robbery of which his younger brother had been guilty, Onias denounced the crime in strong language, which threw the Antiochian Jews into a state of excitement and displeasure, that threatened to prove highly dangerous to Menelaus. He, therefore, by means of a large bribe, prevailed on Andronicus, the king's deputy at Antioch, to put Onias to death. Onias, informed of these intrigues, had taken refuge in the sanctuary of Daphné; but was induced to quit that disreputable place[37] by the assurances of safety and promises of protection he received from Andronicus, who, however, caused him to be barbarously murdered as soon as he had passed the privileged bounds.

This atrocious act raised a terrible outcry among the Jews of Antioch, who hastened to lay their complaints before the king as soon as he returned to that city. Antiochus, to give him his due, was much affected, and shed tears when he heard them. He promised justice, and performed it, at least as far as the evidence before him permitted. Andronicus, whose guilt a proper investigation had made manifest, was stripped of his purple, and put to

---

[37] This was a grove about three miles from Antioch, dedicated to the god of light, Apollo; and which had been made a sanctuary for criminals and a place of pleasure. In the end, the place became so infamous, that no man of character could visit it.

death on the very spot where Onias had been murdered. Menelaus, the more guilty of the two, found means to escape the storm which destroyed the agent of his crime. But the large sums of money that were necessary to enable him to maintain his credit, obliged his brother Lysimachus to resort to such unheard-of exactions, violence, and sacrilege, that the people of Jerusalem rose against him. They scattered like chaff the three thousand men he had got to defend him, and, when he himself fled to the treasury of the temple, pursued and slew him there.

While this was doing at Jerusalem, Antiochus, having completed his preparations for war, led his army along the coast of Palestine, and crossing the frontiers, gave the Egyptians a signal overthrow at Pelusium. (171 B. C. E.) He then left garrisons along the whole of the border, and withdrew into winter quarters at Tyre. On hearing of his arrival there, the Jewish elders sent thither three venerable deputies, to explain the cause of the late riots in Jerusalem, which had led to the death of Lysimachus, and to accuse Menelaus as the author of all the troubles that had happened in Antioch as well as in Judea.

The case they made out was so strong, and was heard with so much attention by the king, that Menelaus felt greatly alarmed for the result. He therefore applied himself to the king's favourite, Ptolemy Macron, and promised him so large a bribe, that he was induced to watch the inconstant temper of the king, whose mind was becoming inflamed by nightly carousals and unrestrained indulgence in wine. Macron availed himself of a fitting opportunity, and got the king not only to absolve Menelaus, but to condemn the three Jewish deputies to death.

This most unjust and horrid sentence was no sooner pronounced than it was executed; for both Menelaus and his confederate Macron dreaded that a return to reason might cause the king to recall the fatal decree. The whole nation of Jews was greatly shocked by the foul deed, which was not less abhorrent to foreigners; so that the Tyrians even ventured to express their sense of the wrong, by giving an honourable burial to the murdered men. The ultimate effect was, that the pride of King Antiochus felt offended at the turn against him which public opinion had taken; and, as is usually the case, having injured the Jews, he began to hate them; while their dislike of him was second only to the strong aversion which they entertained for Menelaus. But, at the same time, the paramount influence of that guilty person with the king seemed so fully established, and was so clearly evinced, that all further thoughts of resisting his authority were abandoned. Accordingly he resumed his station at Jerusalem; while the presence, in the vicinity, of the king at the head of his powerful and victorious army, rendered any general manifestation of the public feeling impracticable.

In the spring of the next year, Antiochus undertook a second expedition against the Egyptians. And as the attention of the Romans was, for the time, absorbed by the war against Perseus, the last king of Macedon, which hitherto had turned to their disadvantage, Antiochus, in order to attack Egypt by sea and land, presumed to violate that article of the treaty of peace with Rome, which restricted his fleet to ten ships of war. Philometor took the field against him in person, but was defeated and taken prisoner. Antiochus treated his nephew with much kindness; and though after the victory he had the Egyptian army in his power, and might have cut them to pieces, he behaved toward them with such humanity, as gained him great favour with that people. Eventually the whole of Egypt submitted to him, with the exception of one city only.

But this city was Alexandria, the strong and wealthy, containing more of pure Hebrew and Grecian blood, and more military resources, than were now to be found in all the rest of the kingdom collectively. Attachment to the dynasty of the Ptolemeans, which so long had ruled in Egypt, induced the Alexandrians to acknowledge as their king the younger brother of Philometor, named like him, Ptolemy, and whom they honoured with the surname Euergetes "the benefactor;" though he is usually distinguished in history by his nickname, Physcon, "big belly," acquired, when he grew older, from his excessive corpulency. Antiochus, in the mean time, had taken possession of Pelusium, a strong frontier fortress, and was placing garrisons in other Egyptian strongholds, when a rumour of his death, before Alexandria, reached Jerusalem and caused general joy.

The deposed high-priest Jason quitted the land of the Ammonites, and with a party, assisted by friends within, surprised Jerusalem, massacred many citizens, drove his brother Menelaus into the castle, and possessed himself of the principality. But he was speedily compelled to quit the city and country, at the news that Antiochus was alive and marching against him with a powerful army. After wandering from place to place, and from one country to another, a fugitive and a vagabond, Jason at last perished miserably, a refugee in the distant and strange land of Lacedæmonia; nor did his wretched end compensate for the innumerable ills which his profligacy and ambition had brought upon his country.

His last inroad into Judea had been reported to Antiochus with such exaggeration, as led him to conclude that the whole nation had revolted; and being further provoked by hearing that the Jews had made public rejoicings at the news of his death, he marched in great wrath from Egypt, took Jerusalem by assault, destroyed forty thousand persons, and dragged an equal number into captivity. He then plundered the temple of its treasures, which are said in value to have amounted to fifteen millions of dollars in the public and private treasury: for, beside the property of the temple, there was money belonging to widows and orphans, and other valuable deposits, the whole of which were carried away to Antioch. The capital being thus drained of treasure and drenched in blood, the country was once more abandoned to Menelaus, supported by an armed force under Philip and Andronicus, two Syrian generals of relentless cruelty.

After having secured his valuable plunder in his own metropolis, Antiochus the next year (169 B. C. E.) returned to Egypt and laid siege to Alexandria. All his efforts, however, were baffled by the determined resistance of the inhabitants. The Jews, in particular, who formed full half of the population of that city, were greatly exasperated at the cruelty and rapacity with which Jerusalem had been treated, and assisted with fierce zeal in repelling the attacks of Antiochus. During the siege, Physcon, in conjunction with his sister Cleopatra, sent an embassy to Rome, to complain of the deplorable condition to which their country was reduced by the ambition of an encroaching neighbour, their own unnatural uncle, whose vassal their unworthy elder brother had submitted to become. This embassy alarmed Antiochus; and as he found that the reduction of Alexandria was a work of greater difficulty than he was at the time prepared to surmount, he made a virtue of necessity, raised the siege, and with his army withdrew to Memphis, where he had caused his captive nephew to take up his residence.

Here he affected solemnly to deliver up the kingdom of Egypt to Philometor, while he himself returned to Antioch. But as Antiochus retained in his own hands Pelusium, the key of Egypt on the side of Syria, his ulterior designs were but too transparent to Philometer, not less than to Physcon. The two brothers soon entered into an amicable correspondence, chiefly through the intervention of the Rhodian ambassadors, who viewed with no friendly eye the revival of the naval power of Syria. Both brothers were earnestly desirous of peace: Physcon, because Alexandria in a great measure depended for subsistence on provisions conveyed by the Nile; and Philometor, because the city held by his brother was the only place strong enough to resist Antiochus, should he, a fourth time, invade Egypt. The brothers, therefore, agreed that they would share the government between them, and resist Antiochus with their united power; and, further, that a joint embassy should be sent to Rome to implore the protection of the republic against their uncle.

This brought on a fourth invasion of Egypt by Antiochus, (168 B. C. E.,) who now threw off the mask he had hitherto chosen to wear; and as their embassy to Rome had produced no result, he declared himself the enemy of both the brother-kings. As had been foreseen, he took possession of all the country except Alexandria, the siege of which city he prepared to resume with forces much more considerable than those under his command the preceding year. But, though the plunder of Jerusalem had enabled him greatly to augment the number of his mercenaries, the circumstances under which he now, for the second time, marched against Alexandria, were widely different from what they had been the year before. The Romans had at length brought the war against Macedon to a close. Defeated at the decisive battle of Pydna, the last king of Macedon died a prisoner; and the hereditary kingdom of Alexander the Great was erased from the list of independent states, and became a Roman province.

After this vast augmentation of their power and resources, the Romans at length found leisure to attend to the urgent cries for help of their ancient allies, the Ptolemies. While, however, to satisfy the clamorous Egyptian ambassadors, a commission was at once despatched from Rome, secret orders detained it at Delos, in Greece, until the campaign against Perseus should be decided. But when the battle of Pydna had secured the supremacy of Rome, the commissioners hastened to carry out their mission. At their head was placed Popilius Lœnas, a man pre-eminently qualified to carry out the haughtiest instructions in the haughtiest manner. After a visit of five days to Rhodes—a commonwealth in alliance with Rome, but which, during the war, had given offence to the senate, and was now to be severely mulcted—the commissioners reached Egypt, and encountered Antiochus at a place called Eleusis, on the sea-shore, four miles from Alexandria.

During his long residence at Rome, King Antiochus had been on terms of intimacy with Popilius; and, seeing him now at the head of the commissioners, the king, rejoiced, stretched forth his arms to embrace him. But the Roman sternly repelled the salute, demanding first to receive an answer to the written orders of the senate of which he was the bearer. The official tablet which he handed to Antiochus contained but one single sentence: "Antiochus, thou wilt abstain from making war on the Ptolemies."

On reading this haughty missive, the king felt equally indignant and grieved. Still, dissembling his feelings, he said calmly to Popilius, "I will confer on the matter with my friends, and let thee know the result." But the haughty Roman refused to grant the king even the semblance of free will: instant, abject submission to the mandate of the senate was what he required and exacted. With his staff, Popilius drew a circle round the king on the sand, and said, "I require thy answer before thou steppest out of this circle." The struggle in the king's mind between pride and fear, though fierce, was brief. "I will obey the senate," was the faltering answer reluctantly wrung from the conscious feeling of his impotency, as his eye imperious quailed beneath the steadfast gaze of the stern republican, and his royal head bowed humbly in token of submission. Then, as if in pity for the mental anguish he had inflicted on the *king*, Popilius extended his hand to his old *friend*. A year before, the conduct of either party would have been very different. But the conquest of Macedon once achieved, the supremacy of Rome was no longer to be disputed by any of the terror-stricken successors of Alexander the Great.

In obedience to the commands of the senate, Antiochus at once withdrew his army from Egypt. As that army defiled before him, and he saw the thousands upon thousands of brave, highly-disciplined, and well-accoutred warriors who were ready to "do or die" at his bidding; when he reflected that, notwithstanding all this mighty array, he himself, its chief, was nothing more than the abject dependant and slave of a remote commonwealth, his mortification and rage knew no bounds. And as the agitation of his mind was still further heightened by the large quantities of wine which he continually swallowed, his phrensy increased to such a degree, that his favourite, Macron, deemed it absolutely necessary that the king should vent his pent-up indignation on some hated object which, to his distempered imagination, might serve as a substitute for detested Rome.

Judea—Jerusalem unfortunately lay in his way. Ever since the foul murder of the Jewish delegates, committed by his orders at Tyre, the reproaches of his own conscience and the sullen discontent of the Judeans combined to render them hateful to him. In the fulness of his power, their proud metropolis had manifested its joy at the tidings of his death, and had been punished with plunder and slaughter. Doubtless his present humiliation was, to that city, a source of revengeful satisfaction. But he ought to mar its joy. Though he could not defy Rome, he was still able to destroy Jerusalem; and the work of desolation which he had commenced in his prosperity he could and would complete even now in his deepest adversity.

The proposal was no sooner presented to his mind, than he determined to carry it out. During the four successive years that King Antiochus had invaded Egypt, the march of his troops through portions of Judea had subjected that country to much suffering. And when the inroad of Jason, and the storming of Jerusalem, had once aroused the fury of Antiochus, he handed over that city and the whole country to the tender mercies of officers known and notorious for their relentless cruelty and ever-exacting rapacity. Andronicus, Philip the Phrygian, "more barbarous than his master," and Menelaus, the recreant high-priest, "worse than all the rest," vied with each other in pandering to the king's hatred of the Jews. The two years, 169 and 168 B. C. E., beheld the Syrian mercenaries living at free quarters in Judea; and those portions of the country that laid on the line of march of the Syrian army were impoverished by the continual billetings of soldiers, and oppressed by their brutality. At the same time, and while the ordinary traffic of the country was interrupted by the war, and its resources were daily growing less, the exactions of Menelaus, whose tax-gatherers wrung from the people the scanty pittance which the rapacity of the soldiery had not carried off, were unceasing. It was, therefore, no wonder that, when the king entered Judea, he found the inhabitants gloomy, dissatisfied, and little disposed to welcome him with any outward demonstrations of joy or affection. And as the spirit of discontent, which he himself had called forth, reacted on his furious frame of mind, he intrusted the execution of his immediate vengeance to fitting ministers; while he himself hastened on to Antioch, there to prepare the final blow that was forever to extinguish Judaism as a religion, and the Jews as a peculiar people.

It is doubtful whether Menelaus was sufficiently in the king's confidence to be instructed officially of the blow meditated against Jerusalem and the temple; but the private relations between him and Macron were of such a nature that it is extremely probable the high-priest had a hint of what was intended, that he might provide for the safety of his personal friends and adherents. Menelaus, in his inmost heart, hated the people of Jerusalem. They had slaughtered his brother and representative, Lysimachus; they thirsted for the blood of Menelaus himself, and he knew it. Fratricide, assassin, traitor to his people and to his God, Menelaus knew that throughout the whole of his administration, from the instant he supplanted his brother Jason until now that the ruffian mercenaries of his despot master were to be let loose on an innocent and unsuspecting people, not one redeeming trait could plead for him; and that his own personal safety required that he should crown his career of guilt by exterminating his enemies—a designation in which he justly included the entire orthodox population of Jerusalem.

He had already at Antioch declared *his* readiness to adopt the polytheism of Greece, and thus to second the favourite scheme of Antiochus—religious unity throughout his empire. His adherents—those who wished to set aside the usages of Judaism, and to break down the partition wall that separated the Jews from the heathen world—were quite ready to go with him to any length in the renunciation of Jewish customs and observances. They contended that, while it was absolutely necessary to distinguish between the principles and practices of Judaism, it was also highly desirable there should be a fusion between the Jews and Gentiles; that, therefore, no importance whatever ought to be atached to the external rites and observances of religion; and that sacrifices, festivals and days of rest, forbidden meats, and all other institutions peculiar to Judaism, should at once and forever be renounced, to make room for that freedom from restraint, and those graceful and pleasing observances which distinguished the Grecian world.; that by this means the Jews, instead of being a feeble minority, obnoxious to the king because they thwarted his great purpose of national amalgamation, would become incorporated in that universal (pagan) church, the altars of which rose everywhere throughout the civilized world; and would, moreover, obtain honours, dignities, and offices from the favour of the king.

Thus Menelaus and his adherents publicly professed their readiness to renounce the Law of Moses, while in their private life they made no scruple in violating its precepts; and nothing but the dread of the vast majority of the people prevented Menelaus and his party from publicly abolishing the sabbaths and festivals. The two parties, the orthodox and the apostates, viewed each other with extreme aversion; and as the misfortunes of the times soured men's minds, a conflict between the two was with difficulty prevented by the presence of the foreign soldiery, who, it was well known, were sure to take part with Menelaus, provided only he and his partisans did not begin the affray, and thus might, with some show of reason, claim protection against the people.

Such was the state of public feeling in Jerusalem, when Apollonius, a Syrian general, at the head of twenty-two thousand men, was detached by King Antiochus against that city. As this general was known as the receiver of the king's taxes throughout Judea, and had usually been attended by a considerable body of troops, his arrival and the great force that attended him caused no alarm; and, as his men gave no offence to the citizens, the Jews had not the slightest suspicion of his hostile intentions.

All things remained quiet until the sabbath, on which day it was known the Jews of that age would not fight, even in self-defence. In the midst of the festive rest that prevailed, the soldiers were let loose, and scoured the streets, slaughtering all they met, that suffered themselves meekly to be slain, none being found who attempted to stand on their defence. This is the first instance of that passive courage—resulting from adherence to principle—of which, since then, the Jews have so often had occasion to give proof, and which is the more praiseworthy as it is not the result of cowardice or want of spirit. This same people, the Jews—which suffered itself, unresisting, to be butchered in the streets of Jerusalem on the sabbath day, because they believed that the law prohibited self-defence on that day—shortly afterward surprised the world by deeds of valour and military achievement that placed their active courage above the possibility of question or doubt; but which, not less than their former passive endurance, resulted from adherence to one great and most holy principle—to prefer *duty* to *life*.

While the men were thus cruelly slaughtered, the women and children were spared, to be sold for slaves. All the streets of Jerusalem and the courts of the temple flowed with blood; and the ferocious Menelaus could glut his eyes with the sight of his lifeless enemies. The houses were forced and pillaged, and the city wall was thrown down. All the buildings near Mount Zion were demolished, and with the materials Apollonius strengthened the fortifications of the citadel, which he furnished with a numerous garrison, and held under his own command. This castle was so situated as to give the garrison complete command over the temple, so that the people could no longer visit the sanctuary. And as Menelaus, now all-powerful, refused to perform the public services of the Jewish religion, the daily sacrifices ceased in the month of Sivan, (June,)

167 B. C. E. The priests and Levites who survived dispersed; and Jerusalem, a city numbering from one hundred and twenty to one hundred and fifty thousand inhabitants, was soon completely deserted, as the citizens who escaped the massacre fled for refuge to the towns of the neighbouring Gentiles.

The first act of King Antiochus's revenge had been thus far successful: the proud city that had caused public rejoicings to be performed at the report of his death, was deserted; the citizens, who would have triumphed in his humiliation, were forced, homeless and vagabond, to hide their own heads in humble dependence on those heathen protectors who gave them shelter. But it was not enough that Jerusalem should be brought thus low, that the Jewish people should be thus afflicted; their faith was to be eradicated, their religious nationality was to be forever destroyed, and the only altar consecrated to the worship of "the Lord of heaven," but wrested from him and transferred to the gods of Greece, was at once to attest the crowning measure of the king's revenge, and the full success of his policy of amalgamation. At Antioch a decree was now issued and proclaimed in all the provinces of Syria, commanding the inhabitants of the whole empire to worship the gods of the king, and to acknowledge no religion but his, with the declared object "that all should become one people."

Some historians are of opinion that this measure was adopted by Antiochus in order to give him a pretext for plundering the many rich temples throughout his dominions dedicated to the aboriginal gods of Asia. Thus, among the ancients, Polybius tells us that "Antiochus was the first king of Syria who formed a regular plan for profaning the sanctity of temples," or, in other words, robbing the banks of deposit, and rifling the great magazines of commerce. And among later writers, Hales fancies that "this *general persecution* seems to have been raised by Antiochus not from any regard to his own religion, but from a regular plan and deep-laid scheme of plundering the temples throughout his dominions after he had suppressed their worship." But these writers take too narrow a view of Antiochus's design, which, as we have already stated, was nothing less than once more to raise the Syro-Grecian empire to that independence and power which it had possessed before its unfortunate wars against Rome. This is evident from the fact that there was no *general persecution*, although the edict was general in its terms. The cities containing the wealthiest temples already worshipped the gods of Greece; and subsequent facts proved that none of the other pagan nations would make much difficulty in complying with the royal edict, at least as far as the reception went of a few foreign divinities into their already crowded Pantheon.

Nor can we, with Kitto, admit the supposition that King Antiochus, the madman, was solely actuated "by his insane hatred of the Jews, and which he could not safely manifest without bringing them into a condition of apparent contumacy, which might in some degree excuse, in the eyes of the heathen, his contemplated severities against them." For we must bear in mind that Antiochus did not act from his own impulse, but under the deliberate advice of Ptolemy Macron, a veteran statesman, (Polyb. lib. xxxviii. cap. 18,) and that the fusion of the various nations inhabiting the Syrian empire into one great nationality was a measure that had much to recommend it. And though, during the four successive years that he invaded Egypt, Antiochus's plan of amalgamation had been suspended, it had never been abandoned; while now, that he had been made so painfully to feel his own weakness and the supremacy of Rome, he returned to his schemes with renewed ardour.

But, as will sometimes happen, special and particular

interests, however reasonable they may be in themselves, must yield to the insurmountable obstacles opposed to them by general interests of a higher nature and importance. And when the king of Syria—in order to arrive at the reasonable and, to him, very desirable result of uniting the different portions of his empire into one nationality—sought to enforce a state of things, religious and social, which would have reduced Judaism to the necessity of trampling under foot the principle of its existence, its traditions of the past, and its hopes of the future, there arose a conflict of interests most unequal in their importance to the whole human race. The power and independence of Syria were but as a grain of sand in the destinies of mankind, when weighed against the existence and truth of the Jewish religion. Accordingly, it was this difference in the innate importance of the two interests, and not the relative quantity of physical force by which either was supported, that decided the conflict.

According to the royal decree, the public practice of the Jewish religion and of its observances was prohibited. Circumcision, the keeping of the sabbath, and the reading of the Law, were declared to be capital offences, to be punished with death; and all the copies of the Law that could be found were seized and defaced, torn in pieces, or burnt. It was at this time that, in order to have some substitute in their public worship for the interdicted Pentateuch, the Jews introduced the public reading in the synagogues of such portions from other books of Scripture as had some analogy, or bore some reference, to that special section of the Law which, till then, had been appointed to be read. The portion thus selected is called Haphtorah;[39] for, in perpetual commemoration of that

---

[38] *Haphtorah*, "discharge" or "dismission." So called, because it is the closing portion of Scripture read during the synagogue service.

season of affliction, the custom of publicly reading the Haphtorah on sabbaths, festivals and fast-days, has ever since been retained in the synagogue.

In order to instruct the people in the practices of their new religion, and to enforce the observance of its rites, the king sent to Jerusalem an old man named Athenæus, who became director-general of public worship. He dedicated the temple to Jupiter Olympus, the favourite divinity of Antiochus; and on the altar of the Lord he placed a smaller one, to be used in sacrificing to the heathen god, whose image was erected in the sanctuary. In these events biblical critics find the fulfilment of Daniel's prophecy, (ix. 27,) which speaks of the "abomination of desolation." This altar was set up on the 15th, and the first sacrifices on it were brought on the 25th day of Kislev, (November–December, 167 B. C. E.) Groves were consecrated, and idolatrous altars erected in every city; and the citizens were required to keep a feast on each monthly date of the king's birthday, when they were forced to offer sacrifices to the idols and to eat swine's flesh. The licentious orgies of the *Bacchanalia* were substituted for the national festival of the *Tabernacles;* while the people were compelled to join in these disgraceful riots, and to walk in the procession crowned with ivy and almost naked.

While this was doing in Judea, the king, by the advice of Macron, sent forth overseers, who were to enforce the decree of uniformity throughout his empire. These emissaries pervaded the provinces, escorted by soldiers not only for their own security, but that, wherever necessary, they might propagate their religion by the sword. Their proceedings, equally tyrannical and rapacious, caused insurrections in those parts of Upper Asia still subject to the house of Seleucus. But the nations on this side of the Euphrates, being more within the reach of the controlling Syrian army, complied with the overseers' injunctions before they assumed the tone of commands. (Diodorus, Excerpt. p. 580.)

Even the Samaritans, who often asserted themselves to be of Hebrew descent, and who, under Alexander, had eagerly set forth their claim to a Jewish origin, now wrote to Antiochus to declare that they were of the race of the Medes and the Sidonians. They acknowledged that their ancestors, with a view to prevent certain plagues too frequent in their country, had built a temple to the God of the Jews on Mount Gerizim, and had observed the Jewish sabbaths; but that they themselves, more enlightened than their fathers, had determined in all things to obey the will of their sovereign. They, therefore, begged the king's permission to dedicate their temple at Gerizim to the Grecian Jupiter, under one of his favourite titles, *Xenius*, "the defender of strangers." Thus Antiochus soon found that the only nation from whom his decree was likely to experience serious resistance was that of the Jews; for the mass of that people could not imitate the pliancy of the heathen, but still, with the fervour of conviction and the constancy of true love, clung to the faith of their fathers.

Though all the public services had ceased in Jerusalem, and no voice of adoration was heard in the holy city, unless that of the profane heathen calling on their idols, the people of the country still would steal in to visit, with fond affection, the place of the sanctuary, and there to offer a hasty and interrupted worship. But even this could not be done without danger, as the citadel was so situated that nothing which occurred on the temple-mount could escape the notice of the garrison. And so zealously was Athenæus served by his spies, that two women were discovered and brought before him, who, in the utmost secrecy, had circumcised their infant sons with their own hands. As their *guilt*, in obeying God and disobeying the king, was manifest, they, with their infants, were thrown from the lofty battlements on the south side of the temple, into the deep valley below.

This dreadful punishment, with others of the same nature, had the effect of intimidating many Jews into submission to the king's edict; while a still greater number, ardently attached to the customs of the Greeks, required no compulsion to do that which, with Menelaus at their head, they had long desired to do—to renounce Judaism and its restraints. But by far the greater part of the people fled or kept themselves concealed. And King Antiochus therefore resolved to come to Palestine, that his personal presence might obtain general and ready obedience for his decree. Jerusalem, though almost deserted, was still conspicuous above all other places, and therefore exposed to the utmost fury of the royal inquisitor; and it must be confessed that few of even the most fanatical persecutors in after ages have equalled the ruthless attempts of Antiochus to exterminate the religion of the Jews.

Yet the savage and insane violence of this tyrant was, in fact—and surely we may say providentially—the safeguard of the Jews against the greatest moral danger to which they had ever been exposed: the slow and insidious, but certain and destructive advance of indifference to religious truth, evidenced by the encroachments and gradual prevalence of Grecian manners, Grecian corruption, Grecian idolatry, and Grecian atheism. King Antiochus and his fanaticism aroused the dormant energies of the whole Jewish people, so that the zealous attachment to the Law and truth of the Lord, united with the generous desire for national independence, gave a tone of exaltation to the character of the people, and evoked an enthusiasm, a courage, both passive and active, which set at defiance the utmost power of Antiochus; and which then, and ever since has, in the stern hour of trial, animated and sustained the Jews to such an extent, that it has, in fact, rendered them imperishable.

Had they basely yielded to Antiochus, they might have escaped the ills he inflicted on them; they might, like the other inhabitants of geographical Syria, have merged into a nationality so contemptible, that in the Greek and Roman plays, the words "slave" and "Syrian" were synonymous; and that even before the war which crushed Syria, the Roman consul Titus Quintius Flamininus, in reply to a pompous harangue of the ambassadors of Antiochus the Great before the Greek National Assembly at Ægium, (192 B. C. E.,) could take upon himself to declare that "the vile name of Syrian comprehended every form of baseness, vice, and servility." (Plutarch, in Flamin. and Tit. Liv. lxxxv. cap. 49.)

With this corrupt, effeminate, and base, but elegant, highly-polished, and pleasure-loving nationality, the Jews might have been amalgamated. But what would have been the consequence to them? Like those base Syrians, they would have been swept away from the face of the earth; their identity would have been at an end; their national existence obliterated; their influence on the destinies of mankind gone forever. The sacred mission, however, that had been intrusted to them, did not permit so miserable a consummation to their wondrous history; the high and holy truth of which they were the guardians and witnesses, forbade so ridiculous a downfall of their lofty aspirations.

The Midrash, commenting on the plea of Moses—"For they are a stiff-necked people, and thou shalt pardon our iniquities, &c.," (Ex. xxxiv. 9,)—raises the question, "As a stiff-necked, stubborn disposition is sinful, how came Moses, instead of attempting to exculpate his people, to hold up this very sinfulness in the Israelites as the principal reason why their iniquities should be pardoned?" "Because," replies the Midrash, "Moses spoke in the spirit of prophesy. A time will come, when every means will be employed by the mighty ones of the earth to lure or drive Israel to renounce the Law. But Israel is a stiff-necked people; and, therefore, force or fraud, torture or temptation, will equally fail of success against them." And this stiff-neckedness, or rather this firmness of purpose, this high-souled constancy, long dormant, but now called forth by the persecution of cruel Antiochus, has never since ceased to maintain itself in Israel.

And thus, by the wise and merciful dispensation of Providence, even Antiochus became a benefactor to the Jews. His ruthless fanaticism was the painful but effectual remedy that the corruption of the times rendered necessary, and that cauterized the gangrene in the priesthood and people, which threatened certain destruction alike to the body politic and to the religion of Israel. For the influence of Menelaus and his brothers had corrupted the ministers of God to that degree, that, on the return of better times, an entire division of priests—*Bilgah,* "the fifteenth order," (1 Chron. xxiv. 14,)—were severely punished for their want of faithfulness to the God and law of Israel. And though the individual descendants of that order could not be excluded from the performance of sacerdotal functions which were their birthright, yet the entire division Bilgah was branded with a public and lasting stigma.[39]

---

[39] In order that animals intended for sacrifice might be slaughtered with greater facility, each order of priests had assigned to it, in the outer court of the temple, an iron ring, to which the head of the animal was to be fastened. Each order also had a chamber or store-room of its own. Of this, as well as of their iron ring, the order Bilgah was deprived. As an instance of the bad spirit which prevailed in this particular division or order of priests, the Talmud (end of tr. Succah) relates, that during the persecution under Antiochus, a daughter of Bilgah, named Miriam, renounced

Nor did these priests stand alone in their defection. Many of the wealthy and educated classes were, as we have already stated, so infected with Grecian skepticism, and so short-sighted, that they did not perceive the dignity of their national existence, nor that the preservation of Israel was inseparable from the law of God and its observance. On the contrary, these Greeklings, unworthy of the name of Israelites, were so effeminate and cowardly, so sensual and worldly, that while they looked with an eye of contempt on those Jews who remained steadfast in the Law, they themselves even went beyond what the king required in seconding his views and enforcing his decree, because, like him, they were eager to destroy the distinct nationality of the Jews. Antiochus' persecution, therefore, came to have the wholesome effect of most strongly identifying the true patriot with the devout worshipper, and taught the Jew that he owes his allegiance first to his God, and next to the land in which he lives.

On his arrival at Jerusalem, King Antiochus applied himself to enforce his decree of conformity and uniformity by every means in his power. Those whose ready obedience disarmed his wrath were viewed with favour, and in some instances rewarded. But those who proved refractory were exposed to his utmost rage, since he considered their disobedience at once as rebellion against his royal authority and sacrilege against his gods. Accordingly he commanded and in person superintended the most hor-

---

her religion, and married a Syro-Grecian officer of high rank. When the king's troops took possession of the temple, Miriam, who accompanied her husband, struck the altar of burnt-offering with her shoe, exclaiming— "Thou insatiable wolf, how much longer art thou to consume the wealth of Israel, though thou art not able to help them in their hour of need?" Her conduct is imputed to the bad example to which she had been accustomed in her father's house and among her nearest connections, who subsequently were subjected to the degrading stigma above related.

rible tortures of the recusants, and seemed to derive a degree of pleasure from these inhuman spectacles, which kept pace with the increasing agonies of his victims. Josephus, in his history of this period, exhausts his Greek eloquence in highly-wrought descriptions of those heroic scenes of martyrdom; and in so doing, he contrasts strongly, but not at all to his advantage, with the sublime brevity of the 1st Book of Maccabees: "Howbeit many in Israel were firmly resolved not to profane the holy covenant—SO THEN THEY DIED." (Chap. i. 62, 63.) We will not imitate him; but will content ourselves with briefly noticing two instances, out of the many recorded by the national historians, as the noblest examples of that fortitude which is to be derived from trust in the Almighty, confirmed by the testimony of a good conscience.

Eleazar, a man in his ninetieth year, venerated for his piety, and respected for his social position, was denounced as a rebel against the king, inasmuch as, notwithstanding the royal decree, he still adhered to the Law of Moses. As this had been proclaimed a capital offence, his life was forfeited; but the royal clemency was offered to him on condition of his publicly eating forbidden meats. On his refusal to do so, the king's officers, with whom he had previously been acquainted, struck with admiration for his firmness, and with pity at the idea of the torture the feeble old man would have to endure, offered to provide him with meat which it was lawful for him to eat, but which they would proclaim to be swine's flesh; and this simulated but public submission to the king would be received as sufficient to save his life. His reply deserves to be recorded: "I am now ninety years of age, and have all my lifetime served my God uprightly, and with a good name among my people. Shall I now, on the brink of the grave, and in order to save the few days that in the ordinary course of nature I yet may live, give the lie to my whole life, and become a cause of offence and scandal to my people, some of whom may even be seduced by my example, and may look upon my apostasy as an excuse for their own weakness? Besides, I am too old to learn to lie. As an honest man I have lived; as an honest man let me die." *So then he died.* Truly saith the poet, "An honest man's the noblest work of God."

A widow and her seven sons were brought before the king in person. He interrogated them separately, beginning with the eldest; and as each of them in succession refused to worship the king's idol, or to renounce the Law of God, Antiochus caused them, one after the other, to be put to death in the most horridly painful manner. The mother stood by; and as each victim was in turn called forth, she encouraged and strongly urged them to remain true to the God and Law of Israel. At length the mother and her youngest son, a mere child, were the sole survivors of that noble band of martyrs.

Even King Antiochus the madman began to relent. Spite of himself, he could not help admiring that firmness of principle and unyielding constancy which his victims had sealed with their hearts' best blood. He owned, with a sigh of regret, that such men, could they have been gained to his cause, would have proved the most trustworthy support of his throne. The beauty and innocence of the brave boy, who with undaunted eye had witnessed the cruel murder of his brothers, and who now with firm bearing confronted him, interested the king. He entered into a conversation with the boy, painting the charms of a life spent in the fulness of royal favour and its fruits, wealth, and honours, and contrasting them with the horrors of a death instant, untimely, and most painful. Antiochus used every argument, and held out every promise in vain: the youthful martyr was not to be seduced.

The king was vanquished: the desire to save this infant

hero became almost irresistible in the royal mind. But thousands were crowding round the king's tribunal, and watching this species of duel between the monarch of all Syria and a child. The royal dignity must not be compromised: some outward act of submission must vindicate the supreme authority. The king therefore proposed to the boy that he would grant him life and liberty on one condition—that he should not be required to worship the idol the king had erected, but that the king would drop his signet-ring from his hand on the ground, and that the boy should kneel and pick it up. This was an act of respect and courtesy due to his sovereign which the Law of Moses did not forbid, and which, therefore, could be performed without any scruple of conscience. But the boy perceived the drift of the subterfuge. The surrounding crowds, who could not hear what passed between the king and himself, but who could see whatever was done on the lofty platform on which he stood and the king was seated, would naturally look upon his kneeling or stooping as an act of prostration and of worship to the idol. He would then be execrated by his own people as a traitor to his brothers and an apostate from his God; and probably this act required of him, and apparently so simple, would eventually leave him no alternative but suicide or apostasy. He therefore refused compliance.

As a last means, the king had recourse to the intercession of the mother, and strongly urged her to preserve the life of one, at least, of her seven sons, by persuading him to comply with the king's wish, and to perform an act, innocent, and of no moment in itself, but which became of importance to the king's dignity. The mother, however, was not less firm in her faith than her children. In terms the most pathetic, she urged her only surviving son, her youngest and best beloved, to remain steadfast and faithful, that he might soon rejoin his brothers in heaven. They had again and again declared that the Supreme King of the world "would raise to everlasting life those who died for his Law." Joining in this declaration, and adding the prophetic menace that his and their tormentor "should have no resurrection to life, but would receive the just punishment of his pride through the judgment of God," the boy declared his determination to share the fate of his brothers. The king's patience was exhausted. His pity, baffled, turned into rage. At a given signal, the executioners rushed on their victim, and while his body became a prey to tortures the most revolting, his pure spirit returned to its Father in heaven. The mother followed him. But in her last moments she exultingly exclaimed, "Father Abraham, I have surpassed thee, for thou hast only raised one altar for the sacrifice of one son; whereas, I have raised seven altars for the sacrifice of seven sons." So THEN SHE DIED.

We must refer our readers to the 1st and 2d Book of Maccabees, and to Josephus, for further accounts of Antiochus's destructive presence in Jerusalem; and how, after his departure, his emissaries spread over the country, and ruthlessly enforced the king's decrees. Never before had the Jews been exposed to such extreme misery, for never before had they been persecuted on account of their religion. Every public act of worship was at an end; every private observance was certain destruction as soon as discovered. Apostates became numerous, but martyrs were still more numerous. For nearly six months the persecution throughout Judea was unrelenting. In every other portion of the Syro-Grecian empire the Jews were subjected to similar ill-usage, while the Ptolemean princes in Egypt began to second the fanatical spirit of their uncle, and to prohibit the practice of Judaism throughout their kingdom. Every Jew who refused to adopt the worship and customs of the Gentiles was to be put to death. (2 Macc. vi. 8, 9.)

Thus, on the verge of apostasy or extermination, the utter ruin of Jews and of Judaism seemed inevitable, when it pleased Divine Providence to save the remnant of the people; not indeed by a direct or miraculous interposition, as in the days of old, but by pouring forth the spirit of zeal and of patriotism, arousing in the minds of virtuous men that noble daring which urges them on to conquer or to die, and that true and generous valour which considers life of no value, unless devoted to the cause of God and of their fatherland. Such were the sentiments which induced the aged Mattathias to raise his sword against the oppressors of his people, and which prompted his five sons nobly to stake their lives in defence of their faith and country. As the Jews were the only people to whom, nationally, a positive religion had been revealed, the dogmas of which excluded all worship but that of God alone, while all around them pantheism and idolatry, with their ever-shifting mythology, prevailed, the Jews, among all nations or religious systems, were the first to make a stand in defence of their faith. Theirs was the glory of being first called upon to uphold the truth of their belief at the price of life, and to seal their conviction with their hearts' best blood.

But as they were the first martyrs persecuted for conscience' sake, so they were likewise the first champions in the cause of religious liberty. The Greeks who conquered at Marathon fought for national independence; the Romans who expelled proud Tarquin gained a triumph for civil liberty. But the handful of Jews who under Judah the Maccabee and his brothers drew the sword against the overwhelming power of Antiochus and his successors, made their stand for religious freedom and the rights of conscience. One by one these pious brothers fell, willing victims to their sacred and most important cause. But their noble blood was not poured out in vain. Civil and

religious liberty, peace, and the undisturbed worship of
God were the glorious rewards of their toils, their dangers, and their death. If Scotland glories in her Wallace;
if William Tell in Switzerland, and Gustavus Vasa in
Sweden, have merited the gratitude of their people and
the admiration of posterity; if, greater than all these,
the glorious name of George Washington, his heroic
struggles and genuine patriotism, enlist the sympathy and
command the veneration of every true friend of humanity,—that sympathy and veneration are, even on higher
grounds, due to Judah the Maccabee and his worthy brothers; for they were the great prototypes to him, and to
all who, in after ages, have merited the blessings of their
oppressed and injured fellow-men.

In Modin, a small town of Judea, on an eminence commanding a view of the sea, about one mile from Joppa,
(Jaffa,) lived an old man named Mattathias, the son of
Jochanon, the son of Simon, the son of Asamoneus,
from whom the family took its name. He was a priest
of the order or division Joarib, the first of the twenty-four orders appointed by David, (1 Chron. xxiv. 7,) descended from Phineas, the son of Eleazar, the elder
branch of the family of Aaron. This aged man was the
father of five stalwart sons, named Jochanon, Simon,
Judah, Eleazar, and Jonathan, all in the prime of life. He
often, before his sons, lamented the wretched state of
their people; and was accustomed to say that it was every
way preferable they should sacrifice their lives in defence
of their religion, their laws, and their country, than to
live disgraced as apostates and slaves.

The opportunity to vindicate his principles, and to
prove that they were those of his soul, not merely of his
lips, was soon afforded to him. Apelles, a royal officer,
arrived at Modin, with full power to enforce the edict of
conformity, and to abolish the religion and law of the

Jews. He first applied to Mattathias, the man whose priestly birth and high moral character gave him the first rank in the place, and the influence of whose example would most likely insure ready obedience to the decree of Antiochus. Promises and threats were in succession resorted to by Apelles in vain; for this true priest of the Lord repelled the proposal to worship the king's gods with indignation and abhorrence. Nobly replying, that though every other person submitted, he would rather die than forsake the Law of the great God of Israel, Mattathias, with a loud voice, and in the hearing of the assembled townsmen of Modin, proclaimed his refusal to sacrifice to idols, and exhorted his five sons to stand by him and to follow his example.

The altercation which ensued became aggravated by an apostate, who, to curry favour with the royal emissary, and to show his zeal in the royal cause, approached the altar which Apelles had erected, and, in the presence of his indignant countrymen, prepared to offer sacrifice to the idols whose worship the king's decree commanded. Mattathias, hurried on by an irresistible feeling that "it was time to be doing for the Lord," leaped forward, and, with his own hand, struck down the apostate rebel against the God of Jacob. This was the earnest-blood of the great war which followed. Kindled by his own act, and fired by his example, he, his sons, and the men of Modin rushed on the royal commissioner. In the *melée* that ensued, Apelles and his retinue were slain, and the idolatrous altar was torn down.[40]

---

[40] This is the historical account of the rising as given in the first book of Maccabees, (ii. 15,) and in Josephus. (Ant. lib. xii. cap. 8.) Tradition, as preserved in the morning service of the Sabbath, Hhanuka, speaks of a *jus primæ noeti* that the Syrians enforced against Jewish brides as the occasion of the rising; and though it strangely mixes up the history of Judith with that of the Maccabees, there is reason to believe that its

Alive to the consequences of his deed, Mattathias proclaimed through the town, "Whosoever is zealous for the Law and maintenance of the covenant, let him follow me;" and then, with his sons and four adherents, withdrew into the mountains of Judea. But though this band of pious and patriotic outlaws did not number more than ten, their bold purpose of resistance quickly spread throughout the land; and as soon as the banner of their faith was raised, numbers of God-fearing Israelites hastened to rally around it. Success attended their undertakings, which were conducted with equal enterprise and discretion. For a time, Mattathias and his followers carried on a kind of guerilla warfare, which the nature of the country and the good-will of the people greatly

---

narrative may not be altogether destitute of foundation, as it is in a degree confirmed by a work of some authority which forms part of the first volume of the Beth-ha-Midrash, a collection of miscellaneous pieces of ancient Hebrew literature, lately published by A. Jellineck, of Leipsig, some of which have never before been printed. The most interesting of the pieces thus for the first time, brought to press is the Mid. Hhanuka, copied from an ancient and very scarce Codex, in the possession of the City Senatorial Library, at Leipsig. It contains many curious and important particulars relating to the wars of the Maccabees, and explains many circumstances not sufficiently clear in the Apocrypha and Josephus. From the narrative of these two authorities it departs, in so far as it ascribes the first rising of Mattathias and his sons, not merely to the indignation the old man felt at the sight of an apostate offering to idols, but to an outrage offered to a young virgin, betrothed to one of the sons of Mattathias; that Hannah, the daugther of Jochanon, a most beautiful maiden, was about being married to Eleazar, a son of Mattathias; when on their wedding-day (the 17th of the 6th month, Elul) a Syro-Grecian officer attempted to violate her person, but was prevented by Eleazar, the bridegroom, who cut him down on the spot; and that this was the first act of resistance that inaugurated the long war—a circumstance which shows to what extent of outrage and oppression the Syro-Grecian dominion in Judea was carried, and the more to be noticed as neither the Apocrypha nor Josephus speak of any *such* indignities as offered to the Jews.

favoured. As opportunity offered, the champions of the Law sallied forth from the mountain fastnesses in which they had lain hidden, attacked the Syrian garrisons, entered the towns, destroyed the heathen altars, performed circumcision, re-established public worship, and drove off such of the king's officers as were appointed to enforce idolatry.

These conscientious warriors and their adherents—in order the more strikingly to evince their opposition to the loose principles of those who, by adopting Grecian views and neglecting the Law of God, had brought all this misery on their people—carried out all the obligations of the Law in the most rigid and literal manner. Hence, they held it to be imperative to abstain from the use of arms on the Sabbath-day. The Syrians, and the apostates who had joined them, were not slow in discovering and taking advantage of this scrupulous observance of the Sabbath. A thousand persons, who had taken refuge in a cave near Jerusalem, were attacked on that day, and allowed themselves to be slaughtered without the least resistance.

This fatal event, while it spread the utmost grief and consternation among the pious and devoted followers of Mattathias, led him seriously to reflect on what was his duty in this important respect. While reading the Scriptures, his attention rested on the words of the Law, (Leviticus xviii. 5:) "Ye shall keep my statutes and my ordinances, which man shall do, that he may live by them. I am the Lord." This, it struck him, plainly meant that life, not death, was the result to be attained by the observance of the statutes and ordinances of the Law; and that, therefore, to perish unresistingly by the murderous hand of exulting idolaters, who, even while they slaughtered the wretched Jew, blasphemed his God, and ridiculed his Law which exposed him to so horrid a fate, could not be in conformity with the spirit, and even with the letter, of the Law of life. Accordingly, after mature deliberation, Mattathias and his council decided that it was not only lawful for the Jews, but that it was their absolute duty, to stand on their defence on the Sabbath-day, though they still held themselves bound to abstain from voluntarily becoming the assailants on that sacred day of rest. He and his followers used every means to make this decision known throughout the land; and, as his authority was universally respected, with such success, that henceforth no further scruples were entertained on the subject of self-defence on the Sabbath-day.

This wise decision, and the continued success which attended all his enterprises, caused the party of Mattathias steadily to increase, until he saw himself at the head of a considerable body of men who were prepared to hazard every thing in defence of their religion. But his advanced age could not endure the fatigue of his new and hazardous mode of life ; for, like the Chouans (*chat huans*, night owls) of Brittany, during the French Revolution, night was the main season of his warfare, when he suddenly made his inroads into the habitable country, and as suddenly disappeared, after causing great loss and injury to the Syrians and their adherents, the apostates. And though his band was yet too feeble to maintain possession of the places he surprised, the terror of his name and arms, and the rigid retribution he inflicted on those who tortured and slaughtered faithful Jews, became a protection to the latter, not only in the districts directly adjoining his mountain strongholds, but throughout a great part of Judea, which laid open to his inroads.

During the greater part of one year, his zeal and wisdom made up for the infirmities of old age and the decay of bodily strength. But at length his worn-out frame sunk under his labours ; and feeling the approach of death,

Mattathias, like the patriarch of old, summoned his sons around him, and gave them his last blessing and directions. Strongly exhorting them to continue the work he had so well begun, he appointed his third son, Judah, the bravest among the brave, to be their military leader, associating with him his second and most prudent son, Simon, as chief counsellor. With the fervent hope of pious patriotism, he prayed for and predicted the success of his and their cause, which indeed was the cause of God, of conscience, and of freedom. His parting injunction—"And ye, my dear sons, be ye valiant zealots for the Law, and give your lives for it"—was strictly obeyed by every one of the five; while these same words in after ages found a powerful response in the breasts of thousands of Jews.

Thus this heroic father of heroes, this true descendant of Phineas, who in his generation had been "zealous for his God," (Numbers xxv. 13,) after having devoted his last breath to God and fatherland, died amid the tears and blessings of his people. And so highly and justly is his memory still revered by that people, that in the thanksgiving and prayer which each year perpetuates the deliverance of Israel from the cruel fanaticism of Antiochus, the name specially mentioned is not that of Judah, the youthful chief who victoriously carried on what his father had begun, but that of the aged Mattathias;[41] for his noble and pious zeal gave the first impulse to that long, glorious, and holy war, the extraordinary result of which was, that a small province, the scanty population of which was even divided against itself, without any foreign assistance, and by its own firm and unyielding determi-

---

[41] In this thanksgiving Mattathias is styled Cohen-Gadol, "high-priest," and as such he probably was regarded by his adherents, who must have refused to recognise the usurper and apostate, Menelaus. But there is no proof that Mattathias ever held the dignity of high-priest in the temple at Jerusalem.

nation, triumphed over a great and powerful monarchy. From the first blow struck by Mattathias at Modin, this sacred struggle for the rights of conscience and the freedom of opinion continued twenty-six years (from 168–142 B. C. E.) under five Syrian kings; and after destroying above two hundred thousand of the best troops belonging to those princes, it terminated in the independent government of the grandson of Mattathias, the heir of his valour and zeal, and whose descendants, the Asmoneans, as high-priests and sovereigns, reigned in Judea above a century.

Hales (Analysis, ii. 551) remarks, that "such a triumph of a petty province over a great empire is hardly to be paralleled in the annals of history." But to us it appears that the qualifying term *hardly* is altogether uncalled for. The two most remarkable triumphs, after years of protracted warfare, of "petty provinces over mighty empires," recorded in history, are that of the United Dutch Provinces over Spain, and of the North American colonies over Great Britain; and these two instances of success are, in some respects, not unlike the struggle of the Jews against Antiochus and his successors. In each case, the conflict was one of right against might. Religious liberty in Holland, civil rights in America, were the great principles at stake. In either case there was no comparison between the power and resources of the contending parties; so that, when the sword was first drawn, the cause of right and freedom appeared utterly hopeless, and its defenders were scouted as desperate and lawless rebels. But beyond this, and the final success with which Providence in its mercy crowned the better cause, the resemblance between Judea's triumph and the other two ceases.

The United Dutch Provinces, during their long struggle against Spain, had powerful allies. Queen Elizabeth of England, and the English people, Henry the Fourth of

France, and the French Huguenots, the Protestant princes and people of Germany, afforded aid and assistance. Even Cardinal Richelieu, and the house of Braganza in Portugal, indirectly promoted the success of the Dutch; while their great wealth, the fruits of a commerce at that time the most widely extended and lucrative in the world, enabled them to enlist in their cause and service veteran mercenaries from every part of Europe, so that eventually their armies were fully as numerous as those of Spain.

The American colonies, likewise, were not left to encounter the might of Great Britain without foreign aid. France, Spain, and Holland armed in their behalf. Russia, and the northern powers, were also favourable to their cause. In their hatred and jealousy of the rising power of England, the despots of Europe, the sovereigns of the Bastile and of the Inquisition, strained every nerve to fight the battles of freedom in America; while some of the most generous and heroic spirits of the old countries, hastened to draw their swords and to shed their blood in the righteous cause of the New World.

But the Jews had no such auxiliaries. Alone and reluctantly they entered on the conflict. Without human aid they carried it on. No ally embraced their quarrel; no foreign sword was drawn in their defence. A mere handful of men, they began the war: in several of their glorious fields they were outnumbered in the proportion of ten to one; and the disproportion between them and their enemies was seldom less than three or two to one. When, therefore, they triumphed, they freely and thankfully raised their eyes to heaven, for God alone had been their help. And when in their annual thanksgiving they declare that it was God alone who, "in his abundant mercy, had stood by them in their distress, had judged their cause, had vindicated their right, and avenged their injuries," and that he, blessed be his holy name! had "given up the strong to the weak, the many to the few, the tyrant and oppressor to the God-fearing defenders of his Law,"—when, annually, they make this declaration, they state that which is strictly and literally true. And therefore this triumph of a "petty province over a great empire," is NOT PARALLELED ANYWHERE in the annals of history.

While the virtuous Mattathias breathed his last, and his sons prepared to continue his efforts, King Antiochus, finding no one specially worthy of his notice either to torture or to convert in Jerusalem, had returned to his luxurious palace at Antioch. And as the nascent insurrection in Judea did not reach the capital of the province, while the statue of Jupiter still continued to desecrate the temple and altar on Zion's holy mount, the king reserved the mutinous proceedings of Mattathias and his adherents for matter of future vengeance. For the present, and in order to celebrate the success of his decree and the triumph of his gods, the king, with his court, his generals, and almost every distinguished individual in the state or army, were preparing for a solemnity at Daphné, near Antioch, that was to eclipse the games recently celebrated by the Roman proconsul Paulus Emilius at Amphipolis, and even to surpass the still greater splendour exhibited at Alexandria during the coronation festival of Ptolemy II. Philadelphus. It must, however, be remembered, that the magnificence displayed by the Roman was a triumph over conquered Macedon; and the solemnities with which the first Ptolemy delighted his people on associating his son to the government, (283 B. C. E.,) showed the still nobler triumph of skilful industry and bold commercial enterprise; whereas the gold, the gems, the spices and perfumes, the embroidered textures of curious fabric, the innumerable paintings and statues so ostentatiously exhibited by Antiochus, were the merciless extortions of rapine aggravated by sacrilege. But such was the fondness of the Greeks for public solemnities and gymnastic exercises, that "sacred embassies," as they were called, came from nearly three hundred cities to join in the religious games, and to bring the accustomed offerings. (Polyb. lib. xxxi. cap. 3, et seq.)

The festivities lasted thirty days, during which time the strange follies of King Antiochus were not the least singular and, to some, amusing part of the spectale. Himself vilely mounted, he would with mock humility, conduct the splendid cavalcades of Nisæan horses, and the pompous procession of Indian elephants, sometimes hurrying on their progress, and again as capriciously retarding it. "At the banquet, which daily succeeded the religious procession and military reviews, he would run jesting from lodge to lodge, show the guests to their seats, snatch a mouthful from one table, drink hastily at another, and at length conclude with playing the fool among the hired buffoons and mimics, to the scandal and disgust of all who saw him." (Gillies, viii. 13.)

Such were the extravagancies exhibited by Antiochus at Daphné, such the riotous debaucheries in which he squandered a great portion of the treasures he had stolen at Jerusalem. Judah, the son of Mattathias, was differently employed. Succeeding to the designs of his aged father, he carried them on with youthful ardour. And as every fresh success increased the number of his followers, his troop gradually became a little army, numbering six thousand men. These he tried in many gallant adventures, till he could place full reliance in their steadiness. He then went a step further than his father. The cities he surprised he kept possession of, fortifying them, and providing them with trustworthy garrisons, that they might serve as places of refuge to his persecuted brethren. Apollonius, governor of Judea-Samaria, the recent plunderer of Jerusalem and murderer of its inhabitants, thought it high time to take the field to crush the rebels at one blow. He raised a large army, chiefly consisting of Samaritans and Jewish renegades, with which he marched against Judah, who, nowise terrified by the numerical superiority of his enemies, did not decline the battle. Coming forth with his handful of men, Judah attacked and totally defeated Apollonius, who himself was slain, (according to the Midrash, in a hand-to-hand combat with Judah himself,) and his sword became a trophy which ever after the gallant victor used in battle. The camp of the Syrian army, with all the rich spoil it contained, fell into the hands of Judah, many of whose men, who were but indifferently armed before the battle, thus obtained the means of getting properly accoutred.

The first battle in the open field had been fought and won; the first glorious victory in the good cause had, with the help of God, been achieved by Judah the Maccabee. The etymology of this surname is very uncertain. Among the various opinions adduced on the subject, the one most generally received is, that this word is formed by the four initial letters of the text, "Who is like unto thee among the gods, O, Lord," (Ex. xv. ii.,) in Hebrew, *Mi camoca ba-elim Adonai,* which were inscribed on Judah's banner. According to some, however—who from 1 Macc. ii. 4, maintain that Judah wore this name long before he had raised any standard against the enemies of his people— the word is derived from *makab,* hammer; and Judah, from his great personal strength and the weight of his blows, was called Maccabee, as the Carlovingian chief, Charles, from the same reason, was called *Martel,* "the hammerer." Certain it is, that Judah bore this designation by way of eminence; and among his own people, the Jews, he is the only one who had that honour.

Among Gentile writers, the name passed from him first

to his brothers and successors, then to his adherents, and to all who took up arms or who died as martyrs[42] during the persecution by Antiochus; and lastly, that name has been extended to the books which contain the history and legends of those wars and persecutions as far back as Ptolemy Philopator. But whether the surname be intended to give to God on high the glory, which is the opinion that has in its favour the authority of tradition, or whether it was only intended to describe the personal qualities of him who had been appointed to vindicate the glory of God and the freedom of Israel against the blasphemy of impious renegades and the tyranny of cruel heathens, he who bore the surname of the Maccabee had to make good his right to that designation in many a stricken field.

Seron, the lieutenant, in the government of Cœle-Syria, of Antiochus's favourite, Ptolemy Macron, aroused by the tidings of Apollonius's defeat, raised a force still larger than that which had been routed, and marched in search of Judah, who shrunk not from the proffered battle. The hostile armies unexpectedly met on the rocks of Bethoron, between Jerusalem and Shechem. According to their usual custom before engaging, Judah and his men had kept a fast; and, faint with fasting and marching, the handful of Jews felt reluctant to engage, and despaired of success when they contrasted their own weakness with the strength of Seron's large host. But the magnanimous Judah soon dispelled their fears, by reminding them of the generous declaration of Jonathan, the son of Saul, on a similar perilous occasion: "There is nothing can prevent the Lord from giving help, whether there be many or few," (1 Sam. xiv. 6;) and concluding with the soul-stirring appeal, "We fight for our lives and our laws," he encouraged his small troop

---

[42] The widow who, with her seven sons, so piously died for the Law of God, is generally called "the mother of the Maccabees," though there is no reason for supposing that she belonged to the family of Mattathias.

boldly to confront the oppressors of their people. On the descent from Bethoron, Judah suddenly "leaped" (1 Macc. iii. 23) on the enemy, whose long array was painfully toiling up the steep ascent. Seron fell at the first onset; and his army, confused and without a competent leader, was routed with dreadful slaughter.

The second great victory was thus gained; yet Judah, not less prudent than bold, did not overrate the real value of his achievements. It is true that two armies, each many times more numerous than the small force which he led, had been routed; but it was also true that these armies were composed of effeminate and unwarlike provincials, without discipline, without experience, and, as compared to his own men, without zeal or courage. Their numbers, instead of adding to their efficiency in the field, had only swelled the multitudes of slain during their flight. Judah felt that to his own troops, and still more to his brethren, the Judeans, these extraordinary and little-expected victories must appear as achieved by the direct and wondrous interposition of the Most High, and that the moral effect must be to raise their confidence and valour to the highest degree.

But would their valour be equal to a conflict with the regular armies of Syria? Would their confidence be proof against the terror which could not fail to attend the disciplined skill and trained valour of veteran mercenaries, led on by the most experienced generals of a warlike monarch? These were questions that forced themselves upon his mind, and which were urged upon him by his cool and prudent brother Simon. They admitted of but one reply. If, as Judah felt and believed, it was the help of God, and not their own strength, which had achieved these victories, that help was as fully able to grant a triumph over the veteran phalanx of disciplined Greeks, as over the tumultuous band of effeminate Syrians. All that he (Judah) could do was to trust to God, to pray to him, to obey, strictly and literally, the precepts of the Law, and to devote himself, body and soul, to his sacred cause, without allowing worldly ambition or selfish motives of any kind to mislead his mind. His followers were to a great extent inspired by his lofty faith, and shared his pious hopes. Like him, they felt that obedience to God's law was their best shield. The more ardent among them assumed the designation *Hassidim*, "the pious," while the apostate Grecianizing Jews were called *Abaryanim*, "transgressors"—party-names founded in fact, and which, for a length of time, made their influence felt in Judea.

Antiochus, informed that the Jews, a people hitherto oppressed with impunity, had at length been goaded into successful resistance, determined to take signal vengeance on these *rebels*. But along with the tidings of Judah's exploits, came alarming intelligence from the northern and eastern parts of the empire, where the rapacity of the king's overseers and missionaries had excited such general discontent, that many provinces had determined to withhold their contributions. This, to Antiochus, was a matter of far greater importance than disturbances raised by a handful of Jews in the small province of Palestine; for his nephew Demetrius, the rightful heir to the crown of Syria, was still detained as a hostage in Rome. By servile flattery to the Roman commonwealth, and still more by immense bribes to the commissioners whom Rome from time to time sent into the East, Antiochus had been permitted to reign. But he could hope to retain the crown, and to transmit it to his son, only by the same means that hitherto had kept him in possession. Money, therefore, was to him the most important consideration. Accordingly, upon the emergency that now presented itself, the king determined to move in person into Upper Asia with part of the forces he had recently passed in review at Daphné. And as the expedition would cause him to be absent for some years, he named Lysias, "a nobleman, and one of the blood-royal," regent of all the western provinces, from the Euphrates to Egypt; Antiochus at the same time appointing him guardian to his son, a boy seven years old. His parting commands were that Lysias should march an army into Judea, exterminate the Jews, and plant a foreign colony in their stead. (166 B. C. E.)

Quite resolved to carry out the king's orders to their full and fell intent, Lysias, after concerting with Ptolemy Macron, governor of Cœle-Syria, diligently collected his forces, so that, early next year, he was able to march forty thousand foot into Judea, under Nicanor and Gorgias, generals of approved merit. They encamped at Emmaus, in the heart of the devoted province, where seven thousand horse joined them. And so confident were they of victory, that Nicanor proclaimed beforehand a sale of captive Jews, ninety for a talent—about eleven dollars a head —for the benefit of his Syrian majesty's exchequer. This drew crowds of slave-merchants to the camp, each loaded with ample means to profit by the good bargain thus offered, and attended by a great number of servants, with chains and other *necessaries* to carry off the human cattle.

Kitto (History of Palestine, 688) remarks that this was *not* a peculiar circumstance, and refers to Polybius as his authority that it was then usual for the march of armies to be attended by slave-merchants. This, however, we opine, does not contradict, but on the contrary confirms, the fact that the great public auction announced by Nicanor, and the consequent gathering of purchasers, were *indeed peculiar and unusual circumstances*, as otherwise Nicanor would not have deemed it neccessary to "cause proclamation to be made in all the cities and seaports round about." (1 Macc. iii. 41.) Nor does Polybius, or any other historian of that period, give any instance of a similar auction announced before battle, as was now done by Nicanor, in order that he might lose no time, but at once carry out the king's order, to root out the Jews and to locate another race in their land.

The Maccabee heard of this unusual gathering in the enemy's camp, and knew what it portended, but did not lose heart or faith. The small troop under his command took post at Mizpeh, a mountain of extensive prospect that overlooked the tents of the Syrians, and which had been a place of great religious and public importance to the house of Israel in former days. Long before David had conquered Jerusalem, or Solomon consecrated the temple-mount, the people had assembled at Mizpeh. There the war against the tribe of Benjamin was resolved and declared, (Judg. xxv. 1;) there the prophet Samuel had erected the *Eben-ha-ezer*, "the rock of help," when the Lord gave victory over the Philistines; there the same prophet had proclaimed Saul the first king in Israel; and many other historical events had taken place at Mizpeh. (1 Sam. passim.) Here, then, Judah and his people—shut out from Jerusalem and the temple, once holy, but now defiled—assembled. Like their fathers in the days of Samuel, they fasted and prayed, (1 Sam. vii. 6;) while Judah, in strict conformity to the commands of the Law, (Deut. xx. 5–8,) caused proclamation to be made that every man who, in the course of the passing year, had built a house, planted a vineyard, or betrothed a wife, and all those that were afraid, should enjoy full liberty to withdraw from his standard.

Many availed themselves of the permission; so that, by this strong act of faith, his little army was reduced from six thousand to three thousand men—less than one-tenth of the host opposed to them. But those three thousand Hassidim, strong in their trust to God, felt no fear. At worst, they could but die, and how glorious to die in such a cause! But death was not the only and inevitable prospect before them, as Judah took care to remind them. Their God was all-mighty, as well as all-merciful. The host of Sennacherib had been countless, yet it was overwhelmed in one single night. Nay, in times immediately preceding their own, eight thousand Jews had defeated one hundred and twenty thousand Gauls in the great battle of Babylon. (2 Macc. xiii. 20.) If, therefore, it pleased God to help them, as hitherto he had done, Nicanor and Gorgias would fall before them, even as Apollonius and Seron had already fallen.

The Syrian generals had sent out scouts, who soon discovered and reported that half of Judah's encampment was empty, and his army reduced to a mere handful. Hearing this, the two generals deemed it superfluous to employ the whole of their large force against so small a body. Gorgias, therefore, with a chosen band of five thousand foot and one thousand horse, marched out to surprise and attack Judah by night, and to intercept his retreat to his mountain strongholds. But diligently as Nicanor and Gorgias were served by the well-paid zeal of hired spies, Judah was still better served by the faithful attachment of his devoted people. No sooner had Gorgias begun his march, than Judah was made acquainted with the movement. That vigilant leader at once penetrated into the design of the enemy, and prepared to counteract it, by taking advantage of the separation of the two commanders. With the utmost celerity and silence he marched forth early in the evening, and fell upon the camp of Nicanor by night.

That general, in full reliance on the forward movement of his colleague, apprehended no danger, and had taken no measures to guard against a surprise. In the midst of his fancied security he was aroused from his sleep by the war-cry of the Jews. He beheld his whole camp in confusion, and his soldiers panic-stricken and routed beyond the possibility of being rallied, so that he himself was hurried along by their flight. The victory of the Jews was complete; some thousands of the enemy were slain; many soldiers and slave-merchants were made prisoners. The camp, with all the wealth that it contained, fell into the power of the victors. During the first confusion of the attack, some tents had been set on fire; but Judah forbade either to extinguish the flames or to plunder the camp, because the detachment of Gorgias had still to be encountered and defeated.

That general had, in the night, reached the post recently occupied by the Jews, and on finding it deserted, he exclaimed, with scorn, "The banditti have fled to the mountains." But Nicanor's flaming tents soon undeceived him; and, before he could decide on his line of retreat, the glad trumpets of the priestly Maccabee announced the impending attack. At the first sight of Judah's victorious standard, Gorgias's detachment, the choicest troops in the hostile army, fled precipitately. The Jews pursued: in the two routs (for they cannot be called battles) nine thousand Syrians fell. Gorgias took refuge within the fortress of Jerusalem; Nicanor reached Antioch disguised as a slave, and justified his want of success by declaring to the regent Lysias that "the God who fought for the Jews was indeed mighty, and that it was worse than useless to attack them." (1 Macc. iv.)

Upon returning from the pursuit, Judah and his men took possession of the Syrian camp, in which they found not only great quantities of provisions and valuable merchandise, but also the large sums of money brought by the slave-merchants who had come to buy, and whose fate it was to be sold; for as many of them as fell into the hands of the victors were, with just retribution, sold for slaves.

This signal victory was gained on a Friday. On commencing his perilous march to the enemy's camp, the watchword given by the Maccabean chief was, THE HELP OF GOD! By means of that help, the Jews had achieved a great triumph almost without loss; and as the day of rest commenced, it found them reposing after their glorious toil, enjoying the wealth of their tyrants, and ready, without let or molestation, to "keep holy the sabbath-day;" to "remember" and to "observe" which, those self-same tyrants had forbidden under penalty of death. But now, in their camp, in their very tents, the Jews kept the Sabbath; and the persecutors, the tormentors, whose duty and pleasure it was to prevent that observance, where were they? Thus was the help of God most signally manifested; and with devout thanksgiving to their great Protector, the Jews celebrated the Sabbath. And they had cause, for their victory proved doubly advantageous to their future progress. It furnished the Maccabee with quantities of arms and ammunition for his men; and the fame of his success drew to his standard numbers of his people, who, from all the places of their dispersion, hastened to join him. As there was no hostile force capable of keeping the field against him, he became actual master of the greatest part of Judea. And though he was not yet in a condition to batter down the walls of the heathen fortress at Jerusalem, his activity in the smaller towns and in the open country was incessant. Everywhere the idols were thrown down, and their worshippers expelled.

The clamours of these wicked fugitives induced Timotheus, governor of the country beyond Jordan, and Bacchides, a Syrian general of great military skill and experience, to march against Judah with a numerous army. But the help that had hitherto been extended to the Maccabee was not withheld from him. In a pitched battle, Timotheus and his associates were defeated with immense loss.

Twenty thousand stand of arms, vast stores of provisions, and great wealth fell into the hands of Judah, whose beneficence rejoiced over the means which victory placed at his disposal, and whose generosity in the distribution of the spoil even outstripped the rule laid down by David. (1 Sam. xxx. 24.) For, while by that rule those only were entitled to share who had actually fought, or been left in charge of the baggage, Judah caused a considerable portion to be distributed among his indigent brethren; so that the old and lame, the sick and decrepit, the widow and orphan, were made partakers of the fruits of his victory, and had ample cause to give thanks to God, and to bless his champion.

In the midst of the fierce passions which ruled the ascendant in this struggle between the Jews and their foes, it is pleasing to meet with such traits of charity and humane feeling, especially as humanity was by no means the order of the day. On the contrary, the usage the Jews had received and were still receiving had exasperated them to the utmost; the merciless conduct of their oppressors met with retribution as merciless. The legend of the times, which loves to trace the finger of Providence in the triumph of the Jews, relates with visible satisfaction, the avenging justice which overtook the cruel tools of Antiochus. In the battle which Timotheus lost, Philarchus, one of his chief officers, and a bitter tormentor of the Jews, was slain. Callisthenes, another officer, who had first set fire to the gates of the temple in Jerusalem, escaped, and concealed himself in a hut not far from the battle-field. Here he was discovered, and a detachment of Hassidim set fire to the hut and burnt him in it; "a just punishment for his sacrilege," says the legend. (2 Macc. viii. 30, et seq.)

These tidings of repeated disasters, the route of the army he had sent into Judea, and the confession of Nicanor that the Jews were invincible, aroused Lysias, but did not dishearten him. He made haste to assemble the forces he could best rely on, and at the head of sixty thousand foot and five thousand horse, he marched forth in person, fully determined to avenge the disgrace and disasters the Syrian army had suffered, and to extinguish the rebellion of the Jews in the blood of the rebels. Advancing through Idumea,[43] he encamped before Bethzura, a strong frontier fortress, originally built by Rehoboam, King of Judah, (2 Chron. xi. 7,) and now held by a garrison of the Maccabee's troops.

Here Lysias was encountered by Judah, at the head of ten thousand Jews, a larger number than any that hitherto had followed his standard. The two armies soon engaged; and when night put an end to the battle, Judah had gained decisive advantages. For though the Syrians had lost no more than five thousand men, yet observing that the Jews fought like men who were determined "to conquer or die," while his own troops appeared heartless and discouraged, Lysias did not deem it prudent to renew the engagement, but retreated from Judea and returned to Antioch. There he made preparations for a campaign on a grander scale for the next year, drawing together the veteran bodies garrisoned in the strongholds of Syria, and

---

[43] This name must be understood as distinguishing the more modern territory of the Edomites from their original and more southern home of Edom, in Mount Seir—the wide and stony deserts between the Red Sea and the Lake Asphaltites which, in the days of Judah the Maccabee, were held by the Nabatheans. This new country of the Idumeans laid west and south-west of the lake, and had originally formed the inheritance of the tribe of Simon and of part of the tribe of Judah. During the Babylonish captivity, the lands of these tribes long lay desolate, but were finally occupied by the most industrious portion of the Edomites, who made Hebron their capital, and rebuilt Bethzura. Subsequently, the country was conquered by John Hyrcanus, and reunited with the kingdom of Judea.

causing vast levies to be raised even in the remotest provinces under his government.

The writers in the "Universal History" consider this victory as the one most difficult to account for among the many gained by the Maccabee, as it seems to them incomprehensible that Lysias, at the head of seventy thousand men, and attacked by ten thousand only, should, after a loss so small in comparison to his numbers as five thousand men, become so disheartened as to retreat and abandon the entire province of Judea to the rebels he came to exterminate. These writers (vol. x. p. 282) are of opinion, that "if the Jewish authors have not exaggerated the number of their enemies, we may very well suppose they have their character; and by their defeat, and their generals so suddenly retreating from Judea, it may be reasonably concluded that his army, instead of consisting of such choice horse and foot, was only an undisciplined multitude gathered up in haste, and easily scared at the sight of so brave and resolute an enemy."

To us this opinion appears hasty, and not warranted by the facts. It is not likely that Lysias, warned by previous defeats, and taking the field in person, would trust his life and reputation to an "undisciplined multitude," when he, as regent and supreme commander, could take his choice of the best troops of Syria. But while we believe that the army of Lysias was what the Jewish writers describe it to have been, "all of the choicest troops he could get," we admit that a wide line must be drawn between the *morale* of Judah's men and those of Lysias. The former, uninterruptedly victorious in successive battles against immense odds, replete with religious enthusiasm and the conviction that God himself fought for them, and animated by the strongest motives that could urge them on to defy death and to fight for victory. On the other hand, the Syrians, called to the field without any of the powerful and exciting sentiments that stimulated the Jews, discouraged, probably, by the report of previous defeats, and still more by the declaration of Nicanor, an experienced and renowned warrior, that "the Jews were invincible," and, therefore, notwithstanding their superior numbers, reluctant to attack, and standing on the defensive.

It is no wonder that Lysias and the generals that were with him, on contrasting the ardour of the Jews with the backwardness of their own men, and seeing the difficulty and loss with which the first attack of the Jews had been repelled, deemed it advisable to break off the battle, and to retreat from the field while it was yet in their power to do so with their forces unbroken; and it was only the superior generalship of Judah, and the extreme bravery of his men, that, pressing on their retreat, compelled them to abandon their camp with all its operose magnificence; which, however cumbersome to the late owners, was of high importance to the Jews, since it enabled them to execute a design which they formed immediately after this decisive victory. And this difference in the *morale* and spirit of the two armies must not be taken as a proof that the army of Lysias was cowardly and undisciplined, since the experience of all ages proves that even veteran troops of high discipline and bravery, are not able to resist that conscious feeling of inferiority which repeated discomfitures are sure to cause, while repeated success begets a corresponding feeling of superiority, such as appears to have animated the Jews.

The retreat of Lysias left Judah undisputed master of the whole province of Judea, with the sole exception of *Acra*, the heathen fortress at Jerusalem; and he now determined to carry out one of the objects which he and his adherents had most dearly at heart—namely, to cleanse the temple of Jerusalem from the defilement of idolatry, and to restore the worship of the God of Israel, the Lord of the universe. Amid the privations in their mountain retreats, and the dangers of their precarious guerilla warfare, the hope of seeing the temple restored to its purity and glory had still animated Judah and his Hassidim. Their efforts had been crowned with success; victors in every well-contested field, they now entered Jerusalem. They found the gates of the temple burnt and the sanctuary dilapidated. In the deserted and neglected courts of the Lord's house shrubs were growing, "as in the forest or on the mountain."

When Judah and his host beheld the desolation of that holy place, they all rent their garments, cast ashes on their heads, and cried toward heaven. But their active zeal did not permit them long to waste their time in idle lamentations. With tearful eyes, but heartfelt gratitude, the Maccabeans set about their task of repairing, cleansing, and consecrating the sacred buildings. To guard the city from surprise, and the work from interruption, Judah stationed his bravest troops in the various avenues; and then appointed those Cohanim (priests) who were most respected for their zeal and sanctity, to enter the temple, and to clear it of all its profane and defiling lumber; while the rest of the people were at work in the outer courts and throughout the city. The old desecrated utensils, especially the altar of burnt offerings, were broken up and buried; a new altar, made of unhewn stones, was erected; the table of shew-bread, the candlestick, and the altar of incense, were made anew of pure gold, out of the spoils of their enemies, and replaced in the sanctuary. The work of restoration was carried on with such ardour, that the inauguration of the temple could take place, and the public worship could again be performed, on the 25th of Kisleu, the self-same day on which, three years before, Antiochus had caused the worship to cease, and had defiled the temple by dedicating it to Jupiter Olympus.

This anniversary of a profanation predicted centuries before as the "abomination of desolation," (Dan. xi. 31,) but from which the Lord had now vouchsafed, with "a strong hand and outstretched arm," to cleanse his altar and his sanctuary, so that the day had indeed been changed "from sorrow to joy, from mourning into feasting,"—this anniversary, now so glorious, was ushered in with all imaginable solemnity. At the earliest dawn, the priests' trumpets were sounded; a new fire was kindled by the striking of two firestones, and as soon as the flames ascended to heaven, the lamb of the daily sacrifice was offered; the lamps were lighted, the usual portion of incense was burned, and every other part of the divine service performed according to the Law of Moses; and from that day it was not again discontinued until the last siege of Jerusalem by Titus.

The Talmud (tr. Sabbath, chap. ii.) relates, that when every preparation for the inauguration was completed, no consecrated oil could be found for the sacred lights; and the scrupulous Maccabee feared to contaminate the purity of the restored utensils by using oil desecrated by idolaters. In this strait, a small jar of oil, with the seal of a former high-priest still intact on the cover, happened to be found; and though the quantity of oil which it contained was barely sufficient once to light the sacred lamps, yet, by a special blessing, it proved sufficient for the consumption of a whole week, during which period new oil was obtained and consecrated. The festival of inauguration which the Maccabees celebrated in Jerusalem lasted eight days.

Josephus (Ant. lib. xii. cap. 11) informs us, that during all this time the front of the temple was adorned with crowns, garlands, escutcheons, and other ornaments of the best gold. Every house was illuminated; and to perpetuate the signal deliverance and blessing which the Lord had vouchsafed to extend unto his people, an annual festival of the like duration was instituted, which to this day is kept up by the house of Israel in every part of the world. During the eight days of this commemoration, called Hhanuka, "dedication," lights are kindled, and special prayers are offered, giving thanks unto the Lord, for that he nerved the arms of his servants, and saved his people from extermination and apostasy.

BOOK II.

THE MACCABEES.

CHAPTER V.

Death of A. Epiphanes—Polybius, the historian—Antiochus V. Eupator—Death of P. Macron—Judah's campaigns—Truce, and renewed hostilities—First siege of Acra—Death of Eleazar the Maccabean—Siege of Jerusalem—Lysias and Philip—Peace—Judah appointed governor for the king—Death of Menelaus—Alcimus.—(From 165 to 161 B. C. E.)

WITH the reopening of the temple at Jerusalem, and the public observance of the Jewish religion throughout the land, the actual rule of the Syro-Grecian kings over Judea may be said to have terminated. For though the war between the province of Judea and the empire of Syria continued many years longer, though the successors of Antiochus always claimed, and often exercised, supreme power and sovereignty over Palestine, and the Jews themselves did not proclaim their independence till nearly a quarter of a century later, yet, from the moment Judah the Maccabee took possession of Jerusalem, he, and after him his brothers, became *de facto* rulers of the land. He and they were at the head of the armed force; he and they conducted the internal administration and the foreign policy of Judea; he and they treated with the kings of Syria as an independent power against another independent power, and entered into treaties of alliance with foreign governments, without the sanction, and contrary to the will, of these kings, whose authority in Judea extended no further than the spot momentarily held by their army, and ceased altogether as soon as that army was forced to retreat.

Some historians place the end of the Syrian domination about a year later, and date the administration of the Asmoneans from the time Judah the Maccabee was recognised as governor of Palestine by the regent Lysias. But this recognition added nothing to the real power of the Maccabee, and did not in any degree influence the political fortunes of the Jews. We, therefore, prefer to date the end of the Syrian domination from that glorious day when, in spite of King Antiochus, his veteran armies, his elephants and horsemen, the "sweet savour" of Judah's offering once more arose from Zion's mount; while thousands of grateful voices, who, without fear or molestation, proclaimed their confession of faith—"Hear, O Israel, the Lord, our God, the Lord is ONE"—(Deut. vi. 4,) gave glory to God in the high heavens, and honour to the Maccabee, his servant on earth.

After having restored the public worship, and recalled many of the inhabitants to Jerusalem, Judah's next care was to secure the temple, as well as the people, against insult and molestation from the hostile garrison stationed in the fortress on Mount Acra, a hill higher than the temple-mount, and which nature and art combined to render impregnable, especially to an assailant situated as was the Maccabee. For Acra was defended by a numerous force, composed partly of Syrian veterans and partly of apostate Jews, both equally detested by the Maccabeans, and obnoxious to retribution for their enormous cruelties. The fortress had, moreover, been abundantly victualled and furnished with many and various engines of destruction, such as were used in the wars of those days. Judah, on the contrary, could not undertake the siege, as he was altogether destitute of instruments to batter down the strong walls; and the forces under his command were not numerous enough to permit him even to blockade this last stronghold of the oppressor.

But, though he could not attack Acra, he could defend the temple and its worshippers against annoyance from the enemy. For that purpose he caused the mountain of the temple to be protected with new walls, and towers of great loftiness continually manned by a powerful and vigilant garrison. And as the experience of Lysias's last invasion had taught Judah the great importance of Bethzura as a protection on the most exposed frontier, he caused that fortress to be strengthened with additional works.

Judah's care and diligence were thus exerted to the utmost; but not more than what the dangers that threatened him and his people imperiously called for. The uninterrupted success which hitherto had attended him, roused the fear and envy of the neighbouring nationalities. Those old and ever-active enemies of the Jews were alike alarmed at the rising power of the Maccabee, and enraged at the triumph of the God of Israel. As the return of King Antiochus from his Eastern expedition had been announced, and was soon expected, they all determined to join their forces to his, and entirely to exterminate the Jewish people. And that they might not lose their time while waiting for him, they gave an earnest of their intentions by murdering such Jews as happened to be living among them or within their reach. (1 Macc. v. passim.) Fortunately for the Jews, King Antiochus did not return; and the valorous enterprise of the Maccabee, stepping between his persecuted brethren and assassination, once more rescued them from destruction.

During the war in Palestine, so disastrous to the Syrians, Antiochus had prosecuted an expedition not less disastrous in Upper Asia. (166 B. C. E.) His proceedings in his march thither are very imperfectly explained. (Appian. de Reb. Syriac, cap. 66.) But on his return, having detached part of his army to collect tribute, Antiochus, with a powerful escort, advanced to plunder a temple and rich staple of trade at Elymais, the southern appendage to Mount Zagros, and the main caravan communication between Susiana and Media.

It seems that this place contained more than one wealthy temple, as it was in an attempt on the temple of Jupiter, at Elymais, that Antiochus the Great had lost his life. His son Antiochus Epiphanes, who professed especial veneration for Jupiter, directed his attention to the treasures under the protection of Venus or Diana,[1] whose altars had been honoured and enriched by the great Alexander. But though he escaped with life, Epiphanes's attempt was not more successful than that of his father. He was disgracefully defeated by the inhabitants of the district, and forced to save himself by flight to Ecbatana, the capital of Media.

There he first learned the repeated discomfitures and routs of his armies in Judea—tidings which exasperated to fury the wounds which his pride had received in his late repulse from Elymais. Transported with ungovernable passion, he swore, in the excess of his rage, that utter destruction should be the lot of the Jews, and that Palestine should become their grave. While he urged the march of his troops westward with the utmost precipitation, the immoderate quantities of wine which he unceasingly swallowed caused him to be attacked with a painful and incurable disease of the intestines. Yet on he went, his mouth, amid deep curses, uttering the fell purposes of his heart, till, in his reckless haste, his chariot was upset. He himself was thrown out and much hurt; and the foul and

---

[1] Appian (cap. 66) says the temple Epiphanes attacked was dedicated to Venus; but Polybius (lib. xxx. cap. 11,) maintains that it was Diana's temple. The treasury attempted by Antiochus the Great was, according to Justin, (lib. xxxiii. cap. 2,) in the "templum Elymai Jovis."

diseased state of his body, acting on his wounds, caused them to breed vermin, and to emit so pestiferous a smell that his attendants dared not approach him. In this loathsome and horrid condition, he died at the obscure village of Taboe, situated near the extremity of Mount Zagros, on the road to Babylon. (164 B. C. E.)

Both Jewish and Greek writers attest that his death was attended with extraordinary circumstances. Polybius (lib. xxxi. cap. 11) reports, that Antiochus was seized with a phrensy in consequence of conspicuous manifestations of divine displeasure—wonders which the respectable historian ascribes to the tutelary divinity of Elymais, whose temple and treasure the king had recently destined to depredation. The Jewish legend (2 Macc. viii.) relates how the force of conscience, acting on the restless mind and debilitated body of Antiochus, led the proud monarch to perceive the hand of God in a disease so horrid and peculiar as that under which he suffered; how he acknowledged that his barbarities and sacrilege were justly punished by the torments he endured; how "he wearied heaven with fruitless vows" of penitence, and wrote a letter to Jerusalem, restoring to the Jews and their religion all the rights of which he had sought to deprive them, and requesting the people he had so cruelly ill-used to pray for him to their God, that in his mercy he might spare the wretched life of the king.

Josephus (Antiq. lib. xii. cap. 13) deems it necessary—as in his times it unquestionably was—to reply to Polybius, and to remark, that "it was more likely Antiochus should have been punished for actually plundering the temple of Jerusalem, rather than for a simple attempt on that at Elymais, which failed in the execution." We are not disposed to join Josephus in what we consider a very weak argument in a strong and good cause. Besides, Time, that great teacher and umpire, has long ago decided on the rival claims in this instance advanced for Jerusalem and Elymais; the first, indestructible in fact and in idea; the other, a "baseless fabric," forgotten, or only remembered to be laughed at.

But though we do not find fault with Polybius for believing (or rather for stating, like a good pagan as he was) that the tutelary divinities of Elymais wrought vengeance on the would-be plunderer of their shrines, we blame the great historian very much, for that he, the contemporary, who so fully relates every remarkable event of his times, and whose authority is so justly respected, should have made no special mention of the struggles of the Maccabees. The same remark applies equally to the other contemporary Greek historians that we still possess; so that if it were not for the evidence furnished from other sources, the silence of the Greek writers might be urged in denial of the deeds of the Maccabees, just as that selfsame silence is urged in denial of Alexander's visit to Jerusalem.

Salvador (Histoire de la Domination Romaine en Judée, i. 70) explains this silence in various ways. He says: "Even if time had not destroyed most of the historical works of that period, as well as several books of Polybius, this omission would find its explication in more causes than one. In the -midst of the agitation prevailing throughout Egypt and Western Asia, owing to the encroachments of the Romans, and the fall of the kingdoms which constituted the Greek world, Judea—a narrow strip of land on the shores of the Mediterranean, painfully struggling to recover its independence, and the principal efforts of which were confined within a narrow mountainous territory—did not offer any thing sufficiently striking or interesting to the eye of historians of Greek lineage, and was most frequently included in the general designation of Arabia. Moreover, it so happened that at

Alexandria, and in all the most important cities of those regions, the Jews and Greeks were engaged in an unceasing conflict of mind and of interests. They were continually disputing about the pre-eminence of their respective races, of their antiquities, usages, and laws. And if the Jews contrived to relate many a circumstance calculated to do them honour, the Greeks, on the other hand, who were by no means scrupulous, contrived to destroy, to falsify, or to neglect many a useful evidence."

"Finally, Tacitus mentions one cause, a last and convincing one, in his Annals, on an occasion where that historian does justice to one of the most brilliant heroes of that universal national resistance against the Romans, which was not less active on the banks of the Rhine than on those of the Jordan. 'Arminius,' says Tacitus, 'was, without doubt or question, the liberator of Germany. He attacked the Roman people, not during its nonage, as so many kings and chiefs had done, but during all the splendour of the empire. Though Arminius lost battles, he was never subjugated. He died at the age of thirty-seven, after twelve years of sovereign power; and his fame is still cherished by the barbarians. But his name has not even been mentioned in the annals of the Greeks, WHO NEVER ADMIRE ANY EXPLOITS BUT THEIR OWN.'" (Annal. lib. ii. § 88.)

Thus far Salvador; but while we are quite ready to adopt the reasoning he adduces, we are, nevertheless, free to condemn the intentional silence and omissions of Greek historians. Nor can we exempt Polybius from blame, when he enters so fully into the history of King Antiochus's reign, and yet can find no room for actions, the most glorious and dignifying to human nature, connected with that reign.

To the Jews the death of Antiochus proved, as we have already stated, a most fortunate and providential deliverance. On his deathbed, the king expressed his dissatisfaction with Lysias, and appointed Philip, one of his generals, guardian of his infant son and regent of the kingdom; and in token of his appointment, the king placed the royal crown and signet-ring in his hands. But Lysias, who probably had received timely intimation of the king's intention, availed himself of the advantage of having the heir in his hands. Upon the first intelligence of the king's death, he placed his young charge on the throne under the name of Antiochus Eupator, ("well-fathered,") and assumed for himself the exercise of government as lord protector.

When Philip, who had hurried on in advance of the army, arrived from Upper Asia, he found himself forestalled, and unable to vindicate the authority intrusted to him by his deceased master. To avoid the danger to which his high pretensions might expose his life, Philip fled to Egypt, purposing, however, to vindicate his claim to the regency by the aid of that kingdom and of the mercenaries then on their return from the East.

But there was another and more dangerous competitor for the supreme power in the person of Demetrius, the lawful heir to the crown, and who, during the whole reign of Antiochus Epiphanes, had been detained as a hostage at Rome. He was now twenty-three years of age, and failed not to urge his claims upon the attention of the senate. But that astute body decided that it was more to the interest of Rome that a child should, under a questionable title, occupy the throne of Syria, than that the ardent and able Demetrius should make good his undoubted right to the crown. Accordingly Antiochus V. Eupator was, by the Romans, recognised as king, and Lysias as his guardian.

As these various negotiations, and the necessity for establishing his own authority, fully occupied the attention of Lysias, the Maccabee obtained a short respite from the vast forces which the regent had assembled for the invasion of Judea. The heroism of Judah had gained admirers for him even at the council board of Antiochus. Among these the most conspicuous was Ptolemy Macron, the favourite of the late king, and long the bitter persecutor of the Jews. He had despised them: the tameness with which they had allowed themselves to be slaughtered in Jerusalem on the Sabbath-day, and the misrepresentations of the recreant Menelaus, had led Macron to believe that the Jews were a people of turbulent cowards, fit only to be slaves. But the valour of Judah and the bravery of his men now undeceived Macron, who was too experienced not to perceive the immense injury a prolongation of this war of principles must inflict on the power of Syria. So long as Epiphanes was alive, Macron—who, better than any other person, was acquainted with the king's temper and disposition—did not venture to express his altered opinions. But after the "madman" had breathed his last at Tabœ, Macron did not hesitate to urge the regent to grant the Jews peace.

But his high favour with the late king had rendered Macron, a foreigner, obnoxious to the Syro-Grecian courtiers. Lysias himself was not sorry for the opportunity which presented itself to seize upon the important government of Cœle-Syria, which Macron held: he therefore joined in a conspiracy formed against the hated favourite, the result of which was that Macron was accused before the king of treason; and though he was not convicted, he was deprived of his government, which was bestowed on Lysias, banished from the king's presence, and deserted by all his friends and sycophants. The solitude to which he now saw himself reduced became insupportable to him. Blighted ambition, joined to the pangs of conscience, overwhelmed his mind, and he put an end to his mortifying reflections by a draught of poison. (2 Macc. x.)

Thus the king and his favourite, the head that planned and the hand that executed the horrors of Jerusalem, perished alike' miserably at brief intervals; and the sole survivor of this guilty triumvirate, the apostate high-priest Menelaus, did not long escape his fate. However much we detest the crimes and cruelties of which these men were guilty, we are divided from them by too great a space of time to share the personal feeling which animated against them the writer of the second book of Maccabees, or to join with him in triumph over their wretched end. Moreover, the history of the last eighteen centuries has made us acquainted with too many persecutors, not less guilty than Antiochus and his coadjutors, that after a life of crime died quietly in their beds in the midst of all worldly prosperity; we know too many of these criminals and their history to join in the view the legend labours to inculcate—"that the persecutors of Israel meet with condign punishment here on earth." But though we know that this rule by no means holds good in every case, yet we sometimes meet with instances of retribution so singular and providential, that, with all our philosophy, we are bound to confess "there is a God who judgeth on earth!"

Though Judah and his people—thanks to the death of Antiochus Epiphanes—enjoyed a short respite from the formidable invasion the regent Lysias had prepared, they were not permitted to taste the sweets of peace. Gorgias first, and then Timotheus, (the former at the head of an army of Idumeans, the second commanding the tribes east of the Jordan,) attacked and were defeated by Judah, who, in the interval between their attacks, had to turn his arms against the children of Bean. Whether this was the name of a man, a city, or a tribe, is uncertain. Probably the Beni-Bean were a tribe of Idumeans or Ishmaelites, of whom it is recorded that "they were a snare and decoy to the Israelites, and lay in wait against them on the highways, as they passed to and from Jerusalem." (1 Macc. v. 4.) Judah compelled these assassins to seek refuge in some of their strongest towers; and as he understood they were abundantly supplied with everything necessary to hold out a siege, he determined to leave his brother Simon with a portion of his forces before these towers, while he himself, with the rest of his army, marched across the Jordan against the Ammonites, whom he defeated; after which he took and garrisoned the strong fortress of Jazar, and then marched back into Judea.

During his absence, his brother Simon had pushed the siege of the two strongholds in which the Beni-Bean had taken refuge, and reduced them to extremity. The Maccabean brothers had determined to root out this tribe, which had been so "sharp a thorn in the side of the Jews." But Judah had the mortification to find that even in his army, devoted as it was to the cause of God and fatherland, there were men who preferred their private interests to the general welfare; and who prostituted bravery, talent, and honesty to the acquisition of gold. The besieged succeeded in bribing some of Simon's principal officers with the sum of seventy thousand drachmas, and by the connivance of these traitors a considerable portion of the garrison found means to escape. The vigilance of the Maccabees, however, detected the treason, and frustrated its further success. The culprits were denounced, tried by the heads of the army, convicted, and put to death. Judah then took the two towers in which the defenders were cut down to the last man, by assault, and burnt them to the ground, after which he hastened to meet Timotheus, who had gathered a large force and penetrated into Judea. In the battle which ensued, the Jews were again victorious; and the general of the defeated army took shelter in the fortified city of Gazarah, where his brother Chereas commanded. The Maccabee invested the place, and, after a siege of five days, took it by assault, in which both Timotheus and his brother, and another renowned Greek general, Apollophanes, lost their lives.

These repeated defeats exasperated the confederate Gentile tribes to the utmost. Their numbers were such as to leave no reasonable doubt of the destruction of the Jews, and yet, whenever they met on the battle-field, the valour and skill of Judah and the bravery of his men triumphed. As his enemies could not prevail in fair fight, they had recourse to assassination. Upwards of a thousand Jews residing in the land of Tob fell victims to the popular fury; their wives and children were carried into captivity. The Jews of Gilead must have shared the same fate; but, fortunately for them, they received timely notice of the intended massacre, and fled to the fortress of Dathema, where they provided for their defence. They were soon besieged by an army of Syrians and Sidonians, commanded by the younger Timotheus, the son, probably, of him who had fallen at Gazarah. The besieged, however, found means to acquaint Judah with their desperate condition, and to implore help. At the same time, similar applications came from Galilee, where the Jews had barely found time to place themselves on the defensive against their raging foes.

Judah summoned a council of war, and dividing his army into three divsions, he himself and his brother Jonathan hastened to Gilead, where the danger was the most pressing. His brother Simon, with the second division, marched to Galilee; while the defence of Jerusalem and the command of the third division were intrusted to the two brothers Joseph and Azariah, with the strict charge not to undertake any offensive operations, but to stand altogether on the defensive until either Judah or Simon should return.

The two expeditions were eminently successful. Both in Gilead and Galilee the enemies were routed, and the Jews rescued. But as the Maccabeans found it impossible, with their small forces, to protect or secure the further abode of the Jews in either of these countries, both Judah and Simon resolved to remove the Jews, with their families and property, into Judea. And as many cities laid waste, and a great part of the land was depopulated, the Maccabee assigned to these refugees locations where they might dwell in safety and prove of great use in augmenting the resources of the patriot army.

On their return to Jerusalem, the Maccabean brothers found that their own success had been more than counterbalanced by the loss incurred through the disobedience of their lieutenants. Joseph and Azariah had for the first time found themselves at the head of an army; and as they did not know how soon the return of Judah or of Simon might supersede them in their command, while at the same time they were most anxious to distinguish themselves, they determined, though contrary to the express orders of Judah, to perform some exploit that should entitle them to fame and honour.

The opulent seaport town of Jamnia[2] attracted their attention: to achieve the conquest thereof before the return of their superiors seemed an object worthy of their ambition. Accordingly, thither they marched with their little army. But Gorgias, who commanded in Jamnia, was both vigilant and enterprising. Twice defeated by Judah, he was burning with eager thirst for vengeance;

---

[2] This city, which in sacred Scripture is called Jabneh, (2 Chron. xxvi.) is situate on the Mediterranean, between Joppa and Azotus. After the destruction of Jerusalem, it acquired considerable importance as the seat of the patriarch, and, as such, we shall have occasion to speak of it again.

while the experience he had acquired of the extreme activity with which the Maccabees conducted their operations, called forth his utmost watchfulness.

No sooner had Joseph and Azariah begun their march, than Gorgias obtained intelligence of their movements; and when he ascertained that the dreaded Judah was not with them, and that their numbers were greatly inferior to his own, he at once determined to forestall their attack. Accordingly, he sallied forth and fell upon them when he was least expected. Neither Joseph nor Azariah were equal to the emergency in which they were thus suddenly placed. Expecting to surprise the enemy, they had taken no measures to prevent being surprised, and could form no disposition to repel their assailants. Their men, who were not animated by the presence of Judah, nor directed by his matchless valour and skill, lost heart and fled. Two thousand were slain during the fight and pursuit; and the small remnant that escaped sought refuge in Jerusalem, disgraced and utterly dispirited, while Gorgias returned to Jamnia to enjoy the triumph of having destroyed the *prestige* of Jewish invincibility.

Nor was it long before Judah and his people experienced the consequences of this triumph. The regent Lysias, who, notwithstanding the immense preparations he had made for the invasion of Judea, had not yet put his forces in motion—prevented partly by the internal affairs of Syria, and the negotiations pending at Rome, but principally by his fear of defeat, and doubt of any favourable result—now, encouraged by the success of Gorgias, and envious of the laurels gained by his lieutenant, put his immense army in motion. (164 B. C. E.)

His forces numbered eighty thousand foot, eighty elephants, and a considerable body of horse. With these he again laid siege to Bethzura. His declared intention was to extirpate the whole Jewish nation, to repeople their country with heathens, and to enrich his master and himself by the plunder of Judea and by the sale of the lands to new settlers. As irresolute and timid as he had been since his first discomfiture, so extravagantly arrogant the victory of Gorgias and the vast forces under his command now rendered him.

Judah, who was then at Jerusalem, prepared to meet the invader. As was his custom before battle, he and his army fasted, special prayers were offered, special sacrifices were brought, and then they again marched forth "for their wives and their children, their lives and their laws." The legend relates that on their march there appeared to the Jews a man on horseback in rich shining armour, and brandishing his spear against the enemies. This sight, whatever it was, inspired Judah's men with such courage and confidence, that they fell upon the Syrians like lions, killed eleven thousand foot, and put the rest to flight.

This fresh defeat revived all the regent's fears, and convinced him that the Jews could not be overcome, because of the omnipotence of the God by whom they were helped. Lysias, therefore, offered Judah terms of peace. After some negotiation, a treaty was concluded, by which the king of Syria granted a general amnesty to all the Jews that had appeared in arms against his father or himself; he further revoked the edicts issued against the religion of the Jews, and restored to them the right to live according to their own laws and to administer their own internal affairs. In return for these concessions, the Jews promised to be loyal to the state and to pay tribute as heretofore.

The 2d Book of Maccabees (chap. xi. 1–13,) preserves three letters, which on this occasion were addressed by the young king and by the regent to the elders of the Jews and to the governor of Judea. There is also one letter from the Roman commissioners in Syria, Q. Memmius and T. Manlius, who had employed their efficient aid in behalf of the Jews. Another dignitary, whose good offices had been exerted to promote this peace, was the high-priest Menelaus, who hitherto had been with the Syrians, but now, as we learn from the king's letter, was to be included in the peace, and who actually returned to Jerusalem to resume his high functions in the temple, or, in the words of the king's letter, "to comfort and confirm the Jews." (163 B. C. E.)

The peace thus concluded was of no long continuance. The hatred against the Jews which rankled in the breast of the heathen nations contiguous to Judea, prevented their approving or joining in a measure which, as they well knew, fear alone had extorted from the court of Antioch. And the Syrian generals who commanded in Idumæa on the south, Samaria and Galilee on the north, the sea-coast of Phœnicia on the west, and beyond the Jordan to the east, from Damascus to the southern extremity of the lake Asphaltites,—all these Syrian governors and generals, envious of Lysias, and little mindful of his commands, were ready to join in every undertaking that could bring loss and suffering on the Jews. The consequence was, that although the war with the kingdom of Syria was formally at an end, yet in reality the Jews, neither in Judea nor any of the adjacent countries, were permitted to enjoy any peace.

Among the Syrian generals who carried on this unauthorized warfare the first rank is due to Timotheus, the next to Gorgias. Timotheus, who had the death of his father and uncle to avenge, held the chief command beyond Jordan. Gorgias, twice defeated by Judah, but proud of his own victory over Joseph and Azariah, fancied that he and his Idumeans were alone able to conquer the Maccabees.

Nor did the enemies that everywhere sought the destruction of the Jews limit their efforts to open war. The foulest modes of assassination were unscrupulously resorted to. Thus the inhabitants of the seaport of Joppa, under some pretence of festivity or amusement, treacherously invited a number of Jews who lived in the city, with their wives and children, on board some barges by the sea-shore, rowed them farther into the deep, and then flung them overboard. This premeditated atrocity, which cost the lives of about two hundred Jews, was soon heard of at Jerusalem, and Judah justly provoked, hurried against these murderers, came upon them in the dead of the night, set fire to their port and shipping, and killed all those that had saved themselves from the flames.

A similar act of nefarious treachery, planned by the inhabitants of Jamnia against their Jewish townsmen, was prevented from succeeding by the extreme activity of the Maccabee, who, on proof of the murderous purpose of the Jamnians, hastened from Joppa, and punished Jamnia so terribly, that the flames of ships, ports, and magazines were seen at Jerusalem, though at a distance of two hundred and forty furlongs.

It would be equally monotonous to writer and readers, were we to follow the Maccabees into every field they had to fight, or to every fortress they had to assail. As specimens of their prowess, let it be recorded that at Raphon, Timotheus, who had assembled an army of one hundred and twenty thousand foot and twenty-five hundred horse, was most disgracefully defeated; for as soon as Judah, at the head of his vanguard, came in sight, the immense host arrayed against him were seized with a panic, and made such haste to fly from him, that, in their hurry to get away, they wounded one another with their own weapons. In this running fight Timotheus lost thirty thousand of his men;[3] and as he found it impossible to rally them, or to get any number to make a stand, he himself was also forced to betake himself to flight.

A portion of the fugitives, finding themselves closely pursued, fled into the city of Carnion, and took possession of the fortified temple of the Syrian goddess Atargatis, where they attempted to defend themselves; but were destroyed by the victors, who burnt the city and temple to the ground. Timotheus himself was taken prisoner by Dositheus and Sosipater, two of the Maccabees' most gallant captains. But he ransomed his life and liberty by releasing a great number of the Jewish inhabitants of Galilee whom he had made captive, and some of whom were nearly related to his captors. (2 Macc. xii.)

After this signal victory, Judah returned to Jerusalem. On his march, he requested permission of the governor and magistrates of Ephron to traverse their city, which was so advantageously situated that "he could neither turn to the right nor to the left of it." But as the city was strongly fortified, abundantly victualled, and manned by a strong garrison, Judah's request was not only refused, but the governor caused the gates to be walled up. The consequence was, that Judah attacked Ephron, and, after a fierce conflict, which lasted the whole day, the city and citadel were taken by assault, many thousands of the enemy were put to the sword, and a large number were carried into captivity. After carrying off the richest plunder, the victors burnt the city, and completely razed the fortifications. Thence Judah continued his march homeward, extending protection to his menaced and persecuted brethren,

---

[3] The judicious reader may perhaps, here and on other occasions, suspect the numbers. But in the books of Maccabees they are given in words, at length, not in letters, the usual numeral signs of the Greeks; and "famæ verum standum est," as Livy says in a similar instance.

whom, wherever he found it practicable, he carried with him into Judea.

The city of Bethshean—then called Scythopolis, from a colony of Scythians long settled there—contained a considerable Jewish population, the safety of which gave Judah great uneasiness, as, amid the general ill-usage the Jews everywhere experienced, he had reason to fear the worst from a tribe so fierce as the Scythians were reported to be. On his return from Raphon, he spread his victorious army along the plains of Bethshean, while he caused inquiries to be made as to the treatment the Jews had experienced in that city. When he found that these much dreaded barbarians had protected and befriended their fellow-townsmen, Judah sent a message of thanks to Scythopolis; and exhorting the citizens to continue their friendship to his people, he assured them of his own.

He then continued his march to Jerusalem, which proved very fatiguing, as the country, almost depopulated, could afford but scanty supplies; and his army was encumbered with the aged and infirm, with women and children, whom his victories had released from captivity or rescued from destruction. Judah remained with the rear-guard, that he might encourage those who lagged behind, and succour those who most stood in need of assistance. Thus he brought them all safely to Jerusalem about the time of Pentecost, when Judah and his people went to the temple to return thanks to God for their quick and wonderful success.[4] (1 Macc. v. 46, et. seq.; 2 Macc. xii. 30, et seq.)

---

[4] "Quick and wonderful indeed, if we consider that the peace could not be broken as soon as made, and that it was concluded on the fifteenth of Xanthicus, answering to the beginning of our April, and that the feast of Pentecost, fell either in the latter end of May or beginning of June; so that in less than two months' time they burnt the two havens and fleets of Joppa and Jamnia; beat the Arabian nomades; took the city of Caspis;

We know nothing of the private life of Judah the Maccabee, and even in the record of his public services the brilliancy of his patriotism and military virtues scarcely permits us to get a glimpse of any other traits in his character. It is only incidentally, as on the occasion of this march to Jerusalem, that we discover the kindness and beneficence that found room in the breast of this unyielding patriot and formidable warrior. When we read how his sword gleamed foremost in the thickest throng of battle, how his arm dealt the death-blow on the bravest, and his voice levelled to the dust walls and towers, cities and temples, we are apt to imagine the dreaded Maccabee as a gloomy, relentless avenger, whose sole mission it was to execute judgment on the enemies of the Lord, and whose heart was a stranger to all the milder feelings of humanity. It is a remarkable fact, that during the civil wars of England, when Oliver Cromwell and his Ironsides took for their prototype the Maccabee, it was only the sterner traits of his character that presented themselves to their mind. And as they generally were fond of adopting the strong and figurative language of the Old Testament, it has been asserted by many a historian, that the rigid and stern character by which the Puritans generally were distinguished, was owing to their having received their training chiefly from the old Law.

But when we read how Judah the Maccabee, during the gloomy period of his first and doubtful successes, could venture to affront the cupidity of his few followers, and to deprive them of a portion of those spoils which

---

defeated Timotheus and his numerous army; burnt and destroyed Carnion and Ephron, besides several other strong fortresses; released a vast number of their brethren, and were returned to Jerusalem loaded with spoils and a vast multitude of female captives; and all this without any loss to themselves." (Universal History, vol. x. p. 295, note T.)

law and usage declared to be theirs, that he might obey the dictates of his own benevolence, and relieve the indigence of the widow and the orphan, of the aged and the infirm; when we next read how, in the full noontide blaze of his highest fortunes, the victor in battles numberless did not disdain in person to comfort the weary and to support the fainting; and when we then remember that this beneficent warrior, this tender-hearted champion of God's holy Word, had received *all* his training, mental and moral, from that Law which in him found one of its most pious defenders,—we are bound to admit that the Old Testament is equally capable of inculcating the kindliest feelings that adorn the heart of man, and the loftiest emotions that dignify his mind.

The great victory which Judah gained over Timotheus was easily achieved, and was altogether due to the panic caused by his name and presence, or rather to that feeling which Scripture designates as the "terror of God." (Gen. xxxv. 4.) But the battle which, directly after the festival, Judah had to fight against Gorgias and his Idumeans called for greater exertions, and was so fiercely and obstinately contested, that all the generalship, as well as all the piety of Judah, and the bravery of his men, were brought into requisition, to compensate for the inferiority of numbers, before the enemy could become routed. Gorgias himself, who bravely did his duty as general and as warrior, was seized alive by Dositheus, one of the captors of Timotheus, but was saved by a Thracian horseman, who cut off the Jewish captain's arm close to the shoulder. This forced him to quit hold of his prisoner, who, seeing the day irretrievably lost, fled from the field, and found shelter in the strong fortress of Maresa.

Judah did not pursue him; but permitting his own troops to recover from their exertions and fatigues, by resting over the Sabbath at Adullam, the Maccabee directed his arms against the strongholds of the Idumeans, took their chief city, Hebron, as well as Azotus, a principal city of the Philistines, together with many other fortresses. Wherever he passed he pulled down the idols and destroyed their altars, and returned to Jerusalem loaded with fresh laurels and spoils.

These various exploits, while they added to the military fame and power of the Maccabee, contributed also to the greater security and welfare of his people. And Judah felt that there was but one great effort more required to cleanse the land of its oppressors, and to place the temple and its worshippers beyond danger or insult; and this was to reduce Acra, the strong fortress held by the Syrians and apostate Jews at Jerusalem. During Judah's absence, the garrison had been active in its hostilities, and not only hindered many Jews from visiting the temple, but greatly annoyed those who did. On his return from the expedition against Gorgias, the Maccabee learnt the breach of the peace of which the commander at Acra had been guilty, and determined, if possible, to take this fortress, and thus at once, and forever, to pull out this thorn in the side of the Jews, which, grievous as it had been, their want of skill and experience as engineers had hitherto compelled them to endure. Accordingly, Judah collected his whole force, prepared engines for throwing stones, and other battering implements of surpassing efficacy, and laid siege to Acra.

The place was very strong, the garrison numerous, and well furnished with arms and provisions. Numbers of apostate Jews, who formed a portion of the garrison, and who knew how odious they were to their orthodox brethren, were bent on the most desperate resistance. Judah was acquainted with all these difficulties, but he also knew the extent of his own resources; and he therefore felt convinced

that though the fortress could and would hold out a long
'time, yet, if he could prevent its being succoured by the
king of Syria, it must eventually fall into his hands. He
therefore invested Acra so closely, that no messenger could
leave that fortress without being taken by the besiegers.
And as there was no intercourse between Judea and the
adjoining provinces, so that no tidings of what was doing
in Jerusalem were likely for some considerable time to
reach Antioch, Judah fully expected that before the king
and regent would become acquainted with the danger impending over their last stronghold in Judea, or could assemble forces for its relief, the banner of Israel would be
planted on the walls of Acra.

But the apostate Jews in the fortress penetrated his design. They felt, with him, that however desperate and
well-conducted their defence, they must eventually succumb, unless relieved by Lysias. And as they saw, from
the vigilant manner in which Mount Acra was invested,
that no emissary would be able to leave that fortress, they
advised the commanders to make a vigorous sally, in order
to give an opportunity to some of them to escape from the
fortress, and to repair to Antioch. Their advice was
adopted; and the sally was so well managed, that a number
of these renegades, accompanied by some officers of the garrison, contrived to force their way through the besiegers,
and to reach Antioch.

The regent had already heard of the unauthorized hostilities which the neighbours of the Jews had carried on
against them, together with the retaliation the Maccabees
had inflicted on their adversaries; and though reluctant to
recommence the war, Lysias began to assemble his forces,
for he felt the necessity of putting an end to these intestine commotions, which threatened to become fatal to the
power and resources of the Syrian empire. While he was
yet undecided in his own mind as to what measures had

best be adopted, the fugitives from Acra presented themselves before the king, to inform him "that the lawless Maccabee had broken the peace; that he persecuted with merciless rancour all that dared to show any fidelity to Syria; that he plundered, sacked, and put to fire and sword all that came in his way; and, lastly, that as a preparatory step to his altogether renouncing his allegiance, Judah had laid siege to Acra; while such were the means at his command, that unless the besieged fortress were speedily relieved, it would, like Bethzura and so many others of the king's strongholds, fall into the hands of the rebellious Jews; and that the king would not then possess, throughout the whole province of Judea, a single city or fortress held by his own troops."

This representation at once decided both the king and the regent. The forces already assembled were immediately put in motion; reinforcements and auxiliaries were hurried off to join them with the utmost speed; and at the head of one hundred thousand foot, twenty thousand horse, fifty-two elephants, and three hundred war chariots, Antiochus and his guardian Lysias again invaded Judea, and for the third time laid siege to Bethzura with an army which, not only in point of numbers, but also and still more in point of warlike qualities, was greatly superior to any that had as yet been led against Judea.

On the tidings of this formidable invasion, Judah at once raised the siege of Acra, and with his little army hastened to confront the enemy. On the first night of his arrival in the vicinity of the king's forces, Judah, with a few resolute men, fell on them, killed a large number, threw the whole camp into the utmost confusion, and at break of day retreated, without the loss of one single man.

This bold attack confirmed the Syrian generals in their high opinion of Judah's enterprise and the bravery of his men, against which no vigilance could sufficiently guard their camp. But then the king, as well as the regent, felt certain that in the open field their superior numbers, their elephants, and war chariots could not fail to overpower the Jews. Leaving, therefore, a force to blockade Bethzura, Lysias marched in search of Judah, determined to bring on a general engagement, which the Maccabee at first did not decline; nay, at the head of his small army he even began the onset, and inflicted some loss on the Syrians. But the heroic valour of the Jews was exhausted and at length overpowered by the desperate odds against them; and Judah now gave proof of his prudence and superior generalship by manœuvering so as successfully, and in time, to extricate his forces, that were in danger of being surrounded, and making good his retreat to Jerusalem without any material loss.

It was in this battle that Eleazar, the brother of Judah, lost his life in a gallant attempt to retrieve the fortune of the day. Perceiving an elephant larger and more royally accoutred than any of the others, he erroneously concluded that the king himself was mounted on this lofty animal; and under the impression that the fall of the king would lead to the retreat of the invaders, Eleazar, by resistless fury and great havoc of the enemy, cleared his way till he reached the elephant, when he stabbed it in a mortal part with such fatal effect that the huge animal instantly dropped down, overwhelming and crushing the heroic assailant with its weight. (1 Macc. vi.)

When the relieving army of the Jews had thus been driven out of the field, the king's forces again returned to the siege of Bethzura. The garrison made a long and vigorous defence; but, unfortunately for them, it happened to be the sabbatic year of rest to the land, during which all agricultural operations were suspended. And as during the preceding years of persecution and devastation, the greater part of Judea had remained desolate, the store of provisions throughout the land was but small. The supplies at Bethzura had, therefore, of necessity, been scanty from the very first; and when they were totally exhausted, and no hope of relief remained, the garrison was compelled by famine to capitulate. They, however, did not yield till they had obtained very honourable conditions from the besieger; but the treacherous regent kept his word with them no further than the bare saving of their lives, turned them all naked out of the town, and placed in it a garrison of Syrians.

After the reduction of Bethzura, Lysias led the young king and his army to Jerusalem, and laid close siege to the temple, which was bravely and successfully defended by Judah and his most gallant and devoted followers. All attacks were repulsed; all the effects produced by battering machines were repaired by counter-works. The real danger, that which the garrison could by no means avert, was want of provisions. The same cause that had compelled Bethzura to surrender threatened Jerusalem likewise. Great numbers of the Jews had already found themselves obliged to slip out of that city for want of food, so that there were hardly hands enough left to defend the place. And Judah, with an aching heart, saw the near approach of the fatal day when, completely worn out with famine and disease, the few survivors of the garrison would have to surrender, and Judea would once more lie prostrate at the mercy of the heathen and of the apostate.

But man's extremity is God's opportunity. When the Maccabee was reduced to the utmost, and all the advantages that had been gained were on the point of being again and forever lost, Providence was pleased to relieve the besieged, and to frustrate the hopes of the besiegers, through the instrumentality of a man who, though more fully determined to destroy the Jews than even Lysias or the young king himself, yet, on the present occasion, involuntarily proved the most efficient auxiliary of a people that he had pledged himself to exterminate.

Philip, whom the late king, Antiochus Epiphanes, on his deathbed, had appointed regent, to the exclusion of Lysias, had hastened on to Antioch to assume his office. But on his return from the East, without an army, he found the power of his rival too firmly established, and had, as we have already related, been obliged to consult his personal safety by seeking refuge in Egypt. The troops, however, who had accompanied Epiphanes, at length returned from their Eastern expedition, fully determined to carry out their king's last intentions, and to remove Lysias from his high office, of which his repeated miscarriages against the Jews proved him unworthy. Philip contrived to join this Eastern army, that recognised his authority, and at the head of which he unexpectedly marched against and took possession of Antioch, at the very time that Lysias was vigorously pushing the siege of the temple at Jerusalem.

The unexpected tidings of this calamity reached Lysias, with the addition that Philip was marching full speed against him at the head of an army not less numerous than his own. This intelligence induced Lysias to raise the siege, as the total subjection of the Jews appeared to him a matter of much less consequence than the preservation of his own authority and the recovery of Antioch, the metropolis of the whole empire. On this trying occasion Lysias evinced considerable ability and diplomatic skill. The resolution to raise the siege was kept secret both from the Syrians and the Jews; while in order to disarm them, overtures reached the Maccabees to the effect that the breach of the late peace had been unauthorized by the king, who had invaded Judea solely in order to succour his fortress of Acra, and to vindicate his authority; that these objects having now been attained, he did not wish to reduce the Jews to extremity; that, therefore, if they would at once submit, he would again grant them peace on the same terms as before—that they should be allowed to live according to their own laws.

Judah and his adherents were but too happy to accede to terms so advantageous and honourable. And as soon as they were agreed upon and sworn to on both sides, King Antiochus, with his guardian, the regent Lysias, were admitted within the fortifications of the temple. But the same want of honesty that had disgraced the regent at Bethzura, also, to a certain extent, characterized his conduct at Jerusalem. Under the pretence that the fortifications of the temple were too strong to be intrusted to the Jews, he ordered them to be immediately pulled down and demolished, in manifest violation of the peace to which he had so lately sworn.

After this act of treachery, which again exposed the temple to insult and annoyance from Mount Acra, Lysias marched his army from Jerusalem; and having now no enemies behind him, the king and regent, by a return nearly as sudden as the irruption of Philip, regained Antioch, defeated and killed the pretender to the regency, and dispersed or destroyed his followers.

The whole of this episode in the history of the Maccabees is so singular and complicated, that if it were not sufficiently attested by the evidence of history, it would almost appear incredible. Epiphanes removes Lysias from the regency, and appoints Philip in his stead, solely on account of the ill-success in Judea; and the consequence of that appointment is, that at the very moment when Lysias is on the point of most fully retrieving his past miscarriages by the total subjugation of the Jews, he is compelled to abandon all the advantages he had gained, being forced to it by Philip, the man especially sent to secure those advantages. This claimant to the regency, Philip, derives his authority solely from the ardent desire of his late sovereign that the rebellious Jews should be exterminated; and yet the moment he is able to make use of his authority, he causes the deliverance of these self-same Jews from utter and unavoidable ruin. It is true that the result is, on his part, involuntary; but for that very reason the Jews were all the more justified, when in this singular complication of *accidents*, counteracting each other, they saw the finger of a Providence watching over their preservation.

The treachery of which the regent had rendered himself guilty, both at Bethzura and at Jerusalem, renders it doubtful whether his victory over Philip would not have been followed by a renewal of the war against the Jews. But difficulties with Rome, and other events which we shall presently relate, rendered the preservation of peace throughout the whole empire a matter of the highest importance both to Lysias and to his pupil, the young king. The court of Antioch, therefore, not only itself abstained from any breach of the peace, but also in relation to Judea, adopted two measures, the best calculated to prevent the unauthorized warfare of the neighbouring tribes, and also to check the outbreak of internal strife between the orthodox and Grecianizing Jews.

The first measure was the appointing of Judah the Maccabee as governor over the land, " from Ptolemais to the Gerrhenians." And as he thus became the king's officer, invested with lawful authority by virtue of the king's commission, the pretence for attacking him and his people as "rebels and outlaws" was altogether removed.

The second measure was the bringing of Menelaus to justice for his many crimes. This turbulent and ambitious personage had, on the conclusion of the first peace, repaired to Jerusalem to resume his functions of highpriest. But as the Maccabeans held the apostate in the utmost detestation, and refused to admit him into the temple, he was compelled for his personal security to take refuge in the fortress of Acra. Here, it appears, he was the main instigator of the hostilities which the heathen garrison carried on against the temple, and which became the cause of Judah's laying siege to Acra. On the raising of that siege by the royal army, Menelaus presented himself before the king and regent as the accuser of the Maccabee, and as a competitor for the office of governor.

But his time was at length come. The regent soon became convinced that Menelaus was utterly and irreconcilably hateful to the Jews, and that any attempt to place this odious personage in authority over them, whether spiritual or secular, must lead to fresh commotions. Lysias also discovered that the cause of this deeply-rooted abhorrence on the part of the Jews was well founded, as the crimes of Menelaus were so atrocious and so manifold, that the permitting him to outrage justice with impunity, as he had hitherto done, was one of the worst misdeeds of the preceding reign. And as Menelaus with his usual restlessness kept urging his claims, Lysias determined to get rid of this troublesome criminal, and accused him before the king as the sole author and cause of all those intestine wars that during the last few years had afflicted Syria.

Menelaus was found guilty, and sentenced to such a death as his treason, if not to Antiochus, yet to God and his own people, fully deserved. He was conducted, under a strong guard, to Berea, where he was consigned to the Ash Tower. This was a mode of punishment invented by the Persians, who considered it as a kind of privileged death, to be inflicted only on offenders of the highest birth and rank, whose blood was not to be spilled, and whose bodies were not to be degraded by the rope. The punishment of ashes is variously described. According to Valerius Maximus, (lib. ix. cap. 2,) a place was enclosed with high walls, and filled with ashes. A piece of timber was made to project over the ashes, on which the criminal was placed. He was liberally supplied with meat and drink until, overcome with sleep, he fell into the deceitful heap and died an easy death. The Syro-Greeks, who borrowed this punishment from the Persians, sometimes inflicted it on the most odious offenders, making it an engine of slow and suffocating torture.

Such was the end of Menelaus, the last and most guilty of that triumvirate who conspired against the Law of God and against Israel.

In removing Menelaus from the high-priesthood, and in appointing Judah royal governor of Judea, the regent had yielded to the necessities of the times, and to the wish that the Jews and the adjacent nationalities should be pacified. But fully determined to uphold the royal authority, the regent's next measure was of a very different character. The lawful heir to the office of high-priest was Onias, a nephew of Menelaus, and a son of that high-priest Onias who had been murdered at Antioch. But the regent Lysias judged it most for the king's interest that the high-priest to be appointed should be altogether dependent on the court of Syria. He therefore advised Antiochus to set aside the legitimate line of succession, of which young Onias was the sole survivor, and who, from that very fact, became independent of the king as soon as his right to succeed was acknowledged.

In his stead, Lysias appointed Jakin, or Eliakim—better known by his Greek name, Alcimus—who, though of priestly descent, had no other claim to succeed to the highest office in the priesthood than the king's will. Of the previous life of this Alcimus we know next to nothing. The Medrash Rabbah (in Genesis, ch. 65) relates that he was a native of Zerudoth, and a sister's son (nephew) of José ben Joëzer, of Zereda, at that time chief of the Sanhedrin, and who subsequently suffered martyrdom at the instigation of his kinsman, Alcimus. But though we know so little of that which the French style his *antecedents*, his career, subsequent to his appointment of high-priest, is sufficiently known to prove that for treachery, cruelty, and impiety this Alcimus was fully equal to his predecessor, Menelaus.

When he presented himself at Jerusalem to enter on his office, the Jews refused to recognise him as high-priest, because he had obtained and sullied that dignity by open apostasy, and by conforming to the religion and customs of the Greeks. And as the inhabitants of Jerusalem were supported by the royal governor, Judah, in their opposition to Alcimus, the would-be high-priest had no choice but to return and lay his complaint before the throne. But, by the time he reached Antioch, he found that both his protectors had been destroyed by a revolution as sudden as it proved irresistible, and that a new sovereign wielded the sceptre of Seleucus Nicator, which he claimed as his rightful heritage.

CHAPTER VI.

Demetrius I. King of Syria—His flight from Rome—Death of A. Eupator—Invasion of Judea—Massacre of Hassidim—José ben Joëzer—Nicanor—His blasphemy, defeat, and punishment—First treaty between Judea and Rome—Discontent of the Hassidim—Bacchides—Battle of Eleasa—Death and burial of Judah the Maccabee—His character—Gentile testimony to his military talents.—(162 to 161 B. C. E.)

DEMETRIUS, the son of Seleucus IV. Philopator, had in his infancy been sent as a hostage to Rome, where he remained thirteen years after the death of his father. His uncle Antiochus had been assisted to ascend the throne from which he had hurled the assassin and usurper, Heliodorus; and subsequently, by extreme servility to the senate, and large bribes to the Roman commissioners, he had been permitted to reign, notwithstanding the remonstrances of his nephew Demetrius. For the senate at Rome, which always professed to do justice, but which in reality was guided solely by its own interest, preferred a prince of doubtful title to one of unquestionable right; and from the same motive the son of the usurper, Antiochus, was acknowledged as king of Syria by Rome, because the senate preferred seeing that monarchy governed by a child, rather than by a young man of ability and ambition. The senate, therefore, turned a deaf ear to all the reclamations and arguments of Demetrius, though he declared that, from his residence among the Romans since his childhood, he looked on the senators as his fathers, and on their sons as his brothers, and that the wrong done to him was as if done to their own kindred. (Polyb. lib. xxxi. cap. 12.)

To prevent any rash measures on the part of their hostage, the senate even sent ambassadors to Antioch to confirm the coronation of Antiochus Eupator. At the head of this embassy was Cneius Octavius, who had commanded the Roman fleet in the last Macedonian war, and whose name, after four generations, was raised to the highest lustre by his descendant Octavius Cæsar Augustus, successively the tyrant and the father of the Roman world. This ambassador, Octavius, acted harshly and tyranically in Antioch. His attention was attracted by the vast assemblage of forces which the regent had marched, first against Judea, and then against Philip. Among these forces there was a considerable number of elephants, although the kings of Syria, by their treaty with Rome, were bound not to keep any of these warlike animals.

Octavius further found that, in violation of the treaty, the kings of Syria had fitted out a greater number of ships of war than they were allowed to possess. He therefore proceeded to enforce the treaty by causing the elephants to be killed and the ships to be destroyed, as he had the unquestionable right to do; but the manner in which he executed this odious business was so arrogant and offensive, that a Syrian Greek, named Leptines, stung with indignation at the brutality with which his country was insulted by the Roman, seized an opportunity to assassinate Octavius in a bath at Laodicea. The news of this event, so disgraceful to the government of his rival, encouraged Demetrius to renew his importunities with the senate. But they proved again unsuccessful; and the heir to the Syrian crown began to fear he should have to end his days in Italy, when fortune threw in his way two Greeks, then resident in Rome, who inspired him with better hopes, and enabled him to realize them.

The first of these was the historian Polybius, with whom Demetrius had contracted an intimacy, as both were greatly addicted to field-sports; the second was Menyllus, the ambassador of Ptolemy Philometor, King of Egypt.

These men, united in mutual friendship, exhorted the young prince never again to apply to the senate, but to trust to their management and his own good fortune for effecting his escape.

Their advice gained additional weight from the reports brought by Diodorus, who had been intrusted with the care of Demetrius in his childhood, and who just then arrived at Rome from Syria. He assured Demetrius that such was the general discontent excited by the unpunished murder of Octavius, and such the suspicion with which the regent and the army viewed each other, that should the rightful heir appear in Syria, he could not fail to recover his kingdom. It was therefore determined by his two advisers that Demetrius should at once, and before any suspicion arose, attempt his escape.

Though a hostage, and in some respects a prisoner in Rome, Demetrius lived there in princely magnificence. He was accompanied by many Syrians of distinction; spent his time with them in mutual visits and entertainments, and enjoyed the privilege of hunting the wild boar at a great distance from the capital.

It was decided that he was to avail himself of this privilege in order to escape, by means of a Carthaginian vessel which laid at the mouth of the Tiber. This vessel was bound for Phœnicia, to carry the annual acknowledgments or presents from Carthage, the colony, to Tyre, the mother country. And as Menyllus, the Egyptian ambassador, was about to return home, he hired a passage for himself and his retinue, examined the accommodations, and laid in stores without creating the smallest suspicion. Before the day fixed for sailing, Menyllus again went on board, and told the captain that unforeseen events had arisen which would prevent him personally from embarking, but that, nevertheless, their agreement should stand good, as he wished to send part of his family back to

Egypt, and that the passengers would join the ship about midnight, at which hour the captain said he would be ready to receive them.

On the same day, Demetrius and his confederates partook of an entertainment at the house of one of his Syrian companions, with the declared purpose of proceeding that evening on a hunting party to Anagnia, forty miles distant from Rome. He chose not to give the entertainment himself, for his own parties were usually numerous, and suspicion might have arisen in persons not invited. Polybius was prevented by indisposition from being present, but knew from Menyllus every step taken in the business.

As the evening advanced, the historian began to fear that Demetrius, who was a hard drinker as well as keen sportsman, might frustrate his own success through intemperance in wine. Polybius therefore sent to him a box with a tablet containing some verses from the Gnomic poets, recommending sobriety, vigilance, distrust, and, above all, expedition, and extolling these qualities as the sinews of successful enterprise. Demetrius read, recognised the writer, and prepared at once to follow his admonition. On pretence of a nausea from drinking, he left the company. The other guests followed him. Those not in his secret were sent forward to Anagnia, with orders to proceed with the dogs and nets some twenty miles farther, to Mount Circæum, a place almost surrounded by the Pomptine marshes, and abounding with wild boars.

As soon as Demetrius, and the intended companions of his flight, eight in number, were left by themselves, they equipped themselves as travellers, and each, attended by a single servant, rode off at a rapid pace, to take shipping at Ostia, fifteen miles from Rome. As the wind was favourable, and the Carthaginian only waited for his passengers, he sailed as soon as they were on board; and the fugitive had nearly reached the straits of Messina before his flight, though rumoured, was authenticated. It was then too late to pursue him. The senate, however, sent Tiberius Gracchus, at the head of a commission, to inspect the affairs of Syria and the neighbouring kingdoms. (Polybius, lib. xxxi. cap. 19–22.)

But before this commission arrived in Asia, Demetrius had seated himself on the throne of his father. Landing at Tripolis, in Phœnicia, he thence proceeded to Apamea, where his ancient tutor, Diodorus, who had left Italy several days before him, had prepared every thing for his welcome reception. With increasing bands of adherents, he marched toward Antioch, every city that he came to declaring in his favour; for his return taking place so soon after the murder of Octavius, no one doubted that his enterprise had the full approbation of the Romans.

As he approached Antioch, a mutiny broke out in the army commanding that capital. Lysias, the regent, with his pupil Eupator, were made prisoners by their own troops, who proclaimed their allegiance to Demetrius, at the same time desiring to know his pleasure with regard to their prisoners. "Let me not see their faces," was his reply and their death-warrant. Unresisting and unlamented, Antiochus V. was put to death as a usurper, in the twelfth year of his age, and the third of his nominal reign; and his guardian Lysias shared his fate.

We have seen that Menyllus, the ambassador in Rome of Ptolemy Philometor, took the most active part in enabling Demetrius to escape. This he was induced to do from resentment at the manifest injustice the senate had committed against his master. Philometor had, as we have already related, been compelled to associate his younger brother Physcon in the government, which, as both were but boys, was conducted by Eulœus, a eunuch, who lent his aid to the assault Epiphanes made on the Jewish religion, by prohibiting its observance in Egypt. But as Philometor reached man's estate, he freed himself from the tutelage of the eunuch, and not only recalled the decree against the Jews, but generally evinced a character far superior to any of his predecessors since the third Ptolemy, Euergetes.

But while his mild virtues gained him the love of his subjects, the turpitude and ferocity of his younger brother Physcon excited the people against him, so that they drove him in disgrace from Alexandria. But he was still the favourite of the Romans, who considered him a useful instrument for dividing the power of Egypt—a kingdom that remained intact after the expulsion of Epiphanes, and which now began gradually to recover its vigour. Philometor was therefore commanded to resign to Physcon the kingdom of Cyrene, with all the Egyptian dependencies in Lybia; and when this order had been complied with, the isle of Cyprus—recently recovered by Egypt from the crown of Syria—was also adjudged to Physcon, that his dominions might stand on a nearer footing of equality with those of his brother.

In the course of these transactions both the brothers visited Rome; but while the senators respected Philometor, they favoured his brother. After the departure of the two kings, their ambassadors appeared before the senate. But though justice and reason were on the side of the elder brother, Roman selfishness decided in favour of the younger.

His miscarriage in this affair induced Menyllus to assist the views of Demetrius, who on the throne of Syria might prove a valuable friend and auxiliary to Philometor. But upon first recovering his inheritance, Demetrius was involved in so many anxieties at home, that he could pay no attention to foreign politics. The death of his rivals had put him in possession of Antioch and the western provinces of his kingdom. But the most important portion of his heritage, the wealthy satrapy of Babylonia, was still held by two powerful instruments of the late government —Timarchus, the governor, and Heraclides, the treasurer, both appointed by Epiphanes, deeply embarked in his schemes of amalgamation, and detested by the people for their severities. Against these two officers Demetrius had first to turn his arms; and from their overthrow he acquired the name of Soter, "the Saviour," by which he is known in history.

His next care was to disarm the probable resentment of the Romans, and to court their favour by embassies, and presents, and professions of the most perfect respect and devotion. To show his zeal in their cause, he made diligent inquiry into the murder of their ambassador, Octavius; but all his researches did not enable him to implicate in that crime the government which he had overthrown. The murderer Leptines openly gloried in his deed; while at the same time this firm patriot, with equal sagacity and confidence, predicted that no harm would befall him for his glorious misdeed. Demetrius sent him to Rome along with a Greek named Isocrates, who had publicly lectured against the rapacity and insolence of the Romans, and had extolled the assassination of Octavius as an example worthy of imitation. Along with these two prisoners, the king sent the senate a present of a large golden crown. On their arrival at Rome, Isocrates provoked general disgust and contempt for his cowardice and grovelling meanness; whereas Leptines gained respect, as he appeared before the senate bold, firm, and with aspect erect and immovable. As he had uniformly predicted, no harm befell him. The Romans accepted the present Demetrius had sent them, but dismissed the prisoners, declaring that the guilt of the Syrian nation and government could not be washed out in the blood of individual delinquents.

When Demetrius had thus recovered his dominions and made his peace with Rome, his next care was Judea. Alcimus, on his arrival at Antioch, found his former protectors utterly ruined; and fearful of being involved in their fall as their protegé, he laid by for a little time, and assembled around him the numerous apostates whom the Maccabee had banished from Judea, and with whom Alcimus now made common cause. At the head of these exiles he presented himself before the king, and, in their behalf and his own, accused Judah and the Maccabeans of treason against the king, and of tyranny and cruelty against the acusers themselves.

They stated that they had been banished from their native home for no other crime than for their attachment to the religion and customs of Greece, which were doubly endeared to them because they were the religion and customs of the king himself. They forgot not to represent Judah as the minion of the late regent Lysias, who, regardless of the true interests of the crown, and intent solely on strengthening his own authority by placing in power men who were altogether his own creatures, had rewarded the rebellion of the Maccabees with the government of Judea. And though Alcimus himself in reality was a minion and creature of Lysias, with no other claim to the high-priesthood than the will and favour of the late regent, he possessed skill sufficient to divert the king's attention from the origin of his appointment, by representing himself as a victim unjustly deprived of his high office by that malignant traitor to the king and kingdom, the rebel Maccabee.

Demetrius had been too long absent, and had been returned to Syria too short a time, to be well acquainted with persons and affairs in that kingdom. It is also probable that the men whom he consulted were more inclined to favour Alcimus, with his Greek name and Greek pliability, than Judah, the stern champion of his faith and people. The fact of the Maccabee holding his appointment as governor of Judea from the late government, would also contribute to exasperate the king against him. The result of Alcimus's application was, from all these causes, perfectly successful. Bacchides, Governor of Mesopotamia, was ordered to march against Judea, to reinstate Alcimus in his dignity, and to bring Judah and his adherents to condign punishment. The governor of Mesopotamia and the high-priest of Jerusalem were joined in the same commission; and Alcimus, eager for power, hurried the Syrian general, who was altogether devoted to him, so that he marched forthwith against Judea.

It was not merely on the force of arms that Alcimus relied for success against the Maccabee; treachery was one potent auxiliary he called to his aid, while the altered character of the war, and the consequent change in men's minds, was another and even more powerful ally. It was no longer a war of extermination or apostasy that was carried on against the Jews by the king of Syria. The regent Lysias had, in the name of Antiochus Eupator, secured to them the right to live according to their peculiar laws and usages; and Bacchides, in the name of King Demetrius, declared that he did not come to abrogate that right.

The mass of the Jewish people, who had just begun to taste the sweets of peace, were by no means inclined rashly to renew the horrors of war, which had exposed their country and families to losses and sufferings for which no amount of booty and no degree of military glory could compensate. With this state of public feeling Alcimus was doubtless well acquainted; and he therefore concluded that provided the most prominent leaders, civilians as well as military men, could be removed, no great resistance to his installation as high-priest was to be apprehended from the bulk of the Jewish people. These views he urged strongly on Bacchides; and as that general entertained a wholesome dread of Maccabean prowess, he readily joined into Alcimus's schemes for entrapping Judah and his principal adherents.

Both high-priest and general sent deputies to invite the Maccabee to a conference, at which all disputes might be settled in an amicable way; and they spared neither promises nor vows that he and his friends should come and go in perfect safety. But the prudent Maccabee suspected their design; he rightly judged that an army so powerful as the Syrian, under a commander so distinguished as Bacchides, would not have been marched against Judea for the sole purpose of deciding the title of an intruding priest; but that some project more dangerous to his people and to himself must be hidden under the friendly professions and apparently harmless purpose of the invader. While, therefore, he recognised the supremacy of King Demetrius, and declared his willingness to pay the customary tribute, Judah declined the proposed conference; and though he did not take the field against Bacchides or oppose his march, the Maccabee began to prepare for a vigorous defence.

But, as Alcimus had foreseen, the mass of the people did not wish for a renewal of the war. Even the Hassidim thought Judah's suspicion groundless, ill-timed, and unjust. They contended that an amicable settlement was the fairest and best, and therefore to be greatly preferred by pious men; that moreover, Alcimus a descendant of Aaron the priest, "the friend of peace and promoter of peace," should not be lightly suspected of treachery and perjury while engaged in his hereditary duty of peace-making. When, therefore, they found that their remonstrances with Judah were unavailing, and that he persisted in his distrust of Alcimus, the Hassidim determined to try how far their mediation would work toward the desired peace; and having obtained an oath of safety from the treacherous high-priest, they waited on him to the number of sixty, and at first met with a most friendly reception.

But though Alcimus could plan and concoct schemes of treachery with the utmost coolness, his violent temper did not permit him to carry out his own devices with that self-command which was necessary for their complete success. Had he permitted his visitors to depart in peace, had he repeated his friendly interviews with them again and again, there is no telling whether the practical refutation thus given to his suspicions, and the growing pressure from without, might not at length have induced even the wary Maccabee to fall into the snare. But Alcimus could not wait. When he saw so many of his enemies in his power, when he saw before him the men who had shut him out from the temple and driven him from Jerusalem, his thirst for vengeance became irresistible. And though Judah was not among his victims, he caused his sixty visitors to be seized and cruelly put to death.

Among them, and probably at their head, was José, the son of Joëzer of Zereda, senior president of the Sanhedrin, and nearly related to the high-priest, whose mother was his sister. After the death of Antigonus of Socho—of whose antagonism to the philosophy of Epicurus we have already spoken—the presidency of the Sanhedrin was intrusted to two officers, of whom the senior had the title of Nasi, (president,) and the second that of Ab-Beth-Din, (vice-president.) José ben Joëzer was of the lineage of Aaron, distinguished in the priesthood as a Hassid, and as such holding a prominent rank among the champions of Judaism.

The writer in Frankel's Monatschrift, whom we have

already quoted, is of opinion (No. 11, p. 406) that when we read (1 Macc. ii. 42) that "an assembly of Hassidim joined Mattathias," and when the traitor Alcimus, in his complaint before King Demetrius, (2 Macc. xiv. 6,) declares that "the war is kept up by the men called Hassidim;"—in each of these two instances it is José the son of Joëzer who is chiefly alluded to as the first civilian among the defenders of the Law, and at the head of the principal authority which they recognised.

It is possible that his near and twofold connection with Alcimus—his own sister's son, and like himself, a Cohen—may have somewhat biassed the pious José, and rendered him loth to treat his nephew as a perjured traitor; and it is probable that his opinion and example greatly influenced the Hassidim. But they and he paid for their overtrustfulness no less a penalty than life.

His brief dialogue with his murderer is related in the Midrash (Bereshith Rabba, 65) in a manner equally simple and impressive. He was led out to death on a sabbath-day, the scaffold or platform for his execution being carried before him. Alcimus, mounted on a splendid charger, met him, and causing the procession to stop, he jeeringly addressed his aged kinsman, saying—"My lord, look at the horse my master has given me, and that on which thy master is about to make thee ride." "Ay," was the brief reply, "if thus to those who offend him, how much more to those who obey him!" meaning, "If those who offend God can enjoy such prosperity in this life, how much greater by far must be the felicity that in the life to come is in store for those who obey God!"

Nothing daunted, Alcimus rejoined "My lord, who has ever obeyed him with more sincerity than thou?" José answered with the same brevity as before, "If thus to those who obey him, how much more to those who offend him!" meaning, "If those who obey him can suffer such misery in this life, how much greater by far must be the suffering that in the life to come awaits those who offend him!"—a remark that in proper time did not fail to produce its due impression on the mind of Alcimus. For though the statement by the Midrash, that directly he left his victim he committed suicide, is contradicted by the First Book of Maccabees, (vii. 20 et. seq.,) and also by Josephus, (Antiq. xii. 10,) and it appears he continued his career more than a year after the martyrdom of José the son of Joëzer, yet both these authorities agree so far with the Midrash, as to state that the death of Alcimus was untimely and violent.

His treachery, however, defeated its own purpose, and was of singular service to the Maccabee and to the friends of resistance, since it fully justified his suspicions, and proved to the people that nothing but the blackest perfidy and cruelty was to be expected from the perjured pontiff and his equally treacherous colleague; a conviction which induced the Hassidim once more to stand up for their religion, their liberty, and their heroic but prudent chief. Nor was this all; but Bacchides—whether stung with the reproaches to which this useless perfidy exposed him, or disgusted with a colleague incapable of deliberately carrying out his own plans—quitted Judea, and returned to Antioch, leaving with the high-priest a body of troops sufficient, as he thought, to maintain that functionary in his new dignity; and proving his own fierce hatred of the Jews, not only by causing a considerable number of them to be-seized and slaughtered at Bethsetha, on the road to Antioch, but also by denying the rite of sepulture to his victims, whose corpses he caused to be flung into pits and wells.

Alcimus, thus left to himself, spared neither pains nor cost, flatteries nor cruelties, to strengthen his position and party. The many Grecianized Jews and renegades whom Judah had banished, were especial objects of the high-priest's attention. His emissaries sought them out in their various places of refuge, and under the most liberal promises invited them to rally under the standard of Alcimus. His generosity and caresses, not less than their eager desire to return to their native land, induced numbers of these unfortunate exiles to join him. Not a day passed but that some reinforcement added to the strength of these outcasts; and as they were impelled by the fiercest passions of revenge and hatred against their orthodox brethren, Alcimus, at their head, and supported by the Syrian troops, made continual incursions into various parts of the country, plundering, burning, and destroying all that refused to recognise his high priestly authority.

Judah—who during the presence of Bacchides, and so long as the Syrians had committed no actual hostilities, had abstained from opposing the royal arms—now took the field against Alcimus, defeated him in several engagements, and inflicted such severe punishment on the cruel renegades that fell into his hands, that the remainder of them dared no longer act against him, but either fled from Judea, or sought refuge in Acra, the heathen fortress at Jerusalem.

Their desertion proved to Alcimus that they considered his case as hopeless, and convinced him that unless he procured a much larger army with which to force the Jews into submission, he would never be able to master his enemy, nor yet be permitted to approach the sacred altar. He therefore returned to the court of Syria, and once more urged his complaints and accusations, which, as before, were backed by all the enemies of the Jews then at Antioch. His forays against his own people had placed much booty in his hands, which he had carried off with him, and part of which he now employed in bribing the

king with the present of a magnificent crown of gold and
other rich gifts; and as Demetrius was already sufficiently
incensed against the Maccabee, the creature, as he
thought, of the late regent Lysias, all that Alcimus
required was readily granted. A large army was placed
under the command of Nicanor, one of the bitterest
enemies of the Jews, with the express orders to cut
off Judah and his partisans, to disarm and to disperse
his army, and to settle Alcimus in his power and
dignity beyond the possibility of any future opposition.
(1 Macc. vii. 21, et. seq.)

Though the royal commands were thus explicit and peremptory, and though Nicanor, who entered Judea at the
head of a numerous army, would have been but too happy
to carry them out to the letter and to their fullest extent,
yet in his own mind that general was more than doubtful
of his ability so to do. Nicanor's hatred of the Jews was
neutralized by his dread of the Maccabee, by whom he
had already once been so signally defeated, that he felt
another such discomfiture would be utter ruin to his fame
and future hopes as a military commander. He therefore
resolved to leave no means untried to bring Judah to accept of a peace, deeming it less dangerous to modify the
king's orders than to hazard another battle against the
never-vanquished Maccabee.

On his arrival in Judea, the apostates who so lately had
deserted Alcimus again joined the Syrian banner, and in
such crowds, that before he reached the neighbourhood of
Jerusalem, Nicanor found his forces increased exceedingly.
On the other hand, the Maccabeans who had early tidings
of his approach, went to the temple to implore the Divine
assistance by fasting and prayers, and then prepared themselves for a vigorous defence. But when Nicanor reached
Dessau, a fortress not far from Jerusalem, where Simon,
the brother of the Maccabee, was stationed, and that leader

went forth to meet him, the sight of the immense army arrayed against him so terrified the Jewish commander, that without attempting to fight, he at once fell back on Jerusalem; and, as he was known to be valiant as well as prudent, his hasty retreat produced an unfavourable impression on the minds of the people.

No increase of force or apparent success could, however, tempt the Syrian general to depart from the plan he had traced out for himself, or to commence hostilities against Judah. On the contrary, he caused that valiant chief to be waited on by three of the principal officers in the Syrian army, who were authorized to offer peace to the Jews. Judah, who with pain had observed the disheartening effect which Simon's retreat had produced on the minds of his men, and who knew that the majority of them were become averse to war, deemed it his duty to communicate these proposals to the people; and as they were received with great gladness even by the most zealous of his adherents, he agreed with the emissaries of Nicanor on time and place for an interview with that general, so that the two chiefs in person might settle the terms of peace.

As Judah from past experience had cause to dread treachery,—if not from Nicanor himself, at least from Alcimus,—he caused a number of his best men to be so advantageously posted, that in case any violence was offered to him, they might instantly hasten to his relief. But his precaution for once proved needless, as Nicanor was so earnestly bent upon concluding peace, that their conference was carried on to the satisfaction of both parties. Articles of peace confirming the treaty of Lysias were agreed on and sworn to; after which Nicanor paid a visit to Jerusalem, and stayed there some time, without giving the Jews any cause of complaint or at all interfering with their internal affairs. To avoid giving them any umbrage, he even went so far as to disband the greater part of his army, and for a time lived in perfect friendship with Judah and the Jewish nation.

This harmony, however, was disturbed by Alcimus, who, though his title as high-priest was nominally recognised, yet continued excluded from his sacerdotal functions, and who, consequently, thought the peace not sufficiently advantageous to himself. He therefore returned to Antioch, and once more appeared before the king to complain, not only against the Jews, but also against Nicanor as a betrayer of his master's interests, and a friend to his mortal enemies; in testimony of which, he urged the peace lately concluded between them contrary to the king's expressed will.

Demetrius was alike incensed and surprised that his general should venture to take so important a step, not only without the king's permission, but even without his knowledge; and the first outburst of the royal anger threatened to prove fatal to Nicanor. But that general had powerful friends at court, and at their intercession the king was induced not altogether to withdraw his favour from Nicanor, or to recall him from his command, though the peace he had concluded was declared null and void, Demetrius refusing to ratify the treaty. The general was, moreover, commanded under pain of the king's severest displeasure, instantly to renew the war against the Jewish chief, and not to sheathe the sword until the Maccabee should be killed, his party wholly suppressed, and Alcimus enthroned as high-priest in the temple of Jerusalem.

The royal orders were accompanied by letters to Nicanor from the friends at court who had protected him, upbraiding him for his presuming to disobey the king, and assuring him that though their intercession and influence had been so far successful, yet they felt convinced his continued disobedience, or indeed any departure from the strict letter of the royal commands, would lead to his certain destruction, which no efforts of theirs could avert; that, therefore, if he wished to escape being treated as a rebel, he must put Judah to death, and install Alcimus in the temple; and that, if he deemed the forces already under his command insufficient for the purpose, reinforcements to any extent he might require would be despatched without delay.

The receipt of orders and communications so little expected, caused Nicanor the greatest perplexity and uneasiness of mind. For while, on the one hand, the peremptory command of the king left him no choice but obedience, on the other hand the terrible defeat which he, with a large army, had once experienced from Judah and a handful of men, had stamped on his mind the conviction that God himself fought for the Maccabee—a conviction which no event in the subsequent career of that never-conquered leader had weakened. The Jews, moreover, had strictly kept the peace, and given no fresh cause for hostilities; so that in violating an agreement which he himself had proposed, and to which he had sworn, Nicanor would become guilty of perjury in the eyes of God and man; a reflection not at all likely to tranquillize his mind.

The conflict which these contending emotions raised within him showed itself in his outward demeanour, especially toward Judah. Instead of treating him with that cordial intimacy and friendly equality which till then had characterized their intercourse, Nicanor's manner became changeful and abrupt, sometimes haughty and imperious, at other times fawningly friendly, and in either instance without any apparent cause.

These inconsistencies in the conduct of Nicanor did not escape the keen eye of the Maccabee; he easily perceived that Nicanor was at strife with himself, while at the same time he was hatching some design against Judah, which might be carried out when least expected. The Jewish chief, therefore, deemed it prudent to provide for his personal safety; and this he did with such speed and secrecy, that it took Nicanor completely by surprise. The Syrian had at length made up his mind that the king must be obeyed, and that Judah must be destroyed; but as an appeal to arms still "cowed his better part of man," treachery was to effect that which he had not the courage to attempt by open force.

The sudden disappearance of his intended victim, however, deranged his plan, the success of which depended altogether on Judah's confidence and the facility thereby afforded to seize his person. Nicanor was now, much against his inclination, obliged to resort to public measures of hostility; and alleging Judah's flight as the cause, he hastened to raise a new army by reassembling the troops he had disbanded, and reinforcing them with veterans, chiefly apostate Jews, drawn from the numerous garrison at Acra. At the head of thirty-five thousand men Nicanor marched against Jerusalem; but the numbers at his command were not sufficient to restore his courage. He still dreaded war; and, clinging to his first scheme, endeavoured to surprise his opponent by some foul stratagem.

For this purpose he sent emissaries to Judah to assure him that the Syrians had no wish or intention to renew the war; that the assembling of royal troops was the consequence of Judah's ill-advised, uncalled-for, and suspicious disappearance. Nicanor therefore proposed an interview at which they might once more meet, and restore that state of peace which had been disturbed without any real cause for complaint on either side. Judah consented to meet the Syrian general at the place appointed, where their first greeting appeared friendly and peaceable. But Judah soon discovered the purpose of his antagonist, which was to keep him in talk, and to lull him into security until the ambush previously prepared should be ready to pounce upon and seize him. He therefore suddenly broke up the conference and withdrew, and from that time refused to see Nicanor any more.

As all his treacherous schemes miscarried, Nicanor at length, reluctant and fearful, had recourse to arms, and advanced to Capharsalama, in the vicinity of Jerusalem. Judah marched forth to meet him, and forced him to retreat with the loss of five thousand men. But this half success disheartened the Jews; they feared that, as they had not been able to overthrow Nicanor's army, even before it received the numerous reinforcements that were hastening to his aid, they themselves would be overthrown and defeated by him if they were again to meet him in the field. Many of them, therefore, forsook Judah and sought shelter, some in the temple and some in the city, while Judah himself, with the few true hearts that adhered to him, retreated to the north, toward Samaria.

This result was far more favourable than Nicanor had dared to expect. And as he had escaped the utter and disgraceful rout which he had dreaded, he began to look upon his own loss of five thousand men, and consequent retreat, not as a defeat, but as a success, and merely as the price at which the dispersion of the Jews and the discomfiture of Judah had been cheaply bought. Thenceforth his arrogance became as great as his fears had been; and leading his army, reinforced by several thousand men, to Jerusalem, he ascended to the fortress on Mount Acra. There he was met by a deputation consisting of the heads of the people and some of the priests, who, in a submissive manner, assured him of their faithful allegiance to the crown of Syria, and pointed out to him the sacrifices which at that very time were offered up in the temple for the prosperity of King Demetrius. But Nicanor scouted their assurances of loyalty; and after casting many an insolent and blasphemous reflection on what he chose to call their

base superstition, he vowed the utter destruction of them
and their temple, and swore unless Judah was immediately delivered up to him, he would pull down the altar
and burn the temple, and in their place erect an altar and
temple to Bacchus.

The surrendering of Judah, however, was a demand
which the priests and heads of the people had it not in
their power to grant, as the Maccabee, unconquered, was
still in the field, though his followers were but few. But
Nicanor refused to listen to any thing they could urge,
and determined, until Judah should be in his power, to destroy such other leading men among the Jews as the people
most confided in. The legend (2 Macc. xiv. 37–46) relates the heartrending and sickening circumstances attending the immolation of an aged and eminent member of the
Sanhedrin, whose piety and patriotism had gained for him
the title of "father of his people," but whose identity the
mutilation of his name (*Razis* he is called in the legend)
does not enable us to establish.

Modern commentators of the Bible assign the 74th, 79th,
and 80th Psalm to this period of Nicanor's brief sway, and
also to the foul murders committed by Alcimus immediately
before and after this period; and as far as the intrinsic
evidence of the Psalms themselves can throw any light on
the subject, there is no portion of time in Jewish history
to which the expressions used in these Psalms so fully and
truly apply, as to the gloomy days of Nicanor, of Alcimus,
and of Bacchides.

In the midst of his cruelties and his blasphemies, Nicanor felt any thing but easy in his mind. It was not by
the murder of a wretched old man like Razis, nor yet by
the use of insulting and vain-glorious threats against a few
feeble priests and their worship, that the war could be
brought to an end, or the king's peremptory orders enforced. The decision was to be sought on whatever field

the Maccabee chose to make a stand; and when Nicanor heard that many Jews, exasperated by his blasphemies and cruelties, again flocked round the standard of the Maccabees, he mustered nearly forty thousand Syrians and Jewish apostates, and marched forth in search of Judah; nor had he far to seek him. Judah, whose force again numbered three thousand men, no sooner ascertained that Nicanor was encamped at Bethoron, than he took a position at Adasa, a place about thirty furlongs distant from the enemy; and there Nicanor resolved to attack him.

The legend (2 Macc. xv. 1, et seq.) has taken care to clothe this, the last of Judah's great victories, with many details alike interesting and marvellous. The day on which Nicanor, who still trusted more to his cunning than to his prowess, resolved to attack the Jews, was the Sabbath; in the full expectation that, rather than desecrate the day by fighting, they would allow themselves to be butchered without resistance, as he had once seen them do in the streets of Jerusalem.

He was, however, assured of the contrary by Jewish apostates who were in his army; and some of them, recalled to better feelings, perhaps, by the sufferings of their people and the imminence of Nicanor's advance, even ventured to beg of him that he would pay a regard to that holy day which the God of heaven had consecrated to his service. With scornful taunt Nicanor asked them whether there was indeed a mighty God in heaven who had ordered the sanctification of the Sabbath; and being answered in the affirmative, he replied, "And I, who am powerful on earth, do command you to fight for the king, your master, and to obey his orders." When we remember how long and how greatly this same Nicanor had been trembling at the idea of an encounter with Judah, because of his mighty protector in heaven, it appears to us that all his blasphemies were so many rhodomontades, in which he indulged in order to conceal from others, and perhaps also from himself, the fear which still was busy at his heart and brain.

Judah also prepared for battle, not by any blustering or rant, but by directing the hearts and hopes of his people toward their Father in heaven. The date of the battle happened to be the 13th of Adar, (161 B. C. E.,) the anniversary of Queen Esther's fast, and of the deliverance of Israel from the murderous plot of Haman. Judah recalled that circumstance to his fasting but not fainting warriors; and—still more to encourage them, he related to them a dream or vision by which he himself had been greatly comforted, and in which he saw, first, the late pious high-priest, the murdered Onias, and then the prophet Jeremiah, interceding for the people of Israel; and that, at the close of this vision, the prophet had addressed him, presenting him with a splendid sword, and had given him the assurance of a complete victory.

This address of Judah's produced an effect on his men fully equal to any he could have anticipated. Confident of help from above, they attacked the enemy with a degree of valour and enthusiasm which nothing could resist, and at their very first onset broke and routed the Syrian army. As Nicanor himself was one of the first that fell, his troops were seized with a panic, threw down their arms, and vainly sought safety in flight. For not only were Judah and his little army unwearied in the pursuit, but from all the country round, the people, as they heard of the victory and saw the fugitives, rose against them with a degree of exasperation that enables the legend to relate that not one of the Syrians escaped to carry the disastrous news to Antioch.

The day after the battle was Purim, the feast of Esther; and that day of general rejoicing has probably never been celebrated with more pious and heartfelt joy than by Judah and his men after their most signal deliverance and triumph. The body of Nicanor being found among the heaps of slain, Judah ordered that his head and his right hand, which he had so lately lifted up with threatening oaths against the temple, should be cut off and carried in triumph to Jerusalem. There they were exposed to the view of Jews and of Gentiles, with the impressive proclamation that these were the head and hand of the profane and cruel Nicanor, who had sworn the total destruction of God's holy temple. The fierce act of posthumous retaliation received its completion by the tongue of the wretched blasphemer being cut out of his head, minced up, and thrown to the birds, after which his head and hand were hung up on two of the highest towers in the city, but where these horrid trophies of vengeance were destined not long to remain.

This complete and brilliant victory gave the Jews a short breathing-time of peace; for their enemies, astounded at the continued success of the Maccabee, left him unmolested in possession of Jerusalem and Judea. But that chief, powerful and victorious as he then was, could not contemplate either the past or the future, his own people or the king of Syria, without serious misgivings. For on the one hand he saw that his people were tired of war; they had once abandoned him, their oft-tried leader and champion. They had forsaken him in the time of his utmost need, and when the ferocious Nicanor proclaimed aloud that nothing short of Judah's life would disarm his rancour.

On the other hand, Judah knew that King Demetrius viewed him (Judah) personally with intense hatred, because he considered him not only as a rebel against the majesty of Syria, but also as the creature, the only surviving and successful representative, of the faction of Lysias. It was therefore to be apprehended that the king would send army after army to destroy Judah, while it was very uncertain whether his people would stand by him to defend him. And what was worse, it was to be feared that since the people proved thus unsteady and lukewarm in the cause of God, the protection of God might be withdrawn from them. For himself, Judah felt no fear; he had devoted his life to God and his country, and was alike ready to live or die for his most holy cause. His fears were for his country and nation; and therefore he deemed it wise and prudent to secure to them an auxiliary whose alliance might act as a curb on the bitter hatred of King Demetrius, and the assurance of whose help would deter the neighbouring nationalities from hostilities against Judea.

Rome had already once exerted her influence at the court of Antioch in behalf of the Jews. The power of Rome thus began to be known to them, and they were assured that the Romans faithfully and effectually protected their allies. According to Salvador, (Hist. de la Domination Romaine en Judée, vol. i. p. 76,) the Romans themselves, who watched the resistance and victories of the Jews with interest, because these contributed to weaken and embarrass the Syrian monarchy, had, by means of their occult agents in Judea, who held out the most brilliant promises, indoctrinated the Jewish people with the desire for an alliance with Rome; so that Judah was forced to yield to these advances made by the Romans, which, indeed, he could not decline without drawing down upon himself the resentment of that proud and implacable people.

Two Jewish ambassadors, Eupolemus the son of John, and Jason the son of Eleazar, who had already in former years given proofs of their diplomatic skill in successful negotiations with King Seleucus Philopator, were therefore sent to Rome, where they concluded a treaty of alliance, offensive and defensive, on terms of equality and perfect reciprocity between the Romans and Jews. Nor did the Roman senate scruple thus to recognise as independent the revolted subjects of its older ally, the king of Syria; for it was part of the systematic plan of subjugation practised by that most astute and politic body, to grant liberty to those nationalities who were under foreign dominion; which served the twofold purpose of directly weakening the ruling power whose subjects were thus detached from it, and of subsequently enslaving both when fit opportunity should offer.

Accordingly, the senate at Rome passed a decree which was engraven on copper, in order to be sent to Jerusalem, importing that the Jews were thenceforth acknowledged as the friends and allies of the Romans; that both nations should be ready to succour each other and the allies of either with all their power, and in no case should assist their enemies; and whereas Demetrius, King of Syria, had been complained against to the senate as an oppressor of the Jewish nation, a letter should be sent to him, strictly charging him for the future to forbear all hostilities against them, and threatening him with an invasion of his country by sea and land in case he did not comply with this decree. (1 Macc. viii. 25, et seq.)

The concluding of this treaty with Rome has exposed Judah to blame from two very different sets of reasoners. One party blames him for that, being manifestly protected by God, he should still have sought human aid. But then the word of God nowhere commands that pious men are never to listen to the wholesome counsels of earthly wisdom, nor does it condemn the adopting of measures of human prudence as incompatible with a perfect trust in the Lord.

The second party condemns Judah's shortsighted policy, inasmuch as he did not penetrate the designs of Rome, which was first to supersede, and then to succeed to, the supremacy of the Syrians in Judea. But then it is certain that Judah did not fight for national and political independence, but for religious liberty and freedom of conscience. If that had been conceded by the Syrian king, the Jews would readily have returned to their political dependence, and indeed were anxious so to do. And if, on the contrary, the right freely to worship God could only be secured by political subjection to the Romans, Judah and his people would not have hesitated to purchase religious liberty at that price. Since their return from Babylon, they had been dependent successively on Persians, Macedonians, Egypto-Grecians, and Syro-Grecians, and if that dependence was now to be again transferred, all that the Jews then cared for was the right to live according to their own laws. Judah is then not to be blamed for concluding a treaty which subsequent events proved to have been well timed.

The tidings of Nicanor's wretched end, and of the utter destruction of his army, no sooner reached Antioch, than King Demetrius took such measures to avenge the defeat and to repair the disaster as the greatness of the emergency seemed to him to require. Till then he had looked upon the war in Judea as a mere provincial outbreak, such as was frequent in the unwieldy monarchies of the East. The full extent of previous losses and defeats—so little creditable to the glory of the Syrian arms—had probably been concealed from him; those discomfitures which it had been necessary to confess, were ascribed to the mismanagement of the late regent Lysias, or to the incapacity of the generals he intrusted with command; and Alcimus had probably described the ferocity of the Jews and of their leader as greatly exceeding their valour and his generalship. But the annihilation of the army commanded by Nicanor, a veteran general of acknowledged reputation, at once dispelled all these illusions, revealed to the king the extent of the danger in Judea, and showed him that the best troops and the best general in his service must be marched against the Maccabees.

It was the custom of the times—as we have stated in our account of the battle of Raphia—that when the king in person took the field, he was stationed at the head of the right wing of his army; and therefore the best soldiers were drafted into the *corps* that formed this royal wing, which thus embodied within itself the flower of the whole military force of the monarchy. This right wing, consisting of twenty thousand foot and two thousand horse, Demetrius now despatched into Judea; and the command he intrusted to Bacchides, who had already on a former occasion led an army against the Maccabee, and whom that prudent leader had not deemed it expedient to attack.

Alcimus the high-priest again accompanied the Syrian army, which directed its march to Galilee, and commenced its operations with the storming of Maseloth, or Massadoth, a considerable city, and in which a great number of Jews were slaughtered. From thence Bacchides advanced toward Jerusalem; but on receiving intelligence that Judah and his forces had retreated from the capital to Eleasa—also called Adassa—the Syrian general determined at once to attack him, fully convinced that if the Maccabee was defeated, Jerusalem would offer no resistance to the royal arms.

While Judea was thus threatened by the most formidable army that during the whole war had invaded that hapless country, the Jews at no time since the defeat of Apollonius had been so little prepared to meet the invaders. The mass of the people, as we have already stated, had become tired of a war which seemed interminable, since even the most complete victory procured but a short respite, and the destruction of one hostile army was followed by a fresh invasion of forces more threatening; moreover, with the death of Epiphanes, the war had changed its character of resistance to religious persecution. There was more of politics mixed up with it, and with that change the ardour of the people had greatly abated.

Those among the Jews who had been foremost to support the Maccabees and to fight the battles of the Lord, the Hassidim, were no longer attached to that chief as they had been. He entertained friendly relations with the Parthians, who were also at war with the Syrians; and he had, moreover, by way of response to the advances made by the Romans, sent an embassy to Rome to conclude an alliance with that mighty commonwealth. Both these measures were loudly condemned by the Hassidim as impious, and implying a doubt of the power of God to help his people. The Midrash Hhanuka[5] preserves the very words in which the leader of the Hassidim expressed his dissatisfaction to the Maccabees: "Then Jochanan became wroth, and said to the Asmonean, Is it not written, 'Cursed be the man who placeth his dependence on flesh, while from the Lord his heart departeth; but blessed is the man that trusteth in the Lord, for the Lord will be his trust.' (Jer. xvii. 5, 6.) Thou and thine, I and mine, we represent the twelve tribes of Jah, (the Lord;) and through us, I am assured, the Lord would have wrought wondrously."

After this severe reproof, it seems that Jochanan and his adherents left Judah, who thus, at the time of Bacchides's invasion, found himself deserted alike by the mass of the population, who were averse to war, and by a great body of his bravest supporters, whose excess of zeal condemned his foreign policy. The whole number

---

[5] See page 240 note. 40.

of his followers at Eleasa did not exceed three thousand. With these, however, Judah determined to attack the enemy who was approaching. But as Judah caused the usual proclamation (Deut. xx. 5–8) to be made, the terrific sight of the serried ranks of veteran warriors that confronted the handful of Jews so acted on the fears of the latter, that, availing themselves of the permission to withdraw, the greater part hurried away from the battle field, on which their intrepid leader was left with only eight hundred men.

Thus deserted in his utmost need by his own people, Judah felt more grieved at this sinful public ingratitude and defection than concern for his own impending fate. The few brave men who remained true to their leader and cause, urged him to preserve his valour and their own for another more hopeful occasion. But his answer was, "Far be it from me to run away from the enemy. If our time is come, we will die like men for our brethren, and with fame unsullied." Repeated experience had convinced him that—as he himself on a former occasion had quoted after Jonathan— "There is nothing that can prevent the Lord from helping by means of a few as well as by multitudes." (1 Sam. xiv. 6.) And at the very time the people abandoned him, and the Hassidim forsook him, because, as they insanely insisted, "he had turned away from the Lord, and placed his reliance on mortal men," the pious Maccabee was preparing to give the strongest proof of his "trust in the Lord," when, with eight hundred faithful but dispirited followers, he marched to encounter upward of twenty thousand gallant veterans, led by one of the bravest and most skilful commanders of the time.

The battle began in the morning; and so well-planned had been Judah's attack, so furious and well-sustained the onset of his men, that after some hours hard fighting, the right wing of this "right wing" of the Syrian army, and Bacchides in person, were in full flight for Azotus, eagerly pursued by the victorious Jews. But the Syrian warriors in the field that day were well fitted to meet every vicissitude of battle. The discomfiture of a wing of their army did not disarray the remainder. The second in command, seeing his chief routed, and the Jews in full pursuit, with admirable presence of mind caused his unbroken lines to be lengthened, so as entirely to encompass the small body of Jews, and then fall upon their rear.

Bacchides no sooner perceived, from the relaxing pursuit of the Maccabee, that the main body of his own army had begun to take part in the action, than rallying his fugitive troops, he once more formed them, and led them on to attack the Maccabee in front. Thus encompassed on all sides, outnumbered in the proportion of nearly thirty to one, and that not by effeminate and unwarlike provincials, but by veterans whose trade was war, whose valour had been tested, and whose skill had been acquired in many a well-fought field, it appears next to incredible that the handful of Jews were not at once overwhelmed and trodden down by the multitudes that surrounded and fiercely assailed them.

But such was not the case; and the resistance of the Jews on that day is fully entitled to rank with, if not above, the valour of the Greeks who fought and fell at Thermopylæ. We say it advisedly: if the three hundred Spartans who followed Leonidas, have acquired greater fame and popularity than the eight hundred Hebrews who were led by the Maccabee in this the last and most glorious of his battles, it is not because of their superior merit, but because the exploits of Greeks have met with greater favour from a partial world than the equally and perhaps more valorous deeds of the Jews; the former having been proclaimed by Herodotus, and the latter hidden in the Apocrypha.[6]

---

[6] According to the inscription quoted by Herodotus, (lib. vii. cap. ccxix.) the number of Greeks who fought at Thermopylæ, was four thousand;

The unequal conflict was maintained till night, when darkness separated the combatants; the Jews having not only cut their way through the hosts that surrounded them, but even maintained that portion of the field on which their leader made his last stand.

There was little exultation in the camp of the Syrians; the carnage in their ranks, the resistance they had met with, their experience told them, was unparalleled, considering the disparity of numbers; and it was not without doubt or apprehension for the result that they looked for a renewal of the combat on the morrow. But there was no cause for their fears. The few Jewish warriors that had survived the battle were in the utmost consternation and grief. He, the hero, who had led them forth in the morning, had not returned with them at night. The valiant Judah had fought his last fight. Long before the Roman, (Horace,) who saved his life by flight from the battle field, had uttered the beautiful sentiment that "it is sweet and becoming to die for the fatherland," the Hebrew had realized the glorious thought.

On a heap of slain that had fallen beneath his sword, reposed the noble Maccabee, who died, as he had lived, "without fear and without reproach." Around him lay the greater number of the gallant and faithful hearts who had entered upon and waged the unequal conflict, and who like him, had fallen unconquered, overwhelmed by

---

the Thespians, who voluntarily remained with Leonidas, numbered seven hundred; and the Thebans, whom he compelled to stay with him, four hundred. Isocrates (p. 164) makes the Lacedemonians amount to one thousand, and speaks of a number of other Peloponnesians who also remained to fight. Yet, thanks to Herodotus, and to the celebrated inscription on the tomb of the Spartans—"Go, stranger, and declare to the Lacedemonians that we died here in obedience to their divine laws"—Leonidas and his three hundred have carried away all the glory of the day, and are generally spoken and written of as if they alone had defended the straits of Thermopylæ against the hosts of Xerxes.

numbers, but not defeated. One consolation alone remained to his surviving followers—they had saved his body from insult. The boast of the heathen, that on Judah they would avenge the disgrace of Nicanor, proved idle and vain. Simon and Jonathan, the brothers of the fallen hero, carried his mortal remains to Modin, the native home of his family, and interred it in the grave of his ancestors, by the side of Mattathias, his patriotic father. (1 Macc. ix. 1–22.) The details of this, the last battle of the Maccabee, and the circumstances attending his burial, are involved in much obscurity. Some historians have, without sufficient reason, averred that the battle was followed by a truce, under favour of which his brothers recovered and buried his body. (Kitto, 694.) But neither the Apocrypha nor Josephus, (Antiq. lib. xii. cap. ult.,) know any thing of this truce, which moreover is altogether contrary to the character of the war waged by Bacchides, who looked upon and treated the adherents of Judah, not as honourable foes entitled to the benefits of truce or treaty, but as rebels and outlaws, to be hunted down and slain without pity or remorse.

We are therefore convinced that, notwithstanding the obscurity of the original records, our account of these events is substantially correct. That the Jews must have cut their way through the Syrian army is evident, since few as the survivors were, they effected an orderly retreat. That when night put an end to the combat, they must have maintained possession of that part of the field on which Judah fell, is evident from the fact that they could seek out and secure his body, which they carried safely to Modin, where they buried him; and that they did this against the will of the enemy, appears certain, when we remember that Bacchides had denied the rites of sepulture to the Jews he had slain at Bethsetha, or Beseth; and that he had done this long before his mind had been exasperated by

28*

the indignities practised on the body of his friend and companion-in-arms, Nicanor.

When the tidings of Judah's death reached Jerusalem, the whole city was plunged in the most poignant grief. Those who deserted him when alive, bitterly wept for him now that he was dead. Throughout the land the mourning was universal, and continued for some time. In imitation of the elegy which David wrote on the fate of Saul and Jonathan, the poets of Judea lamented the death of their hero in lofty strains, repeating "How is the mighty fallen! how is the preserver of Israel slain!"

And well they might lament; for Judah the Maccabee was decidedly the greatest and best of Jewish "public characters" since David. During the six years that the Maccabee administered the affairs of Judea, his merits, military, civil, and religious, and the services he rendered his country, were such that, notwithstanding the very limited sphere he had for his activity, they are entitled to our highest admiration. He found the country depopulated, Jerusalem and other cities of note deserted, the fields lying waste, commerce utterly destroyed, and the general ruin aggravated by the cruel and brutal outrages in which a ruffian soldiery, apostates as well as foreigners, were permitted to indulge. At his death, the country was again teeming with population, Jerusalem flourishing, agriculture prospering, and commerce reviving under the security which his vigorous administration afforded to life and property.

If such, notwithstanding incessant warfare, had been the success of his civil services, his merits in the cause of religion and public worship were to the full as important. Not only had he, under Providence, rescued Judaism from utter ruin, and restored the temple of Jerusalem to a condition somewhat approaching its pristine splendour, but the zeal with which he watched over the purity of the public worship and its ministers, the vigour with which he resisted the intrusion of Menelaus and of Alcimus, though backed by all the power of a mighty empire, and, above all, the piety and honesty with which, during three eventful years, he officiated as high-priest, assign to him a lofty rank among these functionaries.

But as both his civil and sacerdotal services were the offspring of his military prowess, it is as a warrior, as the proto-champion of religious freedom, that he is best known and most admired. An eminent French writer on military tactics, the illustrious Chevalier Folard, in his "Commentaries on Polybius," (lib. ii. cap. 1,) has the following remark on the generalship of the Maccabee: "After the reign of David, the Hebrews were frequently involved in great wars. We find much bravery in the soldiers, but no general who can be compared to Judah. The records are sufficiently particular in relating his actions, his tactics, his strategy, and his mode of combat. Marches, battles, retreats, crossings of rivers, attacks of camps, intrenchments, surprises, mountain-warfare, stratagems in the art of attack and defence, sieges, escalades—indeed, every thing that the science of war offers most grand and most sublime, are there found together. In vain the Maccabees are confronted by warlike and formidable troops, or have to deal with skilful and experienced generals; vain is the inferiority of numbers to which they are constantly condemned: nothing can daunt them or put them out of countenance. The actions of Judah and his brothers are numerous, and replete with profound and admirable instruction. Military men ought to make them their study, as there is much to be learned from them."

Such is the testimony which an eminent Gentile tactician offers to the great deeds of the Hebrew leader, to whose glorious career we are now forced reluctantly to bid farewell. Take him for all in all, he was a man the like of whom Israel has not yet seen again.

CHAPTER VII.

Jonathan succeeds his brother—Battle of Tekoah, and retreat across the Jordan—Alcimus—His death—Ariarethes VI.—Jonathan returns to Judea—State of parties—Bacchides invited by the apostates—Siege of Bethlagan—Syrians evacuate Judea—Internal peace and good government restored—Troubles in Syria—Conspiracy of the three kings—Balas claims the crown of Syria—Immunities granted to the Jews—Jonathan high-priest—Defeat and death of Demetrius I.—Reign of Alexander Balas—Onias builds a temple in Egypt—Samaritan temple and controversy.—(From 161 till 149 B. C. E.)

If the Jewish people fancied that, because the king of Syria had promised they should enjoy undisturbed the privilege of living and worshipping according to their own laws, they no longer needed the aid of the Maccabee, they were soon undeceived. The pæans that at the tidings of his death so joyfully resounded among all their enemies, were of themselves sufficient to open their eyes to the extent of their loss; and the course of events soon convinced them how injurious to themselves had been the apathy and timidity with which they had deserted their noble leader. Bacchides advanced to Jerusalem, and took possession of the city and temple, installing Alcimus as high-priest with great pomp. Under the protection, and at the invitation of these two chiefs, the numerous apostates whom the vigour of Judah had forced to quit the country now from all parts returned, eager to avenge on the orthodox population the ills they themselves had suffered during their banishment.

It is a just remark of the Greek historians, that no enemies are so rancorous or implacable as exiles who return to power. Those banished apostates, who, on their return home, found their party in the ascendant, neglected no opportunity to harrass, vex, and oppress the orthodox, not only by the public and unrestrained practice of idolatry, with all its hateful rites and abominations, but also, and still more, by denouncing to the Syrian authorities, or to Alcimus the high-priest, all such Jews as were known or supposed to be friendly to the cause and memory of the Maccabee; that is, in other words, the most pious and respectable personages in the nation.

The weight of these denunciations fell chiefly on the Hassidim, who now had ample cause to lament and to repent of that sinful bigotry which had induced them, the pledged and sworn defenders of the faith, so cruelly and ungratefully to forsake the purest and most highly-gifted of its champions. Not only did Alcimus, that Grecianizing assassin whose hands were red with the blood of slaughtered saints, bear supreme rule in the temple of the Lord to which, so long as Judah lived, the traitor had never been able to approach; not only was there evident proof that the worst corruptions of Jason and Menelaus would be re-enacted and outdone by their unprincipled successor,—but, in addition to the danger thus impending over the religion and the whole people of Israel, the Hassidim as a political body were especially singled out for destruction by the king and his lieutenant Bacchides.

For Demetrius had not forgotten the denunciation of Alcimus, "that the war was kept up by the men called Hassidim," (2 Macc. xiv. 6;) and his general was ambitious of the glory of being the pacificator of Judea, which, as he thought, could only be acquired by destroying the Hassidim, root and branch. Several of the principal officers that served under him were especially commissioned to make diligent search after the friends and supporters of the Maccabee. Their efforts were seconded by the returned apostates with all the rancour of exiles and the bitter zeal of renegades, denouncing to the Syrian commissioners, as Hassidim and adherents of Judah, those very men who had been the foremost to desert him, but who now were hunted out and put to death with a refinement of cruelty and torture surpassing every thing that the Jews had suffered since their return from Babylon. Modern biblical commentators are of opinion that during this time of persecution by Bacchides the 79th Psalm was composed, and with especial reference to the sufferings of the Hassidim, who are indeed introduced by name in the second verse: "They (the heathens) have given the dead bodies of thy servants as food unto the birds of heaven; the flesh of thy Hassidim (pious ones) unto the beasts of the earth."

Their misery was still further enhanced by a grievous famine that raged in Judea, crowded as that country was by the return of all the exiles and the numerous Syrian army and garrisons, which completely paralyzed the energies of the people, and forced every man to be so fully occupied with care for the subsistence of his own family, as to render him indifferent to every thing else; and to complete this hopeless condition of the Hassidim and of the orthodox Jews, they could find no leader. The monstrous ingratitude with which the people, the blind bigotry with which the Hassidim, had treated the Maccabee, were enough to deter any one from picking up and wielding the staff of command that had fallen from the grasp of the dying hero; since they proved how little reliance could be placed on public firmness or party constancy, and that even the most eminent public services do not carry with them a guarantee for public support in the hour of need.

The cause of Judaism seemed once more on the verge of destruction. All that during six glorious years of incessant and successful exertion had been gained by Judah was lost; and though no royal decree commanded the cessation of Jewish observances, or enacted the abrogation of the Law of Moses, that task was tacitly taken up by Alcimus, the high-priest, whose intention of effecting a fusion between Jews and heathens every day became more manifest.

But it was not to be. The parting charge of the venerable Mattathias, "to be zealous for the Law and to die for it," had not yet been forgotten by his sons; and when the few who still retained a love for their faith and their country repaired to Jonathan, a younger brother of Judah, and requested him to become their chief, that brave man readily accepted the dangerous distinction, and prepared to gather some force with which to stop the cruel progress of Bacchides.

The king's lieutenant, however, was too well served by his spies, the apostates, to remain long ignorant of the effort of Jonathan; and before the Jewish chief had half completed his preparations, the Syrian, at the head of a considerable body of troops, was marching to surprise and slay him. But the friends of the good cause were likewise on the alert: Jonathan had timely warning of the approaching danger, and with his few adherents retreated to the wilderness of Tekoah. There he fixed upon a spot almost inexpugnable, leaning on the river Jordan, the flanks covered on one side by a dense wood, and on the other by a large impassable morass; and thus inaccessible on three sides, his position could only be approached by a narrow defile or pass, which he thought might easily be defended by his brave followers, notwithstanding their great inferiority of numbers.

Jonathan was a man of dauntless courage, and of energy not inferior to his brother Judah; but he was not gifted in an equal degree with that intuitive quality which military men call the *coup d'œil*, and which enables a general with one rapid but unerring glance instinctively to take in *all* the advantages and disadvantages of the position he is about to occupy. Accustomed to be guided by the superior ability of his elder brother, the new chief, on first assuming supreme command, was far better qualified for the station of second-in-command than that of generalissimo; a discovery which he was not long in making, but which experience and military tact gradually enabled him to rectify.

Having placed his followers in a position of security, Jonathan's next care, on hearing that Bacchides was marching against him, was to place their equipage and goods, which were considerable in value and quantity, beyond the reach of the enemy. For this purpose he despatched his brother John, at the head of a convoy, to the Nabathean Arabs, who were at peace with the Maccabees, and to whose care these movables were to be intrusted. On his march, however, John was surprised by the Iambrians, who, suddenly issuing from their city of Medaba, fell upon him, slew him and his men, and seized upon the property they were conveying. These Beni-Iambri were a tribe of plundering Arabs, and their city was one which the Moabites had taken from the Israelitish tribe of Reuben, beyond the Jordan, (see Josh. xiii. 16, and Isa. xv. 2,) and of which subsequently these Arabs had obtained possession.

This act of unprovoked treachery which they committed against John and his small troop, soon became known to Jonathan, and was not long left unpunished. Having been informed that a great wedding was to be celebrated at Medaba, between a chief of the Iambrians and an Arabian princess, Jonathan further ascertained the day on which the bride was to be conducted home. He then placed himself with his men in ambush behind a hill; and as soon as the wedding-party, which was very numerous, came near enough, he fell upon and cut down four hundred of the escort, and carried away the plunder of their camp.

This daring act of highhanded retribution caused great excitement throughout Judea, as well as in the adjoining countries, and proved both to Jews and Gentiles that the old Maccabean spirit was not yet extinct, and that the cause of Judaism was still upheld by brave hearts and sharp swords. Bacchides was at once roused to action. His experience in the wars of the Jews was limited to the battle in which Judah had fallen; but this one specimen of their prowess had inspired him with a wholesome respect for Jewish valour; and he had arrived at the conclusion that it was far more safe to deal with them when they did not resist, than to assail them under harness.

Like most of Epiphanes's principal officers, he had been present at the sack of Jerusalem, and had seen how passive the Jews were on the sabbath-day; and though he must have heard that their views on this subject had undergone great change, and that Nicanor and his host had been destroyed on the sabbath-day, still the scene of unresisted slaughter he had witnessed at Jerusalem had left so strong an impression on his mind, that he determined to try whether the sabbath might not once more paralyze the defence of the Jews.

Accordingly, on a sabbath-day he attacked the narrow pass that led to Jonathan's camp, and by which alone it could be reached. His expectation of turning the holy day to his advantage was almost realized; for Mattathias and Judah both dead, the Hassidim began to question the lawfulness of self-defence on the sabbath-day. Moreover, the superior numbers of the enemy and their martial bearing produced a bad effect on the Jews, whose inferiority in numbers, armament, and discipline was not compensated for by confidence in the superior generalship of Jonathan. Indeed his deficiency in this respect now at once struck all his followers. For, while on the one hand it was true that the position he had chosen was one into which the enemy would find it very difficult to force their way, on the other hand it was equally true that, in case a retreat should become necessary, the Jews would find it next to impossible to force their way out, hemmed in as they were on every side by the same obstacles that kept the enemy out.

All this—the dread of violating the sabbath, the fear of the enemy's superior hosts, and the perilous position they held, acted so strongly on the minds of the Jews, that they were reluctant to engage the enemy, who had already entered the defile. But Jonathan had inherited from his brother Judah that species of military eloquence which goes right to the heart of the soldiers, and never fails to arouse their courage and to inflame their ardour. He now addressed his men, saying, "Come on, and let us fight for our lives, for it is not now with us as it was in time past. You see plainly that the battle is before and behind us: the Jordan on this, the morass and wood on that side. Nor is there any place left for us to turn aside to. Therefore cry ye now unto Heaven, that ye may be delivered."

As soon as he ceased speaking, his men, encouraged by his short but telling address, and urged on by the utter desperation of their condition, fell upon the enemy and killed a great number at the first onset. But the dense masses of Syrians had already advanced too far up the narrow pass to be borne back by the handful of Jews opposed to them. Gradually, and step by step, the Jews were compelled to recede as the Syrians pressed upon them, until the pass was forced, and the leading files of the enemy began to appear in the open space before Jonathan's camp. But the energy of Jonathan saved his little army, although their condition was hopeless. At his bidding, the Jews, all armed and accoutred as they were, rushed into the Jordan, and with sinewy arms swam to the opposite shore, where they took post.

This was a line of retreat on which Bacchides did not deem it advisable to pursue them. The Syrian general had now ascertained that the Jews would fight on the sabbath-day, if attacked. The forcing of the pass, though but half defended, had been attended by a heavy loss of men. According to Josephus, it cost the Syrians not less than two thousand killed. Content, therefore, with having expelled Jonathan and his "faction" from Judea, and with driving them across the Jordan into the midst of tribes hostile to their cause, Bacchides led his army back to Jerusalem, from whence he issued his orders for the fortifying and garrisoning such cities as where best adapted to keep the Jews in subjection, and to compel the Maccabean party either to submit, or at least to render any future attempts of theirs difficult of success.

Among these fortifications, Bethhoron, Emmaus, Bethel, Thimnatha, Gazara, and Bethzura completely bridled the entire province of Judea, while Acra commanded Jerusalem and the temple. In this last fortress, which received fresh and large supplies of men, arms, and provisions, the Syrian governor also placed the children of several of the most prominent families in Judea and Jerusalem, who were kept as hostages to prevent their parents and kindred from going over to Jonathan and his party.

While Bacchides was thus occupied in fortifying and building, Alcimus exercised his authority to demolish and pull down. As a first step toward his projected fusion of Jew and Gentile, the high-priest directed one of the inner walls of the temple to be demolished. This wall the First Book of Maccabees (ix. 54) calls "the wall of the inner court of the sanctuary," while Josephus (Antiq. lib. xii. cap. 17) designates it as "the wall of the old sanctuary," and adds that it had "formerly been built by the direction of the prophets Haggai and Zachariah."

Modern writers on Jewish history, are of opinion that the wall meant was that low stone partition or screen which divided the court of the uncircumcised from that of the Jews; and that Alcimus intended to give the former access to the privileged parts of the temple. But he lived not to see his orders carried out. He was suddenly seized with a palsy or paralytic cramp, which deprived him of speech, so that he died in great misery, and without being able to utter a word. As the king appointed no successor to his high office, matters in the temple remained as they had been before Alcimus assumed power.

The battle which Jonathan had fought against the Syrians, and which ended in his expulsion from Judea, had, nevertheless, been of signal advantage to that chief. His men had noticed that during the action the efforts of Bacchides had been principally directed against Jonathan's person; a circumstance which showed them what importance was assigned to the life of their leader by the enemy. Then the happy union of valour and skill with which Jonathan had defended his own person, and at the same time performed every duty of a commander, had excited their admiration; while the singular manner in which they had effected their retreat from their inextricable position by swimming across the Jordan, without loss—a feat never before performed by any army—led them and the Jewish people generally to believe that the especial protection of Providence was vouchsafed to Jonathan, as it had long been extended to his brother, the Maccabee.

In this belief they were further confirmed by the wretched end of Alcimus, and the sudden departure from Judea of Bacchides and his forces—events which followed close upon each other, and the last-named of which appeared to them altogether inexplicable. We, who are better acquainted with the annals of foreign nations in those times, know that the recall of Bacchides had been ordered by King Demetrius, in obedience to the mandate addressed to him by the Roman senate, in consequence of the treaty with Judah the Maccabee.

King Demetrius had never been recognised as lawful sovereign of Syria by the Romans; and was equally afraid of their enmity, and desirous of their friendship. (Polyb. legat. cap. xx.) When he received the letter of the senate, which ordered him to cease all hostilities against the Jews, he at once obeyed, and recalled his general and his army; but he did this so privately, to prevent the Jews from becoming too arrogant on the strength of their Roman alliance, that the cause of Bacchides' departure from Judea did not at the time transpire, and is not mentioned either in the Book of Maccabees or by Josephus. As it was, it gained for the Jews a respite of which they stood greatly in need; and thus we see that the very measure, for which wild fanatics had condemned and deserted Judah, became a means under Providence of greatly assisting the Jews, whom the wisdom and patriotism of the Maccabee continued to protect even after his death.

After Bacchides and his army had withdrawn from Judea, that country during two years enjoyed profound repose. For though Jonathan and his party had early tidings of Bacchides's departure, and at once returned to Judea, the Maccabean chief was careful not to commit any breach of the peace, and avoided every collision with the Syrian garrisons; who, on the other hand, were restrained by the king's command from exercising any hostilities against any portion of the Jewish people, so long as they themselves were not attacked.

The numerous apostates, with the loss of their great chief Alcimus, and the withdrawal of their great protection, the Syrian army, had lost much of their influence and all their active power. Conscious of their own weakness, and of the strong feelings entertained against them by the great mass of the people, the most obnoxious of these apostates took up their abode at Bethzura, or under the shelter of the heathen fortress Acra at Jerusalem, and thus avoided coming in contact with their enemies, the Hassidim. And those of the apostates who did not reside in these two strongholds lived quietly among their neighbours, giving as little offence as they could, and abstaining from every public display of their apostasy, except when under the safeguard of the Syrian garrisons, in whose heathen rites they joined. But this state of internal tranquillity did not suit the leaders of the apostate or Grecianizing Jews; for as their party was not sustained by any inward principle, the cohesion of its members could only be secured by the stimulus of a pressure from without, either crushing, as had been the vigour of Judah, or propelling, as had been the activity of Menelaus and of Alcimus.

To a party thus constituted, peace and quiet were the most dangerous destroyers; and accordingly the leaders saw with regret that each day of peace chilled the zeal and lessened the number of their adherents. Many of these, especially such as were not deeply stained with public apostasy, or who had adopted Grecian customs from caprice or fashion, were anxious to return to their own people, and to the faith and habits of their fathers.

The temple at Jerusalem, where the Cohanim, (priests,) freed from the pestiferous influence of Alcimus, had restored and carried on the public worship in its purity, unmolested by the garrison of Acra, greatly contributed to this revival of Jewish feeling; and thus the patriot or Maccabean party daily acquired strength and consistency, while the anti-national or apostate party was as visibly declining. Jonathan, assisted by his brother Simon, took advantage of this change,' and adopted every measure to consolidate the power and security of the Jewish people; so that when the hour of trial came, he was once more, and this time successfully, able to resist the invader.

During these two years (159–158 B. C. E.) of respite, King Demetrius had succeeded, by rich gifts and gross flattery, in obtaining from the Roman senate his pardon and a recognition of his right to the throne of Syria. The death of Judah, the expulsion of Jonathan from Judea, and the subsequent cessation of armed resistance in that country may probably, along with other events, have exercised some influence on the senate, which renewed its alliance with the king of Syria; so that from this quarter he had apparently nothing to fear.

But Demetrius had resided too long at Rome, and knew the Romans too well, to suppose that they would ever sincerely forgive his having deceived them, and gained the crown of Syria, which the senate had awarded to his cousin, the young Antiochus. King Demetrius had, therefore, soon after his accession, applied himself to conciliate the Greek kings in Asia Minor, and to court their alliance. Among these kings, the one whose friendship, from his personal character and the warlike qualities of his subjects, Demetrius was most desirous to secure, was his near kinsman, Ariarethes VI. of Cappadocia; a prince who had just mounted the throne—young, brave, and beloved by his people. The first advances of the king of Syria were cordially received; but when, still further to cement their friendship, Demetrius sent an embassy to the young king, offering him in marriage his own sister, Laodicé, the widow of Perseus, the last king of Macedon, Ariarethes became alarmed at this direct attempt to embroil him with the Romans, to whom at that time both Laodicé and her brother seemed equally obnoxious.

The king of Cappadocia, therefore, without hesitation rejected the proposal; and by so doing provoked the hatred of Demetrius, whose pride construed this refusal into an affront to him personally, as well as to the widowed queen. Thenceforth he was at no pains to conceal his resentment, which very peculiar circumstances in the royal family of Cappadocia soon enabled him to gratify.

The father of Ariarethes had espoused Antiochis, a daughter of Antiochus the Great, and aunt to King Demetrius. During the earlier years of her marriage this princess proved barren; but fearful lest her husband should repudiate a childless wife, she deceived him with several supposititious children. At length, however, she actually gave birth to a son; when her feelings as a mother getting the better of every other consideration, she confessed the frauds of which she had been guilty, obtained pardon, and procured her genuine offspring, Ariarethes, to be declared successor to the throne, and which, at the demise of his father, he actually ascended.

All this, however, did not pass without the highest dissatisfaction of Orophernes, the eldest of the sons the queen had palmed off on her husband; and who now complained that, through the unnatural artifices of a woman unworthy of all credit, he had been deprived of his right of primogeniture. The sincere or well-affected indignation of Orophernes might have evaporated in useless reclamations in the soft climate of Ionia, where, after the story of his pseudo-birth became known, the old king had sent him to reside. But the resentment so loudly expressed by Demetrius against the actual possessor of the throne of Cappadocia seemed to hold out to the pretender the assurance of a welcome reception at the court of Syria, and induced

Orophernes to hasten to Antioch, and to explain his wrongs to his kinsman, Demetrius.

His appeal for justice and aid was favourably heard and readily granted. The army which Bacchides just then had marched back from Judea, and which was ready for immediate action, was placed at his disposal; and the experienced generalship of Bacchides was opposed to the hasty levies of Ariarethes. The two armies met at Mazaca; the Cappadocians, partly deceived and partly defeated, threw down their arms. And notwithstanding speedy assistance from Eumenes, King of Pergamus, the hereditary foe of the kings of Syria, Ariarethes was driven from his kingdom, and sent to sue for aid to the Roman senate, the ordinary refuge of dispossessed kings. (159 B. C. E.)

The fruitless aid given on this occasion by Eumenes closed his eventful life and long reign of thirty-eight years. To the last, his exertions were always on the side of justice—a characteristic by which, in that profligate age, he stands most honourably distinguished. (Polyb. lib. xxxii. cap. 20.) Unfortunately for his *protegé* Ariarethes, the aged king of Pergamus did not stand well with the senate, as he had of late years given many plain indications that he was no longer to be duped by the artifices under which Rome disguised its lust of power. A splendid embassy from Orophernes, his presents, his promises, and flattery, outweighed the petitions of an abdicated king, low in circumstances and broken in spirit. All that Ariarethes could obtain was a decree appointing him to reign conjointly with his rival. (Appian, de Rebus, Syriac, cap. 47.) A decree barren and nugatory, since, toward carrying it into effect, no forces were raised, nor any orders issued. Orophernes remained in possession of the whole kingdom; and Bacchides having thus successfully carried out the mission of vengeance intrusted to him by his sovereign, led the Syrian army back to his government of Cœle-Syria. (158 B. C. E.)

His return had been anxiously expected by the leaders of the apostates in Judea, who witnessed the daily decay of their party, yet were so situated that, without the assistance of this Syrian general, they could do nothing to retrieve their affairs. Since the death of Alcimus, there was not among them any one man of sufficient rank or standing, to gain ready access to a monarch so difficult of approach as Demetrius. Moreover, Jonathan managed his affairs with such consummate prudence, that no overt act of recent disaffection or resistance to the royal authority could be laid to his charge. And as the king did not harbour against Jonathan that deep personal rancour with which he had pursued Judah—whom he had been persuaded by Alcimus to consider as a creature of the late regent Lysias, and the only remaining chief and representative of his faction—the apostates saw plainly that with the king their case was hopeless. But not so with Bacchides. Many of them were personally known to and trusted by that general, whose hatred of Jonathan and the whole Maccabean party was not less deeply rooted than their own.

Accordingly they entered into a correspondence with him soon after his return from Cappadocia, and invited him to surprise and destroy Jonathan and his whole "faction," which, they said, could be done in one night. Bacchides applied for permission to act to the king, who readily consented to a measure which at once might remove all the men who were likely to give him trouble, either in Judea or at Rome; and his general lost no time in marching to Judea, and in directing his partisans there to seize upon Jonathan as had been agreed upon.

But notwithstanding the secresy with which this plot had been carried on, it had not escaped the vigilance of the Jewish chief, whose measures, rapid and decisive, not only defeated the scheme against him, but also enabled him to punish the traitors who were trying to reopen the wounds of their long-bleeding country. For as the apostates were gathering to fall upon him, he suddenly came upon them, took fifty of the chief conspirators and put them to death, after which the rest dispersed and the whole design was discomfited. (1 Macc. ix. 57–61.)

Josephus (Antiq. lib. xiii. cap. 1) will have it that these fifty apostates were put to death by Bacchides in a rage of disappointment; but we prefer the authority of the First Book of Maccabees, the account given by which carries truth on the face of it. For it is far more probable that the Jewish chief should punish with death traitors that were plotting his ruin when they fell in his power, than that the Syrian general should slaughter his own unoffending partisans after they had escaped from captivity.

Nothing daunted by the miscarriage of his plot, Bacchides marched against Jonathan with all the confidence which superior power and previous triumphs could not fail to inspire. Jonathan and his brother Simon were, however, prepared for the attack. As they doubted whether they could at once, and with any chance of success, meet him in the open field, they had caused the dilapidated fortress of Bethlagan, also called Bethbasi, in the desert of Jericho, to be repaired and strongly fortified. And having laid in a large store of provisions and arms, they now, as the Syrian general advanced, retreated before him and threw themselves, with such forces as they had with them, into this stronghold, in which they were invested by Bacchides, who summoned all his adherents in Judea to join his numerous army.

The Maccabean brothers justly expected that their castle's strength would laugh the siege to scorn; and that the difficulties and losses to which their vigorous defence exposed the Syrian general would eventually compel him to retreat. But finding, after a time, that the obstinacy of Bacchides was equal to their own perseverance, Jonathan left his brother Simon in command of the fortress, while he himself, at the head of a small brigade, sallied forth to gather reinforcements. The organization which, during the two years of peace, the Jewish chief had been engaged in preparing and perfecting, now came into operation. While the Syrian army was detained before Bethlagan, Jonathan marched through the open country. Every town, every village, sent forth its contingent of armed men, and he soon saw himself at the head of an army sufficiently strong to resume the offensive, and to operate against the besiegers.

Odonarches, a Syrian general, and the Beni-Phasiron, an Arab tribe in league with Bacchides, who had been posted so as to cover the besieging army, were successively attacked and defeated by Jonathan. As the rear of Bacchides's army thus became exposed, Jonathan followed up his successes by attacking the camp, and forced the Syrian general in person, with the elite of his troops, to undertake its defence. Simon, however, who commanded in the fortress, did not remain inactive. Making a vigorous sally, he destroyed the works, and burnt the battering train and engines of the Syrians; and then falling on the besieging army, he discomfited that portion of it which was opposed to him, while his brother Jonathan inflicted great loss on the troops commanded by Bacchides himself.

That general now found his position no longer tenable. Vexed at heart at meeting with defeat where he had expected an easy victory, and discovering, too late, that he had been made the tool of an unprincipled faction, he vented his rage on the apostates who had invited him into Judea, and caused several of them to be put to death. It is doubtless this act of rage in Bacchides which Josephus confounds with Jonathan's act of justice.

After having thus sacrificed to his disappointment the

unhappy men who had caused so much ill to their country, and who, in their last moments might bewail their infatuation, Bacchides resolved to raise the siege; but he soon found himself so closely beset by the victorious Jews, that to retreat with honour seemed impossible; and his whole care evidently became how to extricate himself from his perilous position with as little disgrace as might be. Jonathan now enjoyed the satisfaction of having placed his enemy in the same hopeless condition as that from which he himself had escaped by swimming with his men across the Jordan.

But too honest a patriot to seek the gratification of his personal feelings where the good of his country required their sacrifice, Jonathan was no sooner informed of the altered frame of mind of the Syrian commander, than he hastened to prefer the lasting blessings of peace to the momentary advantage of military triumph, and despatched messengers to Bacchides with proposals of a pacific nature. These Bacchides was but too glad to accept; a treaty was negotiated and soon after ratified by both parties. And Bacchides, having solemnly sworn that he would never again act offensively against Jonathan or the Jews, marched with his army into Syria, and faithfully kept his oath as long as he lived.

By the articles of the treaty, all prisoners on both sides were to be released, and the authority of Jonathan as governor or sub-governor of Judea was recognised. As soon as Bacchides left the country, Jonathan took up his abode at Michmash, where he "judged" the people, or governed according to the Law of Moses, and much in the manner the ancient judges of Israel had done. He began with making a severe example of the apostates who had so frequently involved their people in bloodshed; and having cleared the country of their baneful presence, he next, to the extent of his power, reformed the public abuses which had sprung up during the late troubles; so that from this time (156 B. C. E.) Judea began once more to enjoy the advantages of internal peace and a regular government. (1 Macc. ubi supra, v. 62, ad fin.; Antiq. lib. xiii. cap. 2.)

The discomfiture of his great general Bacchides in Judea, was not the only nor yet the worst disappointment that King Demetrius at this time experienced. The recovery of the throne of Cappadocia by his mortal enemy Ariarethes was a blow by far more painful to his pride; while the discovery of his intrigues against Egypt, in its consequences became ruinous to himself. Ariarethes had returned from Rome with a barren decree of the senate in his favour, but without any means to enforce it. His friend and protector, Eumenes, King of Pergamus, had died during his absence in Italy; and that monarch's successor and brother, Attalus, however much inclined to support the cause of Ariarethes, was not sufficiently powerful to undertake his restoration, upheld, as his successful adversary was, by all the power of Syria and the partial recognition of his right by the Roman senate.

Thus left to his own most scanty resources, the first gleam of hope dawned on Ariarethes from Cappadocia itself, where the vices of his opponent became his most useful auxiliaries. Instead of atoning by superior merit for the defect in his title, Orophernes no sooner fancied himself firmly seated on his throne by the favour of Rome, and released from the control which the presence and counsels of Bacchides and his army imposed upon him, than he began to display the wanton arrogance of confirmed hereditary despotism. He trampled on the laws of the Cappadocians, and introduced among that simple and rustic people all the corruptions and effeminate vices he himself had acquired in Ionia, aggravated by brutal inebriety.

His last and insufferable outrage was the plunder of the revered Cappadocian temple at the foot of Mount Ariadné.

His enraged subjects revolted. Ariarethes, assisted by the king of Pergamus, was at hand to avail himself of their general rising; and Orophernes, afraid to encounter his rival in battle, fled precipitately to Antioch. Before his flight, however, he found means to secure a large sum of money, which he deposited at Priené, a city of Ionia, and long the place of his residence. (Polyb. lib. lxxii. cap. 12 et 20.)

The expulsion and restoration of Ariarethes are intimately connected with the affairs of Judea, as that country enjoyed two years of peace while the Syrian veterans were employed in Cappadocia; and afterward repaid the obligation by keeping those veterans so fully employed, and inflicting on them so severe a loss, that they were unable to march back against Ariarethes.

When Orophernes appeared in the presence of his Syrian ally, he found that there was but little prospect of retrieving his affairs by the means of Demetrius. During the period of that king's short-lived prosperity, his success in Cappadocia had tempted him to cast a longing eye on the island of Cyprus, an old possession of the crown of Egypt, which had been betrayed to, and during several years held by, Syria; but had been recovered by the Ptolemies not long before Demetrius's flight from Rome.

He was at peace with Egypt; he was indebted for his successful escape from Rome and Italy to the king of Egypt. Nevertheless, Demetrius was sufficiently unprincipled to enter into a secret correspondence with Archias, governor of Cyprus for Ptolemy Philometor, and by a bribe of five hundred talents (half a million of dollars) had engaged him to betray his trust and to surrender the island to Syria, as had been done once before by Ptolemy Macron, who, as a reward for his treason, became the friend and confidant of Antiochus Epiphanes. But Archias possessed less ability than Macron, or was more unfortunate.

The conspiracy was brought to light; the traitor hanged himself; and Demetrius incurred the twofold mortification of losing a large sum of money, and likewise all credit for good faith among his neighbours.

King Demetrius was by nature of an indolent and thoughtless disposition. The energy displayed in his escape from Rome, the prudence and decision which dictated and carried out his plans on that occasion, and during the first measures of his reign, were not his own; and as soon as the influence and counsel of men like Polybius, Menyllus, and the king's foster-father, Diodorus, were no longer afforded to him, and he was left to his own guidance, his reign became a series of faults and follies. After having wantonly provoked the enmity of Cappadocia by his pride, and of Egypt by his rapacity, he felt his own inability to control or soothe the hostility he had aroused. His only care was to shut out all knowledge of the consequences of his own acts. He has already been described as a hard drinker and a keen sportsman. But with increase of years his slothfulness increased; and renouncing the pleasures of the chase as too fatiguing, he sought and found his sole delight in the wine-cup.

To enjoy his degrading carousals unmolested by the intrusion of business, he built in the neighbourhood of Antioch a strong castle fortified with four lofty towers; there he shut himself up with the companions of his revels, in careless and drunken oblivion of his crown and of his subjects.

In an age when kings, though seldom qualified to be their own ministers, were still obliged, according to the usage of the times, to answer petitions, to judge causes, and to assist personally at the public ceremonies of religion, Demetrius's total seclusion from affairs could not be tolerated. His subjects complained that they wanted the protection of government, and a conspiracy was formed against him, in which Orophernes had the ingratitude to join. But the treasonable design was discovered in time; and of all those concerned in it, Orophernes alone escaped death, because his person was still deemed important to embroil the affairs of Cappadocia whenever the opportunity should offer. However, during the many years of Ariarethes's prosperous and peaceful reign, Orophernes never could find any such opportunity; and as his protector relapsed into his former drunken habits and seclusion, the pretender to the throne of Cappadocia retired to Priené, where he lived and died in obscurity.

King Demetrius in his strong castle was no inapt image of the ostrich, who, when pursued, is said to hide his head in a bush, and fancies that, because he cannot see his pursuers, they cannot see him. But though the king of Syria no longer troubled himself about his neighbours, they were all the more intent on taking advantage of his total disregard of his kingly duties, and of the wide field he thereby opened for the plots and machinations of his many enemies at home and abroad.

The kings of Egypt and of Cappadocia had been personally wronged by him; the king of Pergamus was his hereditary enemy. These three kings entered into a conspiracy against Demetrius, the object of which was to ruin him by raising a pretender to his throne. To insure the success of this scheme, the confederates admitted into their confidence Heraclides, who had been treasurer of Babylonia under Antiochus Epiphanes and the regent Lysias, but had been disgraced and expelled by Demetrius in the early part of his reign, and who since then had resided at Rhodes. With him the three kings entered into a correspondence, and encouraged him to raise up a rival against Demetrius who, through their assistance and the disgust of the Syrians, might deprive that monarch of his crown.

Heraclides readily consented, and soon discovered a Rhodian youth of obscure birth, named Balas, who seemed well qualified to personate Alexander, a deceased son of Antiochus IV. Epiphanes, and as such to lay claim to the throne of Syria. As soon as he had been sufficiently tutored in the part he was to act, he publicly advanced his pretensions, which were at once acknowledged by the three confederate kings. (153 B. C. E.) He was then sent to Rome, together with Laodicé, a true daughter of Antiochus, who readily entered into his views, out of revenge for the murder of her brother Antiochus V.

The senate soon detected the imposture. But mindful of their traditional policy, to weaken by intestine commotions those kingdoms which yet preserved the power of resistance, and actuated by their old grudge against Demetrius for having contrived to seize on the crown of Syria without their consent, the senators solemnly recognised Balas as the son of their old ally, King Antiochus. As such, they empowered him to raise forces for the recovery of a kingdom in which he could have had no just pretensions to supersede Demetrius, the son of the elder brother, even had his alleged birth been true. Fortified by this recognition, Balas now assumed the name of ALEXANDER, and the title of king of Syria; and attended by an armed force, he sailed to Ptolemais (previously Accho, now Acre) in Palestine, where he was joined by numbers who had become disaffected to Demetrius. That infatuated prince was now fairly roused from his lethargy, and came forth from his disgraceful retreat; but it was too late.

Among the various nationalities interested in the transfer of the crown of Syria, and who might be expected to side with the one or the other of the competitors, the Jews held a prominent rank. Three years had now elapsed since Bacchides had been compelled to retreat from Judea. During the whole of that time the country had enjoyed peace under the government of Jonathan, whose authority was recognised by the whole people. And though the Syrians still held and strongly garrisoned Fort Acra at Jerusalem, and the other strongholds erected by Bacchides, in the first-named of which the hostages taken by that general were still confined, yet as the apostates, comparatively few in number, alike dispirited and powerless, hid themselves under the protection of the Syrian garrisons, and the latter received no orders from the king to molest or interfere with the Jews, the public peace was not disturbed; while Jonathan grew so powerful, that his alliance became of the utmost importance to each of the contending parties.

Demetrius, in particular, who had been so feelingly convinced of the strength and bravery of the Jews, had most cause to use all possible means in order to prevent their declaring for Alexander Balas. To effect this, Demetrius wrote a letter to Jonathan full of expressions of friendship, appointing him his general in Judea, with power to levy what forces and to fabricate what arms he pleased, as the king's friend and ally. To this letter was added an order for the instant release of the Jewish hostages still detained at Acra, and who, in violation of the treaty with Bacchides, had now been confined nearly eight years. As soon as Jonathan received this royal rescript, he repaired to Jerusalem, caused the king's orders to be communicated to the garrison, and demanded that, according to the tenour thereof, the hostages should be delivered up to him. The commanders of Fort Acra, on seeing the great power intrusted to Jonathan by the king, dared not hesitate about the matter, but at once complied with his demand; and Jonathan had the satisfaction of reuniting parents and children who had so long been separated, that they scarcely hoped ever to meet again in this life.

Jonathan further availed himself of the authority with which he was now invested to raise an army, which, as there was neither check nor danger to prevent men from joining him, soon became very numerous. At his summons, the commanders of the different fortresses garrisoned by the Syrians throughout the country, and who found themselves too weak to resist, surrendered these strongholds to him, and with their men retreated out of the country. The only fortified places in Judea still held by the Syrians were Acra and Bethzura, in which the apostate Jews had found shelter; and as these were afraid that on their retreat they might be attacked and destroyed, they determined to die sword in hand, unless they could obtain such terms as should secure to them and theirs life, liberty, and property.

But Jonathan was too wise a politician to allow personal or party resentments to lead him astray into the diverting of his means and attention from the great struggle at hand, or to embark in an enterprise so hazardous as the attack of the strong fortress of Acra, garrisoned, moreover, by the troops of King Demetrius, under whose authority Jonathan professed to act. He therefore contented himself for the present with removing from Michmash to Jerusalem, where he took up his residence, and caused the repairs of the fortifications, both of the city and temple, to be forthwith commenced under his own personal direction.

The efforts made by Demetrius to secure the support of Jonathan could not long remain concealed from Balas. When he understood how powerful a friend Jonathan was able to prove to the party for which he should declare himself, and ascertained the favours with which Demetrius had lately attempted to bribe the Maccabean chief, he determined to outbid his rival, and to draw Jonathan to his own side. For this purpose he wrote him the following letter, which Josephus has preserved, (Antiq. lib. xiii. cap. 5,) and which we transcribe as a proof of the importance attached to the friendship of Jonathan and the support of the Jews:

"King Alexander to his brother Jonathan sendeth greeting: Being informed of your power and valour, and that you are worthy of our friendship, we constitute you high-priest of your nation; and it is our pleasure that you be enrolled in the number of the king's friends. To this end we have sent you a purple robe and a golden crown, not doubting a suitable return from you for our affection and friendship."

This most obliging letter, together with the high dignities it conferred, and the robe and crown that accompanied it,[7] Jonathan did not hesitate to accept; and at the ensuing feast of tabernacles (153 B. C. E.) he assumed the high-priestly office, and put on the vestments peculiar to that dignity amid the acclamations of the people. For not wishing to hold the first rank in the Jewish hierarchy solely by the appointment of one whose royal birth and claim to the Syrian crown were so strongly suspected, nor yet to enter the Holy of Holies with no better right than what the selfishness or caprice of a heathen could confer, Jonathan submitted his advancement to the high-priesthood to the choice of the people, who readily elected him. Nor does it appear that at the time there was any claimant whose title was superior to that of the Asmonean family, which recognised Jonathan as its chief.

The last legitimate high-priest of the line of Jehozadak was Onias III., who was expelled by his brother Jason, and assassinated at the instigation of his younger brother, Menclaus. These two usurpers, who succeeded each other,

---

[7] This circumstance explains why Haman demanded a royal robe and golden crown for the "man whom the king delighteth to honour," (Esth. vi. 8,) and why such particular importance is attached to Mordecai's coming forth from the king's presence "in royal apparel, and with a great crown of gold." (Ibid. viii. 15.) These, it appears, were the highest insignia of the king's favour, and conferred only on his special and personal friends.

purchased the office from Epiphanes to the exclusion of their nephew Onias, the son and legitimate heir of their murdered elder brother. On the execution of Menelaus, that exclusion was, by the advice of Lysias the regent, made perpetual, and Alcimus was appointed by royal authority.

After his death the office remained vacant for seven years. In this interval, the young Onias, finding that his just claims had been disregarded, and that there was but little likelihood of their ever being recognised and acted upon by King Demetrius, in his impatience fled from Antioch to Alexandria, where he entered into the service of King Ptolemy Philometor; and being a man of great abilities and valour, he rose to the chief command of that king's armies and to a high place in his councils. He also introduced another Jew, named Dositheus—like himself, a man of superior abilities—to the king's confidence; and these two men so entirely engrossed the king's favour during his whole reign, that the jealousy and hatred they provoked subsequently caused great suffering to the Egyptian Jews.

This Onias, though not an apostate, was suspected of not being strictly orthodox. He was known to have adopted foreign habits; and from his long absence from Judea and constant residence among heathens, was not only become a stranger to the feelings of the Jews, but was viewed by them with an eye of suspicion, which his subsequent conduct fully realized. To appoint him to the highest dignity in the priesthood, was out of the question, at a time when not only the utmost purity of religious principle, but also the most active zeal for strict orthodoxy, were deemed indispensable to the first functionary in the temple.

And when thus the hereditary rights of Onias had been set aside, no one could compete with the claims of the Asmoneans. They were descended from the order of Joarib, the first among the priestly families. To their public services it was, under Providence, owing that the temple of Jerusalem, instead of being desecrated by a heathen altar, was again restored to the worship of the One True God. In that temple Judah had, during three years, performed the duties of *sægan*, *i. e.* representative of the high-priest; and when Simon, the elder of the two surviving sons of Mattathias—three had already fallen in battle for their country—voluntarily stood back, no other competitor could balance the title of Jonathan.

He thus became the first of his family who, by the voice of the priests and of the people, as well as by the appointment of the sovereign, enjoyed the pontifical dignity. After him his brother Simon was elected by "the priests and the people," as was subsequently Simon's son Jochanon. The succession then became hereditary, and continued in the family of the Asmoneans till the days of Herod, who caused the last legitimate inheritor to be assassinated. After that, the appointment became venal and arbitrary, as will hereafter be related.

Jonathan's political abilities were too fully equal to the exigencies of his singular position to permit his committing himself prematurely, by declaring for either one or the other of the two competitors, each of whom had, of their own accord and without his solicitation, granted him valuable advantages, of which he did not hesitate to avail himself. For while he accepted from Balas the offices of high-priest and ethnarch, or prince of Judea, it was as general commanding for Demetrius in that province that he raised forces, manufactured arms, and took possession of the strongholds held by the Syrians.

Nor must Jonathan be accused of duplicity, because he accepted from each of the rivals whatever each of them was disposed to give him; for he was certain that neither of them was actuated by friendship for him, or kindly feelings toward the Jews. Demetrius, like Balas, looked only to himself; and placed between the two, Jonathan acted on the same principle; for well he knew that the crisis then impending might secure to the Jews peace and prosperity, or involve them in utter ruin; and that the alternative depended on the circumspection of his own conduct. And it must be confessed that he steered his frail bark with such consummate prudence, that he not only weathered the storm, but also secured to his people many and great advantages.

When Demetrius found how greatly his first advances to Jonathan had been outbid by Balas, but that, notwithstanding this, the Maccabean chief had not openly declared in favour of the pretender, the legitimate king of Syria conceived the hope that he might in his turn be able so greatly to outbid Balas as to leave nothing for him to offer. And as he supposed that Jonathan, as well as the Jews generally, were actuated by one sordid motive only—gain for themselves—he took a last step to secure their support.

The letter he despatched on that occasion, and which has been preserved to us, is a masterpiece of state craft. Balas had addressed himself to Jonathan only, and had bestowed on that leader, personally, every boon his utmost ambition could crave. The first rank as spiritual and temporal chief of Judea, the distinction of being declared the king's friend, and the endearing epithet of "brother," had all been granted to him. But to the Jewish people Balas had granted nothing. Demetrius now addressed himself "unto the people of the Jews." Content with confirming to Jonathan by implication the power and dignities of which he had already assumed possession, and designating him as the "high-priest," but not by name, Demetrius speaks to the "people," and promises them exemption from actual burdens, and also future privileges of the most important kind. His letter[8] is extremely curious,

---

[8] "King Demetrius unto the people of the Jews sendeth greeting: Whereas ye have kept covenant with us, and continued in our friendship, not joining yourselves with our enemies, we have heard thereof, and are glad. Wherefore now continue ye still to be faithful unto us, and we will well recompense you for the things ye do in our behalf, and will grant you many immunities, and give you rewards. And now do I free you, and for your sake I release all the Jews, from tributes; and from the customs of salt, and from crown taxes, and from that which appertaineth unto me to receive for the third part of the seed, and the half of the fruit-trees, I release from this day forth, so that they shall not be taken of the land of Judea, nor of the three governments which are added thereunto, out of the country of Samaria and Galilee, from this day forth forevermore. Let Jerusalem also be holy and free, with the borders thereof, both from tenths and tributes; and as for the tower which is at Jerusalem, I yield up my authority over it, and give it to the high-priest, that he may set in it such men as he shall choose, to keep it. Moreover, I freely set at liberty every one of the Jews that were carried captives out of the land of Judea into any part of my kingdom; and I will that all my officers remit the tributes, even of their cattle. Furthermore, I will that all the feasts, and sabbaths, and new moons, and solemn days, and that the three days before the feast, and the three days after the feast, shall be all days of immunity and freedom for all the Jews of my realm. Also, no man shall have authority to meddle with them or to molest any of them in any manner. I will, further, that there be enrolled among the king's forces about thirty thousand men of the Jews, unto whom pay shall be given as belongeth to all the king's forces. And of them shall be placed in the king's strongholds, of whom, also, *some* shall be set over the affairs of the kingdom, which are of trust; and I will that their overseers and governors be of themselves, and that they live after their own laws, even as the king hath commanded in the land of Judea. And concerning the three governments that are added to Judea from the country of Samaria, let them be joined with Judea, that they may be reckoned to be under one, nor bound to obey other authority than the high-priest's. As for Ptolemais, and the land pertaining thereto, I give it as a free gift to the sanctuary. Moreover, I give every year fifteen thousand shekels of silver, out of the king's account, to the places appertaining. And all the overplus which the officers paid not in, as in former time, from henceforth shall be given toward the use of the

showing the extent and ramifications of the manifold and vexatious "exactions" which the kings of Syria imposed upon their subjects. As such it bears a remarkable resemblance to the decree passed on the memorable night of the 4th of August, 1789, by the Constituent Assembly, which consecrated the opening of the French Revolution, and forever abolished the "exactions" imposed by the "feudal system" on France and the greater part of Europe.

In addition to this singular enumeration of taxes and dues, and the curious information respecting the fiscal regulations of the ancients, this letter affords valuable proof of the extreme populousness of Judea; for since the king offers as a boon to the nation to enlist thirty thousand able-bodied men in his service, it shows that such a number could be easily spared from the labours of agriculture and the trades of cities and towns. According to the rule of computation adopted by modern statistics, it would give us for Judea, as it then was, exclusive of Samaria, Idumea, and the land beyond Jordan, a population of nearly three millions. The three days before and after the feast, of which the king speaks, also convey to us information of which we shall have to say more hereafter.

But all the diplomatic skill with which King Demetrius and his advisers had drawn up this curious document, failed to produce the effect desired. The very magnitude

---

temple. And beside this, the five thousand shekels of silver which they took from the uses of the temple out of the accounts, year by year, even those things shall be released, because they appertain to the priests that minister. And whosoever they be that flee unto the temple at Jerusalem, or be within the liberties thereof, being indebted unto the king, or for any other matter, let them be at liberty, and all that they have in my realm. For the building, also, and the repairing of the works of the sanctuary, expenses shall be given out of the king's account. Yea, and for the building of the walls of Jerusalem, and the fortifying thereof round about, ex penses shall be given out of the king's account, as also for the building of the walls of Judea."

of the promised concessions and privileges served to defeat the aim intended, since it was evident they were extorted by the distress or fears of the moment, and carried with them no guarantee that they, or any of them, would be faithfully observed the moment King Demetrius again became freed of the "pressure from without."

Then, again, the omission of Jonathan's name from the whole letter was not calculated to inspire that chief with any great confidence in the king's good feelings toward him, as the title "high-priest" might designate any person whom Demetrius at any time might please to appoint; and, lastly, the public feeling was strongly against King Demetrius. The people could not but remember that when Nicanor wished to remain at peace with the Jews, the king's positive and peremptory commands had compelled that ill-fated warrior to renew those hostilities which he carried on with such ferocity against the Jews, and with so fatal a result to himself and his army. Nor could Jonathan and the Maccabeans forget that it was the king's groundless but personal rancour against Judah which had persecuted and pursued the hero even unto death. All these considerations combined to induce Jonathan, with the full consent of his people, to throw the whole weight of his power and influence into the scale of Balas; and to do this at a time when the pretender had met with a check, so that the joining him became, in his estimation, all the more meritorious.

King Demetrius, who, when sober, was destitute neither of courage nor conduct, attacked Balas, and defeated his army with great loss. But the party of the pretender, strengthened as it was by the addition of Jonathan, was too widely spread to be crushed by one defeat, as long as its chief survived. The three confederate kings hastened to support their ally, and reinforced his army so strongly, that in the next campaign Balas felt justified in staking the decision of the contest on a great battle; and fortune favoured him to the utmost of his wishes. Demetrius was defeated and put to flight. His horse plunging into a bog, he was thrown off, intercepted, and slain by his pursuers. He fell in the thirty-fifth year of his age, and the twelth of his reign, (151 B. C. E.,) leaving two sons, Demetrius and Antiochus, destined successively to fill his throne. These young princes owed their immediate safety to the precaution their father had taken of sending them, before the battle, to the free city of Cnidus, on the coast of Caria. Their enemies either knew not the place of their retreat, or attempted not to wrest them from it, in violation of the neutrality maintained by that small but respectable commonwealth. (Justin, lib. xxxv. cap. 2.)

Balas, or King Alexander, as he now was universally designated, thus became master of the Syrian throne, and hastened to evince the gratitude he entertained for Jonathan's seasonable support. In order to fortify himself in his newly-acquired kingdom, Alexander Balas solicited in marriage Cleopatra, the daughter of Ptolemy Philometor. The king of Egypt, though fully cognizant of Balas's humble birth and bold imposture, granted his request; and sailing with his daughter to Ptolemais, he there met the low-born but fortunate usurper whom he had helped to place on the throne of his kinsman of Syria, and whose nuptials he now honoured with his presence. Jonathan, with a numerous retinue, likewise repaired to that city, presented himself before the two kings, and was received with great marks of friendship and esteem.

During the marriage festivities, which were celebrated for several weeks and with great pomp, some apostate Jews appeared before King Balas with accusations against Jonathan. But the king, resolved not to hear any thing against his friend, caused a proclamation to be made through the city, expressly forbidding any such complaint to be brought before him. Still further to mortify the enemies of the Maccabean chief, the king seated him, clothed in purple, next to himself, confirmed all his former grants, made him commander-in-chief of all the royal forces in Judea, and also gave him titles and governments in other parts of his kingdom. All this so greatly terrified Jonathan's accusers, that fearful of what mischief might befall them for presuming to appear against the king's favourite, they secretly departed from Ptolemais, and were not heard of again during the remainder of that reign. Jonathan, on the other hand, having made considerable presents to the king and queen and to their court, returned into Judea highly satisfied with his reception, and congratulating himself and people on their wise and fortunate choice of such a sovereign.

From this time the Jewish nation became more and more considerable, not only in Judea and throughout the Syrian monarchy, where they enjoyed the fullest equality, civil and religious, but also in other countries, especially in Egypt, where, as we have already stated, Onias and Dositheus held the highest rank in the king's confidence, had the chief command of the army, and the direction of the affairs of state. The king of Egypt and his sister-wife Cleopatra were both favourable to the Jews, intrusted them with the guard of their principal fortresses, and gave many of them high offices at court, which brought them into continual intercourse with their sovereigns. In return for these favours, the Jews firmly and bravely supported the cause of King Philometor in his long wars against his brother Physcon; so that the four years of Balas's reign form an especially prosperous episode in the annals of the Jewish people.

Indeed, the favour, influence, and wealth which the Jews of Egypt enjoyed, induced their sacerdotal chief, Onias, to attempt and carry through a singular undertaking—namely, the raising in Egypt of a temple in which the sacrifices should be brought, and all other ritual observances, peculiar to the temple of Jerusalem, should be fully adhered to, although the Law of Moses expressly restricted these rites to the ONE place, which "the Lord should choose in one of the tribes," where "the Lord would cause his name to dwell." (Deut. xii. 11, 14.)

Onias had attended his sovereigns on their visit to Ptolemais, and had there convinced himself that Jonathan was too firmly seated in his high office to leave any room for hope to any competitor. At the same time, Onias, with envy and indignation, compared his own position as a servant (high in dignity, trust, and power, but still "a servant") to the king of Egypt, with that of the prosperous usurper—for as such he considered Jonathan—who was installed in that pontifical chair which was his (Onias's) birthright; and who, as high-priest and chief of the Jews, was little inferior to the kings into whose companionship he was received almost as an equal. The temple of Jerusalem, with its Holy of Holies and the vestments of Aaron, were—Onias felt it—forever beyond his reach. But it might be possible to raise a rival temple that should also boast of its Holy of Holies, and in which he himself, arrayed in the vestments of high-priest, might on the day of atonement perform those solemn rites which formed the peculiar privilege of "the priest, who shall be anointed and who shall be inducted to minister as priest in his father's stead." (Lev. xvi. 32.)

It is true that this new temple would be destitute of that halo of glory which its holiness and high fame spread around that of Jerusalem. But then—whispered his pride—whatever defects the temple might be taxed with, would be fully compensated by the superior sanctity of his own claims as the legitimate successor of Eleazar the son of Aaron, and sole representative and inheritor, by indefeasible hereditary right, of Jehozadak, the last high-priest on whose breast the *Urim* and the *Thummim*, those oracles of the living God, had been permitted to rest.

Nor was he altogether unable to adduce something like scriptural warranty to authorize his raising a second temple out of Jerusalem and beyond the limits of Judea. The prophet Isaiah has the remarkable prophecy—"On that day shall five cities in the land of Egypt be speaking the language of Canaan, and swearing by the Lord of hosts. The city of HACHAIRES shall one be called. On that day shall there be an altar to the Lord in the midst of the land of Egypt, and a pillar at its border to the Lord; and it shall be for a sign and for a testimony unto the Lord of hosts in the land of Egypt, for they shall cry unto the Lord because of the oppressors, and he will send them a helper and a chief, and he shall deliver them. And the Lord will be made known to the Egyptians, and the Egyptians shall know the Lord on that day, and will do service *with* sacrifice and oblation; they will also make vows unto the Lord and perform them." (Isa. xix. 18–21.)

This prophecy, though ambiguous enough in itself, was yet sufficiently clear to suit the purpose of Onias, who no sooner returned to Alexandria than he submitted to the king and queen his plan, in which the political interests of Egypt were brought as prominently forward as his own rights and hopes of pontifical dignity. King Philometor readily gave his consent to an undertaking which, if approved of by the Egyptian Jews, would effectually dissolve their connection with, and dependance on, the temple of Jerusalem.

But the difficulty was to obtain the consent and support of these Jews in the face of a positive prohibition of the Law. The prophecy which Onias adduced in his support was differently construed by the learned Jews of Alexandria from what it had been by him. The *Ketib*, or text of the prophecy, had *Ir hachaires*, "city of the sun;" the

Keri (amended and usual reading,) however, had *Ir haires,* "city of destruction." This usual reading Onias rejected, preferring the text as it stood. And as *Heliopolis* in Greek corresponds to *Ir hachaires* in Hebrew, Onias, in order literally to fulfil the prophecy, fixed upon the ruins of an ancient Egyptian temple in the *nome* of Heliopolis whereon to build his temple.

This circumstance gave great scandal to the Jews of Alexandria, who looked upon the place as defiled, and offered every opposition in their power to Onias, his reading, and his temple. It is, however, singular that, subsequently, the great Targumist, Jonathan ben Uzziel, (in loco,) as well as the Talmud, (*tr. Menachoth,* f. 119, A,) read with Onias, "city of the sun," while most of the latter Jewish commentators render it "city of destruction."

Notwithstanding the strong opposition he encountered, Onias was too fully determined to carry out his plan, and too firmly supported by the king's favour, to renounce his undertaking, or even to choose another site for his temple. One learned writer (Scaliger, in chronol. Euseb. sub. an. 149) asserts that in persisting in his choice Onias was influenced by another motive besides that of carrying out the prophecy to the letter,—that he was governor of the *nome* or district of Heliopolis, in which he had built a city named after him, Onion, and which he had peopled with Jews, chiefly refugees from Judea and Syria.

His temple was built after the model of that at Jerusalem, but was neither so large nor so sumptuous. The whole temple area he caused to be surrounded by a strong stone wall; and within the temple itself he placed the altars of incense and of burnt-offering, the table of shew-bread and the veil, in all respects like Jerusalem, the only difference being, that instead of the seven-branched candlestick, Onias contented himself with a stately golden lamp, which hung from the roof by a chain of the same metal. In this temple Onias inducted himself as high-priest, (149 B. C. E.,) but could not succeed in placing it in the general estimation, or even in that of the Egyptian Jews, on a level with the temple at Jerusalem, where those priests who had once officiated at Heliopolis were never suffered to minister or to eat of holy things. Both edifices, however, experienced the same fate by the same hand. That of Jerusalem was destroyed, and five years later that of Heliopolis was shut up, by the Roman emperor, Vespasian.

The warm debates which Onias and his building at Heliopolis had caused among the Jews of Alexandria, served to drag from their obscurity the claims of a third temple, that of the Samaritans on Mount Gerizim. This temple had been built upward of two hundred and fifty years before by Sanballat the Horonite, the greatest of the adversaries of Nehemiah and of the rebuilding of Jerusalem. His daughter, a heathen woman, had been married to Manasseh, a grandson of Eliashib the high-priest, and, like Onias, a descendant of Jehozadak. When Nehemiah annulled these mixed marriages, and compelled the priests and the people to repudiate their non-Israelitish wives, Manasseh refused to submit or to part from his wife, and was, in consequence, expelled from Jerusalem. (Neh. xiii. 28.)

Josephus tells us (Antiq. lib. xi. cap. 5,) that this Manasseh, having been banished from Judea, fled with his wife to her father Sanballat, governor of Samaria, who, in order to reward him for his faithful attachment to his wife, and to compensate him for his losses in Judea, caused a temple to be built on Mount Gerizim, where the Lord was to be worshipped with offerings and services similar to those of Jerusalem. Of this establishment, Sanballat appointed his son-in-law—a genuine descendant of Aaron—high-priest; and in his family the dignity remained hereditary, though the orthodox priests at Jerusalem denied the legitimacy and purity of Manasseth's successors, because of their descent from a heathen mother, contrary to the express prohibition of the Law. (Lev. xxi. 14.)

This establishment of Sanballat's attracted to Samaria great numbers of Jews, who, like Manasseh, had married strange wives from whom they could not bring themselves to part, or who had rendered themselves amenable to punishment by other transgressions of the law, and who thenceforth found an asylum and ready welcome in Samaria. By these means the population of Samaria received a strong infusion of Jewish blood; a circumstance that doubtless caused and kept alive the bitter feeling of rancour that these two races entertained toward each other; for the exiles and their descendants would naturally hate the Jews as tyrants and oppressors, while the Jews would as naturally detest the exiles and their descendants as renegades and traitors.

The temple of Samaria, like the Samaritans themselves, had undergone many changes and vicissitudes, though always greatly influenced by the aspect and condition of Jewish affairs. When, through the favour of Alexander the Great, the star of Judah was in the ascendant, none were so eager as the Samaritans to proclaim their affinity with Jews and Judaism, in order to obtain a share in the privileges and immunities which the generous conqueror granted to the chosen people. When, on the other hand, Antiochus Epiphanes proscribed Judaism, and almost exterminated the Jews, the Samaritans indignantly repudiated all affinity or connection with the rebels of Judea, and requested permission to dedicate their temple to Jupiter Xenius, "the defender of strangers." Now, that an ambiguous prophecy was brought forward in favour of an Egyptian city and temple, the Samaritans thought the time had come to vindicate the superior sanctity of their own temple both over Jerusalem and over Heliopolis.

Their pretensions were no sooner announced than they were most strenuously rejected, not only by the adherents of Onias, but also by those Jews who were opposed to his undertaking. The disputes waxed fierce, and were fomented by the Greeks and Egyptians, who, in their impartial hatred of Jews and Samaritans, derived a malignant satisfaction and pleasure from setting them by the ears. At length the controversy rose to such a height as to endanger the public peace, when the spokesmen of the two parties were summoned before the judgment seat of King Philometor. There the rival claims were fairly investigated. The Samaritans alleged the superior sanctity of Mount Gerizim—a spot twice appointed by Moses for a blessing. (Deut. xi. 30; xxvii. 12.) The Jews replied, that though this was true, Moses himself had not assigned any superior sanctity to Mount Gerizim over Mount Ebal, on which the curse was to be pronounced, but that he classed them together, saying, " Behold, they are on the other side of Jordan." (Ib. xi. 30.) That, subsequently, he speaks of " the place which the Lord shall choose in one of thy tribes," (Deut. xii. 14,) without the most remote allusion to Mount Gerizim, which had already been chosen for a different purpose. The Jews further proved that the temple of Jerusalem had been chosen by the Lord, who had permitted a visible sign of his divine presence to rest thereon, (1 Kings, viii.10,) a distinction never conferred on Mount Gerizim and its temple.

This great suit, IN WHICH THE LITIGANTS AS WELL AS THE JUDGE FULLY RECOGNISED THE AUTHENTICITY AND TRUTHFULNESS OF THE FIVE BOOKS OF MOSES, was eventually and solemnly decided in favour of Jerusalem and its ancient and most holy temple. Moreover, as in the course of the proceedings it was discovered that the designs harboured by the representatives and advocates of the Samaritans were highly dangerous and injurious to the public peace, these advocates, two in number, were sentenced to death, and executed by the king of Egypt; a rigour which did not at all tend to reconcile the Samaritans with the justice of the decision.

CHAPTER VIII.

Demetrius II. recovers the crown of Syria—Battle of Azotus; Waterloo—Death of A. Balas, and of Ptolemy VI. Philometor—Treaty between King Demetrius and Jonathan—Troubles in Antioch suppressed by the assistance of Jonathan—Perfidy of King Demetrius—His expulsion from Antioch—Tryphon—Antiochus VI.—His treaty with Jonathan—Civil war—Battle of Azor—Jonathan renews the alliance with Rome, and treats with Sparta—The pirates of Cilicia—Jonathan entrapped and murdered by Tryphon—Simon elected to succeed him—Death of Antiochus VI.—Sepulchre of the Maccabees at Modin—King Demetrius II. declares Judea independent.—(From 148, to 143 B.C.E.)

WHILE thus, without any fault of Jonathan's, rival high-priests and rival temples in vain sought to deprive Jerusalem and himself of their pre-eminence, King Balas, by his bad government, invited rivals far more formidable and successful. During his contest with King Demetrius, the impostor had evinced both talent and courage; and the ability with which he had brought that struggle to a successful issue, was the principal motive which induced Philometor to bestow the hand of his daughter on a low-born usurper. But when King Balas believed himself firmly seated on his thone, he began to indulge without restraint the mean vices of his nature. Intoxicated with a prosperity completely undeserved, he committed the government to ministers who flattered his passions while they abused his power and confidence. His own time was altogether given up to a life of unbounded voluptuousness. His wife Cleopatra was neglected, while his court was crowded with the most ostentatious courtesans of Greece, whose accomplishments, by emblazoning his profligacy, rendered his disgrace the more conspicuous.

His subjects, though by no means over-fastidious, were

nevertheless shocked and offended by the public display King Balas chose to make of his libertinage. King Demetrius, though a drunkard, had carried on his revels in privacy; his harem of humble concubines never intruded on public notice. But Balas, whose open and ostentatious debaucheries violated every rule of Oriental life, seemed to despise and set at defiance the better feelings of the Antiochians; while at the same time the cruelty and extortion of his ministers completed the general dissatisfaction.

Thus Balas became an object not only of hatred, but of contempt—a feeling the most dangerous to sovereigns. Several of his generals and governors began to turn their eyes toward the son of their late king Demetrius, named like his father, who, as we have related, had escaped to Cnidus, and in the first stage of manhood gave indications of an active and energetic character. Being provided with a large treasure, which had been sent with him to the place of his retreat, and encouraged by the certainty of finding adherents even among the most powerful of Balas's officers, the young prince Demetrius hired a considerable body of troops, especially in Crete, and invaded the province of Cilicia, proclaiming his own right to the crown of Syria, and denouncing Balas as an impostor and usurper. At the same time, Apollonius, governor of Cœle-Syria and Phœnicia, one of the most important officers in the Syrain monarchy, openly revolted from Balas, to whose government he had never been well affected, and with the forces under his command declared for Prince Demetrius.

In his younger years, this Apollonius, following the fortunes of Demetrius Soter, had remained with him during his long residence as a hostage at Rome, and was one of the eight Syrians of distinction who accompanied him in his flight when he returned to recover possession of his kingdom. (Polyb. lxxxi. cap. 19 et 21.) Upon the restoration of his fellow-fugitive and patron, Apollonius was appointed governor of Cœle-Syria and Phœnicia, which offices he was permitted to retain by Balas, notwithstanding his well-known devotion to the person, cause, and house of Demetrius. But though nominally in the service of Balas, he was in reality only on the watch for an opportunity to serve the son of his former master; and probably had a principal share in planning the enterprise which young Demetrius was about carrying into execution. For as soon as that prince unfurled his standard in Cilicia, Apollonius declared for him, and was fortunate enough to secure the adhesion and concurrence of all the inferior commanders in those parts; so that the rebellion at once assumed an aspect most threatening to Balas.

Amid this general defection, Balas had at least one friend in that portion of his kingdom, whose fidelity equalled his power; and that was Jonathan, the high-priest and governor of Judea. When he became acquainted with the open rebellion of his neighbour Apollonius, he at once prepared to check his progress and to defend the cause of King Alexander, for such Jonathan really believed the impostor to be.

Apollonius, having got a considerable army together, and ascertaining that Jonathan was hostile to his party and views, marched against him and advanced as far as Jamnia. But as the portion of his forces on which he principally relied was his cavalry, and he feared to lose the benefit of their services were he to advance farther into the mountainous region of Judea, he encamped and sent a bold and insulting message to Jonathan, daring the Jewish chief to quit the shelter of his rocks, and manfully to come forward and give him battle in the open plains. Jonathan accepted the challenge, and with ten thousand chosen Jewish warriors advanced from Jerusalem to Joppa. On his march thither he was joined by his brother Simon, who brought him reinforcements. Joppa was garrisoned by the troops of Apollonius, who shut their gates against the Jewish chiefs and barred their further progress. Jonathan was obliged to attack Joppa, and speedily took it, almost in sight of the rebel army which marched against him.

Apollonius had eight thousand foot and three thousand horse. Besides these, he left a detachment of a thousand chosen horse in ambush, with orders to fall upon Jonathan's rear as soon as he should be seriously engaged in front with Apollonius himself. He then feigned a retreat, as if he was marching southward toward Azotus. His stratagem in so far succeeded, that Jonathan, as he expected, came out from Joppa to pursue him; and Apollonius, suddenly facing about, fell upon him, in the full expectation that the unexpected charge of his ambush would throw the Jews into confusion and cause their defeat.

But Jonathan was too experienced a commander to permit the success of any such evolutions. The feigned retreat and sudden attack of Apollonius roused Jonathan's suspicion; and, penetrating the design of his enemy, he anticipated a probable attack by a force in ambush, and drew up his men in the form of an oblong square, not unlike the Macedonian phalanx; and as Apollonius's ambushed horse came thundering along, the rear ranks of Jonathan's compact square had only to wheel about to present a double front.

This manœuvre the Jews executed with great precision, and with unusual firmness bore the brunt of the battle on both sides. In vain Apollonius exhausted his cavalry in repeated charges; he could make no impression on the phalanx of the Jews, who repelled every attack with great slaughter. At length, toward evening, Jonathan, observing that the enemy's cavalry, men as well as horses, were completely spent and incapable of further efforts, suddenly and unexpectedly passed from defence to attack. Opening his square, he rushed upon the enemy's foot, and, unsupported as they now were by the cavalry, totally routed them.

The greater part fled to Azotus, and took post in the temple of Dagon, where they prepared for a vigorous resistance. The Jews pursued, made themselves master of the city, and attacked the temple. But finding that the defenders obstinately refused to surrender, and that the post could only be forced at a great expense of lives, the victors set the temple on fire. The flames spread and destroyed the whole city, as well as all that had found refuge in the temple. The number of Syrian slain during the battle and in Azotus exceeded eight thousand.

From Azotus, Jonathan marched to attack and plunder some other towns that had declared against King Alexander, but spared the city of Askalon, which met him with offers of submission. After a short but important campaign, in which he completely suppressed the rebellion against King Alexander in Cœle-Syria and Phœnicia, Jonathan returned to Jerusalem loaded with rich booty. When Balas heard of Jonathan's faithfulness and victory, he sent him in token of gratitude a rich gold buckle or epaulet, such as only the members of the royal family were permitted to wear, and which fastened their purple mantle to the shoulder. As a more substantial recompense for the important service rendered Balas, he likewise bestowed upon Jonathan the city and territory of *Ekron* as a free gift. (1 Macc. x. 74, ad fin.)

In this battle of Azotus, Jonathan fully established his reputation as a skilful and experienced commander, entitled and worthy to be the successor to the great Maccabee. The battle itself bears a striking resemblance in some of its leading features to the greatest of modern European battles—Waterloo; due allowance, of course, being made for the effect of firearms, and the consequent difference of tactics.

Like Apollonius, Napoleon chiefly relied on his cavalry for the victory; like Jonathan, Wellington drew up his army in solid squares, as best able to resist the attack of horse. Like Apollonius, Napoleon in vain sacrificed his splendid cavalry in repeated but unavailing attacks; he could make no decisive impression on the squares. Like Jonathan, Wellington suddenly and unexpectedly passed from defence to attack, and thereby completed the rout of the French army.

We know that, but for the arrival and advance of Blucher and his Prussians, the result of the battle of Waterloo might have proved very different from what it did. But we also know that the Duke of Wellington was intimately acquainted with the battles and tactics of the ancients, and an assiduous reader of Folard. And when we see the great resemblance in the leading features of the two battles, we cannot help smiling as we ask ourselves, "What share of the glory of Wellington, and the subsequent fortunes of Europe, may be due to the generalship of Jonathan the Maccabee?"

Unfortunately for Alexander Balas, the disaffection against him was so widely spread and so deeply rooted, that Jonathan's victory, however glorious to that chief, could only delay the fall of the impostor, who eventually was ruined by his own obstinacy and the crimes of his minister. The progress of the rebellion, though checked in Cœle-Syria and Phœnicia, was so rapid and formidable, that Balas at length was driven to apply for aid to the father of his neglected and ill-treated wife, the king of Egypt; while Balas, awaiting the arrival of his powerful auxiliary, shut himself up in Antioch, and intrusted the government of that city and the imperial district around it to two generals, Diodotus and Hierax, under the supreme command of Ammonius, his favourite and prime minister.

Ptolemy Philometor, upon hearing of the danger to which his son-in-law was exposed, hastened, with a zeal worthy of a better cause, to his assistance, at the head of a powerful army, accompanied by a fleet not less formidable. He landed at Ptolemais, from whence he prepared to advance to Antioch. On his landing, some apostate Jews, enemies of Jonathan, presented themselves before the king, and tried to excite his anger against the Jewish chief by pointing to the devastations caused by the last campaign, and especially to the ruins of Azotus and the temple of Dagon, as well as to the carcasses of the slain, which yet remained unburied. But the king refused to entertain the accusation, and laid all the blame on Apollonius and his treason. When Jonathan heard that justice had thus been done to his loyalty, he, attended by a splendid retinue, paid the king a visit at Joppa, where he met with a friendly reception, and, after accompanying him to the river Eleutherus, returned to Jerusalem.

The first book of Maccabees (xi. 1, et seq.) taxes Philometor with the design of invading Syria for the purpose of undoing his own work and of ruining the worthless impostor Balas, in order to unite the crown of Syria with that of Egypt. This charge, founded doubtless on after events, seems to express the general public opinion of the times; an opinion which was shared by Ammonius, the favourite and confidant of Balas. This odious minister, judging of Ptolemy's character by his own, believed that the king of Egypt would not have come to Syria, at the head of forces so formidable, except for purposes of his own; and he determined, by an act of real treachery, to anticipate the breach of faith which perhaps his own guilty suspicions had invented. He formed a plot to assassinate the king of Egypt at Ptolemais, which, however, miscarried; and Philometor denounced Ammonius as the author, indignantly demanding that the culprit should either be handed over to him, or meet with condign punishment from his own sovereign.

Balas, however, was so infatuated as to determine, at all hazards, to protect his favourite; and thereby afforded just reason for concluding that he himself had participated in the guilty scheme. Philometor thenceforth renounced his alliance with Balas, advanced toward Antioch, and, having drawn to him from that place his daughter Cleopatra, offered her hand, together with the crown of Syria, to young Demetrius, who not only and gladly accepted the offer, but hastened with all his forces to join his intended wife and his powerful ally, her father. On their arrival near Antioch, the Greek citizens rose in open rebellion against Balas. Ammonius was slain in woman's apparel, as he attempted to escape; Balas fled, and put himself at the head of some troops that still remained faithful to him.

Upon the flight of the impostor, the citizens of Antioch, with whom the son of the drunkard Demetrius was in no great favour, invited Ptolemy to mount the vacant throne; he was even compelled, by their importunity, to wear for a brief period the double diadem of Egypt and Syria. But Philometor was too experienced a politician to act without reflecting on the consequences of his action. It was evident that the Romans would not view with complacency this union of two powerful kingdoms: it was possible, and even probable, that their sword would dissolve the union. He therefore did what, in his circumstances, wisdom and justice required; and—not without some difficulty—succeeded in getting his new son-in-law acknowledged as king. (Polyb. lib. xi. cap. 12.)

Early next spring Balas made a desperate effort to recover the kingdom, and advanced toward Antioch. The two kings went forth to meet him, and a sharp but unequal conflict ensued, in which Balas was defeated, and fled from the field to a petty Arabian prince, Zabdiel, his ally. This robber-chief caused the fugitive to be murdered; and five days after the battle the head of the wretched Balas was presented to young Demetrius, who was saluted as *Nicator*, "the victorious," which designation thenceforth remained to him. Philometor, who had been mortally wounded, died eight days after the battle, in the forty-second year of his age and thirty-fifth of his eventful reign. (146 B. C. E.)

The fall of King Balas and the success of Demetrius were likely to interrupt, if not entirely to change, the character of the friendly relations which for the last few years had subsisted between the king of Syria and the high-priest of Jerusalem. It was to be apprehended that Demetrius, succeeding to the sentiments as well as the crown of his father, might, and with greater justice, entertain against Jonathan a hatred as implacable as that with which his father had persecuted Judah the Maccabee.

The wise and powerful king of Egypt, whose alliance had seated Demetrius on the throne, and whose friendly mediation would have recalled him to sentiments of moderation against the Jews, had died in the arms of victory; and a fierce civil war which, directly after his death, broke out in Egypt, compelled the return home of the army he had led into Syria, and for a time paralyzed the influence of the Egyptian government. Rome itself, involved, contrary to its usual policy, in two great wars at one and the same time, in Greece and in Africa—wars which terminated in the destruction, at the interval of a few months, of two of the most celebrated and commercial cities of the ancient world, Carthage and Corinth, (146 B. C. E.)—Rome itself was not in a condition to afford Judea any effectual protection; and Jonathan, taken by surprise at the complete and sudden change of affairs in Antioch, was compelled once more to prepare for confronting the entire power of the Syrian monarchy with the forces of a single province only.

But these forces were now become considerable. Judea was no longer in that state of utter prostration from which the Maccabee had first raised his country. Her internal resources and population had increased to an extent of which we can only form an idea from the fact that Jonathan, within a few years after the fall of Balas, was able to raise an army of 40,000 men; and that his wealth enabled him to gain the good will of King Demetrius, even when that monarch was most enraged, as we shall presently relate.

As Jonathan thus was left to his own resources, he determined not to await the attack, but at once to secure himself at home by depriving the Syrians of the only strongholds they yet possessed in Judea. For this purpose he laid siege to Acra, the heathen fortress at Jerusalem, which was still held by a strong garrison of Syrians, and in which the most culpable and obnoxious of the apostate Jews had taken up their abode, molesting, as much as they could, the orthodox Jews who repaired to the temple.

For this siege Jonathan had made considerable provision both of men and of engines, convinced as he was that the resistance would be most obstinate. But in the midst of his siege operations he received a summons to appear before King Demetrius, who had arrived at Ptolemais, and had there received complaints of Jonathan's proceedings. As this summons evinced, on the part of the king, the determination not at once to proceed to extremities, Jonathan determined to obey, and, if possible, to avert from his country the horrors of war; and though the risk which he personally ran in trusting himself into the power of the king of Syria was of the greatest, yet this true patriot, who so often had ventured life and limb on the battle-field, did not for an instant hesitate or balance his own safety against the welfare of his country. And this his conduct, under the trying circumstances in which he was placed, fully proved. For while he himself, attended by some of the principal men of Judea,—elders of the Sanhedrin and priests—departed for Ptolemais, he left orders with his brother Simon to push the siege of Acra with the utmost vigour, so that his own absence might cause no interruption to the progress of his undertaking.

On his arrival at Ptolemais, Jonathan found that King Demetrius, though strongly irritated against him, was also impressed with a salutary dread of the strength and national spirit of the Jews; and that, influenced alike by both these feelings, the king and his council were as yet undecided as to the course to be pursued against Jonathan, who was a diplomatist too skilful not to turn their indecision to his own advantage. When the affairs of Judea came to be investigated, Jonathan pleaded his cause so ably before the king, and backed it with such rich presents to the king himself and to his principal courtiers, that the complaint against the Maccabean chief was dismissed, his accusers being compelled to withdraw in disgrace, while he himself was received into the royal favour and friendship.

King Demetrius not only confirmed him in the dignities of high-priest and ethnarch, or prince of Judea, that had been bestowed upon him by Balas, but also renewed and confirmed to the Jewish people all those privileges and immunities which his father had offered to them, but which they and their chief had at that time declined, out of friendship for Balas. The three toparchies, or districts, of Lydda, Apharema, and Ramatha, which some years before had been separated from Samaria and joined to Judea, and which the late king had offered to leave in the possession of the high-priest, were now finally incorporated with Judea. And in order to remove all pretexts for exaction, or claims for arrears of tribute due from the province of Judea or its people to the kings of Syria, King Demetrius consented to cancel all old demands, and thenceforth to receive the annual payment of three hundred talents (about 300,000 dollars) in full of all taxes and contributions from all the territories under the authority of the high-priest. (1 Macc. xi. 20, et seq.)

Successful beyond his utmost expectations, Jonathan returned to Jerusalem, and continued the siege of Acra with renewed vigour. But, persevering as he was in his attack, he found that the energy of despair with which the apostates, who formed the principal part of the garrison, defended themselves, joined to the great strength of the fortress itself, were more than a match for any force he could bring against it; and that to compel a surrender would not only require a length of time, but also a great expenditure of human lives as well as money. The position in which King Demetrius had, in the interim, contrived to place himself, suggested to Jonathan the idea of obtaining from the king himself an order for the evacuation both of Acra and Bethzura, the only places in Judea still occupied by Syrian troops.

Short as had been his reign, Demetrius, by his gross misconduct and cruelty, had already alienated the affections of his subjects. During his exile he had learned to despise and distrust the Syrians—a people, as soldiers, effeminate; as subjects, turbulent; as adherents, fickle and disloyal. As he had recovered his throne chiefly by the assistance of foreigners, Cretans and Egyptians, he determined to intrust the defence of his person and kingdom to none but foreign mercenaries; and one of the first acts of his reign, after the death of Philometor, was to disband the whole of the national troops, who had till then, even in time of peace, been retained at their full complement and pay.

In a letter preserved by Josephus, (Antiq. lib. xiii. cap. 8, ad. fin.,) King Demetrius styles Lasthenes, the general of the Cretans, his "father," because it was by his assistance that he had recovered and trusted to maintain his crown. The mercenaries, as under such circumstances was naturally to be expected, ill used and oppressed the natives, whose complaints to the king, so far from obtaining redress, were stifled by the cruelties practised on the complainants. Lasthenes, in particular, who commanded at Antioch, trampled on the citizens with a degree of insolence and ferocity to which that turbulent though industrious populace was ill calculated to submit. A fearful *emeute* broke out in the capital, which all the force at King Demetrius's disposal was unable to quell, and the crown he had so lately recovered was already tottering on his head. (Diodor. Excerp. p. 592.)

At this juncture it was that Jonathan addressed himself to the king with complaints against the garrisons of Acra and Bethzura, who molested the Jews; and requested that the king would be pleased to command the evacuation of both strongholds. In his extreme distress, Demetrius was but too glad to obtain assistance on any terms; he therefore proposed to Jonathan that, as a preliminary condition to the evacuation of the two fortresses, the high-priest should assist him with a portion of his forces to suppress the rebellion at Antioch; and in return for this service the king promised to withdraw his garrisons from Acra and Bethzura.

This condition Jonathan at once complied with, and a considerable body of Jewish auxiliaries—according to First Maccabees (xi. 41, et seq.) three thousand veterans—hurried to Antioch and joined the king's forces, with the full determination to do him good service; for a bitter feeling of hatred existed between the Jews and the citizens of Antioch. During the reign of Epiphanes, and while Judea was trodden down by the Syrians, among its many oppressors none had been so ruthless, so utterly inhuman, as the Antiochians: and in that city itself the Jewish citizens had not only been treated with equal cruelty, but in every tumult that broke out—and they were frequent—the parts of the city inhabited by Jews suffered rapine and bloodshed at the hands of a lawless mob.

This had more particularly been the case during the riots then actually raging; for as the high-priest of Jerusalem was known to be in favour with the king, the people of the high-priest, the Jews, had been cruelly treated by the rebels. The Jewish auxiliaries at Antioch knew all this, and were determined to have full revenge. In a series of murderous street battles the Antiochians were defeated with great slaughter; and the rebellion was extinguished in the blood, as Josephus relates (Ant. lib. xiii. cap. 8,) of upward of one hundred thousand of the rioters.

In this fearful act of vengeance the Jewish auxiliaries had acted a principal part; and the Maccabean chief could claim the merit of having secured the throne to the son of that Demetrius who had persecuted his own noble brother, Judah, even unto death. But Jonathan soon discovered that, both morally and politically, he had committed a fault in lending aid to the tyrant of Syria; for Demetrius no sooner found himself, as he believed, firmly seated on his throne—the terror of his name, and the dreadful punishment inflicted on Antioch, extorting implicit obedience throughout the wide extent of his monarchy—than he determined to break his engagements with Jonathan, and prepared to renew and aggravate against the Jews the worst outrages inflicted by his predecessors.

For this purpose he not only refused to grant orders for

the evacuation of the two fortresses, which he had promised; but contrary to his express stipulations with Jonathan, the king began to insist on the payment of all the arrears of tribute, together with all the exactions, taxes, and customs which at their interview at Ptolemais he had remitted. Whether the king was influenced by envy or apprehension of the power of Jonathan, or tempted by the wealth of Judea and his own necessities, or whether he was urged on by that painful impatience which possesses the mind of the proud man, when he feels himself under an obligation so great that he cannot repay it, and therefore seeks to get rid of its weight by any means, even by the blackest ingratitude,—certain it is that he not only exasperated the Jews by his demands, but threatened loudly and most violently to punish their exasperation, when a sudden and irresistible revolution drove him out of his kingdom, and left him at his leisure to repent of his tyranny to the Syrians as well as of his perfidy to the Jews.

The usurpation of the Syrian crown by Antiochus IV. Epiphanes, who, after crushing the assassin Heliodorus, ascended the throne to the exclusion of the rightful heir, his nephew Demetrius, then detained as a hostage at Rome, gave a death-blow to the prosperity of that monarchy, by confounding, inextricably, the right and order of succession, and thus paving the way for unceasing revolutions and civil wars; for the fickle Syrians were ever ready through a mistaken loyalty to recognise the title and right of inheritance of any pretender whose father, however unjustly and for however short a time, had worn the crown. In this manner, Alexander Balas, pretending to be the son of Antiochus Epiphanes, had proved successful against the elder Demetrius, surnamed *Soter:* a new pretender, deriving descent from Balas, had every chance of success against the younger Demetrius, notwithstanding his pompous title of *Nicator*.

We have already spoken of two Syrian Greeks named Hierax and Diodotus, confidants of Balas, and who during his reign commanded at Antioch. At the fall of their master, Hierax fled to Egypt and entered into the service of Physcon, whose prime minister he became, and whose throne and government, amid all the capricious cruelties of the prince, were upheld by the vigilance and energy of the minister.

His associate, Diodotus, who gloried in and is better known by his surname of *Tryphon*, "the luxurious," remained in Syria, fully determined to re-establish his fortunes by the restoration of the line of Balas. A boy, the son of Balas, yet remained in the household of Zabdiel, the same Arab prince with whom Balas after his defeat had sought refuge and found death. This boy, so mighty an instrument for working on the minds of the fickle Syrians, and for seducing the turbulent Antiochians, Tryphon contrived to get into his power, and thenceforth rejoiced at the accumulating follies and treacheries by which Demetrius alienated the affections of his subjects and disgusted his friends. The *emeute* at Antiochia, of which we have already spoken, broke out at the instigation of Tryphon; and, but for the effectual aid afforded to Demetrius by Jonathan, must have proved successful, as Tryphon was supported by numbers of disbanded Syrian veterans.

This first miscarriage did not intimidate the conspirator; on the contrary, it encouraged his further attempts, since it proved to him not only how ready the people were to rise against the king, but also how little able the king was to suppress those risings. When, therefore, it became known that the king had broken his promise to the high-priest of the Jews, and that he was about to commence hostilities against that people, so formidable because inured to perpetual warfare, Tryphon once more appeared in the field, proclaiming the son of Alexander Balas, the grandson of Antiochus Epiphanes, as the rightful king of Syria. He was immediately joined by many who were privy to his conspiracy, and gradually reinforced by innumerable malcontents, and especially by the disbanded Syrian soldiers, who from all parts of the country flocked to his standard, and did homage to their young king Antiochus VI., under the title of Epiphanes, "the illustrious," inherited from his supposed grandfather, and of *Bacchus*, bestowed on him by his adherents to express his fine countenance and elegant figure.[9]

Demetrius had to fight for his kingdom. At the head of his foreign mercenaries, he encountered his insurgent subjects near Antioch, and was defeated with great loss; for the Syrian veterans whom he had so ignominiously dismissed from his service now fought against him with a rage and resentment which the hired valour of his mercenaries was unable to resist. The loss of the battle compelled him to abandon his capital; but as the neighbouring cities on the sea-coast, garrisoned by his troops, still maintained their allegiance to him, he took up his residence in the largest and strongest of them, *Seleucia Pieria*. There he shut himself up with his guards, leaving the inland country to provide for its own defence, or to submit to Tryphon, acting as guardian to the young king and regent of the kingdom.

One of the first steps taken by the new government, was to secure the friendship of Jonathan and the Jews. For this purpose, King Antiochus not only confirmed all former grants made to the Jews, especially the remission of arrears, the consolidation of tribute into one annual payment, and the possession of the three toparchies, but also

---

[9] These titles appear on his medals. Josephus (Antiq. lib. xiii. cap. 7) designates this ill-fated youth by the surname of *Theos*, meaning, probably, the god Bacchus.

sent many valuable and honourable presents to Jonathan. At the same time he appointed Simon, the high-priest's brother, commander of all his forces from the frontiers of Egypt to the *Ladder of Tyre*, a mountain so called, nearly midway between Tyre and Ptolemais; stipulating, in return for these advantages, that the two brothers should declare for him and support his cause.

This both Jonathan and Simon were most willing to do, as they had to the very last adhered to Balas, and in return for important services to Demetrius had experienced nothing but perfidy and ingratitude. The two brothers, therefore, at once put themselves at the head of their forces; and having sent an embassy of thanks to Antioch, Jonathan crossed the Jordan, and marched into Galilee against a body of troops despatched by Demetrius to make a diversion.

In this expedition Jonathan was in imminent danger of being cut to pieces by the enemy. He had encamped over night near the Lake *Gennesareth*, and was marching early in the morning toward the town of *Azor*, when he unexpectedly fell into an ambush that had been placed among the defiles of the mountains to surprise him. As soon as he perceived his danger, he prepared for a brave defence, disposing of his men in the best position the nature of the ground would permit. But the greatest part of his men (new levies, who for the first time faced an enemy) were struck with a sudden panic, forsook their commander, and fled; so that Jonathan was left with only fifty veterans and two officers, whose names history has preserved—Judah and Mattathias.

With this handful of brave men Jonathan stood at bay, and fought so desperately that the enemy began to give way. The runaways, who had fled up the hills, from whence at a distance they could see what was doing on the battle-field, and who beheld with what courage and success their chief defended himself, now rallied; and stung with shame and remorse at their own cowardice, they rushed back into the thickest of the fight, and attacked the already wavering enemy with such vigour that they were routed. Jonathan gained a complete victory, and pursued the Demetrians to their fortified camp at Cadish, inflicting on them a loss of three thousand killed.

After this great and unexpected success, Jonathan marched against the city of Ascalon, which opened its gates to him, and against Gaza, which he forced to surrender. At the same time his brother Simon laid siege to and took the important frontier fortress of Bethzura, which the Syrians so long had held; so that throughout all Judea the enemy only retained one stronghold, *Acra*, which still held out for King Demetrius. The two brothers then, after having subdued Joppa and all the cities from Gaza to Damascus, returned in triumph to Jerusalem, where they found all things in peace and prosperity—a condition that Jonathan naturally was anxious to perpetuate by every means in his power.

His past experience had taught him how little reliance was to be placed on the promises of kings, who in their adversity or weakness were ready to enter into engagements which they never intended to keep, and which with the first ray of returning prosperity and power they hastened to disown. He therefore addressed his diplomacy to the mighty commonwealth which, at that time, gave law to the civilized world. Rome had triumphantly ended her wars against Greece and Carthage, and her senate, true to its policy of conquest, again directed its views and despatched its emissaries to the East. Jonathan was too powerful and too prominent a character to escape their attention; and thus he was induced to send an embassy to the senate to solicit a renewal of the alliance contracted by his brother—a request favourably received and readily granted.

The ambassadors were instructed also to visit and to establish amicable relations with the various cities of Greece, especially with Sparta and the Lacedemonians. It is difficult to conceive whence the idea could have arisen in the minds either of the Jews or of the Spartans that the two people were connected by the ties of kindred; yet such was the case. From a letter addressed by "Jonathan, high-priest, and the elders, and priests of the Jews, unto the ephori, senate, and people of Lacedemon, THEIR BRETHREN," we learn that so long ago as the days of the high-priest Onias II., nearly a century and a half back, the Spartan king Arius had written and had claimed affinity for his people with the Jews, "which affinity," says Jonathan, "we acknowledge with greater honour, as we find it confirmed by our sacred books." (1 Macc. xi.; Jos. Antiq. lib. xiii. cap. 9.) Biblical critics, both Jew and Gentile, have laboured hard, but hitherto unsuccessfully, to discover to what portion of Scripture Jonathan alludes;[10] but it is certain that at the time the claim

---

[10] A curious solution of this difficulty is proposed by Dr. Frankel in his *Monatsschrift* for December, 1853, (page 456,) who suggests that the Spartans, to whom Jonathan sent an embassy, were not those who inhabited the Peloponnesus, but those who, since the days of the Persian empire, had been settled at Nisibis, the capital of Armenia, and whom Plutarch designates as genuine descendants of the Spartans. And though Dr. F. admits that the "affinity" between them and the Jews still remains "somewhat obscure," still, as he very justly remarks, an alliance with the Spartans of Nisibis in the very heart of the Syrian monarchy must have been of far more importance to the Jews, who, like themselves, had to resist the tyranny of the Seleucidæ, than any league with the European Spartans, who could exercise no influence on the affairs of Asia, as their ancient power and renown were at this period altogether decayed. And as to the title "king," which Arius, the writer of the letter, assumes, that offers no difficulty, as in Sparta itself the "king" was but a sub-

was allowed with equal readiness by both people, and that Jonathan's ambassadors, who produced a transcript of Arius's letter, met with a most friendly reception from the Spartans.

While these negotiations were being carried on, Jonathan received information that the adherents of Demetrius, whom he had so lately defeated, had assembled a larger army, and were about to invade Judea. Jonathan was most anxious to preserve his own country from becoming the seat of war; he therefore no sooner received tidings of the projected invasion, than he collected his forces and hastened to forestall the attack. His march was so rapid, that at *Amathis,* a place on the frontiers of Syria, he met the enemy, and encamped over against them. They directly formed the design to surprise his camp on the following night; but Jonathan, well served by his scouts, obtained some intimation of their purpose, and kept his troops under arms ready to receive them. The Demetrians marched out of their camp, as projected, but finding the Jews on the alert, they as quickly marched back, without daring to begin an attack.

Indeed, so disheartened were the leaders of the Demetrians by the numbers and good countenance of Jonathan's men, that they renounced the idea of keeping the field against him, and determined on a retreat. For this purpose they caused a number of fires to be lighted in their camp to conceal their flight, while they with all their forces marched off unperceived, and made such speed that Jonathan, when he discovered the *ruse* that had been played off against him, found any attempt at pursuit entirely hopeless; they were already far beyond the Eleutherus before he could reach that river. To make

---

ordinate ruler; and the colonists at Nisibis would most likely bestow a title to which they were accustomed on their municipal chief, even though he and they remained subject to the monarch of Syria.

himself some amends for his disappointment, he fell upon
a band of Arab rovers in the pay of King Demetrius.
These he defeated, and took from them considerable booty,
with which he returned to Jerusalem. (1 Macc. xi. 62.)

Their ill success on this occasion completely disheartened the adherents of King Demetrius from any further attempts in the field. He himself remained shut up in Seleucia, a city strongly fortified, amply garrisoned, and provisioned. Tryphon, it would seem, now had it in his power to terminate the war by besieging and taking Demetrius's stronghold—an enterprise the success of which there was no army in the field to prevent. But before the invention of gunpowder the imperfection of battering-engines left the art of attack far behind that of defence. Tryphon had good reason to assume that the force under his command was not sufficient to reduce a maritime city so well defended as Seleucia, and the port of which, for want of a navy, he could not close or blockade. He therefore contented himself with cutting off his adversary's indispensable resources in the maritime parts of Syria.

Notwithstanding the perturbed state of that kingdom, the maritime cities of Seleucia, Laodicea, Aradus, Tripolis, and Tyre—all garrisoned by Demetrians—carried on a rich commerce by sea, nourished by a great caravan trade carried on through the central regions of Asia. To destroy this commerce, Tryphon armed pirates, chiefly Cilicians, and formed the harbour of Coracesium, on the western frontier of Cilicia, into their common arsenal and stronghold.

To this period, accordingly, history assigns the commencement of the great piratical confederacy of Asia Minor, which grew up in the course of five years under the fostering care of Tryphon, and continued to flourish seventy-two years, until it took all the power of Rome, and all the skill of her then greatest commander, Pompey, to destroy a lawless horde, more formidable and capable of resistance than the mighty monarchs of Syria or of Pontus. (Strabo, lxiv. p. 668; Appian. de Bell. Mithridat. cap. 94–96.)

These pirates greatly harrassed the adherents of Demetrius, nor were they anywise careful to spare the friends of Antiochus. They not only swept the seas and plundered the coasts, but carried their baneful rapacity into the inland country. Slaves constituted the principal object of their pursuit, and these they were alike ready to acquire by purchase or by robbery. The warfare in Syria was thus exasperated by the desire of making prisoners, who were carried to a certain and ready market in the central isle of Delos, where the Romans, enriched by the recent spoils of Carthage and Corinth, were the buyers, the Cilicians the sellers, and the persons of the unhappy Syrians the merchandise. In Delos, 10,000 slaves might find purchasers in a single day. (Strabo, lib. xiv. pp. 668, 699.)

As many Jews resided in the maritime and inland parts of Syria, they likewise but too frequently fell into the power of these Cilician manstealers. And when, in the course of time, we suddenly find numbers of Jews, especially freedmen, in Rome and Italy, while history does not tell us how they came there, we may be sure that these unfortunates were victims of that kidnapping and piracy which so long devastated the eastern coasts of the Mediterranean and the countries adjacent.

While Jonathan took the field to protect Judea against invasion, his brother Simon was equally active in maintaining the authority of King Antiochus in that portion of his kingdom the command over which had been confided to the Maccabean. The citizens of Joppa, a seaport town which had lately been reduced by Simon and Jonathan, formed the design of transferring their allegiance again to King Demetrius, and to receive a governor and garrison that sovereign was about to send them. Simon, who was then at Ascalon on a journey of inspection, and ever watchful, frustrated the design by placing in the rebellious city a strong garrison of his own. After having reviewed his troops in Galilee, Simon returned to Jerusalem to meet his brother Jonathan, who had convened a council to advise on the best means for reducing Acra, against which stronghold all his efforts had hitherto proved ineffectual. At this council it was resolved to make good use of the peaceful time the country then enjoyed, and to strengthen the defences of Judea, and especially of Jerusalem. Accordingly it was determined that all the fortresses in Judea should be repaired; that new strongholds should be erected wherever they were wanted; that the wall of Jerusalem should be rebuilt; and, lastly, that a new wall should be raised between Mount Sion and the rest of the city, of such height, extent, and strength, as effectually to cut off all communication between the fortress of Acra and the city and country, to the end that the hostile garrison, being thereby deprived of all supplies, might the sooner be starved into a surrender.

These wise and salutary resolutions were at once put into execution, the two brothers dividing the work between them. Jonathan, who remained in Jerusalem, conducted the repairs of the old dilapidated fortifications, and built his new walls so judiciously, that in a comparatively short time the garrison of Acra was starved into a surrender. Simon, who had taken for his share the works outside of Jerusalem, repaired all the then existing forts, and increased their number by the fortifying of *Adiba* or *Adiaba*, westward of Eleutheropolis, on the Syrian frontier. And thus Judea was placed in a condition for defence better than it had ever been in since the return from the Babylonish captivity. (1 Macc. xii.)

The success which Tryphon had hitherto obtained at

sea by means of his Cilician pirates, and on land chiefly by the exertions of the Maccabean brothers, encouraged him to the execution of a most nefarious project, namely—to destroy the youth whom he had crowned under the name of Antiochus VI., and to assume in his own person that royal power which during nearly two years he had exercised in the name of another. He had the less scruple to do this as he well knew that Balas, the father of young Antiochus, had been an impostor, low-born, and not even a native Syro-Grecian, but a Rhodian by birth; and that consequently the claim of Antiochus VI. in the right of his father was a sham and usurpation. Tryphon thought, and the event proved that he was not altogether mistaken, that, provided he could quietly remove the puppet son of Balas, whom he himself had set up, the people, accustomed to his sway, and the soldiery, who so bitterly hated Demetrius, might not be averse to permit him, a high-born Syro-Grecian, to become the founder of a new dynasty.

One obstacle only lay in his way; and that was Jonathan, who as well as his brother and his people, the Jews, had espoused the cause of the young king with equal zeal and sincerity. Tryphon felt that so long as an arm, powerful like that of the high-priest of Jerusalem, upheld the house of the pseudo Epiphanes, his own chance of ascending the throne was but very slight. He therefore determined that the destruction of Antiochus should be preceded by that of Jonathan; and as he was alike ready to employ force or fraud, he marched into Judea at the head of fifty thousand men, and advanced as far as Bethshan, where he was met by Jonathan at the head of forty thousand Jews.

This was an army by far too numerous and formidable for Tryphon to deal with as an enemy. He therefore dissembled; pretended that the purpose of his march, as far as Jonathan and the Jews were concerned, was friendly;

and that he only meant to march through the country the sooner to reach the maritime cities he meant to besiege with the large army which he led on. And as a proof of his friendsip for Jonathan, and of his gratitude for the services rendered to his master Antiochus, he would at once put Jonathan in possession of Ptolemais, the promise of which gift had some time before been made to the high-priest.

Tryphon played his part so naturally, that Jonathan was deceived. Upright and honest in his own conduct, conscious, moreover, of having rendered services as faithful as important to the cause of which Tryphon was the life and soul, Jonathan saw no reason to distrust his friend and ally, bound like himself by gratitude to the memory of the murdered king, Alexander Balas, and to the support of his house and heir. When, therefore, Tryphon advised him to disband his large army, which was both useless and burdensome, Jonathan unfortunately did as he was advised. Dismissing his troops, he only kept 3000 men under arms; and leaving 2000 of these in Galilee, he himself, at the head of 1000 men, marched to take possession of Ptolemais. But he no sooner had entered that city, than the traitor Tryphon ordered the gates to be closed, and Jonathan's escort to be cut down to a man. The high-priest himself was loaded with chains and thrown into a dungeon. (144 B.C.E.)

When the news reached Jerusalem that Jonathan the high-priest of the Lord, the hope of his country, had fallen into the snare that so treacherously had been spread for him, the public grief and consternation were unbounded; and not without cause. During seventeen years that he had conducted the affairs of Judea, his administration had been so prudent, vigorous, and successful, that though the rest of the Syrian monarchy was torn to pieces by wars and rebellions, Judea had ever since the expulsion of Bacchides, or for nearly twelve years, enjoyed comparative peace and positive prosperity. The wealth and population, as well as the extent of the country, had been enlarged, and the friendship of King Antiochus had held out the assurance of further and continued advantages.

But all these fair hopes were at once destroyed, since it was the representative of their friend Antiochus who had been guilty of so foul an action against his own ally and supporter; so that the Jews were threatened at once with the hostility of both the claimants to the crown of Syria, and had every reason to dread that the perfidious Tryphon would soon appear before the gates of Jerusalem, backed by all the apostates and heathen enemies whom Jonathan had so long kept at bay. Nor were their fears unfounded; for Tryphon was making great preparations to march into Judea, and declared his determination to avenge the slaughters at Antioch by extirpating, if possible, the whole Jewish nation; and all the enemies of Judea, who seemed to receive a kind of new life at the news of Jonathan being a prisoner, had began to express an impatient desire to see the land at once invaded, and to threaten the Jews with severe retaliation.

In this extremity all men turned their eyes to Simon, the elder and only surviving brother of Jonathan, as a man not less valiant than the great Maccabee, and at the same time so wise and prudent that his father Mattathias, on his death-bed, and while appointing Judah to be the military leader, had named Simon as his principal adviser. In this capacity he had rendered important services to Judah, while he had likewise, and on many occasions, proved himself a brave and skilful leader in the field.

After the death of Judah, when the public voice called Jonathan to the command, Simon, though the elder brother, advanced no pretensions; and when, subsequently,

Jonathan was elected high-priest, Simon again renounced the right which his elder birth might have conferred on him; and during the whole seventeen years of Jonathan's administration, the elder brother had proved the most faithful adherent and the most competent lieutenant of the younger.

At the crisis of their affairs, when Bacchides for the last time invaded Judea, the services rendered by Simon had been most important. His obstinate and skilful defence of *Bethbasi* (or, as Josephus calls it, *Bethlagan*) had kept the entire force of Bacchides engaged before that fortress, and given time to Jonathan to raise an army for its relief; and at the decisive moment, Simon's well-planned and vigorous sally, which destroyed Bacchides's engines of siege and routed a portion of his army, mainly contributed to the success of the day and of the whole campaign.

Since then, the two brothers had continued to act together in perfect harmony. Whenever Jonathan had occasion to be absent from Judea, Simon took his place at the head of affairs, which he conducted with equal vigour and prudence; and there can be no doubt that had Simon been with Jonathan at the time of his meeting with Tryphon, that traitor would not have succeeded in his vile scheme. To Simon, therefore, the people now appealed; an assembly was convened in the outer court of the temple, and by a unanimous vote he was requested to take upon himself the chief command. This he readily consented to do, not only as the next in succession, but chiefly that he might find the means to release, or at worst to revenge, his unhappy brother.

The speech which Simon addressed to the people on this occasion has been preserved, (1 Macc. xii. 39, et seq.; Jos. Antiq. xiii. 10,) and deserves to be recorded; "You are not ignorant," said he, "how bravely my father, my brothers, and I, have fought in defence of our law and our faith, our temple and our people. They have already sacrificed their lives for that most holy and glorious cause; and of them all, I alone survive to maintain it. God forbid that I should value my life more than they did theirs, as long as I see you groaning under any oppression! Behold me, then, as ready and willing as they have been to stand up in defence of our nation and temple, of our wives and our children." This speech was received with universal applause; and the pious and patriotic sentiments of Simon acting on the minds of the people, they recovered their spirits, and proclaimed him their commander and high-priest, and pledged themselves faithfully to follow him through every danger and difficulty in defence of their religion and country.

The first book of Maccabees, which records this election, seems to hint that some scruple remained in the minds of the people respecting the legality of the whole proceeding. For in the very next chapter, (xiv. 26. et seq.,) which relates how Judea became independent, and Simon its first prince, we find—after a recapitulation of Simon's great deeds, and his descent from the priestly family of Joarib—the following expression: "The priests and the people were well pleased that Simon should be their governor and priest, he and his sons forever, *until there should arise a faithful prophet to show them what they should do;*" an expression which indicates that they look upon the whole arrangement as only temporary. We shall subsequently see what trouble this accumulation of all spiritual and temporal power in one hand caused, when the Jews recovered and enjoyed their national independence.

As soon as Simon was installed in his new dignity, his first care was to finish the fortifications of Jerusalem with all speed, and to get together a force sufficient to make head against Tryphon, who was in full march against Judea. But when this traitor found a Jewish army in the field, and ready to confront him, he once more had recourse to dissimulation. He sent emissaries to Simon and the Jews to inform them "that he had no hostile designs against them; that his quarrel was with Jonathan alone, who was his debtor for the sum of one hundred talents, (about one hundred thousand dollars;) that he would keep Jonathan in prison until the debt was paid, but that his person was perfectly safe; and that if Simon would send him the sum due to him, and also Jonathan's two sons as hostages for their father's keeping the peace, the prisoner should at once be sent back, and Tryphon and his army would withdraw in peace."

This message placed Simon in a very painful position. For, on the one hand, he knew that Tryphon would never set at liberty the man he had so treacherously injured, and whose valour and eminent abilities would be sure, some time or other, to inflict fearful retribution. But, on the other hand, he also knew that if he refused to comply with Tryphon's demands, he would expose himself to the reproach of having sacrificed his brother to his own aggrandizement, or, at least, to the imputation of indifference to his brother's fate. He therefore, with an aching heart, sent the money and the hostages, but no Jonathan came back in return. Tryphon, on the contrary, while he kept the Jewish hero in chains, advanced with his army against Jerusalem; for the heathen fortress Acra, which was closely invested and vigorously pressed by Simon, had in vain applied for assistance to King Demetrius, who had quitted the stronghold of Seleucia for the more voluptuous city of Laodicea, and was there consoling himself, amid feasting and revelry, for the loss of half his kingdom. When, therefore, the Syrians and apostate Jews who formed the garrison of Acra heard of the breach between Tryphon and the Maccabeans, they contrived to apply to him; and, transferring their allegiance from Demetrius to Antiochus, called for immediate aid.

Tryphon, eager to secure so strong a fortress in the very heart of Jerusalem and Judea, hastened to its relief at the head of his cavalry. But his progress was interrupted by a heavy fall of snow among the mountains north of Jerusalem, which compelled him to retreat toward his winter quarters through the land of Gilead. At *Bascama*, in that district, his angry disappointment vented itself in the murder of Jonathan and of his two sons, and shortly afterward in that of King Antiochus VI. To save appearances, the unhappy youth was subjected, unnecessarily, to the operation of cutting for the stone. He died under the hands of a suborned surgeon; and Diodotus, with the surname of "Tryphon," assumed the diadem, joining to the title of *Basileus*, "king," that of *Autocrator*, "emperor."[11]

As soon as the season permitted, Simon marched into Gilead, and having disinterred the remains of the ill-fated Jonathan and his sons, he caused them to be deposited, with due solemnity, in the sepulchre of his fathers at Modin, where he raised a monument to their memory, which he prized so highly that he had it represented on his coins.

This noble piece of architecture stood on an eminence which commanded the whole surrounding country; and being itself raised to a vast height, was seen at a great distance at sea, and served for a landmark. It was constructed of white marble, curiously carved and polished;

---

[11] *Autocrator*, "habens per se imperium," peculiar to the coins of Tryphon, and the more necessary to him as sovereign, because the initials of his name, as guardian to Antiochus VI., had already appeared on the coins of that unfortunate youth. Among modern rulers, the emperor of Russia is the only one who assumes that title, and ostentatiously proclaims his unlimited and irresponsible power.

and around it seven pyramids were erected, in memory of Mattathias, of his wife, and of his five sons. The whole was surrounded with a stately portico, the arches of which were supported by pillars, each cut from a single block of marble, polished and adorned with beautiful sculpture. This splendid specimen of Jewish art survived by some centuries the final fate of Jerusalem and the dispersion of the Jews, and was seen, described, and admired both by Eusebius and Jerome, as well as by Josephus.

But while Simon was thus careful of the dead and of the respect due to their memory, he was not less mindful of his duties to the living and of the safety of the nation that had placed him at its head.

As the Romans at that time were all-powerful, he sent an embassy to Rome to notify to the senate the treacherous murder of his brother, with his own succession to office, and to renew the alliance with them. The same ambassadors were also to visit the Lacedemonians, which they did; and everywhere met with the most honourable and friendly reception. The Romans, and also the Spartans, expressed the utmost resentment at Tryphon's treachery, and readily renewed their alliance with Simon, to whom they sent back letters of congratulation on his accession to the high-priesthood, together with the treaty of alliance and of its ratification by the senate, engraved on a tablet of copper. These important records Simon caused to be read before the great assembly of the people, and then occupied himself with completing the fortifications of Jerusalem, pressing the siege of Acra, and raising new forces against the invasion with which Tryphon still threatened Judea, but which, owing to a singular phenomenon, he was soon after disabled from undertaking. (143 B.C.E.)

The usurper found little difficulty in maintaining himself against Demetrius, as that young and thoughtless prince remained in Laodicea in the delirium of wine and pleasure, while his adherents could only make sudden and occasional inroads into the territories of his rival, in which, however, they could not maintain themselves. But on one occasion, when the Demetrians, commanded by Sarpedon, had made an inroad into the country between Tyre and Ptolemais, they were attacked and put to flight by Tryphon in person, at the head of the numerous garrison of the latter city.

As the victors were urging the pursuit, they were overwhelmed on the coast of Ptolemais by a sudden inundation, caused, probably, by the explosion of a submarine volcano.[12] On the retreat of the flood, Sarpedon, who had taken advantage of Tryphon's remarkable disaster to rally his own men and again to advance, found that though Tryphon himself had escaped, the greater number of his men had perished, drowned in the hollows of the shore, and mingled with vast quantities of fish which the sea had thrown up. The Demetrian general received these fishes as a present from Neptune, to whom he gratefully offered sacrifices for having seasonably intercepted the enemy, and thereby averted the total destruction with which his army was threatened. (Athenæus, lib. viii. p. 333.)

While this was passing between the rivals for the throne of Syria, Simon—who, though he had strengthened himself by alliances, fortifications, men, and arms, was exposed to hostilities from both contending parties—determined to become reconciled to the one of the two whose wrongs toward the Jews had been the less recent and also the less grievous. Accordingly he sent an embassy to Demetrius, and offered to recognise him as king of Syria, and to assist him in the recovery of his kingdom, upon condition that he would confirm him (Simon) in all his dignities, and

---

[12] Strabo simply mentions the circumstance among other inexplicable phenomena, (lib. xvi. p. 758.)

guarantee to the Jews the free enjoyment of all their privileges and immunities. At the same time, and in recognition of Demetrius's right, Simon sent him a rich crown of gold and some other valuable presents.

The king, glad to secure the assistance of so important and useful an auxiliary, readily granted what he had not the power to withhold, and entered into an alliance with Simon on terms of perfect equality. By letters patent under the royal hand and seal, Demetrius agreed to all the demands of Simon, confirmed to the utmost extent all the grants made by his late father, Demetrius Soter, proclaimed a general amnesty and oblivion for all past hostilities, and finally constituted Simon sovereign prince of Judea, with full and entire freedom, and exemption from any foreign yoke or supremacy. (1 Macc. xiv.)

Thus the independence which the Jews, to a certain extent, had hitherto enjoyed *de facto*, was now confirmed to them *de jure* by the only authority that had a right to grant it—Demetrius, the lawful king of Syria. Thenceforth the Jews considered themselves free, and independent of any foreign power. Simon assumed the title of prince and high-priest of the Jews, which was bestowed upon and confirmed unto him and his posterity after him, by the priests, elders, and the people of Judea. A transcript of King Demetrius's letters patent, which were addressed "King Demetrius unto Simon the high-priest and friend of kings, and to the elders and nation of the Jews," was ordered to be engraved on tablets of brass, and to be hung up in the sanctuary, while the original document was deposited in the national archives in the temple. "The first year of Simon, the prince of the Jews," was signalized by making it an epoch by which to compute time. The coins of Simon, and the first book of Maccabees, as well as Josephus, make use of this era.

END OF VOL. I.

HISTORY OF THE WORLD.

By PHILIP SMITH, B. A.

PLAN OF THE WORK.

SINCE Sir Walter Raleigh solaced his imprisonment in the Tower by the composition of his "History of the World," the Literature of England has never achieved the work which he left unfinished. There have been "Universal Histories," from the bulk of an encyclopædia to the most meagre outline, in which the annals of each nation are separately recorded; but without an attempt to trace the story of Divine Providence and human progress in one connected narrative. It is proposed to supply this want by a work, condensed enough to keep it within a reasonable size, but yet so full as to be free from the dry baldness of an epitome. The literature of Germany abounds in histories,—such as those of Müller, Schlosser, Karl von Rotteck, Duncker, and others,—which at once prove the demand for such a book, and furnish models, in some degree, for its execution. But even those great works are somewhat deficient in that *organic unity* which is the chief aim of this "History of the World."

The story of our whole race, like that of each separate nation, has "a beginning, a middle, and an end." That story we propose to follow, from its beginning in the sacred records, and from the dawn of civilization in the East,—through the successive Oriental Empires,— the rise of liberty and the perfection of heathen polity, arts, and literature in Greece and Rome,—the change which passed over the face of the world when the light of Christianity sprung up,—the origin and first appearance of those barbarian races which overthrew both divisions of the Roman Empire,—the annals of the States which rose on the Empire's ruins, including the picturesque details of medieval history and the steady progress of modern liberty and civilization,—and the extension of these influences, by discovery, conquest, colonization, and Christian missions, to the remotest regions of the earth. In a word, as separate histories reflect the detached scenes of human action and suffering, our aim is to bring into one view the several parts which assuredly form one great whole, moving onwards, under the guidance of Divine Providence, to the unknown end ordained in the Divine purposes.

Such a work, to be really useful, must be condensed into a moderate compass; else the powers of the writer would be frittered away, and the attention of the reader wearied out by an overwhelming bulk, filled up with microscopic details. The more striking facts of history, —the rise and fall of empires,—the achievements of warriors and heroes,—the struggles of peoples for their rights and freedom,—the conflict between priestcraft and religious liberty,—must needs stand out on the canvas of such a picture with the prominence they claim in the world itself. But they will not divert our attention from the more quiet and influential working of science and art, social progress and individual thought,—the living seed sown, and the fruit borne, in the field broken up by those outward changes.

While special care will be bestowed on those periods and nations, the history of which is scarcely to be found in any works accessible to the general reader, the more familiar parts of history will be treated in their due proportion to the whole work. It will be found, we trust, by no means the least valuable part of the scheme,—that the portions of history which are generally looked at by themselves, —those, for example, of Greece and Rome, and of our own country, —will be regarded from a common point of view with all the rest: a view which may, in some cases, modify the conclusions drawn by classical partiality and national pride.

The spirit of the work,—at least if the execution be true to the conception,—will be equally removed from narrow partisanship and affected indifference. The historian, as well as the poet, must be in earnest,

> "Dower'd with the hate of hate, the scorn of scorn,
> The love of love;"

but he must also be able to look beyond the errors, and even the virtues, of his fellow-men, to the great ends which the Supreme Ruler of events works out by their agency:—

> "Yet I doubt not through the ages one increasing purpose runs,
> And the thoughts of men are widen'd with the process of the suns."

No pains will be spared to make this history scholarlike in substance and popular in style. It will be founded on the best authorities, ancient and modern, original and secondary. The vast progress recently made in historical and critical investigations, the results obtained from the modern science of comparative philology, and the discoveries which have laid open new sources of information concerning the East, afford such facilities as to make the present a fit epoch for our undertaking.

The work will be divided into three Periods, each complete in itself, and will form Eight Volumes in Demy Octavo.

I.—ANCIENT HISTORY, Sacred and Secular; from the Creation to the Fall of the Western Empire, in A. D. 476. Two Volumes.

II.—MEDIEVAL HISTORY, Civil and Ecclesiastical; from the Fall of the Western Empire to the taking of Constantinople by the Turks, in A. D 1453. Two Volumes.

III.—MODERN HISTORY; from the Fall of the Byzantine Empire to our own Times. Four Volumes.

It will be published in 8 vols., 8vo. Price in cloth   per vol
Sheep   Volume 1 & 2 now ready.

NEW YORK: D. APPLETON & CO., Publishers.

www.ingramcontent.com/pod-product-compliance
Lightning Source LLC
Chambersburg PA
CBHW020104020526
44112CB00033B/813